THE

FOREIGN BIBLICAL LIBRARY.

EDITED BY THE REV

W. ROBERTSON NICOLL, M.A., LL.D.,

Editor of the "Expositor."

SCHLEIERMACHER'S SERMONS.

SELECTED SERMONS

OF

SCHLEIERMACHER.

TRANSLATED BY

MARY F. WILSON.

Wipf & Stock
PUBLISHERS
Eugene, Oregon

Wipf and Stock Publishers
199 West 8th Avenue, Suite 3
Eugene, Oregon 97401

Selected Sermons of Schleiermacher
By Schleiermacher, Friedrich
ISBN: 1-59244-602-7
Publication date 3/17/2004
Previously published by Funk & Wagnalls, 1880

CONTENTS.

BIOGRAPHICAL SKETCH.

IT seems desirable that those who make public references to a man of note should have an opportunity of making themselves acquainted with his opinions and character. A religious paper some time ago filled up a corner with this little piece of intelligence: "It is a very notable fact that a son of Hegel, a son of Schelling, and a daughter of Schleiermacher, are not only orthodox Christians, but most deeply interested in the progress of religion." Another periodical presently repeated the paragraph, prefaced by the remark that what is true in regard to faith—that it is not hereditary—is happily no less true in regard to unbelief. No; faith is not hereditary in the strictest sense, as Schleiermacher took pains to make clear, enforcing in his baptismal addresses, as well as on other occasions, the truth, "that which is born of the flesh is flesh." And yet we know, not only from Scripture, but from the undeniable witness of history, public and private, that there *is* a blessed heritage of faith; that "the seed of the righteous is blessed"; and she were no true daughter of Schleiermacher who should be otherwise than most deeply interested in the progress of true religion. As to orthodoxy, that is a term in these days so difficult to define that the readers of this volume must be left to judge for themselves whether or not it is anything wonderful that a child of the author of these sermons should be an orthodox Christian. This is, on every ground, more desirable than that a translator unversed in the fine distinctions and definitions of theologians, should attempt to give a categorical statement of the views of one to whom has been imputed, on the one hand, every shade of heterodox opinion,—who has been denounced in turn as pietist, rationalist, pantheist, even atheist; and who, on the other hand, has been held to fill a place in the Christian Church not inferior to that of Luther or even of Paul.

The sermons have been selected with a view to as wide a range of subjects as possible, from the four volumes of Schleiermacher's published discourses; and they are arranged, so far as this could be done, according to the order of time in which they appeared, that the reader may be more able to judge of the development and progress of the author's mind. It will also tend to a clearer understanding and a juster appreciation of the sermons, as well as give them a more living and personal interest, that the reader be made acquainted with something of the author's history, and of the times in which he lived and worked.

Friedrich Ernst Schleiermacher, born at Breslau, November 21st, 1768, was the firstborn son of a poor army chaplain of the Reformed faith; a man of earnest, evangelical piety, whose heart, as well as that of the mother, was set on the spiritual prosperity of their children. The little Fritz, in the frequent necessary absences of his father, took his first steps in education under his mother's care. At five years old he went to school, where, as he tells us, by his ready memory and the ease with which he acquired mere verbal knowledge, he came to be thought very clever,—an opinion with which he himself entirely agreed; and so became very conceited. But from the character of his master's school reports, it is plain that the boy was not only clever, but a uniformly good and diligent pupil. The removal of his parents, when he was in his tenth year, to Pless, and then to Anhalt, brought a change that was greatly to the benefit of the delicate child. For nearly two years he lived much in the open air in the country, his mother wisely judging that if he kept up the book-knowledge he had, it was enough for his years. "Fritz," she says, "is all spirit, and Carl all body." So, for the time, Fritz occupied himself in making Latin and French translations, acted as schoolmaster to his wild little brother, teaching him reading and arithmetic, and, these duties accomplished, shared his games and rambles out of doors, sometimes joined by the quiet, retiring elder sister Lotte, the loving, beloved and trusted friend of Fritz through all changing circumstances till the day of her death in 1831.

But even in those earliest years the boy was a thinker; and open and docile as he was to all his good mother's Christian instructions, the active, inquiring mind could take nothing for granted. "I had already," he tells us, "sustained manifold internal religious conflicts. The doctrine of eternal punishment and reward had already exercised a disturbing power over my childish imagination; and in my eleventh year I spent several sleepless nights in consequence of not being able to come to a satisfactory conclusion concerning the mutual relation between the sufferings of Christ and the punishment for which these sufferings were a substitute." A boy of ten losing his sleep, not through anxiety as to his own spiritual safety, but in the endeavour to solve a theological problem which has exercised the minds of devout and scholarly men in every age of the Church! It was clear this boy's life would not run on common or smooth lines. He spent most of two years in a boarding-school at Pless, where scepticism attacked him in the form of doubting the authenticity of all the ancient authors, because he himself did not know any proofs of their genuineness. But a politic fear of losing his much-valued reputation for cleverness, by betraying his ignorance, made him keep a wise silence about those doubts until he should be able to sift the matter for himself.

Before Friedrich was thirteen, he and Carl, as well as their sister Charlotte, were placed under the care of the Moravian Brethren, at first, for a time, at Gnadenfrei, whence the boys went in 1783 to Niesky. Steeped as Germany then was, almost universally, in the benumbing poison of rationalism, or wrapped in the chilling slumber of a deep formalism, the faithful few, like the good chaplain and his wife, with whom the pure gospel light and life still remained, felt themselves a somewhat helpless and discouraged remnant; and the parents thought they found in the pious, tranquil, well-ordered life of the Congregation a haven of safety for their children. And the children themselves, impressed by what their parents represented to them of the depravity and dangers of the world, became, as the father writes, "more and more anxious not to be sent away from us and out into the world, full of their natural corruption, and implored to be allowed to go to Niesky." Here the boy spent several happy years, pursuing eagerly every path of knowledge that was opened to him; the seeds of pure faith and love and Christian fellowship, sown from his tenderest years on good soil, and fostered by this genial atmosphere, already bringing forth fair fruit. His letters to his sister, during his stay at Niesky, show how honestly and earnestly the young heart was set on serving and pleasing the Saviour whom he already loved. "He alone is my stay; the God who died for me on the cross. . . . Ah, did but the love of Christ fill our hearts day and night! . . . did we but cling to Him, so that not even for one moment could we be drawn away from Him!" "In this short period how much have I not experienced; that is to say, much evil as regards myself, and much mercy as regards the Saviour. I have merited wrath, say I, on my side; I have atoned for you, cries the Lamb, from the cross." Expressions such as these indicate what was the prevailing tone of the young student's letters for some years.

But it was necessary that he who was to lead others to new and firmer standing-ground should himself struggle through the flood and test every step; it was fitting that the soldier who was to lead the fight against the deadly evils of his time should learn the use of his weapon in battling for his own life and liberty. Even at Niesky, the earnest, loving heart, longing after real communion with the Saviour, yet as rigidly honest with himself as with others, had undergone sore perplexities and struggles from having never been able to feel sure that the spiritual experiences which he saw and believed to be real in those around him, and which he felt to be very desirable for himself, were, in his own case, anything but inventions of his imagination. And when, in his seventeenth year, he was sent to the seminary at Barby, while these difficulties still perplexed him, he was soon plunged into deeper troubles. These will be most clearly explained in his own words.

In the autumn of 1786 he writes to his father: "With one thing only I am not content. I wish very much to study theology, and that thoroughly; but I shall not be able to boast of having done anything of the kind when I leave this, for, in my opinion, we are kept within too narrow limits in point of reading. Except what we see in the scientific periodicals, we learn nothing about the objections, arguments and discussions raised in the present day in regard to exegesis and dogmatics. Even in the lectures delivered to us sufficient mention is not made of these matters, and yet knowledge of them is absolutely necessary for a future theologian. The fact that they fear to lay them before us awakens in many minds a suspicion that the objections of the innovators must approve themselves to the intellect and be difficult to refute. I do not, however, share this opinion."

This was meant to prepare the father for what the son knew would be a terrible blow to him—the avowal of the change in his views, which he thus makes in a letter six months later: "Alas! dearest father, if you believe that, without this faith, no one can attain to salvation in the next world, nor to tranquility in this—and such, I know, is your belief—oh! then, pray to God to grant it to me, for to me it is now lost. I cannot believe that He, who called Himself the Son of man, was the true, eternal God; I cannot believe that His death was a vicarious atonement, because He never expressly said so Himself; and I cannot believe it to have been necessary, because God, who evidently did not create men for perfection, but for the pursuit of it, cannot possibly intend to punish them eternally because they have not attained it."

Let it be remembered that these are the words of a lad of little more than eighteen; and yet the letter in which they occur is the furthest possible from resembling the utterance of some callow theologian, who imagines that because an idea is new to him it is new to every one else, and whose most profound conviction seems to be, "I have more understanding than all my teachers." On the contrary, its tone is throughout humble, self-distrustful, full of deepest regret for his lost faith and for the conclusions to which he has felt, in the meantime, compelled to come; and full, even more, of reverential tenderness towards his father and bitterest sorrow for the pain which he is so unwillingly inflicting, and which he tries to soften by the hope of a change by-and-by. "Comfort yourself, dear father," he writes; "for I know you were long in the same state in which I am now. Doubts assailed you at one time as they now do me, and yet you have become what you now are. Think, hope, believe that the same may be the case with me." He entreats to be allowed to go to study at Halle; representing that by so doing, and having the opportunity of examining different views, he would be much more likely to change his own; whereas, by remaining among the Brethren, "I should never," he says, "be able to get rid of my doubts. For I am debarred from the possibility of examining for myself in how far the objections of the innovators may or may not be well founded, as I am forbidden to read anything of the kind, and no one here will even refute my own objections."

The correspondence following this letter is pathetic in its painfulness. The father, whose deep affection for his son and pride in his superior gifts only added a tenfold keenness to the sting of the disappointment, could see nothing in the youth's doubts but the pride and depravity of his heart, and a longing after the world and its honours; and poured out tears and reproaches, mingled with entreaties to return from his evil way. He even spoke of feeling compelled to discard him; but this is evidently a mere figure of speech. And the son, on his side, miserable with the strife in his own mind, heart-broken because of his father's grief, meekly justifying himself against misunderstandings, and yet unable to give the only comfort that would avail, suffered probably still more keenly.

The question of leaving Barby was settled by the Brethren, who refused to allow one who had imbibed such views to remain among them even on probation. Thus cut off from all his moorings, external as well as spiritual, his position was sufficiently trying. But in his uncle Stubenrauch, his mother's brother, then a professor of theology at Halle, he found the very friend for his need; one who, while better able than the father to understand the young man's position, gave him sound and Christian advice, and also set things before his brother-in-law in so wise and hopeful a light that ere long the old man's letters to his son regained all their wonted affectionate tone. Under the roof of this kind uncle, Schleiermacher spent two years at Halle, studying with his usual passionate eagerness, but without any definite plan; as he says himself, taking a taste of everything, making a fragmentary study of all sciences, and "hindered in various ways by that conceit which is peculiar to the self-educated." The necessity of self-support led him to cultivate the English and French languages with a view to teaching; and when at the end of those two years the uncle retired to a living at Drossen, the nephew accompanied him, and spent another year chiefly in adding to his knowledge of theology. His life-long gratitude to this fatherly friend finds graceful expression in his own words: "Nothing gives me more pain than to think that I have not availed myself sufficiently of his friendship to be able to say, in lieu of all praise, 'See what I have become, and to him I owe it.'"

What great and essential changes took place in his views during these and succeeding years will be best seen in the following sermons. Throughout his life he retained a most kindly feeling towards the Brethren, with whom a strong tie remained for him through his sister having taken up her permanent abode among them. He often and gratefully spoke of what he owed to his early training among them, and more than once revisited them. On one of those occasions, writing from Gnadenfrei, Charlotte's home, he says, "Here it was that that mystic tendency developed itself which has been of so much importance to me, and has supported and carried me through all the storms of scepticism. Then it was only germinating, now it has attained to its full development; and I may say that, after all that I have passed through, I have become a Herrnhuter again, only of a higher order." And later, in 1805, after spending the Easter as a welcome and honoured guest at Barby—that Barby which had cast him out as poison—he describes to his friend the "beautiful service on Good Friday, based altogether on the great idea of the Atonement," and goes on to say, "there is not, throughout Christendom, in our day, a form of public worship which expresses more worthily, and awakens more thoroughly, the spirit of true Christian piety than does that of the Herrnhut brotherhood! . . . I could not but feel deeply how far behind them we are in our church, where the poor sermon is everything . . . and is rarely animated by a true and living spirit.

"It will soon be my duty to institute divine service here [at Halle], which is to present a pattern, and to act as a stimulus, to new and far-spread generations of religious teachers; but how wretchedly cramped am I as to means, and how much I deplore that I cannot transplant hither the best and most attractive elements of what I witnessed at Barby!"

These long extracts, while showing his own feeling towards the Brethren and their institutions, will also serve to show what estimate they had by that time formed of his Christian character.

In the summer of 1790 Schleiermacher passed his examination as a licentiate of theology, and soon afterwards obtained a situation as private tutor in the family of Count von Dohna of Schlobitten. Here he spent three years very happily, treated with great kindness by the whole family, delighting in the happy domestic life and in the opportunity of forming his manners in polished society; preaching, visiting the sick, and studying as diligently as time permitted. This pleasant episode was brought to a close through his being unable conscientiously to agree with the views of the parents as to the system to be followed in the children's education. After about half a year spent in teaching in Berlin, he was appointed and ordained as assistant to an aged pastor at Landsberg on the Warthe. He writes to his father on entering on this new office: "From my heart I do wish that God's blessing may be upon my sermons, so that they may be sources of true edification and speak to the heart, as, I trust, they will ever come from the heart. To you I need not say how deeply I am moved at the thought of being numbered among those to whom so important an office is entrusted, nor need I assure you that I do not now, and never shall, look upon it merely as a means of livelihood."

After two years of faithful pastoral work at Landsberg, he was appointed preacher to the Charity House in Berlin, a position which he held for the next six years. These years mark a new and most influential era in his life. He very soon became a daily and honoured guest in the house of the Jewish physician, Dr. Marcus Herz and his beautiful and highly gifted wife Henrietta. There he met the most intellectual and cultured society in Berlin, as well as many distinguished foreigners, for whom the Herzes always kept open house. In this congenial and stimulating atmosphere, Schleiermacher's mind revelled and expanded, while ever steadily holding on its own independent course. He carried on his researches now, as throughout his life, in every department of knowledge—literature, science, philosophy, theology; he gave a candid and attentive hearing to the views of others, patiently and without prejudice weighed them, and held to what he accounted truth, whether supported by others or alone. "I do not believe," he says, "that I shall ever attain to a fully wrought-out system, so that I could answer every question that could be raised, conclusively, and in agreement with all my other knowledge. But I have all along believed that the proving and investigating, the patient hearing of all witnesses and all parties, is the only means for attaining at last to a sufficient amount of certainty, and above all to a well-defined boundary between that about which one must necessarily take a side, and that which one may leave undecided without detriment to his repose and happiness."

In this social circle also, not only his intellect but his large, deep heart found the outlet and the sympathy which seemed to him a necessity of life. From childhood onwards he felt it impossible to live without loving and being beloved. To one friend he writes: "I stretch forth all my roots and leaves in search of affection, . . . and when I am unable to drink in full draughts of it, I at once dry up and wither." In forming his friendships he was slow to give confidence till sure of his ground. Intellect and genius no doubt attracted him, but in a friend he demanded more than these. "I cannot," he says, "allow any one to penetrate into the inmost recesses of my mind until I am satisfied of the purity and uprightness of his character. I cannot philosophize with any one whose moral sentiments I do not approve." And again: "For his intellect alone I love no man. Schelling and Goethe are two mighty intellects, but I shall never be tempted to love them." And once more, in defending himself against the charge of having undesirable friends: "Never will I be the friend of a man of disreputable principles; but neither will I ever, out of fear of the world, withdraw the consolation of my friendship from any one who has innocently incurred its ban." But when sure of a pure, true character, he was ready to love in spite of many faults; and having once given his confidence, he was eager to lay open his whole soul to his friend, and to receive a like fulness of communication in return; to have a constant and full and sympathetic interchange of opinions and feelings on all possible subjects. It was perhaps this need of expression that in part made it more natural to him to form friendships with women than with men; though more probably the reason was in the deep, delicate tenderness of his nature. With Henrietta Herz, who was as lovely in character as in person, he formed a friendship that lasted for life; and with several other female friends, all distinguished both by intellectual culture and by personal character, he kept up the closest intimacy.

His faithful sister Charlotte, whom, in her cloistered seclusion, he kept fully acquainted with all his doings and interests, feared, not entirely without reason, that these friendships might injure him in his professional position by exposing his conduct to misconstruction, and also that there might be a danger of his deceiving himself as to the nature of his feelings. He replies at great length, affectionately and patiently going into detail to relieve her loving anxiety. He grants, as to the latter point, that the danger does exist, but assures her that he is always and entirely on his guard, and that between Mrs. Herz and himself any warmer feeling than friendship would never have been possible. And as to the danger to his position, he expresses his conviction that, just because he is a minister, it is his duty to disregard appearances, not, of course, out of mere bravado, but whenever there is good and sufficient reason. And therefore, as he feels sure that these friendships are, on the one hand, essential to him in the cultivation of his mind and heart, and that, on the other hand, they enable him to do much good, he maintains his right to enjoy them.

One faculty which Schleiermacher greatly valued in his friends, that of minutely and exactly observing and describing their own mental processes, was a very strongly marked characteristic of his own mind. This feature indeed comes out so very prominently in his letters that we are obliged to remind ourselves that they are the letters of a German. And yet this habitual, deliberate introspection, which is so commonly an indication and accompaniment of a morbid self-consciousness, was far from being so in his case. Self-conscious he was, in the sense of being fully and intensely aware of every phase and variation in his inner life; but in his relations with his fellow-men his manner had the childlike simplicity that marks every truly great man.

There must have been few more attractive guests in those days at Mrs. Herz's gatherings than the small, slightly deformed man, with keen, flashing eye, and calm, self-possessed manner, who quietly listened and discussed and gave his opinion, and at the same time saw and heard all that was done or said in the room; whose face expressed at once intellectual power and a most winning kindliness.

The most notable of the male friends whom Schleiermacher acquired during this first residence in Berlin was Friedrich Schlegel, who arrived in the city not long after him, and who for some time shared his lodgings. He regarded Schlegel's mental powers with intense admiration, and considered his intimate association with him as the greatest possible advantage to himself. "In regard to intellect," he says, "he is so infinitely superior to me that I cannot speak of his mind but with profound reverence." For a few years his connection with Schlegel occupied a large place in his thoughts and time; a connection of which he said that it would ever remain one of the most remarkable epochs in his life. Mrs. Herz says he was liable to the not very uncommon weakness of greatly exaggerating the merits of his friends; and it is evident that whatever Schlegel's real merits were, his friend saw him through some glorifying medium in his own imagination. "I cannot help," he says, "loving the ideal that dwells in him, although I am very doubtful whether it will not be shivered to atoms before he succeeds in embodying a harmonious presentment of it, either in his works or in his life. However, I see before me, in imagination, the great and truly sublime image of what he may be if he ever attain his true development. How could I then feel otherwise towards him than I do?" It was probably from thus idealising his friend, and also from a generous feeling of his having been unfairly dealt with, that Schleiermacher was moved to write a series of letters in defence of *Lucinda*, a book of Schlegel's which was severely condemned, and, it would seem, not without good reason; and which Schleiermacher himself had at first disliked. Of this incident a German critic remarks, that "the astonishment felt at seeing a healthy and pure mind, such as Schleiermacher's, finding pleasure in the *Lucinda* is exceeded by the admiration experienced at beholding the purified reflection of the work furnished by the pure mind." Schleiermacher probably did in this case like the godly old woman who, after hearing a sermon that was very dry bones to most of the hearers, gave notes of it that were savoury and wholesome food. She had read her own devout thoughts into it.

On his twenty-ninth birthday he writes to Charlotte a lively account of how he had been surprised in the morning by the arrival, first of two young Dohnas, (his former Schlobitten pupils, now officers resident for a time in Berlin,) and then of Schlegel and some of his lady friends; how his table was spread with chocolate and cakes, how "Mrs. Herz gave me a watchguard and Mrs. Veit a pair of gloves and a small wineglass out of which to drink the Burgundy she had ordered for my stomach, and Schlegel a small bottle of perfume for my linen, which he knows I am very fond of." And then he goes on to say how Schlegel had incited the others to join in extorting from him a promise to produce something original in writing before the end of the year; "a promise that weighs heavily on me, as I have not the least desire to be an author." This promise was redeemed by his beginning to contribute short papers to the *Athenæum*, then conducted by the brothers Schlegel.

But he soon found weightier work for his pen. In the spring of 1799, during a short absence at Potsdam, he completed in two months his *Discourses on Religion, addressed to the cultivated Classes among its Contemners.* He was very far from anticipating what was to be the effect of this work, and had doubts of its being allowed to pass by the public censor; doubts not unfounded, for it was barely sanctioned. Its aim was to prove that religion is an eternal necessity in human nature, and to distinguish what is essential in it from the accidental and false additions of men.

The book startled the nation as with the blast of a trumpet. Men awoke, especially young men, from the torpor of unbelief or fashionable indifference, and began to inquire, What is truth? The appearance of the work is regarded as forming a distinct epoch in the religious history of Germany. Harms, who had become dissatisfied with rationalism, relates of himself after reading the book twice through, hardly pausing to eat or sleep: "I suddenly recognised that all rationalism, and all æsthetics, and all knowledge derived from ourselves, are utterly worthless and useless as regards the work of salvation; and the necessity of our salvation coming from another source, so to say, flashed upon me. . . . I may, with truth, call it the hour in which my higher life was born. I received from that book the impulse of a movement that will never cease." The great Neander also regarded the reading of these *Discourses* as the turning-point in his religious life, and many of the most noted thinkers and preachers of Germany were no less deeply impressed and influenced. It is significant of how little the author sought or valued fame that in none of his letters of that period is there the slightest reference to the sensation produced by the book, nothing indeed to indicate that he was even aware of it. On its being sent to the printer he writes to Mrs. Herz: "It is a strange coincidence that one of my sermons should have appeared at the same time as my *Discourses on Religion.* My name thus stands among a number of great theologians and preachers, and in order to excuse himself for having placed it there, B—— has been so bold as to say in the preface that I am highly valued in Berlin on account of my talents and my knowledge. . . . What may I not yet become in this sublunary sphere!"

In the following year he published his *Monologues*, which he describes as "a man's deepest and most intimate communings with himself." These gained him many friends among the best kind of people. Indeed he found it necessary more than once to explain that the *Monologues* presented the ideal to which he desired to attain, not the picture of what he really was. Amiel, in his Journal, after a criticism of the *Monologues* at considerable length, thus winds up. "What a life! what a man! These glimpses into the inner regions of a great soul do one good. Contact of this kind strengthens, restores, refreshes. Courage returns as we gaze; when we see what has been, we doubt no more that it can be again. At the sight of a *man*, we too say to ourselves, Let us also be men!"

In the first year of the new century the first collection of Schleiermacher's sermons was given to the world, dedicated to his good uncle Stubenrauch. This must have been done at the urgent desire of his friends; for even so late as 1824, in referring to the fourth collection which had then been published, he says: "I am still opposed to the publication of the sermons in a printed form; because all sermons, and mine more especially, are only intended to be heard." Something of this he expresses in the dedication to his uncle, and adds, among other interesting explanations: "Others will be offended that the distinction between moral and immoral men, between the pious and the worldly-minded, is so strictly drawn, as among our theologians it has for a long time been supposed to be no longer the fashion to do so; but you know that I could not avoid this offence without being unfaithful to what I hold to be the essential part of Christianity."

In addition to all his other labours, Schleiermacher undertook, jointly with Schlegel, the translation of Plato, from which, however, the latter soon withdrew; and Schleiermacher, after years of toil, completed the task alone.

Schlegel remained only a short time in Berlin, and the increasing difference of their views on various subjects, and perhaps, above all, on religion, gradually made the tie between the two much less close, though Schleiermacher never ceased to speak with warm affection of his early friend.

It should be noted that Schleiermacher carried on all these labours under the burden of wretched health, from which he suffered during most of his life. His eyesight also was weak, and at one time he seemed in danger of losing it altogether; but his resolute will refused to allow even severe physical pain to put a stop to his work, or hinder his enjoyment of social intercourse.

About the same time that Schlegel left Berlin, Schleiermacher was introduced, during a visit in the island of Rügen, to an earnest young preacher, Ehrenfried von Willich, with whom he at once formed a warm friendship —a friendship that was to lead to very important results for his own future life. His remarks to Charlotte show how much more congenial to him was the Christian pastor than the brilliant philosopher. "Willich has not Friedrich Schlegel's great, deep and all-comprehensive intellect; but he is in many respects nearer to my heart, and his sentiments regarding life are more similar to my own." And after each of them had visited him in Berlin: "Willich has been here. . . . That I derive more enjoyment from his presence than from Schlegel's you may easily guess."

One portion of his experience, which began during those six years so full of import and of progress for him, must not be omitted; not only because it for the time so deeply and powerfully affected him, but because it illustrates so strange a state of society, as well as some peculiar views of his own.

One of his most intimate friends was Eleanore Grunow, a highly cultured and gifted woman, most unhappily married to a clergyman in the city. Schleiermacher held very strongly that a marriage in which there is nothing but the outward tie—no inward oneness, no heart union—is an immoral connection, and no real marriage; and that therefore the dissolution of such a connection is a moral duty. Most right-thinking men and women will grant his premisses; but to admit his conclusion would open the door to dangerous consequences. From keen sympathy with the daily sufferings of his friend, as well as the congeniality of mind that had first drawn them together, Schleiermacher's feeling deepened into a strong attachment, which, so far from being frowned on by his conscience, was mixed with his most sacred thoughts and plans. The law of Prussia permitted divorce on the ground of mutual consent, without any criminality on either side; public opinion attached no stigma to the practice; there were instances of it in Schleiermacher's immediate circle; and it was his earnest desire that Eleanore should obtain a dissolution of her miserable union and become his wife. All his intercourse and correspondence with her was carried on with perfect openness, and his best friends, good and pure men and women, knew and sympathised with his wishes. But Eleanore could not come to a decision; and in the distress and trouble of his mind, he accepted, in the spring of 1802, an appointment as court-preacher at Stolpe in Pomerania, thus voluntarily going into what he felt to be banishment.

At Stolpe he consoled himself with long letters to various friends, filled with details of his work, literary and pastoral, criticisms of books read in his solitude, or of prominent literary men, and of course, above all, with minute accounts of mental experiences, or comments on such accounts received. It would be pleasant, if space permitted, to give large extracts from those letters, which present so much more vividly than any description a picture of the man; his unceasing mental activity, his quiet, playful humour, his warm, deep sympathy. The letters are not the less interesting in that they are in some respects so utterly unlike the letters of an Englishman, and still more those of a Scotchman. The effusiveness, the sentimentality, if one may so speak, is probably quite as much a national characteristic as a specialty of Schleiermacher individually. But it seems to us more like a school-girl than a profound philosopher when we read how he, as it were, fell in love with some of his male friends at first sight, as for instance with Willich, with whom he "communed in silence," while the rest of the company sang. Speaking of another, with whom he had exchanged a few letters before they met, he says, when they met accidentally, "We exclaimed in one breath, 'What, this is Hülsen!' and, 'What, this is Schleiermacher!' And then we fell into each other's arms. After having gazed at each other in silence a few moments, it was as though we had been in the habit of seeing each other daily for years." And of his friend Reimer, who published his works, he tells Charlotte, "Yesterday a sudden action took place within us, . . . during which we took possession, as it were, of each other as intimate heart-friends. Do not ask me at present to describe this. I am too much overwhelmed and too perplexed. . . . He folded me in his arms, with the words, 'Henceforward let there be nothing concealed between us!'"

One quotation of another character we must give, as showing both the state of the Church at the time, and Schleiermacher's position and feeling in regard to it. "Last Wednesday the synodal assembly of this diocese took place, and the dean was so kind as to invite me to be present. This occupied almost the whole day. How sad it made me! Ah, dear friend, to find yourself among thirty-five such clergymen! I did not feel ashamed of belonging to the profession, but with my whole heart I longed for and I pictured to myself those future times which, I trust, are not far distant, when such an assembly will be impossible. I shall not live to see it, but could I only in some way contribute to bring it about! Of the openly disreputable among them I will not speak; . . . but the universal degradation, the entire unsusceptibility to all higher influences, the base and sensuous views—depend upon it, I was the only one among them who mourned in heart, the only one; for had there been another I must have found him, I knocked and searched so earnestly."

During his stay at Stolpe, in the autumn of 1803, Schleiermacher published his *Critical Enquiry into the Existing Systems of Ethics*, criticising especially the systems of Kant and Fichte, and giving the highest place to Plato and Spinoza, but formulating no completed system of his own.

But his mind was still disturbed and unsettled, and his heart often deeply distressed in connection with Eleanore, who seemed, just at this time, to have given him up, though the correspondence was resumed for two years more. He calls this book his tombstone—a remnant of the happy past. And yet it was at this very time he undertook to carry on alone the translation of Plato! But it is only fair to add, that he explains his doing this, though with the prospect of a speedy death before him, by saying that, "just as a man ought to do nothing because of death, so also he ought to leave nothing undone because of death."

In May, 1804, Schleiermacher was appointed preacher to the University at Halle, and professor *extraordinarius* of theology. In the interval of comparative leisure, before turning his steps southward, he paid a short visit to Willich, now settled at Stralsund; and in Rügen, where they had first met, was introduced to Willich's betrothed bride, Henriette von Mühlenfels, a charming and beautiful girl of sixteen, then living in the house of her married sister, Charlotte von Kathen. Schleiermacher entered with joyful sympathy into their happiness. He and the young bride forthwith adopted each other as father and daughter, and from that time there was a frequent interchange of letters overflowing with affection on both sides. In October he was settled at Halle, and there, in H. Steffens, professor of natural philosophy, he found another friend in whose companionship he took great delight. He writes about him: "Steffens' profound and inexhaustible mind, joined to his childlike and amiable nature, so susceptible of every generous emotion, gives me new pleasure every time I spend a few hours with him." And again: "Never have I with such sincerity of heart placed another man as high above myself in every respect as I do this one, whom, were it seemly between man and man, I could almost adore. . . . The man is altogether so indescribably attractive—as deep, as spontaneous and as witty as Friedrich Schlegel at his best." And so on, with much more in the same strain. And the feeling was thoroughly reciprocated.

In speaking of a night spent together on a pedestrian excursion, Steffens says: "This night will be to me ever memorable. . . . Never did Schleiermacher seem to me intellectually greater, morally purer. Even to this day that night appears to me one of the most remarkable of my life, as if sanctified. . . . I have a testimony of the impression this night made upon him, in a letter to his dear friend Mrs. Herz. It was the reflection of his own purity that made me appear to him in a glorified light during these truly holy hours. Never did the deep religiosity of his morality strike me more forcibly. The Saviour was with us, as He has promised to be 'when two or three are gathered together in His name.'"

The following Easter Schleiermacher made the visit to Barby which has already been referred to; and later in the summer took another little tour, in the course of which he visited his dear Lotte, and made acquaintance for the first time with his younger half-sister, Nanni, whom he brought with him to Halle, thus making for himself, at last, a little home. One very characteristic passage in his account of the pedestrian portion of this tour may be quoted. "Our longest and most interesting day's journey I went through under intense suffering from cramps in the stomach; yet I did not give in, or allow the state of my health to cause us one hour's delay, nor did the difficulties and sufferings in any way impair my enjoyment, and now they seem as nothing compared with the glorious and lasting impression which the sight of nature in its sublimity has made upon me."

And now, October, 1805, occurred the crisis which Schleiermacher regarded as an unspeakable calamity, but which was in reality a merciful deliverance from a great evil. Eleanore seemed to have decided on the final step. Schleiermacher writes to the Willichs of visiting them again, and adds his hope that it may be "with the excellent Eleanore," "the best loved of all my belongings."

She had gone to the house of her brother, who had undertaken to conduct the business of the divorce, the husband had given his consent, when Eleanore was suddenly overcome by scruples of conscience, and returned to her husband's house, and all communication between her and Schleiermacher was thenceforward at an end.

It came upon him as a crushing, heart-sickening blow; he spoke of it as having destroyed his life and made it utterly worthless; but he lived to take a wiser and sounder view of the position, and to thank, God who had reserved some better thing for him.

But neither sorrow nor any other personal interest was allowed to hinder his work. His influence extended rapidly, especially among the students. He devoted an evening weekly to receiving in his house any of them who chose to come, and of this plan he says, "I do not know which party gains most, the young people or myself."

In the beginning of 1806 he published anonymously the *Christmas Festival*, a delightful little book in the form of a dialogue, in which he introduces several of his friends—Henriette von Willich, with her baby daughter; her sister, Charlotte von Kathen, with her sick child, and others. The book is pervaded with earnest Christian feeling, and bears on the condition of the country in consequence of the French invasion. For now the troubles of war were pressing heavily; and when, in October, the battle of Jena threw Prussia for the time entirely under the heel of the conqueror, the University was suppressed, the students dispersed, and Schleiermacher's professional occupation was gone. He writes to his friend Reimer an account of the pillage of the town by the French, humorously describing his own part in it, in which he and Steffens were deprived of their watches, besides "all my shirts, with the exception of five, and all the silver spoons, with the exception of two." After this he and Nanni united their housekeeping with Steffens and his family; a measure which he says "was imperative, for I had only very little money, which I had borrowed, and Steffens had none at all." And thus they economized fuel and light as well as other items, though Nanni did not enjoy it, as what housekeeper would? But he still held to his post, in hope of better times for the University, and exerted all his influence, which was not small, to stir up a true and noble patriotism and a spirit of determined resistance in defence of all that the nation held dear. A few extracts from his letters during this stirring time may be given.

"Would you desire to be spared any danger, any suffering, at the cost of the conviction of having delivered over future generations to base servitude, and of having exposed them to be inoculated with the despicable sentiments of an utterly corrupted people? Believe me, sooner or later, a great and universal struggle must ensue, the objects of which will be as much our sentiments, our religion, and our mental culture, as our outward liberty and worldly goods, . . . a struggle which will unite sovereigns and people by a more beautiful bond than has existed for centuries." "The general demoralization is fearful; on all sides yawning abysses of infamy and cowardice stare you in the face. Only a few, and foremost among these the king and the queen, form glorious exceptions." "The rod of wrath must fall upon every German land; only on this condition can a strong and happy future bloom forth. Happy they who live to see it; but they who die, let them die in faith." "I have no fear, except, sometimes, of a dishonourable peace, which may save the appearance—but only the appearance—of a national existence and freedom. But even in regard to this I feel tranquil; for if the nations submit to it, it will prove that they are not yet ripe for better things; and the severer visitations, amid which they are to mature, will not fail soon to fall upon them." "The king alone, in his steadfastness, it is gratifying to behold; and I trust, now that he has got over the capture of his capital and the surrender of his fortresses without suing for peace, he will not think of separating his fate from that of the rest of Europe. . . . The conflict must become wider and deeper, if new life and prosperity are to rise out of the universal desolation."

In the following spring, February, 1807, during the siege of Stralsund, young Willich, who had refused to desert his flock, was smitten by a fever that raged in the town, and died after a week's illness. The poor young wife, still only nineteen, turned in her desolation to her "dear father, Schleier," for comfort; and few real fathers could have entered more fully into the sorrows of a stricken child. Henriette returned to Rügen, to be near her relatives, and during the unsettled, troublous times that followed, Schleiermacher maintained a steady correspondence with her and her sister, so far as the distracted state of the country permitted. He lingered in Halle until the winter, in the hope that the University might be restored; but when, in December, prayers were ordered in the churches for Jerome

Bonaparte and his wife as king and queen of Westphalia, it was more than his patriotic spirit could brook, and he betook himself to Berlin, to preach and to lecture in the meantime as he might find opportunity.

Once more, in the following summer, Schleiermacher found his way to Rügen. In personal intercourse, his fatherly affection for Henriette easily and naturally developed into a deeper and warmer feeling, and he carried back with him to Berlin her promise to be his wife when more settled times should come.

Early in 1809 he was appointed pastor of Trinity Church in Berlin, and when, in May, he brought home his bride with her two little children, he felt that his happiness was complete. Even in his much younger days he had delighted in studying family life, and often spoke of it as man's most perfect state; and now he wrote to his old friend Mrs. Herz: "I have taught so much about the beauty and holiness of family life that I ought to have an opportunity of showing that what I have taught has been to me more than empty words, and that the doctrine has in truth sprung from my deepest feelings and from my inward energy." And though he was nearly twenty years older than his Jette, nowhere could he have found a wife more thoroughly suited for him. Thoughtful and intelligent, she grew and developed in contact with his strong nature, while yet retaining her individual character; and their deep, mutual love only deepened through the years until the end. And when, in addition to the two little ones whom he had so fully taken to his fatherly heart, children of his own came to make it a complete family, his cup of joy overflowed. Now at last he had found a sphere in which his rich nature and his great intellect had full scope. His genial, loving, social disposition made him the centre of a wide and ever-increasing circle of warmly attached friends of all classes. He went much into society, and received much at home; not merely because of his unceasing delight in intercourse with his fellows, but because he believed that intimate personal association was the most effective medium of influence for good. And in this he seems to have judged correctly; for those who knew him agree in their testimony that great as was the effect of his written works, and still greater that of his preaching, it was the whole living personality of the man that told most powerfully on all who came in contact with him.

In 1810, when the University of Berlin was re-constituted, with Fichte as rector, Schleiermacher was called to a chair of theology, and the next year became Secretary to the Academy of Science. One public office after another was thrust upon him; while preaching, writing and lecturing went on with unabated diligence. It fatigues the mind even to read the list of the subjects on which he lectured: New Testament exegesis; introduction to and interpretation of the New Testament, ethics, both philosophic and Christian, dogmatic and practical theology, church history, history of philosophy, psychology, dialectics (logic and metaphysics), politics, pædagogy and æsthetics. His preaching drew increasing crowds, not only of the more intellectual classes, but from among the poor and uneducated, who found that they received in it food for the hunger of their hearts, guidance from Scripture for the practical affairs of daily life, and comfort in its sorrows.

It has already been said that Schleiermacher considered all sermons, and his own more especially, as intended only to be heard, not read. The specialty in his own case arose from the fact that his sermons were never written; all his published discourses being printed from notes taken during delivery. They were very deeply thought out; but a few very brief notes were all that he committed to paper; leaving his already well-defined thoughts to take shape as his feelings warmed with his theme and took a special tone from the sympathetic reflex influence of the people assembled before him. This habit of speaking without previous arrangement, with the wealth of ideas that would flow in upon him—one thought suggesting still another—probably accounts in part for the strange, often obscure style of his sermons—the long, involved sentences, reaching occasionally the fearful length of a page and a half; sentences in which, however, one of his constant hearers says he never lost his way (which is much more than can be said of all his readers), and in which he always arrived with certainty at the right conclusion. His friend Wilhelm von Humboldt says of him: "Those who may have read his numerous writings ever so diligently, but who have never heard him speak, must, nevertheless, remain unacquainted with the most rare power and the most remarkable qualities of the man. His strength lay in the deeply penetrative character of his words, when preaching or engaged in any other of his ecclesiastical functions. It would be wrong to call it rhetoric, for it was so entirely free from art. It was the persuasive, penetrative, kindling effusion of a feeling, which seemed not so much to be enlightened by one of the rarest intellects as to move side by side with it in perfect unison." A recent writer says of his eloquence, that it was almost as golden as that of Plato; and a short German notice of him gives the much more valuable testimony, that by his preaching thousands were won to the Saviour. Another criticism from Amiel may here be quoted. "While some shock me by their sacerdotal dogmatism, others repel me by their rationalizing laicism. It seems to me that good preaching ought to combine, as Schleiermacher's did, perfect moral humility with energetic independence of thought; a profound sense of sin with respect for criticism and a passion for truth."

In the pulpit as elsewhere, Schleiermacher was, during those troubled times, a fearless patriot, and laboured unceasingly, in conjunction with Fichte and other noble-hearted men, to arouse in the people a true spirit of freedom, that should lead them to unite in casting off the foreign yoke; his friend Moritz Arndt, who had been obliged, after the battle of Jena, to flee from the wrath of Napoleon, but had now returned, greatly aiding the cause by his stirring patriot songs, especially the one, popular wherever the German language is spoken, "What is the German's Fatherland?"

Schleiermacher's second collection of sermons, published in 1808, twelve in number, all bear on the special circumstances of the country. Eight of them were preached in Halle, and the rest in Berlin. In his preface to them he says: "May this work contribute something to effect what we so greatly need, to arouse and animate pious courage and true desire for thorough improvement, and to make it clear whence alone true prosperity can come to us, and how each one must help towards it."

When at length, in the spring of 1813, Europe began to feel that she had had "enough of Bonaparte"; when Prussia at last aroused herself to cast off her humiliating chains; Schleiermacher felt that Berlin was no longer a safe place for his most precious treasures, and sent his wife and children for some weeks into Silesia, remaining himself, and taking an active part in all the exciting events of those stormy days. He writes to his wife, "As for regular study, that is not to be thought of till the immediate crisis is over. I am continuing my lectures, but I believe I am the only professor who does so." The danger to Berlin, however, blew over; and he was able again to gather his little flock around him. Among the sermons in this volume is one preached at the calling out of the *Landwehr* in that eventful year; and we transcribe a part of Bishop Eilert's eloquent account of one which does not appear in the published collection.

"The students of the University and the gymnasium, who were about to start for Breslau as volunteers, in uniform and armed, had in a body requested Schleiermacher to deliver a sermon and administer the sacrament to them immediately before their departure, thus to consecrate them for their holy undertaking. Their firearms were piled in front or rested against the walls of the church of the Holy Trinity. The beautiful old hymn, 'In all my acts,' sung with heartfelt effusion, had attuned the minds of the congregation to the proper pitch of solemnity. After having pronounced a short prayer, full of unction, Schleiermacher went up into the pulpit. . . . There, in this holy place, and at this solemn hour, stood the physically so small and insignificant man, his noble countenance beaming with intellect, and his clear, sonorous, penetrating voice ringing through the overflowing church. Speaking from his heart with pious enthusiasm, his every word penetrated to the heart, and the clear, full, mighty stream of his eloquence carried every one along with it. His bold, frank declaration of the causes of our deep fall, his severe denunciation of our actual defects, as evinced in the narrow-hearted spirit of caste, of proud aristocratism, and in the dead forms of bureaucratism, struck down like thunder and lightning, and the subsequent elevation of the heart to God on the wings of solemn devotion was like harp-tones from a higher world. . . . And when, at last, with the full fire of enthusiasm, he addressed the noble youths already equipped for battle, and next, turning to their mothers, the greater number of whom were present, he concluded with the words, 'Blessed is the womb that has borne such a son! blessed the breast that has nourished such a babe!' a thrill of deep emotion ran through the assembly, and amid loud sobs and weeping, Schleiermacher pronounced the closing Amen."

When the country was once more restored to freedom, Schleiermacher shared the experience of many another public-spirited man who has cared more for his country's real welfare than for his own advancement. The men who had stirred the people to assert their liberties against a foreign tyrant were regarded with suspicion by the government, as being equally likely to encourage resistance to an undue exercise of power on the part of their lawful ruler. Fichte's pure, beautiful life had already closed, during the war, at the comparatively early age of fifty-one, stricken down by hospital fever caught from his wife, who, with loving devotion, nursed the war-patients for five months, and all but fell a victim as well as her husband. But Arndt and many others of the leading patriots were deprived of office or suspended, and Schleiermacher himself, often in danger of dismissal, probably escaped only because the authorities feared to deprive the city of so bright an ornament, and of a teacher so greatly beloved. Those things did not greatly disturb his equanimity. He calmly and earnestly went on with his work, enjoying the society of his friends, at perfect rest in his happy home circle, and often recruiting health and spirits by a summer tour, sometimes with wife and children, sometimes alone, or in the company of a congenial friend. In 1817 a little change took place in his household. Nanni, who had continued to live with him after his marriage, became the wife of Arndt, and her place was supplied by his own sister Charlotte, the gentle playfellow of his childhood, and his life-long trusted friend, who at last left her retreat among the Brethren to spend the evening of her days beside her beloved Fritz.

It was for Schleiermacher one of the penalties of greatness that his far-seeing wisdom, which made him so much in advance of his age, and his outspoken boldness in stating his independent opinions, compelled him, notwithstanding his peaceable and loving disposition, to be a man of war for the greater part of his life. In the question of proposed Church Reform, he declared that it was vain to attempt to improve the constitution of the clergy if the reform were not founded on a well-organized Christian presbyterian system, with extensive assemblies of elders chosen by the community; just as a truly free state-constitution is based on a free and living communal system.

In the great question of the union of the Reformed and Lutheran Churches he also took a very prominent part. The leading opponent of the union was Claus Harms of Kiel, who, in the beginning of his career, had owed so much to Schleiermacher's *Discourses*. He held that such a union would be an apostasy, not only from Lutheranism, but from Christianity. But Schleiermacher, with deeper insight, pointed out that none of the Reformers had created a new thing; that they had only cleared the old, pure doctrine from the rubbish with which it had been overlaid, and that therefore the work of the Reformation was not to found a Lutheran Church, nor a Reformed Church, "but to bring forth in renewed glory the Evangelical Church, which is guided and governed by its founder, Jesus Christ, the eternal Son of God, . . . the quickening centre of the Church."

From his letters during a holiday tour in 1818, we give a few short extracts:

"The cathedral (Prague) is a noble, but unfinished edifice, in Gothic style; . . . beneath it the history of Bohemia lies interred. . . . The people seem to be quite indifferent to all the beautiful monuments that surround them, and to all the great memories that are attached to them, and appear to be utterly unconscious that, with their Protestantism and their religious liberty, they lost all their dignity. . . . I was actually seized with a shudder—a religious shudder—at the sight of the immense Jesuit college, and with a political shudder at the equally gigantic palace of Wallenstein. But what shall I say of the ruinous state of churches and convents? Protestantism has been wrenched from the people with unheard-of cruelty, but Catholicism they cannot prevent from rotting among them." "We received a visit from a Catholic ecclesiastic, who pleased me so much, that we parted from each other with a brotherly kiss and with tearful eyes." [Munich] "Old Jacobi was actually moved on seeing me. We endeavoured to come to an understanding relative to our views, but we got no further than to understand wherein the difference between us consists; and he always listened to me very good-naturedly when I told him that I thought his great mistake was that he confounded this difference with another."

Schleiermacher's family at this time consisted of two daughters of his own and an adopted daughter, besides the young Von Willichs; and in 1820 his joy received its crown in the birth of a son. He writes to his sister-in-law announcing the event, and says: "This time I had not felt so strong a wish that it should be a boy as on former occasions. I was too much penetrated by the feeling that we do not know what we wish for, more especially in the present times. But when it proved to be a boy, you may conceive with what joy and thankfulness I received him, and that my first prayer to God was, to be inspired with wisdom and power from above to educate the child to His glory."

It was, alas! but a short time that the training of the boy was left in his hands.

In 1821 Schleiermacher published what is considered his chief theological work, *The Christian Faith systematically presented according to the fundamental Propositions of the Evangelical Church*, familiarly known as the *Glaubenslehre*. "The fundamental principle of this classical work" (we here quote from the *Encyclopædia Britannica*) "is that religious feeling, the sense of absolute dependence on God, as communicated by Jesus Christ through the Church, and not the creeds, or the letter of Scripture, or the rationalistic understanding, is the source and law of dogmatic theology. It is therefore simply a description of the facts of religious feeling, or of the inner life of the soul in its relation to God, and these inward facts looked at in the various stages of their development, and presented in their inner connection. It aims . . . to put an end to the unreason and superficiality of both supernaturalism and rationalism, and to deliver theology from dependence on ever-changing systems of philosophy."

This great work caused him fresh troubles, by arousing the bitter opposition of those whose systems he attacked. He also incurred anew the ill-will and suspicion of the government by his boldly contending for the right of the Church to frame her own liturgy, without the dictation of the king and his ministers. In 1824 he writes to Charlotte von Kathen: "My outward position is very precarious, perhaps more so than ever. The suspicions of demagogical tendencies in regard to me have, I trust, been allayed; but the ecclesiastical questions must soon be brought to a head, and should the result be violent measures, I must infallibly be one of the first victims. I cannot say that I am alarmed, or that in itself the thought of this troubles me; for in regard to these matters I know that I have done nothing but what I was bound to do; and I almost think I may say, also, that I have done all that I ought to do."

And again, in 1827, to the same friend: "When you hear how constantly I am engaged in conflicts which I cannot avoid without doing violence to my conscience, you will, I am sure, feel sorry that the last part of my life should be spent amid so much turmoil, and that I should be obliged to waste so much time on these matters, which, according to all appearance, might be used to much better purpose. However, I do not repine, but think, on the contrary, that it is all for the best; and when my book of life is made up, I shall have greater reason for thankfulness than most people. From what I have heard from several quarters, things seem this time to have been very near coming to a crisis. As for myself, I rarely know how these matters stand, and generally do not hear the worst until it has blown over. May it ever remain so; for it is my endeavour to do nothing that I may have to repent of afterwards, and for the rest I leave the result to God."

In the autumn of 1827 Schleiermacher and his wife took a journey into Galicia to bring home a second adopted daughter, a little child of Nanni's sister, who had died there, leaving a young family. Thus in almost continual outward strife, but in home happiness and heart peace, the years sped on.

Schleiermacher's only visit to England, a very short one, occurred in 1828. His companion on this journey was Alexander von Forstner, son-in-law of Charlotte von Kathen. On the way they spent a few days at Bonn with Nanni and her husband; and in a letter to his wife, Schleiermacher gives a pretty picture of Nanni's little flock of five, one of whom "said a little prayer in the true Arndt style." Arndt had been, so early as 1819, suspended from his professorship on a charge of "demagogic movements," though allowed to retain his salary. It was not till 1840 that he was restored, when he was already above seventy. The brave old patriot lived to be ninety-one, and only died in 1860. Schleiermacher preached once in London, at the re-opening of the church of the Savoy.

In the following year a heart-breaking sorrow came upon him in the death of his only son, his little Nathanael, who was taken from him after a short illness, when only nine years old. The blow, he said, drove the nails into his own coffin; yet, with his wonted self-control, he would not allow his grief to hinder his work. He had delighted in helping the child with his lessons for the gymnasium, and having his bright companionship in his study; but on the very day of his funeral the mourning father took up again the burden of his daily duties, and "life," he says, "goes on in its old grooves, but more slowly and more heavily." His discourse at the child's funeral, included in the present selection, is considered one of his finest.

The king seemed at last to become aware that it was possible for thorough devotion to the liberties of the people to exist in perfect harmony with utter fidelity to the sovereign, and in 1831 he conferred on Schleiermacher the Order of the Red Eagle, an honour which was valuable to him only as an assurance of the restored favour and confidence of the king. In the same year his faithful Lotte was taken to her rest. She had in her last days retired to the house of the Brethren in the city, to secure the quiet that had become desirable in her feeble state.

Schleiermacher's habitual feeling towards his opponents may be understood from the following extract.

"Amid the various conflicts which I am necessarily exposed to in my career, and amid the numerous misunderstandings of the extreme parties on both sides, through which I am obliged to wind my way, it is ever a great encouragement to me when I discover even a faint glimmer that leads me to think that we hold the same goal in view, and are labouring for the same end. . . . Thus at least I learn to unite, quietly within myself, with many who believe themselves far distant from me, and herein dwells a peculiar life-giving energy." He only grieved that profitless controversy inevitably consumed so much precious time, which he would gladly have used in more pleasant and lasting work.

In the midst of his other labours he took time to write to his step-son, Ehrenfried von Willich, wise and most loving counsels as to his studies, his companionships, and the future direction of his life. This young man obtained in 1831 a government appointment at Aix-la-Chapelle. To him the mother sends a pleasant picture of Schleiermacher in holiday guise. "I shall never forget the impression it made upon me to see dear father in his blue blouse, with his silvery white hair, as lively and youthful as a young lad about to wander forth into the world for the first time, giving a parting word to all, who pressed round him with joyful emotion."

One other extract from the mother's letters shows us a pleasant part of the family life. "Our Wednesday receptions are very much frequented, so that we cannot be said to live in great retirement. . . . The Wednesday evenings are often rendered doubly cheerful by a great number of young people. The circle of young maidens in our house is a spectacle which gladdens many hearts; and how this fresh and youthful circle gathered round your father embellishes and sweetens his old age, you will readily conceive."

In the summer of 1833 Schleiermacher went, in company with his friend Count Schwerin, of Putzar, in Pomerania, on a tour which he said would be his last, "with the exception of the long one," through Sweden, Norway and Denmark. His home letters during this journey are marked by a deepened tenderness, and still more, as we are assured by the translator of his letters, by the absence of every indication of the fact that his progress through the northern kingdoms was a continual ovation; his arrival in Copenhagen being hailed with the greatest enthusiasm, professors, students and distinguished men joining to honour him by a public banquet, winding up with a torchlight procession.

His last letter was written January 30th, 1834, to Ehrenfried von Willich. In it he speaks of the happy prospect of having all the children assembled in May to celebrate the silver wedding of the parents, refers to arrangements for the approaching marriage of one of the girls to the son of Count Schwerin, playfully enlarges on the wonderful accomplishments of the first grandchild,—probably the child of Ehrenfried's sister; and closes by saying he has been for three days confined to the house by a cough and hoarseness, but hopes to resume his usual work on the morrow. But his ailment suddenly developed inflammation of the lungs, and after a week of intense suffering, the great, brave, tender spirit passed away. His wife, in her notes of that week, relates that after the death film had already overspread his eyes, and his whole aspect was that of death, he suddenly raised himself, and in a clear and strong voice spoke out, "I have never clung to the dead letter; and we have the atoning death of Jesus Christ, His body and blood." He then desired the things necessary for Communion to be quickly brought, and after solemn prayer, administered it to each of those present, while an expression of heavenly rapture spread over his features, and a strange lustre shone in his eyes. Finally he himself partook, adding, "On these words of the Scripture I rely; they are the foundation of my faith;" and after pronouncing the blessing, sank back on his pillow with a farewell word and look of love, and in a few minutes breathed his last, February 12th, 1834.

The sensation his death caused in Berlin, and indeed throughout Germany, was indescribable. The honour which had so often been withheld from him by prejudice and jealousy during his life was abundantly accorded to him in death. The carriages of the king and the crown prince were the foremost of a hundred that formed his funeral procession, thirty-six of the students who loved and revered him as a father shared the privilege of bearing his coffin to the grave, and the streets and the cemetery were thronged with weeping thousands, mourning for a teacher and a friend whose like they might never see again.

I.

THE POWER OF PRAYER IN RELATION TO OUTWARD CIRCUMSTANCES.

TEXT: MATT. xxvi. 36–46.

TO be a religious man and to pray are really one and the same thing. To join the thought of God with every thought of any importance that occurs to us; in all our admiration of external nature, to regard it as the work of His wisdom; to take counsel with God about all our plans, that we may be able to carry them out in His name; and even in our most mirthful hours to remember His all-seeing eye; this is the prayer without ceasing to which we are called, and which is really the essence of true religion.

As to the benefit of prayer there can be no question. Surely, surely we have all experienced it! If our joys have often remained innocent, while others strayed into ways of sin; if our judgments have been mixed with gentleness and modesty, where pride and arrogance might most easily have gained the day; if we have been guarded from the evil which the judgment of man all too willingly excuses; then we owe this beneficent protection to the power of prayer.

Whether prayer has another kind of power in the world besides this, is a question that may easily be raised, and on which, if we are not to have our minds needlessly disturbed, we must come to some fixed belief.

If we are to bring all our thoughts into harmony with the thought of God, then we may and shall direct our wishes to certain things that we desire may occur to, or be averted from ourselves or others. Now if we regard the fulfilment of those wishes as the aim of our prayers, and connect with this idea what is promised in answer to prayer—then, whether we consider this answer, as some do, as a distinct and infallible mark of the divine favour; or if we only believe, as very many do, that our prayers throw some additional weight into the scale; either way, what a narrowing of our mental condition accompanies such a belief; how it sets limits to the reasonableness of our wishes, and even to the humility of our hearts! For thus our minds are filled with hopes, the usually disappointing issues of which disturb our peace, and indeed may bring us into the most painful uncertainty as to our standing with God. Let us therefore consider together this aspect of prayer. The portion of the history of our Lord's passion which we take as our subject is specially suitable for this purpose, as it shows us our Lord Himself engaged in the kind of prayer we are speaking of.

We will consider the nature of His prayer and its results: and you will certainly grant this beforehand, that the disciple is not above his master, and that we cannot expect more from our prayers than Christ obtained by His. For if the granting of our petitions is a token of God's favour, then it would certainly have been given above all to Him in whom God was so supremely well-pleased. If it is only to be given when a man's own strength is not equal to what he seeks, and when there is need of special help, then let me remind you how utterly the Saviour denied Himself all human succour, and what strict limits He set to Himself by the laws which He followed in all His actions. If the success of the prayer depends on the importance, or on the innocence of the thing desired, then you know that no trifle ever occupied His mind, and that though in all points tempted like us, He was without sin.

If, then, we cannot beforehand come to the conclusion that what Christ's prayer effected ours can also effect, this at least is certain, that where His prayer could not prevail neither will ours succeed. This similarity of our position with His must be a soothing thought to us all, whatever may be the result of our inquiry; and therefore I ask the more confidently for your calm and unprejudiced attention.

We have here a direct view of the Saviour, before He fell into the hands of His enemies, in an agitated and anxious state of mind. He knew that there was a plot against His life, which was now on the point of being carried out; and plainly and calmly as He had before talked with His disciples of what was before Him, now that He was to enter on the conflict—now that all, as it came nearer, looked darker and more certain—the various feelings that such a prospect could not but excite in His mind threw Him into a state of stronger agitation than was at all usual with him. He sought solitude, and then fled from it; from prayer He went back to His disciples, who were in no condition to comfort or cheer Him; and from them He went back again to prayer. In circumstances like these, even to those who are furthest from true piety, the old, half-forgotten memory of God comes back, and they turn to Him for help and deliverance; in such circumstances even those whose spirit is bravest, and who are absolutely submissive to the divine will, are yet not quite without anxiety or without wishes; and therefore, in this instance, the prayer of the Saviour took the form of one of the ordinary petitions of men for a result according to their desires.

It is the value and the power of a prayer of this kind that we wish to consider. Let us first examine carefully the case before us, to see what it teaches us, and then, secondly, note any deductions to be drawn from it.

I. First, then, fix it firmly in your minds that you have the privilege of laying before God your wishes about the more important concerns of your lives. It cannot be superfluous, in these times, to strengthen ourselves in this belief. Those who would like to banish everything belonging to religion from the minds of men, by allowing no room for the exercise of it in daily life, do not fail to represent such a prayer as an offence against the Most High. It is irreverent, they say, to express a wish rising out of the narrowness of our intellect and heart, about something which His decree has long ago settled; it is an ill-timed curiosity to say, I wish it might be so and so, when we shall presently learn how He has willed it. Do not be perplexed by such words. Christ did it, therefore we, too, may do it. It is one of the privileges that belong to our position as children of God. That would be a slavish family in which the children were not at liberty to express their wishes in the presence of their wiser father. And is any one able all at once to suppress his desires? If we cannot do so, then let us always speak them out when our heart is moved to do so; for even if we do shut them up within us, they are not hidden from Him. Do not listen to those who tell you that, before you approach God, you must have your mind composed and your heart at peace; that it is unseemly to appear before Him in this agitated state, while the dread of pain and disappointment, the clinging to some good thing which you are on the point of losing, still tosses your heart to and fro, and leaves no room for submission to the holy will of God. If you waited until submission had won the victory, you would feel neither the need nor the inclination for such a prayer, and the privilege of offering it would be useless to you. If the feelings that stir your heart are sinful emotions; if these emotions are kindled by the fire of passion; then the thought of God and prayer to Him can have no place beside them. But that disquietude, so altogether natural to man as God has made him, which agitates us at the touch of loss and misfortune, or when threatened with a check being laid on our activities, or with separation from those we love—such disquietude should not keep us back from God; for only thus will our hearts not condemn us, and we shall have confidence towards God (1 John iii. 21). Christ Himself, as you see here, used no other means to allay this so unusual agitation in His holy soul. Prayer alone was the means He took. In the very midst of His trouble He turned in supplication to His heavenly Father; just when His soul was sorrowful even unto death, He left His disciples to go and pray.

But while I most sincerely encourage you to do this, I just as earnestly entreat you, in the second place, by no means to feel sure that what you ask will of necessity take place because of your prayer. The words of Christ leave no room to doubt that He really and most earnestly prayed that the suffering before Him might be averted; He uses the very same words which He always used in speaking of it; and we know only too well from the close of His history that the event was not according to His prayer. That which He had always foreseen and foretold befel Him; He had the cup of suffering, just as He saw it set before Him in His hour of sorrow and dread, to drain to the last drop. And a result which *His* prayer did not effect will not and cannot be effected by ours. Do not then infer, as many do, from the promises in certain passages of Scripture, that God always gives what is asked of Him in true faith and out of a pure heart. You will not deny that Christ had a faith that might have been pre-eminently a reason for God's favour, and in His filial and submissive entreaty you will find nothing unbefitting to a pure heart. Such an answer then must have been given to Him above all others; and the words spoken by Himself, "Ask, and ye shall receive," must therefore have some other meaning than that which we have indicated, since this was not the sense in which the promise was fulfilled to Him, the Author and Finisher of our faith. And if not to Him, how should it come to pass that God should fulfil *your* wishes because of your prayers? Do you think it might be more possible in your case than in His, because His suffering and death was a part of God's great plan for the restoration of the human race? But in reality everything is taken into account in God's plan, and it is all one plan. Whatever your heart may long for, sooner will heaven and earth pass away than the slightest tittle be changed of what has been decreed in the counsels of the Most High. Or is this your idea: it is true that the Eternal cannot change His purpose, but knowing all things beforehand, He knew when and what His pious and beloved children would ask from Him, and has so arranged the chain of events that the issue shall accord with their wishes? That is to try at once to honour the wisdom of God and to flatter the childish fancies of men. God has not called us to so high a place as that our wishes should be prophecies; but certainly to something higher than that the granting of those wishes should be to us the most precious evidence of His favour. This is really among the most perverted of the devices with which people have tried to adorn religion; but it is only an invention of a warped understanding, not a conclusion drawn from the way in which God reveals Himself in the world. It is dishonouring to Christ to think that He should not have been the first in this respect; and it is dishonouring to men that if God had arranged all this, we should so seldom meet with examples of answered prayer.

Let us see then, in the third place, what really is the effect of our prayers, if it is not to be sought in the agreement of the result with the expressed wish. Just the effect that it produced in Christ's own case. Consider, with me, what passed, on that occasion, in His mind. He began with the definite wish that His sufferings might pass away from Him; but as soon as He fixed His thought on His Father in heaven to whom He prayed, this wish was at once qualified by the humble, "if it be possible." When from the sleeping disciples, the sight of whom must have still more disheartened Him and added fresh bitterness to His sense of desertion, He returned to prayer, He already bent His own wish before the thought that the will of the Father might be something different. To reconcile Himself to this, and willingly to consent to it, was now His chief object; nor would He have wished that the will of God should not be done, had He been able by that means to gain all that the world could give.

And when He had prayed for the third time all anxiety and dread were gone. He had no longer any wish of His own. With words in which He sought to impart to them some of the courage He had gained, He awakened His friends from their sleep, and went with calm spirit and holy firmness to meet the traitor.

There you see the effect that such a prayer ought to have. It should make us cease from our eager longing for the possession of some earthly good, or the averting of some dreaded evil; it should bring us courage to want, or to suffer, if God has so appointed it; it should lift us up out of the helplessness into which we are brought by fear and passion, and bring us to the consciousness and full use of our powers; that so we may be able in all circumstances to conduct ourselves as it becomes those who remember that they are living and acting under the eye and the protection of the Most High.

But prayer will more necessarily produce this effect if some point is not entirely lacking in our conception of the Divine Being. If we lay before God a wish that this or that may so happen in the world as it seems to be best for us, we must remember that we are laying it before the *Unchangeable*, in whose mind no new thought or purpose can arise since the day when He said, "all is very good." What was then decreed will take place; we must not lose sight of the indisputable certainty of this thought. Well, and suppose that which you fear has been decreed? Suppose you are to be torn away from your beloved field of labour, or to lose the friend to whom your heart cleaves, or that the undeserved calumny is still to rest on you? Inevitably our first impulse will be to thrust back those fears. It cannot be, we say; it will not be: it would be too hard; too unfatherly. But the thought, it cannot be, will perish in our hearts when we remember that it is the *Unsearchable* whom our hope seeks to limit in this way. It may easily be—it may easily be, is the voice that reaches us from a thousand examples of unmerited and hardly endurable suffering. And if it should be so—we cannot bend *His* will; then what remains to us but to bring our will into accord with His?

And we are drawn to do this, and to do it from the heart, by the encouraging thought that He to whom we would present our petition is the *Only Wise*. You imagine something to be beneficial and good, and you wish that God may allow it to happen. Does not your wish as well as your judgment stand silent at the thought of Him? How far can you see into the consequences and the connection of those events, even as regards your own well-being? He knows the best and the whole. If according to His appointment you must do without what you desire, you have compensation for that in all the good that you see in the world. And thus will be called forth in us distrust of our own wisdom; humility, that looks on ourselves as only a little part of the whole; benevolence, that will find its satisfaction more in consideration of the world than in our own prosperity.

But the Wise is also the *Kind*. He will not let thee suffer and lack thy desires merely for the sake of others; His will is that to the upright man everything shall serve to his own highest good. And so there comes to us the trust that, little part as we are, account has been taken of us among the whole; and from this comes repose of the spirit; for, whatever befals us, good must come out of it; and thus, at last the quieted and soothed heart can cry, Father, Thy will be done. If we once face the dreaded evil with calmness and submission, we shall readily see in the right light the intention of all that happens to us, and our chief attention will be directed to that. He who prays must remember that everything that befalls us has its end in ourselves, and is intended for our improvement and the increase of good in us. Then he will become conscious that this aim of the Most High, which his excited feelings had for a little while pushed out of sight, is yet in reality his own aim also. And if everything can be, and ought to be, a means to this end, why should he shrink from anything that may come upon him? If both prosperity and adversity draw out and confirm good points of character; if in both he can act worthily and in a way well-pleasing to God; why should he not welcome both as coming from the hand of God and by His direction? When the heart has reached this point it has taken the right attitude. Now we are occupied with something else than our feelings; with the question, What will be required of me should this or that befall? what kind of powers shall I employ? what kind of stand shall I make against it? what acts of thoughtlessness must I avoid? And if we find that it always depends on those same qualities which we have often exercised and studied over; that the whole of what we may be able to accomplish consists of single acts which we have often before performed with good results; then the soul that had shrunk in fear comes back to the consciousness of its powers; then we feel ourselves strong enough to walk in the way that God has traced out for us, strong enough to comfort those who are sad on our account and more disheartened than ourselves; and if the hour comes when the evil does befall, we can say, with a mind composed and at peace, Let us rise and go to meet it.

According to the example of the Saviour, these are the

right effects of such a prayer. I hope they will appear to you all great and important enough to make you willingly forget the impossible and wonderful which so many regard as the main point in prayer. If you count it a better thing to teach those whose training is in your hands to bear all kinds of trouble and hardships, than always to guard them from it, then praise the divine wisdom which, in giving us prayer, has put into our hands a powerful means to the former, but not to the latter.

In order to enable you still further to consider this important subject, let me add—

II. Some general inferences that may be drawn from what the example of Christ has taught us.

1. If nothing is changed on account of our prayers in the course of things ordained by God, we must not attach any special value to occasional apparent answers that we may receive. There seldom elapses any considerable time in which our health, or our outward prosperity, or our relations with those who are dearest to us in the world, are not threatened by various dangers; and I hope there are few among us who do not make such things subjects of prayer. But whatever may be the issue of these critical circumstances, beware of asking in your prayers for the reason of them, or seeking to know how far God has been pleased or displeased. Besides that this is dishonouring God, as we have already seen, it utterly corrupts your judgment of your own and of other men's merits, and teaches you to attach importance to things that have none whatever.

And yet on this judgment, if you are intelligent and consistent with yourself, depends your whole mode of life and action. And this holds good even as to the fulfilment of our purest and noblest wishes, that is, those which are concerned with the progress of good, whether in general or that in which we are instruments and fellow-labourers. Rejoice if your righteous undertakings are successful; rejoice if God makes use of you as direct instruments for the increase of good in the world; rejoice if at last you are specially successful in what has long been the chief object of your efforts, your anxieties and your prayers; but let not those things lead you to the proud belief that they are a distinctive sign of God's satisfaction with your spiritual condition. Many a one with whom nothing succeeds, and whose work in the world seems to be in vain, not only purposes as honestly, but certainly does his duty as zealously and is as thoroughly devout as you. To measure human merit by such things is a dangerous imperfection of faith, and one of those for which very specially Christ became the Mediator between God and us. See how even He seemed to fail in everything, and yet how God made use of Him in the noblest way! How His request was not granted, and yet He was at that moment, as always, the Son in whom the Father was well pleased.

2. You will now, I hope, admit that there is no true prayer but that which I described in the beginning of our meditation; that is to say, the prayer we offer when we have the living thought of God accompanying, purifying and sanctifying all our other thoughts, feelings and purposes. All other forms which prayer may assume in isolated cases must, if you would really please God, resolve themselves into this one highest aspect, which takes in your whole manner of life. Our prayer of thanksgiving is just our thought of God united with our joy at what has taken place; and it will only be pleasing to Him if it hallows and elevates this joy, if it is the means of raising our interest from earthly to higher things. If it is only thanks, mere joy in the new possession that God has lent us, our thankoffering has no value in His eyes.

And it is the same with our petitions, whether they concern our own circumstances, or are brotherly intercessions. If our prayer has not the effect of moderating the wish that it expressed, of replacing the eager desire with quiet submission, the anxious expectation with devout calmness; then it was no true prayer, and gives sure proof that we are not yet at all capable of this real kind of prayer.

3. In the third place, I will say to you frankly that it seems to me a mark of greater and more genuine piety when this entreating kind of prayer is only seldom used by us, and we do not allow our thoughts to be long occupied with it. For why is it, after all, that our prayer takes the form of entreaty? When we desire something that we ourselves cannot accomplish, and at the same time remember God; then occurs to us first of all the thought of His almighty power in contrast to our weakness, and we would like to try to make that power favourable to us. That is prayer as dictated by the weak human heart. But there lies at the bottom of this a defective idea of God. If we called to mind what should always come most readily to our thoughts—His holiness and wisdom—our wish would quickly take the form by which the prayers of pious men must always be distinguished. And, no doubt, the more habitual real piety is with us, the oftener we think of all that we can learn about God, just so much the more quickly will this change take place.

Those who boast that they can persist in prayer, that they do not grow weary in beseeching God to bring about this or that, are still very far from the spirit of true godly fear. It is told us of Christ several times that He retired into solitude, and spent whole nights in prayer. But it was not the fear of anything that might occur, not interest in any event, that drew Him to prayer; but the need of His heart to give Himself up to devout meditation, and to the undisturbed enjoyment of communion with His Father, without a definite wish or a special request. Whereas, when we find Jesus entreating, it is in exceptional and therefore only in rare instances. It needed, indeed, an occasion of strong emotion, such as is not likely to occur very frequently in our lives, to call forth in His holy soul so much that must tend to our comfort in the subject before us. Are you overtaken by such an occasion? Then entreat, until true prayer makes you forget entreaty.

As for those who boast that they often supplicate in this way; that they seek God's presence several times a day to ask about everything, either that has already happened or that they wish to obtain, and to thank Him for every trifle connected with their daily life; it seems to me they have little to boast of. However much they may say of the devotion with which they offer these prayers, I really believe that in such prayers there is no *real* devotion. At stated times they lay their wants before God; their prayers belong, like other little pieces of business, to the order of the day; and from them they go at once to other employments or pleasures in which no trace of religion can be seen; and in the same way they come from the midst of cares and work and merriment to prayer, with their minds filled and pervaded with earthly things. Does that, to a heart whose intercourse with God is habitual, indicate a good state of things? He who is chiefly aroused to the thought of God by a sense of dependence certainly does not think really of Him at all, and the true Christian spirit is utterly wanting in him. Whatever assurances such persons may give us of the blessings brought to their hearts by such prayer, these are certainly only incidental and passing emotions. Do they not always speak the same customary words? Do they not, for the most part, pray with their thoughts far away? We all know how little effect such prayer can have on one's inner life. It is in truth no loss to Christianity when such customs fall into disuse. No; with a light heart would I see all these forms and fixed hours of prayer disappear; free as they may be from any superstitious intention, and whatever bearing they may be thought to have on morality and fulfilment of duty. A heart-stirring thought of the Creator, when our eye rests on His works, out of the quiet delight which we take in His creation; a thought of the Ruler of the world, checking our false estimates, amidst our talk of the fortunes and undertakings of men; a sense of Him whose image becomes manifest in us when we feel ourselves overflowing with love and good-will, amidst the social enjoyment of those noble human feelings; a glad sense of His love when we are enjoying His gifts; when we succeed in some good work, a thankful sense of His support; when we meditate on His commandments, the great hope that He wishes to raise us to His own likeness; this is true prayer: the blessings of which I heartily desire we may all abundantly enjoy.

II.

THE DYING SAVIOUR OUR EXAMPLE.

(On Good Friday.)

TEXT: MARK xv. 34-41.

HEAVENLY Father! On all who are assembling to-day to commemorate the death of the Holy One, in whom Thou wast well pleased, look graciously down! Let not one go away from the cross of Thy Well-beloved without exclaiming, with new, living faith, Truly this was the Son of God! Let not one wipe away his tears of emotion until the heartfelt desire has taken possession of him that his end may be like that of this righteous One! Let not the feeling of holy reverence and admiration, that must lay hold on every one at the remembrance of the dying Christ, be left behind within these walls and bear no fruit; let it go forth with us all into our life, so that it may be more and more consecrated to Thee, and become more like to His, until at last we follow Him, in departing with good courage to Thee. Amen.

A sad and moved heart, my brethren, I take for granted in all of us at this hour, and to this I wish to address myself. Let us, I entreat you, lay aside, at least for the present, all the separate notions that each of us may have of certain particular benefits and blessings from the death of Jesus. I honour them all, if they dwell in a heart that I honour; but it would be sad if the most sacred of days were spent in raising questions, in sifting opinions, in instituting discussions, by which minds are not moved for good, and are often quite turned away from each other, through differences, which of course there must always be, coming to light at the very time when we desire to be most cordially united. No, we wish to unite in such meditations as may be of equal importance and equal blessing to us all, as surely as we all reverence in Christ the Author of our faith, as we all count His death a death of love and obedience, as we all set before us His life even to death as the pattern which we seek to follow; yes, His life even to death, not even excluding the last experiences of His holy soul. Whether we, like Him, shall retain to our last heart-beat the full use of all the faculties of our minds, is a question on which we can come to no decision; it is a special favour of God, depending on the circumstances in which He brings about the close of our life. But the last heart-beat is not really the end of life; life ceases with the last thought and feeling that our spirit brings forth in union with its body; with the last glance in which the surrounding world is still visible to us; with the last consciousness of our earthly circumstances; and if we are then to treat those circumstances, and to regard this world, and to look back on our past life just as He did, that can be the fruit solely of a life led just as His was, and of a mind just as collected. Therefore let us learn to die in seeing Christ die! It is no small thing that I expect from you in calling on you to do this; for it is with the death of the Saviour as it was with His life; let him who seeks only happiness and joy shun likeness to Him; let him alone seek it who covets what is great and perfect at any price. An easier end, a gentler sleeping away than the Saviour's there may easily be; but none that would be more sublime, none more worthy of a pious and virtuous heart.

Let him who covets such an end look now with me at the perfecting of the Holy One of God.

In wishing that we may die as Christ did, I do not mean to advert to that state of mind which for every one who has walked in the right way is a matter of course. That regret for a wasted life may not be our last crushing feeling, that a too fond clinging to the joys and possessions of this world may not make the leaving of it more difficult than it ought to be, that no anxious doubt may mingle in our childlike submission to Him who is leading us into the valley of death; let there be no question of these things among us. There are three other particulars to which I wish to direct your attention as something greatly to be desired; desirable, I mean, just for this reason, that in order to act as Christ did in those circumstances, the close and complete likeness to Him, at which we are all aiming, will be necessary. I desire, then, that in dying we may all have, in the first place, the same sorrow over unaccomplished deeds; secondly, the same calmness under the unjust judgments of the world; and thirdly, that we may be in the same way surrounded by tender and faithful friends. Let your devout attention be directed for the present to these particulars.

I. Oh, that we might all die with the same sorrow over unaccomplished deeds, which was so plainly revealed in the Saviour's sorrowful cry, "My God, My God, why hast Thou forsaken Me?" For do you suppose that this cry was wrung from Him by bodily suffering? Heavy as the pressure of that may have been, yet for Him to whom it still left strength for such expressions of kindness, of care and sympathy as Christ gave from His cross, it could not obscure the principle He had so often asserted, that suffering can just as little be a token of the displeasure of the Most High as success is a pledge of His favour. Or was it that Jesus clung to the joys of life, so that He was afflicted by the necessity of leaving it while so young? Or was it perhaps that His imagination was so filled with ideas of future worldly greatness that He was mortified at not being able to attain to it? No; but He loved His duty with His whole heart; the thought of the great work to which He had devoted His life still filled His soul. And when He reflected how far that work still was from completion; how in fact not one of His disciples had clearly understood His views and feelings or seen into His plan, how little they were prepared for all that must now burst upon them, and how easily the bond that held them together might be dissolved; could we well wonder if He had asked, My God, My God, why hast Thou withdrawn Thy protecting hand from this undertaking? But this He does not ask. He knew how closely the thread of His designs was woven into the plan of Providence; He only wished that it had been appointed to Himself to carry on the great business still further; He only asks, from the depth of a heart that cannot do enough of good, why the Eternal should now call Him away, in order to carry forward the great work without His help; He saw so plainly what more He would have brought to pass; and the Most High was not permitting Him to do it.

It is this very desire and sorrow that I wish for us all in our last hours. It is not needful for this that we be snatched away, as Christ was, in the prime of life from some great work; every one may feel thus, in whatever position he may be. Are you servants of the State, administrators of public regulations; may you grieve that you cannot still reform abuses and introduce improvements! Are you independent and wealthy; may you grieve that you cannot set agoing one more benevolent institution, or do this thing and that for the unfortunate whom you protect! Are you scholars and philosophers; may you be reluctant to interrupt an instructive presentation of your thoughts, or to turn away from a new field of human knowledge!

Are you artists and workmen; may it grieve you that you are not to bestow on one more piece of work at least the new perfection that you have planned or practised! You young men, may you long for even a little while in which to practise and set forth, in your own domestic life, the principles of virtue and religion which you hold dear! You men in your prime, may it break your hearts not to be able to complete the training of your children, to bring on further the young who were trustfully clinging to you! You old men, may it grieve you not to be able still longer to use, for the good of your descendants, the well-earned respect in which you are held, and to support with the counsel of your mature wisdom any good work that is undertaken around you!

In wishing this for you, my brethren, I am, in fact, only wishing that you may never cease to love your work, and to devote to it your whole consideration, your whole strength. If there could ever be a point in human life at which, for those so disposed, the account might be closed, and no work in process, I should be inclined to wish, for the sake of sparing you this pain, that each of you might die at that point of time, before a new series of operations were begun, which you could not complete; but such a resting-point you will not find. There is no rest and no standing still in a spirit that loves duty and work. Every change brought about by the course of nature and of human affairs brings with it new problems and new duties; while you are occupied in meeting the duties of one relationship another has already developed. And even were it not so, the reciprocal influence of action and reflection produces an incessant movement, and ever new desires and efforts. Each action enlarges and corrects our insight into the subject; and all improved insight makes us eager at once to apply it. In the midst of work, therefore, in the midst of unfinished work, death finds every one who is making a right use of life; and from the painful feeling that results from this, he alone can be free who cowardly flees from his obligations and buries himself in vanity and shadows when the voice of duty is addressed to him; such a one may die weary of life, for he has never known its fairest charm. Or the man of slavish spirit, who is content with an empty show of virtue, and knows no higher aim than to have done nothing deserving of punishment—he also, provided his delusion holds out so long, may meet death without feeling; for the future which he is losing has not drawn him with the attraction of new services and completed works, but has only shown him fearful struggles and new temptations.

But, some one might say, even thus there remains also to the sensual and earthly-minded, who is driven from one desire to another, a still unsatisfied longing for some enjoyment; are we, then, with our pain, really in the least degree better than he? Are we better, indeed! We can do what he cannot: we can ask God why He sends us this pain, and He will answer us. Even Christ did not die in asking this sorrowful question. Whatever in it proceeds from the blameless desire that good may be done through us will be lost in the thought that His grace must be sufficient for us; whatever zeal we have for the cause of God will be changed into childlike confidence in Him who will find ways and means for His purposes without us. A divine repose thus soothes away that pain. If it is really only good that we have in view, then let us in commending our spirit to God also commend with comfort our works and plans to Him; and whatever may remain incomplete, we shall yet be able justly to say, It is finished.

II. Again, we could all desire to die with undisturbed tranquility, notwithstanding all unjust and unreasonable judgments, the most unfeeling and hostile behaviour of men. This we see in the case of Christ.

With the meanest cruelty His adversaries found amusement in the sufferings of His last moments, and misconstrued, out of malice or ignorance, His plain words, that they might turn them to ridicule; yet not the slightest sign of displeasure escaped His lips. That treatment from men towards Him who had deserved so much from them appears perhaps the very bitterest ingredient in His cup of suffering; and yet I feel bound to say that even this is a kind of suffering which, as long as things are in their present state in the world, we also shall have to bear, though in a slighter degree; and in the face of which, in whatever way it may come upon us, the composure of the Saviour must be welcome and desirable to us. Unreasonable judgments are something that we must inevitably bear. No one is so high, and no one so low, that they cannot reach him. And a really Christian and upright disposition—why should we shut our eyes to the fact?—is everywhere so rare that men have too little opportunity of observing it to be able to discover and distinguish it. Then why should they presuppose just what is unknown and rare, in order to explain men's conduct by that? They take most satisfaction in what is most improbable; they exhaust themselves in ingeniously imagining what is absurd.

Moreover, it is not at all difficult to attribute every separate expression of this Christian feeling to some other motive. If incidentally something results from it that is agreeable to the ordinary inclinations of men, then the explanation is ready. If it cannot well be said that such a satisfaction was sought or aimed at in what was done, then it was vanity, the desire to appear singular; hypocrisy, seeking to make a show of virtue and unselfishness; or there was some hidden motive at the bottom of it, which the sagacity of a spy quickly discovers. And then if one action, thus explained, contradicts others, the assumptions become the bolder, and scorn is poured more maliciously on so inconsistent a man. He casts out devils by the prince of devils; this is the way in which those who truly honour God and His law in the most difficult positions, where they have acted most nobly, are judged by the great majority of men. They will rather believe that we do good out of hatred, that we care little for the good things of the world out of selfishness, that we expose ourselves to the ridicule of the world from a desire for glory—rather all this than attribute anything to real and unfeigned godliness. If we are obliged during our lifetime to make a considerable experience of this, it will be all the more certainly the case in our last hours.

If we continue to the end vigorous and active in the community, the attention of many will be directed to our manner of withdrawing from the scene. If to the end we are the centre of a little circle of beloved and congenial spirits, with whom our thoughts, our counsels, the expression of our opinions had always some influence, other eyes will be turned with curiosity to our dying bed. And if we have then still strength to express our inmost feelings, those spectators will see in those hours everything that they were unable to understand or reconcile, pressed into very narrow compass. Our unchanged attachment to the occupations of life, which we have loved and earnestly carried on, and the joy with which we look forward to what is prepared for us in the better kingdom of Christ; the calmness with which we shall be ready to part with all that belongs only to our surroundings in this world, and to what is peculiar to the earthly condition; the calmness with which we shall even see our powers decaying, our senses failing, and our limbs growing benumbed under the first touch of the cold hand of death; and, together with that, our continued lively interest in everything that concerns the welfare of our friends and relatives, the prosperity of the Fatherland, the peace of society, the extension of truth, and the unimpeded progress of good in the world;

how can all these things together be anything but incomprehensible to them? Then, that they may not be obliged to admire this greatness of soul, as they call it, they will call to mind every act of weakness, perhaps from long ago; or if they have not that at command, they will remember, as they did with Christ, words and actions which breathed the very spirit of His, but on which they had long ago pronounced a perverted sentence of condemnation; then, even in the last utterances of a pious heart that honours the law of God, they will again discover the old pride, which was long ago their abomination, the fanaticism that they long ago despised, the party zeal that they have always hated, the hypocrisy that they had often felt compelled to expose. Alas for us if then those who love us should be obliged carefully to conceal from us the last hard and false judgments that have been pronounced on us, lest they should awaken us from the sweet dream that men at least know and honour true piety and a moral tone of feeling, though they themselves have no share in it! Alas for us if it were necessary then to deceive us as to the opinion of men, lest some bitter feeling should cloud our last hours! It would be a sign that we had never learned to know men; that we had gone about among them innocently but also very ignorantly, and that if longer life were allotted to us, we should go on being mistaken about them. It is therefore with good reason that I wish for us all in this event the Saviour's calmness and equanimity; for it is the result of the most mature wisdom and the most genuine piety. He whose heart would not even in his last moments be broken by the blindness that degenerates into abuse and calumny, should it come under his notice, must be one who has long known the foolish wisdom and the deep corruption of men. He who, in such a case, is not betrayed into angrily repenting of the kindness he has shown them has certainly had in view in all his doings, not the favour of men, not praise, not gratitude, but only the will of the Most High. He who even then retains enough of goodwill to say, Father, forgive them, for they know not what they do,—his love is of the purest and most divine kind.

III. We could all desire to die surrounded, as the Saviour was, with loving and suffering friends. There stood His tender mother and the disciple whom He loved, and He established between them a heartfelt bond of care and faithfulness; there stood the women who had followed Him, and no doubt many others of His worshippers less known to us. What a comfort must it have been to Him that He could still exert a beneficent influence on them all, and strengthen their faith and their purposes by everything great and divine that was manifested in Him! And as certainly must their fidelity and their presence have softened for Him the sufferings of death, and filled His heart with comforting feelings. If His sorrow at the interruption of His work bore witness that He had worthily maintained His post; if His equanimity under the mockery of His enemies could be a proof of the reality and fulness of His wisdom; on the other hand, this love and faithfulness, enduring even to death, were the best testimony that He, with His loving heart, had enjoyed in His whole sphere of work the highest happiness of life. And it is for such reasons that I wish for ourselves, above all things, to die in such company; nay, as much as lies with ourselves, I demand it of every one.

Do not say that it does not depend on you, but on the free grace of God, whether before your death the fairest ties of nature may be loosed, whether many a one among you may not perhaps remain the last of all his connection, whether death may not come upon many of you far away from parents and children, from brothers and sisters and kindred. I entreat you, honoured and blessed as those affections are which nature itself has created, do not think solely of them. It is the common rule that death has here made many blanks before it takes ourselves away from our place; but though all who are related to us by ties of blood were gathered round our dying bed, we could not experience the comfort afforded by the presence of friendship, unless they were at the same time the confidants of our sentiments, and understood our inmost heart. Behold, said Christ once, pointing to His chosen friends, these are My mother and My brethren; just those it was, for the most part, who now, as sorrowing friends, stood round His cross; and just such ought not to be lacking to any of us so long as we are still on earth. Do not doubt whether you can attain to this happiness; it would be no adverse fortune, but a mournful sign that you had not rightly solved the highest problem of life. The world is not arranged in so malevolent a spirit that from any one who needs and deserves it a friend should be withheld to whom he may open his heart. The power of human nature in drawing congenial minds together is so great that if you only think more correctly and deeply about everything, if you feel anything more heartily and particularly, and express it in your actions, the people who are certain to find this out are just those who know how to value it, or who are like you in that respect. It will only depend on your need of enjoying love and friendship whether a firm and lasting union of spirits is brought about; it depends only on your own will whether you shall still enjoy even in death the peculiar comforts imparted by the presence of friends. Do not fear, when you have found them, that the mutability of the human heart will deprive you of them; that does not reach the depths in which true friendship strikes its roots. Look at Christ; He lost none of His own, but only the one lost sheep, that the Scripture might be fulfilled; and be convinced that in real friendship there can be no instability, no unfaithfulness. Do not fear that death may nevertheless carry off all these from you before the goal of your own life is reached; for that faculty of the human spirit never ceases, and you can never be quite without objects on whom to use it. It is true, a friend whom you have lost will never be replaced; each later connection will take a different form from the preceding; but yet it may be deep and heartfelt, and then it gives the happy consciousness that you enjoy love and respect for your own sake, and influence the depths of a human soul by your own. And fear least of all, I entreat you, the destructive inroads that time may make on your own mind. Do not suppose that dying in possession of loving friends is a special privilege of those who, like Christ, are called away in the flower of their days. Whatever may be said, it is not in the nature of the human soul to become in old age blunted to those joys, to treat the old connections more coldly, and to form new ones reluctantly. If you have ever rightly estimated them, you will always long for them, and never, even in extreme old age, will you stand alone in the world; nay, even if you knew that the next day was to be your last, you would yet, if you met to-day for the first time with one whom you could embrace with hearty love, long to win his affection and try by tender ways to attract it to yourself.

But, you will say, although it is possible and desirable to have friends till the end of life, ought we not then at least to send them away from us rather than to gather them round us? Why increase still more the bitter sensations connected with death by witnessing with sadness and anxiety the sorrow of our friends, and thinking of the critical circumstances in which we are perhaps leaving one and another? Why should we mutually make it obvious, by all that is most vivid in the present, how great a loss we are suffering? We see that Christ did not think in this way. He did not send away His mother and His friend from His cross, but willingly allowed them to be witnesses of His death. A sacred duty calls on us to do the same. We are not by our own fault to break off man's highest ministry even by a moment too soon. We do not know what profitable results the very last outpourings of love may have; and if we show to our friends how a man is exalted even in death by the power of piety and of true wisdom, it will be a blessed impression. But even for our own sakes I desire for us that very sorrow and sadness; for in order not to shrink from such experiences we must be animated by a certain courage, which has the most important effect on a man's whole life, and imparts something great and sublime even to its close. It is cowardly and ungrateful to deny ourselves the last enjoyment of any blessing, because we are obliged to remember that it is the last; for that would lead to casting away from us all the gifts of God, and prematurely to deprive our life of everything pleasant. Even in happy youth does not the feeling of the transitory nature of all earthly things arise? Are we not often involuntarily seized by the thought that each joy may be the last; and ought we not often intentionally to hold fast that thought and look it in the face? but it ought just as little to disturb and discourage a brave spirit in his last moment as in the midst of the hope of a long life. It is an ignoble thing ever to shrink from a pain which is only made possible by the finest instincts of our nature; with so cowardly a state of mind we should have been obliged from the beginning to neglect what was best in us, because we are always exposed in some way to this pain; but a brave spirit will, even at the last moment, feel more strengthened and elevated by the consciousness of having possessed and cultivated this disposition than shaken and weakened by the deepest sorrow.

Let us all strive until our last moment after these purest joys of life! let us bind firmly every tie of love and goodwill, and most firmly of all, not perhaps those which afford us the most lively pleasure, but that which is meant to strengthen and perfect what is highest and noblest in us through real union of minds. Who could help thinking, in this connection, of the union which some of us are about to renew at the Lord's Table, of the covenant of brotherly love and of faithful following of Jesus! The more we value the being fellow-members of Christ, and the more worthy we are, so much the more certainly shall we become like Him, even in our death, in regard to all that we have now been considering. We know that wherever several persons are united in seeking the same end, each one's pleasure and zeal is increased. And if we take this serious view of the fellowship in which we stand with all to whom, in common with us, is committed the promotion of Christ's great work, on whom, as on us, His Spirit rests, how much more opportunity does that give us for all kinds of good! how much more cheerfully can we take up what lies in our own way! how many a call do we meet to lend our support to what others have begun! Oh, none are more diligent in good works than the members of this covenant! Death assuredly finds them in the midst of manifold activities; they certainly look with sad wistfulness, when leaving the world, at their noble legacy of deeds begun!

You are now engaging anew to go on according to our common rule of faith, you make your profession of this publicly and aloud, and there is no doubt that the more honesty and seriousness you show in this act the less can you escape the derision to which those who reverence religion are exposed. But the encouraging approval of your brethren will compensate you for the cruel judgments of the world; the example of so many who have patiently borne what was to be suffered for the faith will strengthen your courage. And what should be the nursery of sincere and faithful friends, if not the Church of Christ, the association of men with whom unselfishness and benevolence, sympathy and helpful love are natural sentiments, among whom every kind of wisdom and perfection ought to exist and to be ready for the service of each? Thus then renew with sincere and devout hearts this glorious covenant, and let us all desire that the Saviour who instituted it may look down on us well pleased, and that His Spirit may rest abundantly upon us.

(*Preached before the King, in the Royal Garrison Church at Potsdam, probably in March.* 1799.)

III.

A NATION'S DUTY IN A WAR FOR FREEDOM.

(*Preached March 28th*, 1813.)

TEXT: JEREMIAH xvii. 5–8, AND xviii. 7–10.

MY devout hearers! Through an extraordinary occurrence we find the order of our discourses on the suffering Saviour interrupted, and our to-day's meeting devoted to a very different subject. How deeply have we all been moved by the events of the last weeks! We saw march forth from our gates the army of a people nominally allied to us, but our feeling was not that of parting with friends; with thankful joy did we feel at last the long, heavy pressure removed from us. Immediately after that came the troops of another nation, nominally at war with us; but with the most joyful enthusiasm were they received when they made themselves known as the friends of the king and the people. And when, not long after them, we saw our own warriors also returning, then no one could any longer doubt, and the word passed joyfully from mouth to mouth: Thanks for the heavenly, unmistakable tokens which God the Lord has given through the fearful turmoil of war in the North; thanks to the noble and brave military leaders who, disregarding the appearance of disobedience and the infraction of the letter, and acting really according to the mind and spirit of the king, dared to take the first decisive step towards freeing us from the intolerable bonds under which we had so long been held; thanks to the king, who when this favourable moment presented itself, could not do otherwise than let his feeling, which was entirely the same as ours, bear sway; thanks to all this, the great change, the transition from bondage to freedom, is in preparation. But openly as we thanked God with joy among ourselves, it was not yet time to do so publicly; for the king had not yet spoken. At last sounded forth to us the long and impatiently expected royal word, which, although certainly the public papers have deeply impressed it on us all, we shall as certainly hear once more with joy and emotion when it is read to-day by the king's command from every pulpit in the city. It runs thus. [Here followed the summons of the king, To my people.]

Thus the king; and I count it only fair to abstain from speaking in laudation of this royal word. It is still fresh in all our hearts, the delight in the certainty of battle which this word gives us, in the high and noble spirit which here gives utterance to what all the best in the nation had long felt and thought. And now, hardly had we heard this glorious call when our ear was greeted by the triumphant shout of a city loved and revered by every German heart, which was the first to be freed from the direct yoke of the enemy; and, as the crown of all, we saw our beloved king himself come among us with a feeling—we may freely admit it to ourselves—that can never before have lifted up his heart, for he never before had an opportunity of feeling so deeply and truly that which is the source of the highest happiness and exaltation to a ruler, the purest harmony between his will and his people's wish; we saw him lead forth on the way to meet the enemy the army which, at his command, had been consecrated and blessed for the battle by prayer. This then, the departure of our army to battle, to decisive battle for what is highest and noblest, is the subject which, as it assuredly fills and stirs all our hearts, is to occupy our attention at this hour, so that for us also this holy war may begin with humble, elevating thoughts of God, and that our hope and our joy may be sanctified to Him.

I have taken these words of the prophet on which to found our meditation, not at all, as it may possibly appear, in order to institute a comparison between ourselves and that nation against whom we are going to war; but merely in order rightly to distinguish what is conflicting in our own history, that we may thus be led up to the essential part in the great change in which we are rejoicing. For, my friends, the joy that befits us in this place is not joy merely because the oppression and suffering under which we have long sighed are now at an end; not the joy which paints for us in anticipation bright pictures of future prosperity which we hope to attain; here this must be only second and last with us. And if, nevertheless, this contrast still presents itself to us, let us apply it to ourselves in this way, that we feel, as the prophet represents to us, that in the individual, but still more in the mass, changes in the lot depend on the rise and fall of intrinsic worth. Yes, let us here consider the great change entirely from this point of our worthiness before God. On two things included in this, these words give us light; first, what, in this aspect, is the exact significance and the real nature of the change; and second, what we must therefore feel called on to do.

I. In order to understand rightly what is the main point in the great change in our position as citizens which is begun by the present declaration of war, we must look back to a former time well known to us all, and through which many of us lived, when deep decay and fearful devastations had fallen on these lands. Then, through the efforts of several wise and strict rulers, through a judicious taking advantage of events, through successfully conducted wars, but most through the growing up of a noble and free aspiring spirit in the people themselves, we became a nation and kingdom regarding which the whole world saw that the Lord would build and plant it and had promised to do it good. And suddenly enough for all those to whom gradual growth is less perceptible, we found ourselves at this height. But gradually, and while dreaming of rising yet far higher, we slipped downwards, and then just as suddenly plunged to the bottom. For we began to boast of our strength, to rely on the fear with which we might inspire other nations, and thus the effects of our former fame were to carry us ever higher without the forth-putting of our own power, without works on our part pleasing to God. We became the man who makes flesh his arm and whose heart departeth from the Lord. Dishonest acquisitions enlarged our territory in a way more apparent than profitable; for we acquired but few true brethren who willingly obeyed the same laws and laboured for the same end. While other States put forth efforts and wore themselves out in constantly renewed wars, partly for the sake of the same great blessings for which we are now about to fight, we thought to become ever mightier and more formidable through repose. Thus our self-confident prudence was gradually followed by despondency, and we became in yet another way the man who trusts in man; for he also who flatters men and fears them trusts in man. And with our fame our very sense of honour became, more and more, as time went on, an empty name. And more and more our heart departed from the Lord. In a puffed-up, unnatural prosperity the old virtues were by degrees lost, a flood of vanity and dissipation laid waste the laborious works of long and better years; and plainly as the voice of the Lord made itself heard warning us to repentance, we did not obey Him; we did evil in His sight, and therefore He repented of the good that He had promised to do us. And suddenly, just as we seemed about to rouse up out of the long blindness and stupidity in which, however, the greater number were still wrapped, though not more deeply than before—suddenly the Lord spoke out against us as against a nation and kingdom which He would pluck up and pull down and destroy. Then there fell upon us that grievous, crushing disaster in war, and this sudden fall from the height into the abyss was followed by the ever more deeply and painfully suicidal calamity of peace. I am not speaking of the privations, of the distress, of the poverty, of the constantly increasing difficulty in all the external relations of life; I speak only of the inward spiritual corruption which was, one hardly knows whether to say, brought to light by this state of things, or actually created and formed by it. The wretched habit of continually bearing indignity, which we practised publicly and privately during those seven dismal years with the feeling that to let righteous indignation have free course could only increase the evil without any beneficial result—that habit and that feeling are the fruit of sluggishness, of enervation, of cowardice; but how did they in turn increase and spread cowardice, sluggishness and enervation, until all confidence in ourselves, every hope, except the foolish hope of a help that was to come merely from without—till even the wish to be able to help ourselves, nay, till even the sense of being worthy of a better condition disappeared; and the miserable idea took possession of men's minds that the living, mental energy of the nation was entirely exhausted, and the hour of utter ruin had come. This fear had power with not a few among us, who were day by day expecting the dissolution of our separate existence, and who, no longer hoping to see any comfort in the future, were only speculating how they could most comfortably accommodate themselves to the foreign yoke. The impossibility which we so often met, of escaping the danger of the moment without falsehood and fraud, the necessity to feign praise and approval, nay, even agreement and friendship, where we could only despise and detest; all this was no doubt the fruit of that loss of shame which for the sake of life ignored all life's noble aims; but how fearfully was this shamelessness developed by that condition of things, and what an amount of humiliation it took even to provoke public indignation! The insecurity of all property and all rights was no doubt in great part a consequence of the thoughtlessness with which, in times of calamity, people so often try to free themselves from the distress of the moment or to enjoy its fleeting pleasure, without remembering what they ruin or risk in the long run; but to what a degree did that insecure condition increase this thoughtlessness! How did we see luxury and extravagance as in the most prosperous times! how did we see usury and regardless violence sucking up the property of others and lavishing its own, as if all were indeed devoted to speedy ruin! This is the deep corruption into which, on the one hand, we had fallen; and if, on the other hand, our fall and these its effects opened the eyes of many for the first time, others made it more plainly visible than before what was wanting in us; if, in many, a noble ardour was kindled to cast off the indignity that oppressed us from without, and to banish what defiled us within, yet even these noble germs of better things, without definite form or connection, could only excite apprehensions of an irregular outbreak, behind which the cowardice and baseness of others would only the more impregnably intrench and fortify themselves.

Such was our condition, my friends, and no one could conceal from himself that if we continued in the same alliances and in the same state of dependence, we must become more and more like the heath in the desert. Now if I regard the renunciation of these alliances and the attitude of war which, on the contrary, we have assumed, and the beginning of which we are celebrating—if I regard these as the beginning for us all of being lifted up from this deep fall; if I hope that God will now repent of the evil that He purposed to do us; this is founded chiefly on the following things.

In the first place, and to begin with what every one must at moments have most deeply felt; this change is in itself the turning back to truth, the deliverance from the humiliating hypocrisy, which every one, the more he believed himself bound to represent in his talk not himself but the State, really carried to a dreadful perfection. Now, thank God, we can again say when we abhor, or when we love and respect; and as every man of honour must stand to his word with deeds, we must surely feel free and strong in this, we must feel that we have a right to hope; for he who yields himself to truth without reservation is trusting in the Lord. But just because the word alone is nothing, and because this word more than any other demands deeds, therefore this change is the return to free action and to independence. How long, my friends, have we really had no will about our common affairs, always accommodating ourselves to circumstances, and to the oppressive foreign force, so far as it chose to reach! Now we have once more a will; now the king, confiding in his people, has declared a determination in which (because after this no reconciliation can be hoped for) there is involved the resolution to enter on a course of brave deeds which can only end, as the royal word says, in glorious ruin or in the firm establishment of this precious blessing of liberty. And hence we found on this change the hope that we shall preserve for ourselves our own distinctive character, our laws, our constitution and our culture. Every nation, my friends, which has developed to a certain height is degraded by receiving into it a foreign element, even though that may be good in itself; for God has imparted to each its own nature, and has therefore marked out bounds and limits for the habitations of the different races of men on the face of the earth. And yet how the foreign element has lately been thrusting itself upon us! how it threatened the more as time went on to drive out our good manners and ways!

And *what* a foreign element! Half the product of the unbridled ferocity of those horrible internal disorders, half devised for the later tyranny. In rising up to cast this utterly off and to keep it away from us for the future, we become once more a kingdom that trusts in the Lord; for in Him is that nation trusting which means to defend at any price the distinctive aims and spirit which God has implanted in it, and is thus fighting for God's work; and only in proportion as we succeed in this can we become as a tree planted by the waters, that fears not when heat cometh, and brings forth its own fruit without ceasing.

But a joyful hope of revival arises very specially from the way and manner in which the great work of which we are celebrating the commencement is developing. First of all, let us not pass unmentioned the gifts which we see offered by rich and poor, great and small, on the altar of the Fatherland. We do not wish to consider those according to their sufficiency for the purpose to which they are devoted—for willingly and abundantly as they are given, they yet meet but a small part of the need—but according to their inward significance and to the spirit of which they are the expression. In offering them we did not wait till a requisition was made and a command given, but as soon as we knew the need we hastened to offer. As it is death to any commonwealth if only the letter of the law prevails, and no one takes more interest in it, by act or feeling, than *that* prescribes; as this is a sure sign that the higher blessings of life are not produced by fixed regulations; so this loyal, living feeling about whatever is necessary for the commonwealth is a sure sign that the life-giving sap of true love has penetrated into the State, and that the leaves of this spiritual tree will remain green even in the heat and in the year of drought. And if many a one has devoted all that he had remaining of earthly jewels and treasures, let us regard this as the necessary avowal that in this war it is not a question of earthly, but of spiritual possessions, and that we are ready, and will be so to the last, to do without and sacrifice all the former in order to gain the latter, and content although we should be obliged, after the successfully decisive battle, to begin the building up of our earthly prosperity from the very foundation. That is what it is to trust in the Lord, and to seek only after His kingdom.

But let us look particularly at the form which the defence of the Fatherland is to take. Among all the divisions that crippled our powers and impeded our progress, there was none more unhappy than that between soldier and citizen, resulting from the rooted opinion that he who was engaged in a peaceful trade or profession could have neither knowledge nor skill to defend his property and the common Fatherland in the time of danger. Hence the special privileges which were granted to those on whom alone the safety of the State depended, and still more to those who were exclusively appointed to command them; hence the jealousy of the citizen as to those privileges, and the general dislike to a class which in time of peace seemed only a burden to all the rest. Many commendable attempts were no doubt made to diminish this evil, but without results of any consequence. Now this separation is to be abolished; the difference is now to exist only between those who, constantly occupied with the proper arts of war, are, in the precision of their exercises and performances, an example to all others as well as the nucleus to which they gather, and those who, scantily instructed and drilled, only take up arms when it becomes necessary; but courage is to be expected from all, all are to know the use of their weapons, all are to take a growing share in the danger, the greater it becomes. We have been wisely led thus far step by step. The brave ardour of our young men was known whenever it became a question of this struggle; they were appealed to, and we saw them at the first call pour in from all ranks, from all nobler occupations to arms. Where a new good thing is to be quickly spread, the fathers must often be taught by the children; we have good reason to hope that it will be so at present, and that after that example of the young, for whom we should venture everything rather than they for us, every one will now be prepared to take part in the defence of the Fatherland according to his assigned order. For this reason the king is now instituting the *Landwehr*. And as this is also to be specially published to-day, hear what he says about it. [Here followed the summons to the *Landwehr*.]

What an exalted feeling this call must awaken in all of us! what a firm confidence in the strength thus united! what a happy foretaste of the harmony and love in which all ranks will be bound together, when they have all stood side by side face to face with death for the Fatherland! what a happy anticipation of the united endeavour to lay in this way the foundation of a life that shall be worth such efforts, and in which unity and strength shall be equally seen!

Thus, my dear friends, we see in this glorious and spirited change in our condition the beginnings of a happy rising again from a deep fall, the returning favour of the Most High, who is again promising to do us good. Let us, then, also reflect how we are obeying His voice, let us further consider, in a few words, what we must in the first place feel called on to do, by this change of affairs. I shall be able to be the shorter about this, as your minds must already, by what has gone before, be directed to what I have to say.

II. I speak first of those who are called directly to the defence of the Fatherland, whether they belong to the armies that are already in motion, or whether, according to their own inclination or by the law of the lot, they are incorporated in that great bulwark which is still to be formed. I do not wish to do what is superfluous, by exhorting them to courage and bravery. He can never be wanting in courage whose mind is filled with the common aim, and who has made it entirely his own. For if, in that case, he finds himself in the great mass of conflicting powers which are organized into a noble whole; if he finds it impossible to think of himself singly, but must regard himself as only a little part of the whole; then his attention and his wishes can also only be directed to the movements of the whole. And that these movements may always accomplish the proposed aim—that alone is what he works for with all his strength; and thus whatever may befal himself in doing so, even were it the final human event, must appear to him only as an utterly insignificant casualty, which he himself regards as little as it can be regarded among the whole. This is the natural courage of him who loves the cause for which he is fighting. But I should like to warn you lest personal ambition weaken the high nobility and the true effectiveness of this courage. Let your emulation never be as to what each one brings to pass; let it be only as to the spirit that each manifests and the virtue he practises. He who strives to do this and that, and not just what always comes to him in his own place, is withdrawing from the natural arrangement of united work, to the injury of the whole. If public distinctions must certainly depend on success, then let every one strive, not to earn them, but to deserve them; let every one remember that all who did their duty faithfully helped to earn those things which others have received; and that the consciousness of having done all that it was possible for zeal and goodwill to do, and the recognition of those who know this, outweigh all other distinctions. I would caution you, moreover, not to let thoughtlessness weaken this natural courage. Not a few seem to think that everything is already done, that there is hardly need of the armies that have already gone forth and are doubtless about to begin the pursuit of the scattered, terrified remnant of the enemy's ruined forces.

to the utmost bounds of the German Fatherland; and that if more men fit for arms were called out, it could only be, not so much for immediate need, as to make use of this splendid opportunity in forming a better and more powerful system of defence for the future. Let such people beware lest the unexpected, which is what oftenest casts men down, come upon them with its terrible force, and they then indeed fear, when the heat cometh. The king's message is very far from countenancing this light view; it does not conceal from us the power of the enemy, nor the greatness of his resources; and we ourselves have some idea of the embittered feeling that he must have against us. Let us secure our courage by being prepared for everything, even for each of us in person to defend or avenge home and hearth.

I speak in the next place of the rest of us in connection with those, the defenders of the common cause; of ourselves as their relatives and friends. The feeling which formerly, when the State was involved in war, was shared by only a few, and as to which they were sometimes pitied and sometimes envied by others—the seeing of their best-beloved ones exposed to the danger of death in battle and to the various disasters of war; this feeling will now become universal. For which of us is there that will not now see among the hosts of the army or of the *Landwehr*, at least relations, benefactors, pupils, heart-friends, if not father, husband, brother and son going to meet those very dangers? And let us then feel that we are not on this account to be pitied, but to be counted happy; that the more highly we value those connected with us, the more ought we to sympathise with and enter into all that is great and glorious in their calling. And the more we love them as ourselves, let us all the more offer and consecrate them to the Fatherland, just as we would yield up our own lives for it were we called on to do so. Much precious blood will flow, many a beloved head will fall; let us not embitter their glorious lot by mournful fears and weak sorrow, but see to it that, worthy of the great cause, we remain green and fresh; let us remember how much happier it is to offer up life as a sacrifice in the noble struggle against this destructive power than in the impotent struggle of medical art against the unknown powers of nature. And the loving cares which, if we could, we would gladly bestow on our own when sick and wounded—let those cares make us entirely a joint community, as the cause is common; let us care for and serve all whom we can, in the firm confidence that in the same way there will be no lack of tender nursing and treatment of our loved ones from others who feel as we do. But, above all, let us take care that the well-deserved honour of those who have dedicated themselves to this sacred struggle be not lost. As we ourselves have been most deeply moved by the distress and humiliation of the past years, and the glorious resurrection of the Fatherland in these days, let us also impress all this most strongly on the rising generation; that this eternally memorable time may indeed be remembered, and that each descendant whom it concerns may say with just pride, There fought, or there fell, a relation of mine.

I speak further, on the other hand, of those who, while others have gone out to defend the Fatherland, are to regulate and direct its internal affairs, and discharge all the various offices which it requires. May this great decisive time arouse them all to redoubled faithfulness and solicitude, to redoubled abhorrence of all neglect at home through indolence or irregularity—for I will not say through self-interest or unfaithfulness — while in the field citizens are offering up their life-blood. May they abhor it as the most shameful treachery to this very blood and to all the virtues that offer it up. Let them remember that every power must be conscientiously applied, every department of the commonwealth faithfully administered, if the great work is to succeed. Above all, let them remember that if the courage of those who have gone to the war is to hold out, they wish to see, in the strength and wisdom of the constitution and government, a guarantee for the higher blessings for which they are fighting. Therefore be it far from any one among us to think himself wise when he is not so; let no one thrust himself, to the exceeding detriment of the commonwealth, into an office which he is not capable of filling; let no one allow himself to be so blinded by friendly partiality as to favour such presumptuous undertakings. But when one *is* wise, then let him strive to act, and to act vigorously and faithfully. Let those who administer justice remember that the sacred sense of the rights of nations and states, which lies at the foundation of this whole struggle, can only be in a healthy state where the rights of the citizens are faithfully observed; let those who have the care of keeping order and security remember that very specially in the exercise of their occupation is to be shown most gloriously that noble and beautiful combination of liberty and obedience in which we have long prided ourselves, and by which, in days of repose as in times of war, we must chiefly mark our difference, both from the former licence and from the later servitude of the nation against which we are contending. Let those who are to elevate the sentiments of the people and to form the minds of the young remember that they, in their quiet work, are the guardians and keepers of the most sacred property; that on their faithfulness in duty and on the blessing resting on it, it depends whether there shall be faculties with which to fight, and above all whether there shall be anything to fight for—a faith, a hope, a love. Lastly, let those who manage the public taxes remember that under the poor earthly form of money and of goods there is offered to them in tribute the efforts of all the noble and intellectual faculties which have established the dominion of man over nature; that it is not the people's superfluity, not their savings which are to be disposed of, but what they have pinched themselves to give. Let all remember how greatly the importance of their work is increased in such times as these, so that, in the first place, they themselves, to whom obedience is to be given, may in their great calling obey the voice of the Lord.

And finally, in contrast with those who are directly at work for the Fatherland, I speak of those to whom this is not permitted, who dare not even wish that the necessity should arise that would call them also to arms. Well, if it is painful to them to devote this great time entirely to quiet work, although they would gladly be waging war, let them consider that we have an internal war to carry on, which is of equally decisive importance. If our real low condition consists in evil of many kinds, let us begin first by lifting ourselves out of that; there is still much to be rooted out, much to be fought against. Let us be brave in this war—it also requires courage; it has its dangers also. Let no one enjoy unshaken respect in society, who still by word or deed preaches despondency or indifference, and who seems inclined to prefer our former condition with quietness to the struggle for a better! Let every one be watched and unmasked who thinks that the more the eyes of all are turned to those at a distance, he may the more securely and secretly indulge in a now more than ever criminal and traitorous selfishness. Let no one remain unchecked, who perhaps in the foolish delusion of preparing for himself a more endurable fate in the event of an unsuccessful issue, seeks to exempt himself from, or in any way to obstruct, the vigorous measures which are indispensably necessary to making the issue successful. And even if narrow-mindedness and baseness of this kind should try in a greater or less degree to creep into the public administration, then, because the danger is doubled, let us also fight with double energy and take no rest until we conquer. Thus shall we also have our own part to sustain, we shall wage the same war as the others, only in a different way; and if those who are placed behind doubtful troops to intimidate those who might think of giving way prematurely, take credit to themselves for a part of the victory, though they have done no fighting, this may also be permitted to us.

These, my friends, are the demands which the present times make on us. Let each of us, then, stand to his post and not give way! let each of us keep fresh and green in the sense of the great holy powers that animate him! let each of us trust in God and call on Him, as we are now about to do together!

Merciful God and Lord! Thou hast done great things for us in calling our fatherland to fight for a free and honourable existence, in which we may be able to advance Thy work. Grant us in addition, safety and grace. Victory comes from Thee, and we know well that we do not always know what we are doing in asking of Thee what seems good to us. But with greater confidence than ever, even with a strong faith, we entreat of Thee prosperity and blessing on the arms of our king and his allies, because it seems to us almost as if Thy kingdom and the noblest gifts that past centuries have won for us would be in danger, if these efforts were in vain. Protect the beloved head of our king, and all the princes of his house, who are now with the army. Grant wisdom and strength to the commanders, courage to the soldiers, faithful steadfastness to all. And grant also, as Thou canst change and turn the fortune of war, that its blessings may not be lost to us; that each one may be purified and grow in the inner man; that each may do what he can, be it much or little; that we may grow stronger in confidence in Thee, and in obedience to Thy will, an obedience reaching even to death, like the obedience of Thy Son. Amen.

IV.

NECESSITY OF THE NEW BIRTH.

(*On Trinity Sunday.*)

TEXT: JOHN iii. 1–8.

WHEN the Saviour promised to His disciples the Spirit, who, after His own departure from the earth, was to come upon them abundantly, He said to them, He will take of Mine and give unto you, and thereby He will glorify Me in and through you. We have once more completed the circle of our memorial festivals, from His birth to the fulfilment of that promise; and now, without being reminded, by the universal custom of the Church, of any specially great event in the times of the founding of Christianity, we have before our Christian assemblies a long period of quiet meditation. What better can we wish for that period, than that this very Spirit who glorifies Christ may be always among us, so that each of our devout meditations may exalt Him in our eyes, and that thus, through His having a more constant and active power in us, He may be also more and more glorified through us.

It is therefore my purpose, in the period on which we are entering, to follow the words of the Saviour that I have just quoted; we will take of His own, that His Spirit may more and more enlighten us and glorify Him before us.

They shall be words which the evangelists have preserved for us as His own; the most direct sayings from His lips, with which we intend during this time to connect our meditations. If, then, His Spirit is actually among us, if Christ becomes increasingly glorious to us through our study of His words, our inward parts more and more enlightened by the eternal, divine light, which He brought from heaven, our hearts more and more purified; we shall then, when the next time of commemorating our Lord comes round, return with new joy and gratitude to the beautiful circle of our Christian festivals, and anew, with yet purer spirit and in a way more worthy of Him, participate in adoring remembrance of His birth, His sufferings and His glorification.

And with what words can we better begin the series of our proposed meditations, than with one of those which most closely connect the festival period just closed with that which lies before us? The Saviour has now, as it were, completed anew before our eyes His work, of the chief points in which our Church festivals were meant to remind us; He has taken to Himself flesh and blood, He has become obedient, even to the death of the cross, He has comforted and instructed His people, He has sent down the promised Spirit after His own final departure from the world, and prepared His disciples for the founding and extension of His kingdom. Now as He generally began His work of teaching by inviting men into the kingdom of God, which had come near to them, we may suitably begin by asking, How are we to attain, or how have we at some former time attained to our part in the Saviour's benefits? How does His kingdom still go on extending in the present day? The remarkable saying of the Saviour which we have taken as the ground of our meditation, gives a clear answer to these questions.

In this whole conversation of the Saviour with Nicodemus, it is very difficult to understand the precise connection, more so than in most of the Saviour's other discourses; but we shall not be surprised at this if we reflect how it is with ourselves when we wish to communicate our most important thoughts, and are limited to a brief conversation in which to do so. We cannot in such a case bestow the usual pains and attention on so arranging our discourse that the other shall instantly take up our meaning; we cannot so enlarge that all the bearings of one thought on another shall become quite obvious; but, knowing that only a little time is granted us, we feel constrained, and strive to give expression only to what is most important, to comprise in few words a real wealth of thoughts and to impress these thoroughly on the hearer, so that he may afterwards reflect more minutely on their import, and may then be able to discover what at present escapes him. It was in this position, so far as such a comparison can be made at all, that Christ here found Himself. He was only rarely in the capital, on the occasions of the great feasts, and this man could only come to Him during the night. Hence the Saviour hastens to point out to the inquiring man the main points on which everything depends; hence the conversation that must contain so much, passes abruptly from one great thought to another; and it is possible that John also may have had too little room to communicate much in the course of the conversation which would have given us here and there clearer insight into the connection.

But the chief of all the weighty matters which our Lord had to say to Nicodemus is just the answer to the question we have proposed. A man must be born anew, else he cannot see the kingdom of God. One life must be destroyed and give place to another—the life of the flesh to the life of the Spirit: that is the only way in which any one can enter the kingdom of God; the new birth is the only manner in which new numbers are ever being won to it. The inquirer has various objections to this, and the Saviour removes them;

but certainly in a way which we may believe left him still much to think about, and intimated to him that nothing but a higher personal experience would help him to a full clearness of understanding. Let us take the same course, by considering that *a man comes into the kingdom of God only through the new birth of the Spirit.* We will first make plain to ourselves, according to the Saviour's words, our common understanding of this in its simple truth; secondly, we will see what objections the masters in Israel have now as then against this doctrine; and thirdly, how we know of no other information or advice to give on the subject than what the Saviour said to Nicodemus.

I. Verily, verily, I say unto thee, except a man be born again, he cannot see the kingdom of God. These are the Saviour's words, and this, rightly considered, may be said to have been always the common understanding of Christians; I mean, the faith of the Church. There is no doubt a sense in which it may be said that every one who is born at all, whatever he may be, sees the kingdom of God and is in it. For as a man's kingdom is there where his will is held to be law, and where he arranges and commands; in this sense the kingdom of God is indeed everywhere, as certainly as God is almighty, and all that live are in it. But we all speak, just as the Saviour did, of a kingdom of God which does not include every one. For as the kingdom of an earthly prince does not, strictly speaking, extend over every place where people act outwardly according to his will, but only where his will is also the real and common will of those who serve him and live under his rule, while the rest—however much outward appearances say the reverse—are in a state of secret enmity against him; so the kingdom of God, in this narrower sense, is only in those who are actuated by a spirit common to them all, making known the will of God in their hearts. Those manifold gifts, which always work in harmony towards the same end, because they proceed from the same Spirit;

those fruits of the Spirit, love, joy, peace, patience, faith, purity; those various ministries which are fulfilled now by this one, now by that one—for if one is gone another is never wanting—and always faithfully and ably, under the one Master; those willing servants, bound for ever, for life and death, ministering in the word of truth, in the power of God, by the armour of righteousness; those unknown, and yet well known; those dying ones, who always live anew; those poor, who make many rich; those strong ones, who are never covetous of vain-glory, so as to envy and hate each other—that is the kingdom of God. And in each individual it is, as the Scripture says, peace and joy in the Holy Spirit; the peace of God, which, confiding in the eternal love and wisdom, is disturbed by nothing; resting in the faith that the Lord will, as time goes on, glorify Himself more and more in the world of spirits; the peace of God, which brings quiet and calmness to the otherwise stormy soul, by which its conflicting passions are brought to rest, so that it is like the pure mirror, in which every object is clearly and correctly pictured. The kingdom of God in each person is joy in the Holy Spirit; the joy, far above all earthly things, in the fellowship of men with God; the joy that wants nothing more eventful than that we always feel the power of God more influential in us, and are always less losing the consciousness of Him in whom we live and move and have our being. But all men do not live in this union, nor experience this peace and joy. We know the great multitude of those who, born of the flesh, are only flesh. It is true they have all, at least many among them, a common aim; but because what each of them seeks belongs only to his worldly existence, the association they form is far from stable, hardly to be compared to that higher kingdom of God; they are only temporarily allied as individuals, and none of them can really regard what another does or enjoys as being also his own and advancing his purpose. And thus they have no peace but in the gratification of their wild passions, their natural instincts, or, it may be, of the gentle, cheerful, social affections; and next to this, from no outward hindrance coming in the way of their doings. Nor have they any joy but that of finding themselves in full possession of the wealth and appliances of life, from which that gratification proceeds; of having new treasures of this kind thrown open to them, and of finding themselves abundantly endowed in comparison with others, so that their enjoyments are secured for a long time or for ever. This is certain, that those persons are not in the kingdom of God, but are leading, far away from it, a life that is rich, luxurious, and in its way, splendidly expanding. It may be highly refined and ennobled; but even the noblest and most refined natural life and motives are still only flesh, and never become spirit. Although in the whole life of such men there occurred no act that might not also occur in the life of him who is led by the Spirit of God, yet so long as truth, integrity, love are regarded only as means towards enjoyment, and that alone is aimed at, of whatever kind it may be; so long as this and no other is the inner motive; so long as the ruling sentiment does not refer to God and to His plans, we perceive the difference most distinctly. From no amount of still higher elevating or perfecting or outward purifying whatever of this life, which, as to its inmost motives, is carnal, can that spiritual life ever be produced; such a life is born of the flesh, and remains flesh although developed to the highest bloom of health and beauty; there is no possible transition, such as that from a state of coarse, carnal life to a cultured, restrained, pleasing condition, and from this to what is really good and holy. If such men are to come into the kingdom of God, they must lead there an entirely different and new life, and the beginning of a new life is a new birth. And we are assuredly, all of us, far from assuming that those who so live could never, just because they have once given this form to their lives, attain to the new life; and that a new birth, although necessary for them, would be impossible—but that what is once born flesh must for ever remain flesh. For from that it must follow that what is spirit must have been originally born of the Spirit; but that is by no means what we know of ourselves. On the contrary, our experience, our distinct remembrance, tells each of us that the peace of God has not always dwelt in us from the beginning, but that it was given to us, that the flesh ruled in us before the Spirit. Though we may never have had a period of gross transgressions, of disgraceful passions or degrading pleasures, yet, beginning from innocence and purity of heart, we did not attain gradually more and more to the complete strength and virtue of a life pleasing to God. Between the beginning of our existence and our present life and aims there lies a time in which lust was the prevailing power; in which it conceived and brought forth sin. If we are honest, we can say that there is a period on which we look back only with the feeling that we appear to ourselves to have become since then different men. That which was then our innermost I and Self has now become something far off and strange to us; and the law of divine appointment, which has now through the grace of God become the law of our life, which we love and obey, was then far off and strange. We were only aware of it as an external force, impeding the free course of our life, just as now the separate stirrings of the flesh and of sin are a force which we do not ascribe to our real life. Thus, then, it is true that one life has ceased and another has begun. But the beginning of the new life is the new birth; and this holds good universally, If any man be in Christ, he is a new creature; the old is passed away, behold all is become new.

Thus Christ makes a division between two periods of the human race, and He is Himself its regeneration. The Christian period is not the continuation of the Jewish and pagan period, but a new one. And so for every nation the appearing of the gospel in it is its regeneration, not only a perfecting of its former condition; for, as we learn from history, much that was really good and beautiful often perishes in the first place, and the whole form is changed, the whole life takes another direction. So almost every great historical event is a judgment on some evil that has gained the mastery, and it thus becomes in one aspect or another the germ of a new life; and only where we find and understand the two things in their connection do we find and recognise a great phenomenon. And the same is true as to individuals; sin must have somewhere gained the upper hand, the flesh must have been active and ruling, that grace may have the mastery when the spirit attains to life; every one must first have tasted the life of corruption, and then, by the second act of divine omnipotence and love, he is born of the Spirit and becomes spirit. We have all, as Christians, an invincible and inalienable consciousness of this transformation; and when we welcome as members of our alliance in a stricter sense some who formerly did not belong to it, we take for granted that they have become such by the new birth which is from God.

Yet, my friends, this very thing is, on the other hand, a hard saying, a much-disputed doctrine; and as that inquiring and well-meaning master in Israel could not reconcile himself to it, but asked, How can such things be? so very many Christians, even masters in Israel, and among them those who are longing for knowledge and honest in motive, have a great deal to object to this demand, that a man must be born again. Let us now, in the second place, consider those objections.

II. When to the Saviour's assertion, Except a man be born again, he cannot see the kingdom of God, Nicodemus made the objection, How can a man be born when he is old? can he enter the second time into his mother's womb, and be born? we are not to suppose that this man, who was a ruler of the Jews and a master in Israel, was so simple as to believe that Jesus, whom he regarded as a teacher sent from God, wished this to be understood literally of the physical birth, or that, if he had believed this, he would have had anything more to do with one who made such an assertion. On the contrary, from the words of the Saviour that follow, when to the question put by Nicodemus a second time, How can these things be? He answered, Art thou a master in Israel and knowest not these things? we must certainly conclude that this form of expression under the figure of the new birth was known to him. And indeed it could not be unknown among a people who made so great endeavours with so confident a hope of extending their faith and their institutions, and who prized the exclusiveness of their descent. It was a glory and a gain with this people when any foreigner was moved to seek participation in their law and in their hopes; but they could only attain fully to this by receiving a share in the nation's genealogy; they must become children of Abraham, and hence the expression of being born again might and must often have been used. This new birth, then, was also the beginning of a new life, which was to be lived no longer after the customs of the pagan fathers, but according to the manner of the new father, and according to the later law, which unite all his genuine and true-born children. But this new life was, after all, only a life according to a new outward law, which became more and more by habit a part of a man's life, otherwise everything remained essentially the same; the same reverence which they had formerly divided among many supposed gods, was directed to the one true God, who yet had been dimly guessed at behind those many illusions; and the same virtue which a right-thinking heathen had no doubt already practised before he became inclined to Judaism, he had to practise and cultivate under that new law. That new birth was thus, as it were, only a new birth from a different flesh, and this Nicodemus could understand. What was born flesh remained flesh, notwithstanding this change. But now, when the Saviour required of all who would see the kingdom of God, even of him and all his brethren, that they should be born again; he concluded, and that most justly, that it was a question of a different and more inward change; and it was just in looking at this as required of himself, that he asked doubtfully, How can a man be born again when he is old? How a man who had so long been flesh should yet be able to be born of the Spirit, and to lead, with all his heart, a life actually and entirely new; this he did not understand.

Very closely related to this are the objections of the men of our own days, and, in part, of the present masters in Israel. Their opinion takes this direction—that a man is of course constantly changing during his life on earth, one in a greater, another in a less degree; and that with one this change may be more a real advance from good to better, with another more a mere variation of conditions the value of which may be pretty much alike. Every man, they say, is at the same time flesh and spirit; thus has God in a similar way endowed all; only in some, through that progress which they make, the spirit gains more and more command over the flesh, and those are the good; with others, on the contrary, the spirit is long kept under, is only rarely seen in its beauty and strength; and the greater part of their life is devoted to various manifestations of carnality, in violent secret or open conflict with the spirit, and those are the wicked; but the great majority of men are those whose lives pass away in continual vacillations, without a decisive preponderance on the one side or the other. But still the spirit is present and at work in all; for otherwise they could not be men, but would be beasts. Now if, after a long apparent resistance, during which, however, the spirit is inwardly gaining strength unseen, it suddenly comes forth with increased power, this looks like a special divine communication and revelation, and if from that point onwards there is a permanent supremacy of the spirit over the flesh, then this is regarded as a transformation, and it is called conversion or new birth. And yet it is not the beginning of a new life; the same spirit has always been in the man and has lived and worked in him, warning, threatening, resisting, punishing, making him ashamed. For, say they, if it is to be supposed that this power which draws man to a higher and better life, and which people are accustomed to call the Spirit of God, is not given to men until later, how could it be said that a man was the same man as before, if an entirely new element were added to his being? and if only some receive this power and others do not, how can it be said that the two beings are of the same kind and partake of one and the same nature? And if that higher life which is the condition of the divine approval and of a man's present and future blessedness, can only be attained by means of a power to be thus specially communicated to him by God, and God imparts this power to some earlier, so that they are able to attain a higher perfection in this life, and to others later, though He does impart it to them, and to others again not at all, what a change takes place in our idea of the divine Being, in whom we strive to imagine infinite righteousness and infinite love united; how does this change into an idea of utterly unintelligible, and for that very reason terrible despotism! For why does He take compassion on the one, and leave the other to his fate? If man is at first born only of the flesh and is wholly flesh, then there is nothing beforehand in any one that would make him more fit for the kingdom of God or inclined towards it, and therefore no ground in the one for being preferred or in the other for being set aside. And can that be regarded as a Christian doctrine, or indeed at all as one, without which the whole of

Christianity is not rightly understood, which brings such confusion into that living sense of God, which is really the source of everything good in man?

And to this they further add, that it is a doctrine that burdens and perplexes the conscience, and on account of it, all that God does for men is for a great many of them fruitless, so that they attain to no real repose and joy in life; and if this is not the case with still many more, that is only because they do not really hold this doctrine very firmly. For if in the midst of a man's life a new life must be begun, one must surely be able to show and give proof when and how it began. With the lower creatures, whose life assumes different forms one after another, this is the case—we can see how the one life dies out and the other springs up—and therefore we ought to be able just in the same way to perceive when the flesh dies and the man is born of the Spirit. Hence among the friends of this doctrine a desire naturally prevails to be distinctly aware of the moment of this change, this new birth. Now the more this new life, as is the way with life in general, has been the outcome of hard struggles amid tears and groans, the more sure every one feels able to be, that he is born of the Spirit; and the less one particular moment stands out distinctly from all others as the starting point of this new life, the more uncertain it seems to be whether the new birth has actually taken place, and everything that seems to indicate the new life is suspected of being possibly an empty show. But, it is said, not without justice, how few men come in a natural way to such a distinctly marked out moment, which perceptibly and, as it were, visibly separates the two parts of their lives! And just because this is so, this opinion has always produced a vain striving after such a moment, with which the conviction of divine grace may be specially connected, and on the remembrance of which the mind may rest in full confidence. Hence it has always stirred up a multitude of tormenting and useless anxieties in the best of men, who though obedient to all the teachings of Christianity, yet could never attain to any real comfort on account of this one opinion, which it was not in their power to verify. Indeed how many examples have there been in every age, that these doubts have gnawed away a man's life, have dried up the inmost marrow of his spirit, and have, not unfrequently, shaken his mind into complete derangement! And this—so it is asked, not, as it seems, unreasonably—this is supposed to be a doctrine revealed by the God who does not even desire the death of the sinner, much less that of the righteous? This is supposed to be the teaching of the Saviour, the friend of man, who came to seek that which was lost, as if He had rather come to cast into awful perplexity those who are walking in the straight and safe way?

These are the objections, not only of worldly people (who are not the persons to whom the demands of Christianity appear too rigorous), but also of many masters in Israel, to the Saviour's words, that a man must be born again in order to enter the kingdom of God. And if we ask them what they propose to make of those words, if they are really Christians and do not dispute the words of the Saviour, then all that probably remains for them to say is, that at the time when Christ spoke these words they had their own important meaning, and that the mistake is only in trying to apply them to the present time. For at that time, they will say, every one, even he in whom a spiritual rule was already established, needed to experience so great a change, in order to enter the kingdom of God through Jesus, that it might really be regarded as a complete revolution. It was necessary that his idea of God, from which all good ways and doings of a man proceed, should be changed; the God of Abraham, Isaac and Jacob, although He was certainly not thought of in a fleshly way as an idol, but spiritually as the source of all good, needed to become for him the universal Father of men, who desires only to be worshipped in spirit and in truth, and who purifies the hearts of the heathen also through faith in His Son. In like manner it was necessary that his whole endeavours to observe the externals of that separating law—which was, nevertheless, a spiritual law, seeing that it told against evil desires in every way—that these endeavours should be directed to the universal law under which all men can unite. His love had to change from the narrow-hearted love of those of his own race, which, nevertheless, being opposed to selfishness, was a work of the Spirit, into that love which embraces in all men alike the image of God; and his hopes of earthly power and greatness, which yet were to be the power and glory of the righteous, behoved to change into joy in a wholly spiritual kingdom of God. But no, there is no such revolution as this, seeing that the very beginnings of what is spiritual in a man born and brought up as a Christian can have no other distinction than this. For this very knowledge is instilled into every one from his youth up; these sentiments are in every way required from all; and as certainly as every man is born at once flesh and spirit, just as certainly every Christian has from the beginning this spirit, which therefore only needs gradually to increase, without any entire change, in order to the man's becoming a man of God, fitted for every good work.

III. Now what are we going to reply to all this? I know nothing else than what Christ answered to Nicodemus, Marvel not that I said unto thee, ye must be born again: the wind bloweth where it listeth, and thou hearest the sound thereof, but knowest not whence it cometh or whither it goeth; so is every one that is born of the Spirit. Just so should we have to tell those objectors, that they seem indeed to know the works of the Spirit very well, and yet not to know whence they come. You think, I would say to them, that this is the way of it, that the right knowledge is now instilled into all from their youth, so that now no one can think less or worse of God and divine things than is according to their amount of Christian knowledge. You think it is enough that every one is called on by all means to have sentiments conformed to the gospel; because, seeing that these sentiments are widely diffused, and that it becomes publicly known how each person stands affected towards them, it is certain that every one who stands in awe of public opinion and to whom the respect of men is of consequence, is very careful not to set them openly at defiance; and if he goes on being thus careful, he becomes naturally more and more unaccustomed to act in direct opposition to them, and more incapable of doing so: and hence, because these sentiments and principles have passed into all social institutions and regulations, the carnality of men is restrained even from childhood, and thus at a very early stage the flesh is, as it were, spiritualized. So that in a kind of casual way, you think, it is to be done? and that if this kind of thing went on continuously, a man would gradually become, without the need of a further great inward change, a man well-pleasing to God and fitted for the work of God! Do you actually fail to see the vast difference between the highest perfection to which man can attain from this point, and the still most imperfect virtue of the beginner in true faith? We, on our side, cannot but say that while the kingdom of God no doubt has an effect on those whom you describe, the latter alone is actually in it, and bears it within him. The evil that the former avoids is, as regards his being in the kingdom of God, just the same as if he had done it; and the good that he does must be forgiven to him just as much as the evil, if he is to enter that kingdom, because it is never the result of faith. Yes, between your perfect man and our beginner there is just as great a gulf as between the man in Abraham's bosom and the one in the place of torment. For what we seek is only effected when that which, as you say, every one now knows,—although this universal knowledge must be of a very subordinate kind, so long as it remains a dead knowledge in so many,—when this becomes in the individual man a living impulse, his only impulse, the essence and the inmost strength of his life; not a law that comes to him from without and which he fears and respects, but his one pleasure and love, without which he does not feel right. And that is the faith of which it is truly said that it comes by preaching, which, however, only means that the grace of God brings it about through the word and life of those in whom it already is; not at all that it develops naturally and of itself out of the dead knowledge. From that knowledge to faith there is no gradual transition; we come to it only by means of an entire change and a new birth. And is it the case in any other sphere that what is dead becomes gradually and of itself a living being; what belongs to others a thing of our own; fear and dislike of anything, not mere habitude and indifference, but delight and love? And yet such is the difference which we have described. For if the opponents of our doctrine appeal to the feelings of approval of good, of shame and regret for evil, which originate and develop as of themselves in the Christian community; and if we further concede, what may be much more rarely the case than is supposed, that those feelings are quite pure and genuine; yet it is certain that notwithstanding all the keenness of those feelings, the will is quite void of what the feeling approves, and leans to something quite different: it is certain that, much reason as there may be for maintaining that man does not of his own accord will evil as evil, just as little does he of his own accord will good as good, and that the strength and persistence of this feeling does not even in the longest time transform the will; but on the contrary, if such a change do not take place through grace, even the feeling itself does not continue in its sharpness and purity, but gets gradually blunted into indifference and obduracy. And if our opponents further appeal to the fact that every man, even the most wicked, has moments in which he feels really moved to good, and that therefore even for such there is no need of a new birth, but only that those moments be made permanent; yet we all know only too well from a former time those unsatisfactory, fleeting emotions, in which there was certainly a hint of the new man; but we know also that we then felt only as if taken hold of by an unknown power. We felt that if this power became a part of us and constantly dwelt in us, we should become different persons; but even the most earnest wishes were not capable of effecting this. Now this very thing, the renewing of the will, which is undoubtedly the centre of the whole being, the continual indwelling, as the Spirit of God, of that which before only stirred the feelings from without, and in a passing way as the power of the Word and of the Church;—this is the new birth, before which, now as in the time of Nicodemus, a man, though possessed of all those advantages, is still only flesh; and of which no one will assert that it is connected with the natural birth into earthly life; for he who should assert this about himself would make himself equal to the Son of God; but on the contrary, we have all come short of this glory that we ought to have before God. The second birth may be easier now than at the time when Jesus talked with Nicodemus; it must be so, otherwise there would be no consistency in the work of God; but it is quite as necessary for entering the kingdom of God; and every one must be so much the more shut up to it, because the servant who is always hearing his Lord's will, and has indeed in himself a warning voice to remind him of it, and yet never does it, is deserving of the greater contempt, and moreover of double punishment.

And as to the difficulties that may arise in adhering to these words of the Saviour, that a man enters the kingdom of God only through the new birth; we have no cause to allow our faith or our feelings to be confused by such fancies. Is there a single one of the doctrines peculiar to Christianity, about which those to whom it is distasteful, or who cannot understand its nature, do not make the same assertions? Believers are not perplexed in this way; it is only those who pervert the terms of faith into sophistries which are beyond man's province, who are caught in their own net. They ask, if it is thus with the Spirit of God, and some may have it and others not, how can it be said, in that case, that men have all the same kind of nature? But are there not in every higher, living nature, faculties, and those indeed the noblest, that are not developed until a later period? Now, if with certain persons this development is delayed, those faculties are imperfectly cultivated, and therefore unhealthy—marred and disfigured in many ways. And we say this freely of those who are without the Spirit of God; for to have that Spirit belongs to the original nature of man, who was created in the image of God. They say, if a man has not been born again, and this can only take place through grace, then it seems a mere arbitrary choice on God's part, that He shows this grace to some and not to others. Is not this the creature speaking foolish words against Him who has formed it? words which are too high for him, and which he does not understand? Well, suppose that you admit no difference between those who are born anew of the Spirit and those who are only flesh; does that, if you are set on reasoning in this way, at all take you past the difficulty of having to think of God as acting in an arbitrary way? You place your comfort, your satisfaction, we will suppose, in virtue, in piety, in the cultivation of your mind; or if you chose to place them in something lower it would be all the same. For some are certainly better and more pious than others, have more virtue and culture, or if you prefer it, more gifts of fortune, more comforts and enjoyments. Now, if you take together all those accomplishments that you possess, all these delightful circumstances in which you are placed, would you really be arrogant enough to maintain that you owe all this to yourself? that you have given much to yourself, or if you have but little, that you have withheld more from yourself? Have not God's leadings a great share in the developing of your faculties, in the determining of your position? And when you look at the inner nature of each one, and find one richly gifted and another but scantily; has each made his own nature, or is it of God? Therefore it is not the new birth that is the stumbling-block of those sophistical objectors; it is that they are trying to contend with God, as no man can possibly contend with Him! Assuredly never yet has a believing soul become doubtful about receiving afresh the divine grace, or been troubled in the lively and vigorous use of it, because he saw that others did not possess it just as he did; and never has a heart that was honestly longing for that grace left off entreating for it from heaven, because all did not possess it in exactly the same degree! The man who really desires what is good will make no such mistake; it is only the vain sophist who becomes a fool in counting himself wise. What can hurt the man who follows after good? Nothing; not even the deepest mystery of the divine will.

And none of us, my friends, must let himself be perplexed by the suggestion that if a new birth were necessary, every one ought to know and be able to point out when this miracle of divine grace was wrought on him. On what alone is it that this demand is founded, which certainly many Christians, because they count too much on certain special experiences, are accustomed to make? It cannot be denied, in regard to such persons, that they certainly argue too much from their own experiences; by which they have perplexed many an anxious heart. But the Saviour says nothing of this; He rather leaves us free to give a wider meaning to the words, Thou hearest the sound thereof, but canst not tell whence it cometh; a meaning in which they less imply a reproach, than express the man's necessary uncertainty. For could it be the same thing to require, Ye must be born again, and You must know when and how you were born again. Do we know it about our natural birth, otherwise than by the accounts of others, such as no one can give us about what has been transacted between God and the soul alone? Is not the beginning of every form of life, from the lowest to the highest, hidden in the impenetrable darkness of divine creation, and is it likely that this would not be the case with the most mysterious creation of the Spirit? that the new life would be just as imperceptibly entered on and developed as the old? And certainly those also are mistaken who think they have actually watched the beginning of this life. It may be that they regard as such one of the many preparatory stirrings of the mind, from which, after all, no continuous spiritual life resulted, or that they confound the first full consciousness of that life with the beginning of it. To this consciousness each of us attains sooner or later; it reveals itself in certain moments of exuberant feeling; it is authenticated by the fruits of the Spirit, which are love, joy, peace, patience; it is the witness of the Spirit of God in our hearts that we are the children of God; and with this let us be satisfied. But let us never sit down so contented with the sense and the certainty of our own life in the kingdom of God, as not to make it our most earnest endeavour to help others forward into this new life. And in this loving endeavour let us aim at nothing less, and set nothing less before them than this great word of the Saviour, so that the little that we can do may be done in the right direction, and that even we may help in the work of the Spirit of God. Amen.

(*From the Author's third collection, published in* 1814.)

V.

CHRIST AND THE UNSTABLE.

TEXT: MATT. xxi. 10–16.

WE have lately seen from several examples that what is properly to be regarded as the suffering of the Saviour, that is, His pain on account of sin, and of the opposition which it offered to His divine work, did not begin merely with the time which, in a stricter sense, we indicate as His period of suffering, but accompanied Him from the beginning of His earthly life, and more especially during His public career. We shall consider this to-day more closely in connection with those events which immediately preceded the sufferings of the Saviour, specially so called. Now, if a meditation of this kind is to be really profitable to us, we must have regard to two things. On the one hand, as we are called and chosen as members of the consecrated body, the Church, of which Christ is the head, to devote ourselves to the work of Christ in order to carry it on according to the measure which God has dealt to each; so in the same warfare against sin, we must also meet with the same opposition which He experienced, and Christ's pain must become ours; and by what He showed Himself to be in the days of His life on earth, He is set forth as the shining example which we are to follow. And on the other hand, as we are invited, with all who are weary and heavy-laden, to enjoy the fruits of His redemption; and as we can only enjoy these with the humble feeling that, mighty as His strength may be in us who are weak, yet sin is never quite eradicated in us, and that the remainder of it in us opposes His work, thus making us the cause of sufferings to Him and His people such as He met with at that time; so, those who caused Him pain in the days of His earthly life must stand before us as a warning and alarming example, lest we sit down idly and indulge that which is like them, in ourselves; causing rather to burn increasingly in us a holy anger against evil, that thereby there may be more and more room for the Holy Spirit to work in us and by us.

The words of our text show us the Saviour in His last entry into the capital of His nation, at the summit of His popularity among men, and at the highest stage of His influence. He is no longer called simply Jesus of Nazareth; His disciples, and after them the people, and, following their example, the children in the temple, cried, Hosanna to the Son of David! the very name by which the expected deliverer of the nation was designated. We see Him exercise magisterial authority, as it were, in the temple, as, besides the existing rulers, it became Him alone to do, who was called to institute a new and higher order of divine things. But how soon, my friends, how unexpectedly soon do we see the whole state of things change! How easily are all the people who have just been shouting their applause around Him, turned away from Him! How soon do we find the Lord, who seemed so lately to have everything at His command, a prisoner and bound in the hands of His enemies! How soon is He who but now had been hailed as the Son of David that cometh in the name of the Lord, brought forward and accused as a malefactor! If we ask the reason of this, we meet, no doubt, on the one hand, the unhappy disciple who betrayed Him; on the other, the enmity of the rulers, restrained only by fear of the enthusiastic people; but how would they have ventured to lay hands on Him, how would hatred and treachery have dared to approach Him, if this enthusiasm of the people had been less evanescent, if the fickle disposition of the people had not favoured their purpose? And the Saviour knew this disposition, even when they were all strewing palms before Him and greeting Him as the Deliverer; we can trace this sting in His heart through all His sayings; and this suffering of soul was present with Him even in the height of His popularity. This then is the subject on which I wish to speak,—the fickle disposition of men as a source of suffering to our Saviour, and in the order that I have already indicated; namely, considering first, how our Saviour bore Himself in regard to this, and how, therefore, we also are to act; and secondly, setting before us, as a warning example, those who prepared this suffering for our Saviour.

I. Yes, my devout friends, we cannot and dare not conceal it from ourselves, the position of those who seek to promote what is good, who are in earnest in labouring at the work of redemption, is still the same as that of the Saviour Himself. They are a little handful—each one of them alone—but, still more where they would like to work in union, beset by enemies and traitors. They meet, no doubt, on the other hand, with much admiration; much enthusiasm is aroused by their courage, their self-sacrifice, their constancy; but often in the most decisive moment this enthusiasm fails to stand the test, and they see themselves forsaken and thrown back upon themselves. Under these circumstances then, surrounded by people of this fickle disposition, what can we learn from the conduct of the Saviour? In the first place, He knew the fickleness of the populace, and hence did not allow himself to be deluded by their ebullition of kindly feeling. Who among us, my friends, in the Saviour's position, if at that feast which drew together many thousands from all parts of the country into Jerusalem, he had been met with such universal favour by the populace—if on every side so much willingness to accept his help had been manifested, so much eagerness to commit themselves to his guidance—who would not have formed the most flattering hopes, which yet no results would have justified; who would not have allowed himself to be seduced into schemes which would have had no relation to the actually existing means that were to be put in operation! Very far was the Saviour from this! Though we do not find that He expressed aloud His suspicion of the real import of these marks of honour, or that He rejected them, yet all His discourses between this brilliant moment and the time of His being seized, of which the evangelists have preserved for us so great an abundance, show plainly how correctly He estimated His position. How many hints there are that the people would, notwithstanding all this, refuse and reject Him; how many open and more private warnings to those who led others astray or suffered themselves to be so led; how many words of comfort because all the good that He had planned for men would not be spread abroad until future generations. He even saw plainly beforehand the temporary painful timidity of His disciples, and foretold that when the Shepherd should be smitten the flock would be scattered. And so He did not allow Himself to be misled into building any far-reaching project on those utterances of the multitudes that poured around Him with their plaudits; no open war against those who, to their own condemnation and the ruin of the people, sat in Moses' seat; no attempt to give to the kingdom of truth a striking, outward form, and put it in the place of the worn-out, dead priesthood; only all kinds of precautions that it might be brought safely, in its unseen form, through all the coming storms. Oh, my friends, that we might learn this from the Saviour! For there is nothing more bitter than hopes and plans for good that have proved vain, and of which we are obliged afterwards to confess that they had not been so well-founded as we thought, and that we might easily have foreseen their unsuccessful issue. But we shall only acquire this wisdom by keeping our zeal for the kingdom of God pure from all culpable thoughtlessness, and by letting the deepest earnestness rule our lives; we shall only learn it if in our judgment of men's state of mind, vanity has no part whatever, and if, in order to estimate it, we always look into the inmost recesses and the former history of our own hearts.

But in the second place, the Saviour by no means neglected to make use of the favourable, though transitory, emotions of the people. If we assume, as we must, that He who had no need that any one should tell Him what was in man, knew the multitude for what they were, even in the midst of their enthusiastic acclamations, we see how little this interfered with His usual manner of acting. Though He knew that these same people who were now shouting their rejoicings around Him, would soon by their acts be against Him, just as His open enemies had always been, yet He did not now hesitate to make it understood that He was indeed the One who was to come: If these should not speak, He says, according to another account, the stones would immediately cry out. What He would gladly have done long before, cast out the crying abuses from the temple and cleanse His Father's house, He felt that He could now do; He felt that these stirrings of feeling, transient as they were, made all opposition to His absolute authority for the moment impossible; and if He knew equally well that in a few days it would all sink back into the old disorder, yet He omitted nothing that the moment allowed, nothing that was an indication of His office, and worthy of His having effected in so short a time. He did not scorn to effect what was to pass away, because even previsions of the future are profitable; and thus He sought to draw from even this transient excitement every advantage which it really offered.

As to ourselves, my friends, as we allow ourselves too

easily to be carried away into indulging extravagant hopes, when we see men better than they really are, so we are also too much inclined to despond when we observe that their movements towards good were only passing and superficial ebullitions. We are disgusted with their praise, their honour, their attachment, when we find how at other times they give the same to those who are utterly different from us, to whose views and mode of action we are thoroughly opposed. We lose all delight in their pious emotions, in their interest in what is good, when we see plainly how soon it is swept away by anything whatever that touches them personally, or how readily the same easily-moved feelings may be enlisted on the opposite side. And, indeed, because what we really love and honour is only real goodness that flows from the pure fountain, we would prefer to have nothing at all in common with such people, and rather fear to injure our work by using the passing impulses of such uncertain characters even as instruments and means towards what we are trying to do. Would that we could in this matter follow exactly in the footsteps of the Saviour! Holy indignation at the changeable character of men was not indeed unknown to Him, nor did He reckon this fluctuating multitude, in their favouring mood, in the number of His people; but He had no hesitation in availing Himself of their mood in order to effect something good by means of it. On men themselves there can certainly be nothing built in such a state of temporary excitement, and nothing that it produces is of much value, in so far as it is *their* work. But why should it not be of value as a work of ours, which yet could not have been accomplished without them? If we can wring from them a contribution or some co-operation in a good cause, which does not on that account become theirs, nor is the worse for it, are we to miss the opportunity? Rather let us avail ourselves the more quickly of the uncertain and brief help, the more uncertain and brief it is;

and let us reflect that this also is a talent that God has entrusted to us, a power that we are to use, each of us where he is placed in the Lord's vineyard, so as to accomplish with it as much as we can. And this will become the more easy to us if, *in the third place*, we become like the Saviour in this, that even in these transient stirrings of feeling we do not fail to recognise their noble and divine origin. For in His conduct this is plainly to be observed. Therefore He bore with, and indeed took pleasure in, the acclamations which expressed the emotions that His superior dignity had aroused, though but for a moment, in their minds. Therefore He did not oppose them with that sullen sternness with which another would perhaps have told them that they were not worthy thus to greet Him. But when the chief priests and elders came and asked Him in doubt, Hearest Thou what these say? or, according to another evangelist, Rebuke Thy disciples and forbid the people; He did neither the one nor the other: on the contrary, He acknowledged it as a good thing, as praise offered to God and to Him, by referring to the Scripture that says, Out of the mouth of babes and sucklings hast Thou prepared praise; He recognised it as necessary, by answering them, as another evangelist tells us, Verily, if these should hold their peace, the stones would cry out. And can we, my dear friends, do otherwise than, like the Saviour, recognise the Spirit of God even in such transient excitements among men? No man can call Jesus Lord, says the apostle, but by the Holy Spirit, and this word we may neither wrest nor explain away. Every impression, therefore, even though transient, produced by the words or the person of the Saviour, that bends the knees of men to the dust in real feeling before Him; every honest, though only momentary testimony of their reverence towards Him, by which they, as it were, glorify His throne set up in the Church; every feeling of horror that seizes their hearts at the thought that His rule round about them, which they themselves have so little supported, may some day come to an end; every service, every contribution which they pay, with their heart's consent, to what we as ministers and servants of our Lord undertake:—all this is the work of the Divine Spirit. And are we not to honour and recognise it? Are the indications of it too many and too various, so that we may easily do without or neglect some of them? If we justly feel grieved that every stirring of this Spirit in the hearts of men does not take a thorough hold and renew and sanctify them, are we therefore to rejoice the less at His every lightest knock at the door of men's hearts, at even the first traces of a life of their own, though it is not yet permanent? Ought we not to be less cast down by the fugitive character of such moments than cheered because there is, nevertheless, a stirring in the hearts of men? Though we do not always venture to prophesy that such stirrings will at some future time lead to fear, and to a point at which men will repent and smite on their breasts and ask, What shall we do to be saved?—even supposing we did not foresee this, are we, on that account, not even to take the pure enjoyment of the thing itself? For what better proof can there be how deep the germ of the divine lies in human nature, and properly belongs to its essence, and hence what can be more moving and cheering to us, than those very fits of piety wrung from hardened or thoughtless men?

May we all thus learn from the Saviour to restrain the natural feeling of aggrieved indignation at the fickleness of men, by striving to find out all that God is effecting, and being set with our whole soul on every good work that our hand finds to do. But do we become altogether like Him in this matter, only by thus acting in regard to the fickleness of others? Must we not also think about banishing it from ourselves? Only remember that in Him there was and could be no trace whatever of this infirmity of human nature;

remember, at the same time, how often you good men, even at heart pious men, have yielded to it in dismissing your weightiest convictions and resolutions; look around you; how much good is forgotten through fickleness, that was begun vigorously and with noble zeal; and you will not fail to acknowledge that even the best are not quite free from this mischievous weakness.

II. Let us therefore, secondly, set before ourselves as a warning, the inward condition of those who in this fickle way forsook the Saviour, and the responsibilities they incurred.

We have certainly no reason to assume that many of those who had celebrated the Saviour's entry, who had publicly directed the hope of the whole nation to Him, and, as His numerous retinue, had supported His strong measures in the temple, would, a few days after, have joined in the cry, Crucify, crucify Him! that the very same people who so confidently proclaimed Him as the Messiah, had afterwards a hand in His death as if He had been a base impostor; or even that their hope of a new and better kingdom of God had entirely vanished, and that just for that reason they would have preferred to see Him utterly destroyed on whom this hope had rested with so decided a predilection. No, the sentiments of men are seldom so entirely turned round, especially from what is good and true to what is perverted and evil! It is not so, assuredly, with any of us, that we could by any possible means become doubtful as to Christ being the foundation-stone of our faith and our salvation, His image and His word the universal standard of all our actions. But just as those people would not likely have thus kept silence, so that we cannot understand what has become of the great host of admirers and adherents, but rather there would have arisen a great and serious struggle, if they had not become doubtful whether supporting Jesus was really after all the means by which that better kingdom of God was to be brought in, or if they must not postpone their hopes to another time; so we also as individuals are often unstable, and what we held with the strongest conviction as good and right, and as necessary for the well-being of present and future generations, and were ready to promote with all our powers, we not unfrequently become again uncertain about, when the decisive moment is at hand. Now, in seeking to point out, from the example of that mixed multitude, what is the cause of this changeable behaviour, I think that many a one is saying to himself, But how are we to know at first, and who is to judge, if such a thing occurs with us, whether it is instability, or rather a later and correct knowledge? for how often it is only through a state of vacillation, and after having inclined alternately to this side and to that, that we arrive at a firm conviction! And how often a man is too hasty with his resolutions, so that it is a real step in the way of improvement when from a false certainty he comes to doubt and uncertainty! But this question need not interfere with the view I have started, for just how these changes of conviction come to pass can only be determined by what has preceded them in us and without us. Let us only, in the first place, not forget that we enjoy a great advantage over those contemporaries of Jesus whom we are setting before us as a warning example. That is, that a Christian guided by the Spirit of Christ will seldom come to a firm decision on any important matter by himself, but through that same Spirit, who is the Spirit of truth; and if he takes up anything in a fit of passionate excitement, a sense of insecurity will arise at the same moment and will go on increasing; and therefore with him it is rarely an advance when from firm conviction he goes back to doubt. Now if with ourselves, what we felt certain about becomes again doubtful, the firm purpose unsettled, whence does that come? This we shall see in those men, in whom we see mirrored both the bold and the cowardly heart.

In the first place, my friends, what is expressed by the

jubilation of that multitude at the entry of Christ, but the hope that He would redeem Israel? They believed that the time was come, or would presently be, when He would come forward publicly, and announce Himself with authoritative credentials, as God's ambassador; everything would then bend before Him, and they, reminding Him at the same time of the way in which they had even now professed their faith in Him, would then renew their profession, and would not only obtain from Him deliverance from all their troubles, but would also share in all the glory of His kingdom. But now they saw Christ Himself in trouble; and if they meant to be loyal to Him, they must have felt called on, instead of merely receiving help and deliverance from Him, to help Him, as it were, in the first place, by making their voices heard in opposition to the demand of the angry crowd. You see here, my friends, how it is not unfrequently with many people. Some prospective undertaking of an individual or of a community appears to us in the highest degree desirable and profitable, perhaps even necessary, to prepare the way for and to support what most concerns ourselves. We long for the moment when they will begin their operations, we receive the first indications of it with rejoicing and exultation, we set ourselves in readiness to apply the hoped-for help to our own uses, and then we join in the cause itself with all our might. But if, meanwhile, the enterprise itself come into danger; if those in whom we hoped meet with difficulties and opposition, and seem to be themselves in need of help; then we become doubtful, and think that in those who are themselves in want of our help there cannot surely be the power that we supposed to help us; we think we must have been mistaken, and are quite rejoiced that we have been warned at the right time and have discovered our mistake. But is not this a very strange way of thinking, opposed to universal experience and to the first principles of all human action? Is there any power in human affairs except by the union of human faculties? Is there any kind of help and support that should not be mutual? Can any one receive help in any way, whether from friendship, or through family connections, or by the public authority, if he has not himself without intermission upheld and maintained those very powers? Is it not, therefore, the greatest folly if, instead of supporting with all our might that from which we expect good—as the friends of the Saviour ought to have showed publicly that the voice of His accusers was by no means the voice of the whole people—if, instead of this, we think that there can certainly be no help and deliverance for us in what will perhaps perish if we ourselves do not support it? Did not the Saviour for this very reason come in the form of a servant, was He not tempted in all things like as we are, that we might understand that God will bestow everything on us only in a human way; that is, growing up gradually from a feeble beginning that stands in need of help?

But, in the second place, it is certainly still worse if the fickleness arises from the fact that it is just we ourselves who ought to afford help to what we have counted good and excellent; if it is when the consummation is to be reached perhaps in doubtful, unpromising circumstances, that the firmness of our resolutions is lost; in short, if a timid disposition or cowardice is the source of our instability. That was certainly the case with many who, when they shouted their Hosannas to the Saviour, had firmly resolved to join Him and share His fate; who at that time were not intimidated by the well-known hatred of the upper classes towards Him, but intended nobly and gloriously to maintain that struggle together with Him; but now, when it was actually begun, they drew back. And how often do we meet with the same spectacle in individuals among men who have recognised what is good. At a distance, opposition, struggles, self-sacrifice cannot alarm them; but when the moment comes they lose heart; anxiety and misgiving master the weak mind, and instead of saying to themselves, The thing you meant to do is still right and good, but you are too timid, too feeble, too weak of will to carry it out, you have given yourself credit for what you are not capable of doing;—instead of this, the desponding heart abuses and deceives the understanding and poisons the judgment with worthless fancies, as if what had formerly been aimed at with lively zeal were neither so good nor so necessary a thing as had then been supposed; as if beneficent time had now for the first time revealed the true nature of the case. Oh, my friends, I cannot begin to tell what deep debasement there is in this condition; with what compassion, bordering on contempt, noble and strong souls look down on it, and how they grieve or reproach themselves for having perhaps reckoned more on us unstable ones than the Saviour did on the men of His time. And how much shame do we prepare for ourselves if that from which we in our cowardice drew back, is yet splendidly carried out! how much reproach if, just because of our cowardly instability, it is discontinued! For we are not, of course, to covet that every good work should be done through us, and we may rejoice just as deeply in that which, through the grace of God, is done by others; but this joy befits only those, and in fact they alone share it, who have themselves done all they could. And if we are disappointed of something that we had desired as a great blessing, there remains to us, it is true, the comfort that all is only for the best as the Lord orders it; but this comfort befits only those, and they alone actually enjoy it, who have risked everything in order to attain what they desired. Shame and confusion, on the contrary, on those who are compelled to say to themselves, If you had continued steadfast, you might now be among those who are thanking God that He has made use of them for the furthering of what is good; but now you have done everything that lay with you to hinder it. And a burning and grievous sting must be fixed in the hearts of those who are obliged to say to themselves, that God will now again prepare praise for Himself only out of the mouth of sucklings; that everything on which perhaps their hopes, with those of many thousands, were set, is again deferred for the next generation; nay, that perhaps only the stones are speaking of that which was then undeveloped and went back, while free and pious men might be joyfully thanking God if it had been accomplished; and that this also is their fault. For where an unstable disposition gains the upper hand, there the little number of the good and strong labour in vain for the present, and none but babes, who are witnesses of the great fault without sharing in it, dare to hope; when faint-hearted hesitation prevents the aim from being promptly met at the right moment, then all that men, moved by the presence of what is great and divine, have felt, is like sterile blossoms from which there remains no fruit. But monuments of ruin will speak; for where precious opportunities are missed for the kingdom of God, there ruin breaks in, there follow close behind, as they did then, the judgments of God.

Yes, my friends, unstable souls are like that fig-tree, the account of which comes soon after our text, the tree to which, in returning to the city next morning from Bethany, the Saviour went to pluck fruit, and found nothing but leaves. So also those people, however much cultivation has been bestowed on them by the stirring and inspiring presence of what is good and beautiful, have never anything to show but the barren decoration of fine feelings and high-sounding words. But the Saviour's heart was vexed; He said to the tree, Be thou forthwith dried up! And what have such people to expect, especially in so decisive a time, but that the power that exhausts itself in empty utterances will entirely leave them, and nothing but the outward life remain, as a warning monument.

Let every one then, trembling at the thought of such results, strive to have his heart kept steadfast, to be ready at any cost to cleave to what he has recognised as true and right. And that we may be able to do this, oh let us be branches in our vine, the Lord, so pervaded by His Spirit and His presence, that, far from being sounding brass or tinkling cymbals, we may enjoy the living faith that makes no difficulty about mountains being removed, and the living love of which our eternal fountain is the Lord, who clung even to the weak disciples with heartfelt fidelity, and bound them together, as may He also bind us, to loyalty in life and in death. Amen.

VI.

FORGIVENESS AND LOVE.

TEXT: LUKE vii. 36–50.

HOWEVER much admiration and honour was given to our Saviour by many of His contemporaries during His life on earth; however powerfully a yet greater number were struck, at least for the moment, by His exalted character; still just His greatest words and His noblest deeds often remained dark even to the noblest and best around Him, and seemed to the rest a piece of insolent pretension. When He spoke of His eternal relation to the Eternal Father, even His more intimate disciples asked in childish perplexity, Lord, show us the Father; while the mass of the people were shocked at His words as at a blasphemy. When He spoke to an unfortunate the great word, Go, thy sins are forgiven thee, they murmured among themselves and said, Who is this that forgiveth sins?

And even the ideas they had of Him were inconsistent with each other. Daily they heard from Him and His disciples that He had come to set up the kingdom of God: could they wonder, then, that He who affirmed this of Himself, also claimed the right to forgive sins? Could they believe in the possibility of a kingdom of God in which the great word, Thy sins are forgiven, would not be spoken to every one belonging to it? Did they believe that through their sacrifices they found forgiveness of sins, although no power could proceed from them to elevate and advance men so far that they should not be always needing forgiveness anew and as much as ever; and yet did it seem to them a strange thing that now at last this greatest and most comforting of all assurances so necessary to them, should proceed from the depths of this divine heart, from Him who so mightily moved the souls of men?

We all feel that true love to the Saviour could have struck no deep roots in hearts that could so marvel.

It is of course different with us, my Christian friends. We acknowledge Him as our Mediator with His and our Father, through union with whom the forgiveness of sins comes to us once for all, and who pronounces it to us ever anew in His word, and by the special manner of His presence with believers. But while those people long ago asked, Who is this that forgiveth sins? it well befits us to raise the question, Who are we to whom sin is forgiven?—are we, at least, in so far worthy of this great word that we thoroughly feel its deep meaning and that it stirs us to fervent gratitude and love? There is an idea very common among us,—which has indeed its true side, and which is founded on living faith,—that if we have once found the way of salvation we should no longer let our thoughts dwell on the weakening and tormenting sense of sin; but that when it is confessed and put away by repentance and faith, it should only serve in the way of instruction and warning; that we should then go forward with alacrity and courage in the work of establishing, specially on this foundation, our relationship of love and fellowship with the Saviour, as the power for a life more honouring to Him flows ever more abundantly into our souls from His word, from His memorial, and from His image present to our minds. This is all quite true; but the one view must not exclude the other, and there is certainly great danger of our relation to the Saviour losing its distinctive character if this thought does not keep a lasting hold of our hearts, that it is He who speaks to us the great word, Go, thy sins are forgiven thee. For He Himself makes this very consciousness at once the ground and the measure of the love that we are able to give Him, and that love is certainly the source of the power that proceeds from Him.

The simple and touching narrative of our text has never failed to take a wonderful hold of every heart not utterly incapable of feeling. In reading it we cannot but be struck afresh with the sense of how glorious a thing it is to be drawn to the Saviour by a feeling of one's own lost condition; and every one must recognise the profound truth of the direct application which the Saviour makes of the incident, when contrasting the weeping woman who was a sinner with the righteous man whose guest He was. But the broader inference which our Lord finally draws from it has always seemed, to many minds, questionable and obscure. Let us therefore, for the present, confine our attention to these last words, "Her sins, which are many, are forgiven; for she loved much: but to whom little is forgiven, the same loveth little." Let us consider the universal connection between the forgiveness of sin and love, as here laid down by the Saviour. Let us note how the conduct of this woman bears on the relation of men to the Saviour, and how all the lessons of the narrative serve first of all to illustrate this; while at the same time there are allusions throughout to everyday human relationships, and the Saviour states His main principle in quite a general way. Let us, therefore, consider first our common relation to Christ, and then our ordinary brotherly relationships with each other.

I. First, then, as to our common relation to the Saviour. Can we accept as universally true this principle which He lays down, Her sins, which are many, are forgiven; for she loved much: but to whom little is forgiven, the same loveth little? Serious difficulties have in fact been raised as to the first part of the statement. Thus, when the Saviour says, She has been forgiven much, for she loved much, He takes the love as the ground of the forgiveness, and so, in fact, places love in the position of claiming forgiveness—even much forgiveness; which will yet be granted for the sake of the love. But he who needs much forgiveness must of course have sinned much. Then is love—at once the deepest and inmost source and the richest and purest outcome of everything good and noble—always to spring out of evil? is sin to be the soil that yields the largest returns, from which good grows the most richly and produces the noblest fruits? And if love is the only true virtue—the sum of all the commandments of God—then must not all sins just amount to this, that love is wanting in a man's heart? But how can you reconcile these things? The more a man needs forgiveness, you say, and therefore the more he has sinned—that is, the further his heart is from love, the deeper he is sunk in lovelessness and selfishness—is he just so much the more able to love? Is he to be made capable of love by its very absence?

Now, how shall we answer such objections? Simply by what experience teaches us. For what, in fact, does produce more love—above all such love as comes from the gratitude of the needy—than a keenly felt sense of need so entirely possessing a man's heart that he is conscious only of the one longing for help and deliverance, and then his actual experience of deliverance? The very name Jesus, Saviour, implies that our love shall be of this kind. The power of sin creates such a sense of need. And when is this great word, Thy sins are forgiven thee, spoken to a man? When can he receive it? Not until his heart, long as it may have been hardened, opens at last to the eternal light; and the more clearly a man recognises, in that light, his own position, just so much the greater must be his sense of the misery from which he longs to be delivered. And it is thus—with this feeling of the guilt of a heart that has become a stranger to love—with this longing to escape from the consciousness of condemnation—that every one who for the first time seriously and truly estimates what is meant by being a Christian, comes to the Saviour. And ever as he sees things more clearly in the eternal light of truth, he becomes more fully conscious that, if he is to be forgiven at all, he must be forgiven *much*. And in order to the full strength of this conviction, and through it to the man's capability of grateful love, there is no need, as objectors fear, that a man should be guilty of great and open sins, of extraordinary and heinous offences; as if the more sins a man should commit, it were the better for him. There is nothing whatever in the words of the Saviour to imply that the power of loving belongs pre-eminently to him who has made himself pre-eminently a mark for the scorn of the world. Christ simply means to deal with the Pharisee according to his capacity for understanding; and therefore He sets before him one man who owes a certain sum and another who owes ten times as much, and bids him decide which will be the most grateful for the remission of the debt. But if we examine this story of His in a spirit of simple desire for truth, and with the honest purpose of discriminating between the mere external and the spiritual, can we really believe that the greatness of the debt is meant to figure a great amount of specially aggravated sins? For the person who has contracted a small debt may have just as far exceeded his means, and may have just as carelessly overlooked the impossibility of restitution, as another who contracts a great one. He must then, naturally, be as grateful as the other for remission. And, just so, the same amount of guilt may attach to very different amounts of sin; and he who, tried by the mere external test of the world, is pronounced pure, may have as much to be forgiven as he who, to the world's eyes, seems laden with sins. But we may be very sure that the Saviour did not mean to measure the need of forgiveness by any such external rule; and it is just as certain that the mind has no measure by which to estimate spiritual corruption, either when we compare men with each other or with the purity of the Saviour. What can we conclude then, but that by these different amounts of debt the Saviour means to indicate the different degrees of the *sense* of sin? And thus shall we see this, first of all, to be no more than true, To whom much is forgiven, the same will love much; he who has seen deep and clearly into the abyss of his sinful heart, will cling with proportionate gratitude to Him who has delivered and raised him up.

But on the other hand the Saviour is entirely right when He inverts the statement, and says, Much is forgiven to her, for she loved much. For, my friends, how do we attain to the pardon of that for which we must be forgiven, be it much or little? Is it not those very people who find the greatest difficulty in the declaration of our Lord, who also say most confidently that God can only forgive, and in point of fact does only forgive, when a man is firmly resolved on a new life, and has set out in the way of holiness?

But is it of any use to think of holiness if we are not thoroughly convinced of the opposition between good and evil? and will holiness not advance the more steadily just in proportion to the abhorrence with which each one regards the evil of which all, including himself, have so much to be forgiven? And if the life of God to which holiness leads is a life of love, then the sense of forgiveness cannot awake in the heart until the stream of Divine love which accompanies the forgiveness has begun to work its way through the hardened crust of the heart, and the living water to flow in; and the heart in which this fountain of love flows abundantly is, without doubt, the heart to which comes most strongly the glad assurance that much is forgiven.

And now we can quite simply take up the other half of the Saviour's declaration, But to whom little is forgiven, the same loveth little, without any stirring of anxious doubts or misgivings, as if it implied that it was an advantage to have sinned more than others; as if grace could go forth most powerfully only on him in whom sin had been mightiest; as if he who, while still far from the life of God, was restrained, possibly by some mere external check, from plunging deep in the slough of sensuality, should now, as if in punishment of that abstinence, be able to attain only to a low degree of the spiritual life; and as if this statement offered a dangerous incentive to hardened and obdurate sinners to persist in their sins; or, as the apostle expresses it, to continue in sin that grace may abound; giving themselves up utterly to their lusts and passions in order that there may be a deeper repentance and therefore a higher measure of gratitude when the hour of grace arrives. All this is mere vain and empty talk. He to whom much is forgiven is not he who has sinned much, but he who feels that, in this respect, the difference among men as a whole is not so great as we foolishly imagine, and that one has little honour above another so long as all lack the honour that comes from God. It is he, in short, who, in his own sin, mourns over all sin—the sin of the whole world; who bathes the feet of the Saviour with his tears, and pours forth on Him the fragrant ointment of a grateful and lowly heart. He to whom *little* is forgiven is not he who has sinned little—for who indeed could stand forth and say, It is I—but he who still thinks too lightly of his sin, perhaps because, unconsciously, he is unwilling to owe too much to the grace of God in Christ.

Such a man was the Pharisee who had invited Christ, but in the worldly wisdom of a cold heart still doubted His being a true prophet, and who was afraid of showing the Saviour too much honour, even in his own house.

And just such as he are all who wish to come to the Saviour, not with the grateful love of the needy, not with the humble love of the outcast, but with the easy, complaisant love of one who, in the strength of his own excellence, can easily afford to acknowledge the excellence and godliness that shine forth from Christ.

And such are all those who readily admit the Saviour's claim to gratitude for bringing blessing to mankind, but are not willing to admit that it was necessary in their own case that this blessing should begin with their being rescued from a state of degradation and ruin. To all such, little is forgiven, and so they love little. Either they have little love, little heart or feeling in any direction, or it goes out chiefly on mere earthly things. Lukewarm is their love to the Saviour. Since there *is* really such a Saviour, they keep up a connection with Him; but in their innermost heart they think they could perhaps do very well without Him. Lukewarm too is their interest in His work. For they do not perceive that all coldness of feeling, all stupid indifference to what is good, all slothful relaxing in our efforts to please God, are really sins; and therefore it is easy for them to boast that little has been forgiven them.

But the true love of the really godly takes quite another view. In the consciousness of our calling, made clear to us only in Him, in the thought of our vows so often made to Him, how can we but feel that to us much has been forgiven, and that there must always be much to forgive.

II. Let us, in the second place, apply these words of the Saviour to our brotherly relations with each other. We are justified in doing this, because He Himself, in the lesson of our text, chooses such a human relation, though but a very external and slight one, to illustrate the relation of His people to Himself; and still further because He, who has manifested Himself to all in order to say to them, Thy sins are forgiven thee, does not shrink from even then calling us brethren.

It is true, indeed, that in our relation to the Saviour, this connection between forgiveness and love is, in two aspects, one-sided. It is only we who are forgiven, while it is He alone who forgives; and again, it is only we who love because much is forgiven us, while He, on the other hand, loves because He has forgiven much; because the consciousness of having raised us up and united us to the Father commends us ever anew to His love.

But in our relation to our brethren the bond is reciprocal. We are forgiven, and therefore we love; we forgive others, and therefore also we love them; and for the same twofold reason do our brethren love us. If the mutual forgiveness is large and generous, so must the love be that springs from it; if it is small, the love will also be poor and lukewarm. Yes, my friends, in every relation of life we must feel this, that much is forgiven us because we have loved much—that we love little, if little is forgiven us. Look at the dearest and closest relationships; those with husband or wife, with children, with brothers and sisters, with all whom God has laid specially on our hearts, and made the objects of our warmest love. Which of us can boast that in these relationships we have sinned little, and that little has been forgiven us? Oh, consider what life is, with all our variable moods, our little unfairnesses, our never-ceasing battle against selfish ways and cowardly sloth; and you will feel constrained to confess that it is only those who love little to whom little is forgiven; those who are satisfied with what can be measured by a mere external and legal standard. But he who requires of himself what the Spirit in His fulness can accomplish—and how much that is, the spirit of love alone can estimate; he who longs for the good of those whom God has given him just as he longs for his own; in a word, he who loves much;—oh, how often will he find cause to entreat for patience and forbearance; how deeply will he feel that to him much must be forgiven.

But just because all who live with him know so well the deep-seated principle of his loving character; because in presence of this master-feeling all roughnesses are smoothed away, all vexations vanish;—for these very reasons he meets with patience and forbearance; and much is forgiven to him, because he loves much.

And just so it is in all the less intimate social relations among men. He who is content with standing in no one's way, injuring no one, neglecting nothing that the rules of a correct life can demand, may readily suppose that there is little to be forgiven him; but then he loves little. He who, on the other hand, lays himself out to exert a kindly and cheering influence on the lives of others,—how many sins of omission, how many moments of lazy indifference or cold reserve will he have to reproach himself with! But if men are only aware that this is the ruling principle of his life, if they feel how much he loves, and see how much he lovingly accomplishes, then much is forgiven to him.

Let us think of what we owe to the fathers, the sons, and the servants of our country. How common it is among us to think that only he who has been guilty of glaring offences against these relationships needs forgiveness. But, alas, how little love there is! How does each of us, under cover of external laws, seek only his own advantage!

Oh that the hard crust of the heart were shattered, and that in the pure vital air, real, unrestrained love might burst forth into a flame! How would the scales then fall from our eyes! how clearly should we then see how infinitely much we all need to be forgiven! but at the same time how surely would the sense of a free, full life of love bring to us forgiveness and oblivion of all the past.

Let us think of our special connection with those to whom we are united by the common bond of faith and of the forgiveness obtained for us by Christ. How much more we could do to purify and strengthen this holy bond, by teaching, by help, and by example; how much more in the way of finding out and helping forward everything good, and in sifting out and suppressing the evil; how much more by counsel and comfort, by forbearance and long-suffering, to be representatives of Jesus! How much we have to be forgiven! and yet how plain it is that nothing but love—the earnest longing and effort always to do more and to be more—can cover the multitude of sins. But think also how much this bond of believers itself, so to speak, forgives; how it acknowledges us notwithstanding our weaknesses; how from it the strength of our oneness in spirit and faith flows into our inmost being and draws us towards the holiness which is our goal.

On the other hand, my friends, how can we as believers—as those who are strong in love and faith—shut our eyes to the fact that others stand to us and to a whole community of men, so far as we represent it, in the same relation which we ourselves bear to the whole Church and to Christ, her Head? Well, once more, then, let us forgive much, that from this cause we may be able to love much and to be much loved! Let us reflect how Christ's forgiveness acts on the feelings; how not those whose closed eyes He opened, not those whom He healed of grievous infirmities, not even those whom He awakened from physical death, clung to Him with such fervent gratitude, or received from Him so lasting a gift of love, as they to whom He could say, Go in peace; thy sins are forgiven thee. And so it is among ourselves. All other benefits and gifts that we can bestow have less power to strengthen the bond of love than gentle sympathy with the inmost feelings, helpful support given to the weak, restoring and raising up and comforting the fallen and penitent. That was the brightest glory of the Saviour, of whom the seer under the old covenant foretold, the bruised reed shall He not break, and the smoking flax shall He not quench. Oh, how many such do we see around us here! Let us bind up every bruised reed with a tender hand; let us gently breathe the breath of love on the expiring spark, if by any means we may revive it; that so we may draw the closer to Him, and feel how blessed are those who gain from Him the name of brethren, and that we may be able to pray with truth, Forgive us, as we forgive. Amen.

VII.

ON MARRIAGE.

TEXT: EPH. v. 22-31.

IN completing lately the annual round of our Christian holy-days, I expressed to you the wish that the holy emotions which our hearts experience at such seasons might not pass away with them; but that the impressions then made might accompany us during the other half of the year, so that without any extraordinary festival incitement we might constantly retain a more lively sense of communion with the Redeemer, and a fuller enjoyment of what the eternal Father has done through Him. Now if we find that this is not the case, and inquire for the reason, we usually hear this answer, That it is the pressure of daily life that continually draws us back from elevating communion with God into the tumult of the world. And yet, my friends, what constitutes the life on which we would so fain lay the blame of our waning feelings of devotion, of our instability and our transient impressions? It consists, in fact, of just those natural relations which God the Lord Himself has established, out of which the Christian community must be built up, and in which, in their turn, all the blessings of true Christian piety are to take root, that they may be more and more widely extended. How then can this life draw us away from communion with God and the Saviour, when it is really His own holy body which ought to be thoroughly pervaded by His own living power? If this does take place, must it not be because we have lost sight of the real meaning of these relationships, or because vain and false ideas that have become associated with them have hidden from us their true nature?

I have therefore thought it might not be superfluous to take a survey of the most important of our life-relationships, and to study them in the glass of the divine Word, in order both to revive in our minds the Christian meaning of them, and that we may more consciously realize that, far from drawing us back from communion with God and devoted love to the Saviour, they are fitted greatly to confirm those graces in ourselves and through us to call them forth in others.

We will begin this series of meditations with the relationship which is the foundation of all others, namely, the holy bond of marriage, which we must regard as the first appointment of God after His almighty Word had called man into existence. Out of this sacred union are developed all other human relations; on it rests the Christian family, and of such Christian families Christian communities consist. Moreover, on this union depends the propagation of the human race, and the transmitting of the power of the divine Word from one generation to another. Therefore let us to-day consider this foundation of the whole Christian Church in the light of God's Word.

The leading idea in this representation of Christian marriage is, that while the apostle reveals to us the inmost depths of love on which the whole fabric of the Church is founded, he at the same time draws our thoughts to the holy relationship between Christ and His people. I say it is the leading idea; for we thus see clearly that in marriage, as the original root of all social life, there should be nothing that could draw us away from Christ our Lord; rather we are taught to refer everything belonging to it to that great union of our hearts with the Saviour. We shall best understand the apostle's ideal of Christian married life by considering two points in his description of it: first, an *earthly* and a *heavenly* view of it, which are yet one; and secondly, a *difference* which resolves itself into a most perfect *likeness.*

I. First, then, let us see how the earthly and the heavenly view of Christian marriage which the apostle presents to us are thoroughly one, and cannot be separated.

He gives us first the earthly view in the words, A man shall leave his father and mother and shall cleave to his wife, and they two shall be one flesh. Certainly it could not be more clearly and strongly set before us than in these words, and we could find no clearer rule by which to judge of the many and varied phases of the married state which we see around us, even in what calls itself refined society. For, alas, how often among Christians does marriage assume, even from this earthly point of view, a truly *dreadful* aspect! How often do we see the two who should be one giving way to anger against each other, separated by dissension and strife, and sometimes even so embittered against each other that, instead of trying to avoid quarrels, they wilfully seek out occasions for them. In such cases it need not be said that two have not become one. Again, how often has the married state a *troubled* aspect, when, for want of any glad assurance of being one in heart, both parties keep watchful guard over themselves, seeking by the most obliging and compliant manner and behaviour, and by self-denying sacrifice, to avoid all occasions for dispute, and trying by the most tender considerateness to make up, if possible, for the absence of true love. And here also, even if it is only one of the parties who is obliged to exercise this self-constraint, while the other is in the right position, it is easy to see that the two have not become one—that there is no true union, but only a carefully maintained contract,

Once more, how often has marriage a *repulsive* aspect, when married people live, it is true, in peace and harmony, but only because in course of time they have become accustomed to each other, and because, while they make as little demand as possible on each other, both find their real satisfaction in other relations of life and in other companionships! That in a connection so indifferent and dead the two are not one flesh is certain, for *that* implies a living union; and it is equally certain that in this case there has been no heart impulse constraining to leave father and mother and cleave to husband or wife, and that therefore even the earthly side of a Christian marriage is wanting. But why should I go on to multiply these illustrations? Let me rather say in a word that, in so far as each has separate joys and sorrows (even supposing that they have much more regard to the interests of each other than to their own); in so far as the wife needs to remind herself to be submissive, and the husband to remind himself to give honour to the weaker vessel; however faithfully they may obey those admonitions of conscience; and in short, wherever there are opposing wishes and aims to be adjusted, fully and generously as those mental concessions may be carried out; just in so far as these conditions exist, the word of the apostle is not yet fulfilled,—the love that makes truly *one* is not and never has been enthroned there.

But let us suppose that a conjugal union, viewed on its earthly side, does fully correspond to the deep meaning of that apostolic word about the life that has become one through love; let us suppose that there is no need for one of the pair to forget himself or herself out of love for the other, because each feels and shares every emotion of the other, and a kind of intuitive perception of the wishes on the one side inclines the other towards the same objects. Let us suppose that no happiness is enjoyed and no pain borne, apart; that the minds are occupied with the same desires and aims, so that they have really one common life; and that even if days of adversity come, the consciousness of their true heart-union will enable them to bear the trial so well and wisely that, when it is past, they will be glad to have gone through such an experience together. Let there be all this, and so a marriage answering, in this aspect, to the word of the apostle; yet, if it is nothing more than this, we can hardly venture to hope that it will continue to be even thus. Rather we should be ready to fear that, as is too often the case, this beautiful harmony was only the effect of the first glow of affection, which might gradually die away as the more lively emotion gave place to a tranquil and customary state of feeling. A union like this is indeed rare and beautiful; and much good, in many ways, may result from it; but if this earthly perfection is not founded on something greater, it still lacks its true proportion, and the marriage still fails to correspond with the picture which the apostle has drawn for us, because there is still wanting the resemblance to the union of Christ with His Church.

For this is the other side of the apostle's picture; setting before us Him who so loved the Church that He gave Himself for it, that He might sanctify and cleanse it.

Here, then, is the heavenly side of Christian marriage union; its higher aim is that each should sanctify and be sanctified by the other. Without this aim, even that perfect harmony that we have described is so wanting in an adequate object, that it can hardly fail to be resolved back into nothing. And what gain worth reckoning could come from a life-fellowship so narrow that it could only be nourished or exercised in connection with outward life? The twofold life would in that case be no better than the single. Where married life is such as this—regular, pure, cultured, it may be, but still, when weighed in the Christian balance, only sensuous, and in the highest sense of the word, unspiritual—we cannot count the difference so very great, whether it is lived by each separately, or by the two for each other and unitedly; nor can that union deserve the high honour which is here put on marriage by the apostle. The results of conjugal love in such a marriage are no doubt great and beautiful. It makes a cheerful and pleasant life even when there are few external helps; it makes it easy to be tranquil on all occasions of difficulty and vexation. But for us Christians this is not enough. Things are only right when all the faculties and energies of the human soul thus developed are at once instruments of the divine Spirit, and, in order to continue such, find their own natural key, and keep it steadily in tune. For if in a thoroughly Christian marriage we had no other joy than this, that it exhibited to us a harmonious play of natural powers, and if this were the highest end of conjugal love, I could find there no resemblance to the relationship between Christ and His Church. Married love is Christian only when each party receives a spiritual stimulus from the other; when that which, in the nature of the one, is opposed to the influence of the Spirit, is restrained and softened by the other; when each, if inclined to grow weak in this direction, is lifted up and supported by the other; when both see more clearly through the eyes of each other how they stand as to their fellowship with God; in short, when both parties feel the power of the Spirit exalted and enhanced in this union as it could be in no other way. Where the manifold blessings which God has associated with this union are thus experienced and enjoyed in all their warmth and fulness, not in a mere earthly way, but each heart saying from its depths, Our conversation is in heaven; where love to each other is thus hallowed by mutual, higher love to the Saviour, so that the wife can say to her husband, You are to me as Christ is to the Church, and the husband to the wife, You are to me as the Church is to Christ; where this love is always growing stronger, as experience proves that with their strength united both make more rapid progress towards their common aim of holiness;—there, my friends, is the heavenly side of Christian marriage. And of such marriages we may say with truth that they were decreed in heaven; for it has been by the mysterious drawing of the Spirit Himself that the wife has been guided to her husband and the husband to his wife; the unaccountable conviction which is daily more clearly proved to have been true, that each has been predestined as specially belonging to the other, as the most peculiar blessing and the most helpful companion on their common way. But where these things are wanting, beautiful and commendable as everything else may be, there must be wanting also the true fidelity and security, and with those, the true Christian value of married life.

But if that earthly part of which we have spoken is nothing without the heavenly, it is equally true that the heavenly part cannot do without the earthly, without the closest fellowship in the pleasures and pains, the cares and the work of this world.

It is an old delusion, already long recognised as such among us, but in earlier times very common in the Christian Church, that the Christian who wished to give himself up to the influences of the Spirit, to obtain the salvation of his soul, and to win even in this life something higher than its transitory things, could do no better than to withdraw himself as far as possible from the world, and to flee at once from its pleasures and its business, its sufferings and its cares. From this delusion—as if the heavenly could exist and dwell in this world apart from the earthly—arose that long-continued and mistaken habit of looking down on this holy state; a habit which was the cause of so much confusion and vice; and now, after we have so long been aware that no one is so good as to be above this God-appointed means of grace, why should we again surround it with this delusion? And yet this is done when it is asserted that, though it would not be justifiable in a single man, yet a united pair would have the most perfect right, because each found sufficiency in the other, to separate themselves as far as possible from the world, and retire from it for the sake of each other. It is a reviving of this delusion to suppose that by a many-sided, active life, the bond of conjugal love is not sanctified, but desecrated; not enriched, but robbed of a great part of the joys designed for it. A dangerous mistake! for even the deepest love can only make men capable of good and purify them from evil in proportion as it strives to fulfil its whole duty, and shuns no part of its vocation; and two human beings united by God can only be sufficient for each other in so far as a life of activity brings to each the temptations and trials against which they need respectively to guard, and sharpens the eyes of both to search into the depths of their hearts and bring hidden things to light. A questionable fancy at the same time, because even in the most beloved ones we can only have lasting joy and pleasure when we see them in the active exercise of their natural faculties, so that when time has stripped off its early blossoms we see the ripening fruits of the life. And how very far this delusion is from being sanctioned by the apostle's words! For when he points us to the connection between Christ and the Church, is *that* union in any sense identified with a morbid, contemplative life? Must it not have cost the Lord toil to take captive all those thousands? And is not His Church made up of servants who are blessed only when the Lord finds them watching at every hour? And when the apostle bids the wives be subject to their husbands, has he in his eye that modest, retiring spirit, which makes the distinction between command and obedience naturally disappear, while every desire to rule might be only a groundless whim about little or nothing? No; undoubtedly he was thinking of the necessary relations in which every Christian home stands to the larger economy of the community with which it is associated; in which the husband alone represents the household, and in relation to which it is therefore he who must act, while the wife takes part, not directly, but only through her connection with her husband. And in laying down as a rule the position that naturally results from this, the apostle shows us that it is God's will that each Christian household should form a part of that wider association, and fill its place in it by fitting and honourable work. Therefore, without regard to their different positions, or to the greater or less facility with which in union they can avoid hard work, each pair entering on the married state is reminded of the divine rule, that the man is to eat bread in the sweat of his brow, and that it is appointed to the woman, not only to bear children with sorrow, but with the most earnest and diligent solicitude to tend and minister to them and to the whole household.

And let us by no means regard this as a matter of necessity, or as an interruption to our spiritual enjoyments, which God has appointed on account of our weakness, lest they should grow commonplace to us and lose their value. It is only in common, social life that men's happiness and well-being have room to grow, and only by a judicious division of work that each becomes most distinctly conscious of his own powers; and so also it is only through this divine arrangement that we find out what special gifts the Spirit of God has created in each family, and both husband and wife, earnestly working together at their everyday duty, at once find out what is their own work, and enjoy their work in the vineyard of the Lord.

II. I have thus laid before you various considerations, in order to prove that if we are to experience the power and blessing of Christian marriage we must not try to maintain the heavenly aspect of it to the exclusion of the earthly. But these same considerations lead us to the second point which I desire you to notice, namely, that while there is in these two sides of marriage a great apparent dissimilarity, it is needful that we be convinced that even this dissimilarity resolves itself into the most perfect likeness.

Look first at the dissimilarity. When the apostle says husbands are to love their wives as Christ loved the Church, we know that this is a love which not only permits but requires love in return, seeing how constantly we are exhorted to love Him who has first so greatly loved us; but we know also that it is from another point of view a love that is raised far above all reciprocal love, seeing that the Church cannot in any way repay Christ her Redeemer, and can do nothing for Him, but only go on receiving from Him a more and more complete redemption. Now if, in the same way, the wife can do nothing for her husband, but be always receiving from him, then the wife is in a bad case as regards her husband, and the woman is always placed at a disadvantage. And again, when we read that the wife is to be subject to her husband as to the Lord, for the husband is the head of the wife, as Christ is of the Church; then if the wife is to be always subject and the husband alone may command—as unquestionably the Church can never in any sense command Christ, but He must always continue to be absolutely Master—in this light also the wife is in a bad position in relation to her husband. And we husbands might seem to have just as little reason to be satisfied with the position here assigned to us, well aware as we are that we cannot worthily fill such a position, and that the more spiritual the marriage union is seen to be, the less room have we for the proud assumption that we have got so far in advance of our wives as Christ is above the Church. But neither could we be satisfied with what some say; that as this epistle was written in a time when the marriage union was only beginning to be understood as a union of holy love, and when women still had a much inferior position to men, therefore the language must be taken less exactly, and in a somewhat different meaning, so as to be adapted to present times. For we could not be willing to have the meaning of anything changed that we find in God's word; nor can we allow ourselves to understand the language less exactly, lest by sophistry and vain interpretation we miss the true comfort which that divine Word contains. Therefore let us rather try to penetrate still more deeply into the meaning of these words, and in order that we may succeed in doing so we must study them in their right connection.

Taking first the words to the wives—that they be subject to their husbands, and that the husband is the head of the wife—let us set alongside of them those other words which recall to us the Scripture narrative of the first institution of this holy union, that a man shall leave his father and mother and shall cleave to his wife. How clearly do these words, which describe the universal divine order, point to a power going forth from the feminine nature which takes possession of and masters the man. As soon as a man is in a position to leave his father's house, justified by education and religion in beginning an independent life, he seeks for himself a wife; he seeks, but woe to him if he chooses merely according to his own will, whether he is led by some prudent calculation, or in the self-will of impatient passion seizes on the object of his choice. No security has he in this way that he has found her with whom he can enter on the true life of love; nothing that guarantees to him an attachment that will compensate him for all that he leaves and gives up. If he is to cleave to his wife, a power must proceed from her that keeps so firm a hold of him that he feels every desire satisfied, every longing stilled; and it must be this same power that at first unconsciously attracts and captivates him. And when the wife pronounces the Yes, by which the man becomes her head—a freely spoken Yes, without which no man can become the head of his wife in Christian communion—she feels that, according to the universal order and special counsel of God, he has become her head, through an unconscious and involuntary exercise of that power which dwells in her; she feels that, for their whole life together, true Christian fidelity, full unweakened affection depends on the continued operation of this power, which raises a Christian marriage union out of the region of change and accident, and shows it as an eternal work of the eternal Love, worthy to stand among the holiest and greatest of such works.

Therefore the divine rule, that the wife shall be subject to her husband, and the husband the head of the wife, stands unchanged, and it certainly could not be changed by us with impunity; it stands, because it is only in the Christian Church and in a civilized community that there can be a Christian marriage; and in both of these it is the part of the man, to whom God has assigned the binding word and the public deed, to represent the household; and it is never well if the wife takes a direct part in those larger concerns. The rule stands; and yet we find no painful contrast with the higher union, but one which resolves itself into the most glorious likeness. For if things, even at home, in so far as they have more or less bearing on those wider connections, are regulated by the husband; if he pursues his daily work from home quite alone, without the help and company of his wife, so causing to the family some measure of pain and anxiety while providing honourably for their comfort; nevertheless, if he always returns with a heart cleaving to the wife whom God has given him, according to that first divine commandment; if he finds refreshment in his weariness, and strength against difficulties in that union of faithful love; then the true wife also feels that *her* power and blessing are in all that he does, and orders, and provides; and thus before God and to their own consciousness, they still stand equal as in the moment when, through that voluntary Yes on either side, the husband became the head of the wife, and she became subject to him.

And now let us look once more at that word, that men are to love their wives as Christ loved the Church, in connection with those other words, that He is the Saviour of His body, and that He gave Himself for the Church that He might sanctify and cleanse it. For when we find how often, from the beginning, His Redemption is spoken of in the same terms that we have used in picturing the seeking love of the husband—for Christ also came to seek;—when we think how, drawn down to us by the sole power of love, He left the glory which He had with the Father to establish a life and kingdom for Himself on earth; when we remember that His own did not first choose Him, but He them, though now, it is true, they love Him with all their hearts who first so loved them; finally, when we realize that Christ now binds Himself up so closely with His people that whatever they ask in His Name He will obtain for them from the Father, and that, though separated from them in body, He is always with them in Spirit; then we are powerfully struck with the resemblance between this deep, holy mystery of love in individual lives and the great mystery of redemption, and we feel that we understand the apostle's injunction to husbands to love their wives as Christ loves the Church. Are we still inclined to mistake here? to feel as if, according to this view, the husband alone must do all, and that the wife could as little do anything for him, or be profitable to him, as the Church can for Christ? Are the wives, and, for their sakes, the husbands, troubled by the thoughts that what we suggested as equalizing conditions—the wife refreshing and strengthening her husband while he plans and rules—must thus come to nothing? Then let us remember that it is impossible that a comparison between Christ and men should apply at every point, and of course the relation of wife to husband cannot, in every particular, present a parallel to that of the Church to Christ. And if we ask, in what special points is this possible, and in what not so, we have the answer in these words,—that Christ loved the Church and gave Himself for her that He might sanctify her. The husband is to take this self-sacrificing love as his example; gladly returning from his wider circle in the busy world to the quiet of his fireside, there to share with the wife of his heart all that is purifying or elevating in what he has met with or done or felt. The likeness is found, not in this, that Christ is our King (as if implying that an exclusive and unlimited authority should belong to the husband), but in this, that to the Church, as His body, He is Saviour and Redeemer. We know that as our Redeemer He has freed us from bondage, for it is the liberty of the children of God to which we are redeemed. Let the husband, then, take this freedom-giving love as his example, and act as the head of his wife in delivering her from all bondage both of heart and life, to which her sex so easily resign themselves, in removing out of her way all restrictions, so that the power of their united life may have unimpeded exercise in her. Then, even on this side, the contrast will pass into likeness; when the husband, although the ruling head, not only is in full sympathy with the body, but draws the brightest gladness and the most powerful stimulus toward everything good from the spiritual freshness and healthfulness of her whose life is one with his own. And thus, in their life together, will be more and more fully realized that which is only promised to the Church in her relation to Christ in the distant future, that we shall be like Him because we shall see Him as He is; as the wife, without leaving her quiet, modest sphere, becomes ever more like her husband, because she both understands and influences him in all his ways and actions. Daily experience teaches this in Christian marriage in the happiest way; and it is thus that our wives enjoy their proper share in all that their husbands accomplish or aim at in the different spheres of public life.

If, then, the wife, while she is and must be subject to her husband, is made more and more free by him who loves her after the pattern of Christ; and the husband, while truly the head, is so only as he cleaves to his wife in inviolable fidelity and deepest love; each merging the thought of rule on the one side and subordination on the other in the nobler and higher sense of a perfect oneness of life; then every appearance of difference from the great model disappears, as even the apostle himself lost sight of his heavenly and glorious ideas in the one thought that two should become one.

When thus every difference is resolved into the mutual and gladsome sense of heart harmony; when to the common life is added a pure spiritual union, that gloriously pictures the Saviour's soul-satisfying love, raising the soul to fellowship with God; when the hearts so purified feel impelled with increased power to labour earnestly in carrying on the work of God in themselves and in those whom He has given them, and among whom He has placed them; then, according to the mind of the apostle, we have the realized ideal of Christian marriage, the foundation stone of the Church of the Redeemer.

But all these glorious things, and whatever besides may be contained in our text, are summed up in another passage of Scripture in the simple words, Let marriage be had in honour among all. These words indeed send us to self-examination and to humiliation. All the great things that the apostle says to us about Christian marriage come just in plain words to this, that we be *honourable* in it. So that wherever in marriage the earthly side is not closely joined to the heavenly; where both parties do not lend their strength to each other, that both may faithfully and perfectly fulfil their vocations; where all distinctions are not being constantly equalized into a perfect and conscious unity; that marriage is wanting in true honour. Either it has not been honourably entered on, and the mutual Yes, instead of being true before God, has been an insult to Him; or it has not been honourably maintained, one or other having gone back more or less, and certainly not unwittingly, from that Yes. And indeed the latter failure naturally results from the former; for we find it easy to take back a little from a plighted word when it has not been given with a deliberate and steadfast purpose. Let all then ponder how much is implied in this, that it is only in the Christian sense that the married state can be maintained with true honour. In truth it can only be so when both husband and wife have received into their hearts our Lord and Master, and He forms the third in the union consecrated to Him through love. For He never goes back from His word, but is ever mindful of His promise that wherever two are together in His Name, there will He, in whom alone we can be strong and happy, be with them.

VIII.

THE CHRISTIAN TRAINING OF CHILDREN.

TEXT: COL. iii. 21.

MY devout hearers! Christian families, founded on the holy bond of marriage, are appointed, in the divine order of things, to be the nurseries of the future generation. It is there that the young souls who are to be our successors in cultivating the vineyard of God are to be trained and developed; it is there the process is to begin of restraining and cleansing away the corruption inherent in them as the children of sinful men; there that their earliest longings after fellowship with God are to be stirred, and that they are to be fitted, by training and exercise, for future usefulness in every good work. Therefore what more interesting subject can we consider than this most important work of Christian parents? which, however, is not the business of parents exclusively. If it were so, the subject would be less suitable for us; for we are not all parents who are met here; not all even engaged in the training and teaching of children. But in this case, as in others, the great, universal law of human life holds good, that two or three are not sufficient for the carrying on of a Christian work. And therefore the bringing up of children is not the work of the parents alone, nor even of the parents in conjunction with those whom they have directly engaged to help them in the way of oversight and instruction.

Rather, because we all live in relations more or less intimate with the young, and exercise an influence on them; because it deeply concerns us all, as members of the Christian Church, that Christian dispositions and faculties should be called forth in them, we may correctly say that the bringing up of the younger generation, as a whole, is a work that belongs to the whole adult community, and we are all bound to see that our share of the work is of the right kind.

But how difficult it seems to treat in a general way a subject like this in a manner suitable for a gathering of this kind. For how is it possible in a few separate discourses to review in a profitable way so wide a field of human wisdom and skill? and what an endless diversity of opinions must be taken into account, which would first have to be reconciled. However, this is not at all the place for setting forth a finished system of human wisdom and art for the training of our children. All that we can do is to awaken or confirm in our minds convictions of duty which shall lead us, at each moment, to the right steps. And when this is all we aim at, we shall be the less disturbed by the differing opinions, though they do indeed seem, at first sight, to present a difficulty. For some people hold that a man is entirely a result of training; that if it is only set about in the right way, and each part of the plan exactly calculated and fitted to the rest, one may make anything he chooses of any child; may draw forth in him, by practice, whatever natural gift he will, and may endue him, by instruction, with all kinds of intelligence and skill. Others, on the contrary, perhaps as lazy and careless as the first are proud and over-confident, maintain that with all our labour and skill we are, after all, helpless against the power of nature; that what we have built up with long toil is often overthrown with a single blow, when the object of our care begins to be more left to himself, and is able to give free play to his real nature; and that in reality every one must accomplish the work of his own salvation and education, in so far as that depends on man. It might, therefore, seem impossible to speak with any profit to those two classes of people together. But if I say to the latter class, Little as you may promise yourselves from training, yet, if you are careful to conduct yourselves according to God's will in all your relations with grown-up people, you must be still more circumspect in your conduct towards your children, and it is only about this we shall speak; and if I say to the former, Much as you think you are able to do, even if you think the whole matter lies in your hand, yet you will not say that it is a matter of indifference how you manage, and all is left to your good pleasure; you will admit that there is a will of God, which you must seek to do: and in this both parties will be agreed, if they wish to treat the matter in a Christian way. And this is the only way in which it can be spoken of here; from no other standpoint can we consider any subject. We can only ask, How are children to be brought up for God? What, if we do not wish to miss this aim, is the will of God for us as regards them; what must we chiefly avoid; to what must we give the greatest amount of attention? Keeping these points in view, then, let us, with God's help, enter on this subject.

It is somewhat remarkable that the apostle, in speaking here of the various relationships of family life, while he treats many other relations much more in detail, on the great subject of the training of children says absolutely nothing beyond the words we have read. In a similar context in the Epistle to the Ephesians, we find, it is true, a further exhortation added; but even there it is prefaced by this same warning of our text, "Fathers, provoke not your children to wrath." This error, then—the only one against which the New Testament Scriptures so emphatically warn us—must be, it would seem, that which we are above all to guard against in the training of our children; indeed, it would almost appear that if we were only watchful enough against that, everything else would be of much less consequence. In the hope then that we have found the most important point in this lesson, let us try to-day to lay to heart this warning, not to embitter our children.

It is evident that, in our relations with the young, we not merely give, but receive; that they are given to us by God, not only that we may mould and guide them, but that they may be to us a strength and a joy. I believe, therefore, that we shall only understand the apostle's warning in the full extent of its meaning if we examine, first, what it implies as to what we are to be to the children; and secondly, how much bearing it has on what the children are to be to the parents.

I. When, in meditating on our text, I put to myself the question, Why, out of all the things to warn us against in connection with the young, the apostle should have singled out just this, as of the greatest consequence, that they should not be provoked to bitterness? it seemed to me this must have been his idea; that, of all treatment, this was the most unnatural and the most injurious.

Man has enemies enough within: corruption of many kinds is deeply rooted in the human heart, and sooner or later springs up and manifests itself in various forms, according to different natural dispositions. And it is a comparatively rare thing that sinful tendencies show themselves for the first time in mature life. It is only in rare instances that, while much that is good and lovely comes out in the character of a child under parental training and teaching, there is no indication, however slight, of the depravity that lies hidden in his nature, and that this depravity only breaks out suddenly and irresistibly when the attractions of a life of excitement and passion seize on the soul. Much more usually all the evil tendencies in the child's nature will have shown themselves very unmistakably before he has exchanged his father's house for the great stage of the world. And if during that time he has been watchfully cared for and guarded by those under whose authority God and nature have placed him; if every influence on his mind has come more or less through the medium of the parents, then does it not look very decidedly as if all the vices and faults that have crept into his character, having come to light during his life with his parents, have done so as the result of that life? I feel pretty sure that Christian parents who walk uprightly before God will not venture to repel this charge. If dispositions like our own have been found in our children, it was the effect of our hurtful example; the sin of the old called forth that of the young. Or, if they have opposite faults from ours, it is generally resistance of the wrong with which our faults threaten them that rouses theirs to activity. How often, too, do we see that even the tenderness of parents, when it takes a mistaken direction, only promotes the development of wrong tendencies and passionate tempers. In all this there is, unhappily, sufficient cause of regret and humiliation; and we are not to try to excuse it, for we are undeniably in fault, and these things only prove how limited are still our attainments in sanctification and wisdom; but as we see the fact daily before our eyes, and can only congratulate him as happiest to whom it applies least, we must conclude that it is at least human and natural. But when children in their daily life with us are provoked to bitterness, and the bitterness makes them shrink from us, and the shrinking grows to a secret repugnance, with all that such a state of feeling necessarily implies; this is a condition of things that the apostle could not bear to enlarge on, and nothing can be more unnatural. For bitterness, beloved friends, is an emotion in the direction of hatred, and therefore contains the possibility of a diminution, or rather, to speak plainly, of an extinction (though, perhaps, but for the moment) of the children's affection. We were lately reflecting on what an unhappy and unnatural state of things it is between married people when variance and discord take the place of love, or are even found where love still exists. And yet we must remember that the marriage union is only entered into after the character and tastes on both sides are fully formed; and that there may be many things in each of which the other is not aware, which may therefore appear unexpectedly and disturb their peace. We must also take into account that married pairs have often come from widely different circles, and that each of them may easily have habits and ideas that are strange to the other, and to which they only gradually become accustomed. But how entirely different the case is between parents and children! The whole being of the child is, in its very origin and essence, related to the parents; a thousand resemblances declare this to us in the most striking way; and it would seem inevitable that every new stage of the child's development must result in increasing love and unity of feeling. The child grows up in the closest connection with the parents; his earliest glance meets the loving eye of the mother; it is her notice that the first bright smile of the little one seeks to attract. The first lesson his mother teaches him is to know and love his father; and as the young minds expand, they cannot but feel more and more how everything comes to them from and through their parents. Here, therefore, is the inmost, inviolate sanctuary of love; and if here, in children, who are at first all clinging affection, there yet arises estrangement, anger, repugnance; if the love which can never be uprooted from their hearts, instead of being set on those who naturally and by God's appointment are nearest to them, turns away to other objects, so that they can bear from others what from their parents would embitter them; this is surely the most unnatural outcome that could be from the home training. And in the same way it is unnatural, though in a different degree, when children become embittered against other grown-up people who take a part in their training, and have an influence on their lives. For though those persons have not so close a natural relation to them, the children are given to their care by the parents; and if they work in harmony with the parents they form a part with them of the sacred family circle. The child feels himself helped forward and supported by them; and this draws forth an attachment strong enough to bear many demands and many prohibitions. It is always thus when things take their clear, natural course; and the contrary condition always stirs in us a sense of repulsion, as from something unnatural.

And as this is the most unnatural state of things between parents and children, it is also the most injurious. It is a responsibility which we cannot evade, though it bears less heavily on the more pious and experienced and wise among us, that we must, by our own weaknesses and faults help to bring out the faulty parts of our children's natural characters. It is inevitable, too, that many tendencies may begin to take shape in their nature without our at once noticing them, and that, even when we do notice them, we may not be able at once to deal with them, but must wait until they become outwardly manifest, so that they can be pointed out to the children themselves. And when we reach this point, the question of the success or failure of our work depends entirely on how far they will yield themselves to us to be cured of their faults; how far they trust us, and believe that we mean well to them and will do well by them, even in many ways that seem hard to them. And if at first many things have been neglected, it is well if, as soon as our eyes are opened to see what weeds the enemy has sown while we slept, we at once set to work heartily, and are sure of finding a trustful heart that believes that, if we weep, there must be some cause for tears, if we are alarmed, there must be actual danger, that if we have recourse to hard measures, it is because milder means would not suit the purpose. If this is the case, nothing is lost as yet. We have in the reverent confidence of the child an ally in the very stronghold which the enemy has seized; and before powers thus united he will be compelled to yield. And even if, as it may and often does happen, we have entered on a wrong path, still there is nothing lost, if at once, when we discover that in labouring against an old evil we have called up a new one, we bravely turn round and begin again. Time may, of course, be lost; many joys may be lost or postponed; but as to the real work of training there is nothing lost; for there is no diminution of our power to combat evil in our children so long as love remains unchilled and confidence unbroken. But how sadly different it is when that which has crept into our children's hearts, without our knowledge perhaps, but assuredly not without our fault, is a bitter, hostile spirit! What shall give us courage *then?* What confident hope can inspire us? Where are we to begin? If the salt has lost its savour, wherewith shall it be salted? If love has perished and confidence is gone, where is the key with which we can once more gain admittance to their hearts? where is the rein with which we can draw away these young spirits from the path of ruin? It is easy to give the answer—unhappily, it is not far to seek for; it may be found in many neglected, disorderly families of professing Christians. For if the hearts of the children have been embittered against us, so that they have learned to shrink from us; if their natural confidence has given place to a sullen mistrust —a feeling that we always consider our own interests rather than theirs; then there is only one way—and God be praised there is still one—by which even this malignant enemy can be overcome: it may be, as it were, starved out, by our withholding from it all nutriment. Only a long experience of an opposite course of conduct on our part, until even the heart that has grown cold and suspicious can no longer resist the conviction that our only desire is to win it back to us,—only this will gradually banish suspicion, and, by making room in the closed heart for love, will give us once more an entrance there. It will call for inexhaustible patience, absolute self-control, thorough self-denial; it is a tedious and toilsome way,—a way which I am persuaded is not followed in every Christian home in which the children have become estranged through provocation. But even if, step by step, we gradually gain a little ground on this tedious and toilsome path, we must at the same time be fighting against other forms of evil, which far from remaining in abeyance because the natural, loving relations are disturbed, will only appear in greater number and gain strength more rapidly. And what means of opposing these new evils remain to us, if our admonitions find no willing ear, our directions to profitable occupations no pliant will? There remains only the harsh way of authority; and that is the plan which, sad to say, we see only too commonly followed around us. And oh, how dangerous a way it is! We see clearly enough in other human relations how little men can be influenced by force, and we always feel drawn as by a secret spell to set ourselves in league against sheer power and its doings. And justly so. For the less a human being yields to force, he proves the more plainly that there is nothing of a slavish spirit in him; that he is conscious of a nobility in his nature that is above mere power; and the more a man tries to gain his ends with others by force, he shows the more clearly that either he is not gifted with reason and love—the only powers that should be brought to bear on a human being—or he does not understand how to use them. And are we to introduce force into the peaceful sanctuary of our homes, and use it towards our children, at an age when they are capable of being influenced by reason and love? Force cannot reach their hearts, where we really wish our influence to tell; it can only restrain the outward demonstrations of their faults that disturb and annoy us. Thus we can protect ourselves against them by force, and have a right to do so, if we find ourselves in the unhappy position of needing such defence: but nothing whatever can we teach by force. It will only make their faults take deeper and firmer root, like plants whose upward growth has been cut off. Indeed the more successful we are in obtaining this mere external improvement, we have the deeper cause for sorrow; because in this way we only make it more apparent into what a slavish state our children have sunk. And therefore it is not unusual with us who are parents, when we grow weary of this struggle, to give up all godly training, and to leave the children to their own way. And being thus, as it were, defeated, we are left behind with nothing but our pious wishes on their behalf, which we have often too much reason to fear are in vain; and for ourselves remorseful tears, which at best can only serve for warning to ourselves and others for the future.

It is very clear, then, that the apostle had good reason for giving this warning the most prominent place in his counsels as to our conduct towards our children. If we only guard against the children becoming distrustful of us, everything else is easily put right; but if we have got into this unhappy condition, it involves ruin and loss in our whole relations with them.

II. But we are to speak not only of how we to whom God has entrusted the hearts of the young are to fulfil His will towards them, but also of what, according to His appointment, the young are to be to us. On this point I cannot expect to say anything new to any of you: I hope I need only appeal to the happy experience of each of you, in proof of how much blessing has come to us through our intercourse with the young; how this, more than anything else, keeps us fresh and cheerful, so that the heart burdened with many cares can still work bravely on; and how by such intercourse we are at once purified from disturbing passions and helped forward in the way of holiness. But such results can only come from an intercourse that is characterized by mutual love and by regard to God's will; for if we provoke and embitter the young spirits, all these blessings are lost. We shall be the more convinced of this if we reflect how it is, exactly, that we derive such profit from the young who are growing up in the midst of us.

Let us consider, in the first place, that the social world around us is a constantly changing scene, a hurrying succession of endlessly complicated situations, in which, at every step, we find more to impede than to help us forward, and must keep a look out on every side lest we come into collision with others. Every one will bear testimony to this, whether he moves in a higher or lower social circle. The external forms may differ, but the essential condition is the same. When we contrast this with what we are told of the peaceful simplicity of former days, we are sometimes inclined to lament that such times are gone, and long to recall them. But let us remember not only that this is out of our power, but that as this simplicity was merely an effect of the isolation in which different communities lived, it must necessarily pass away when commerce and mutual interest begin to be more widely extended. And it is God's purpose that such intercourse among men shall be extended; were it only for this reason, not to mention any other, that God's life-giving Word may be carried everywhere, and may lay hold of all men and all nations who are still strangers to it. But in proportion as this intercourse increases, life becomes for each individual a more difficult thing; it becomes the more needful for every one to take heed against complications in his own concerns; and each one is the more liable to get involved in the cares and mistakes of others, and to be swayed by their wishes and passions. And from this maze of business, from these endless precautions and projects, from the fretting contact with the vain and selfish passions of the worldly-minded crowd, whither can a thoughtful man withdraw to find quiet and repose of mind, but first and best to his own little home circle? It is there that life after the old peaceful fashion should still be found, there that we should be able to forget, as long as possible, the world with its ways and doings, to realize afresh that God has created man with simple tastes, and be anew refreshed and strengthened by the sight of innocent, unaffected gaiety. But from whom, for the most part, do we expect this kind of help? Not from the grown-up members of the family; for either they are themselves taken up with life's troubles and cares, or their sympathy with us has by experience so sharpened their eyes that they are quick to notice when anything has occurred either to depress or to gratify us: and therefore they are often only too likely to recall our thoughts to what we wished to forget. It is only the children, joyous and free from care, who can diffuse around us this atmosphere of oblivion of the world, that is so needful for us. It is they who, when we come back to the home circle, see in our faces nothing but our joy in being there again, and themselves feel only that they have been missing us and now have us back once more. What a strengthening virtue there is in this bright atmosphere, which at once takes us back to man's original state! how quickly it effaces from the soul all traces of even the busiest and most harassing life! Happy is the man who has this as his daily experience!

But this happiness is of course lost for him in whose home the young hearts have become embittered; for he finds awaiting him at home only more painful difficulties than those he has left behind. For from whatever cause the bitterness of children against a grown-up person may have arisen, there must have been something like this to begin with; that he has slighted them and their affairs as of too little importance to be worth his notice; that when they gave free expression to their feelings, they found in him no sympathetic response; that instead of shaking off his variable moods, before coming home, or, better still, getting quit of them altogether, he has brought them with him, and given vent to his ill-humour amidst his family. But for some such coldness on our part, or some such indulgence in uncertain tempers to cause it, no feeling of bitterness can arise. But if unhappily that has taken place, and the children have learned to shrink from us; then of course their ingenuous frankness is lost, and they themselves have only become an additional part of our anxiety and care. The gladness with which they should come to meet us is damped by the feeling that it is not only one whom they respect but one whom they fear, that is coming home; they wait with closed hearts and painful suspense to see what kind of humour we are in, and from each of our moods they have something or another to keep carefully out of sight. In this way all that is trying in our outward life, indeed almost all the vexations and unpleasantnesses that we must encounter there, are transplanted, with their desecrating influence, into the sanctuary of the home: in this way we deprive ourselves of the refreshment and strength that should come to us through the children in our home life. Alas for him whose experience this is, though only occasionally, and through only one or another of the little ones whom God has given him.

Now let us take another thought in this connection. It is

a very complicated state of things that prevails in the wider circle of society in which we move; and from that cause, though not from that alone, a most imperfect state. This is a fact that, indeed, calls for neither discussion nor proof; we all feel it to be so. But it is to be hoped that the more this is felt the more deep and habitual is our longing for the perfect state. And although we live here by faith and not by sight; yet, just as we cannot imagine any life of sight in which there should not be still some mixture of faith; as little can we have any idea of any kind of faith quite apart from some measure of sight, dim and uncertain though it might be. Thus, animated by the faith that things are to improve in the world, we look forward gladly to that better future, and there is nothing so effectual as this hope in strengthening us to be steadfast in our warfare and unwearying in our labours. But how can we look at the future but in our children? It is they who are to come after us and fill our place; it is for them we ought to lay up an inheritance in a better order of things. And we are the more content to lose sight of ourselves in the thought of them when we recall the comforting words of the Saviour Himself in a similar connection; His prediction that the kingdom of heaven, into which the men and women at that time refused to enter, should belong to their children. Therefore if it is our inevitable lot to see our own or kindred infirmities manifesting themselves in our children, we long to see, at the same time, indications of the presence of faculties that will lighten many a struggle for them, and hasten on many a victory; we long to see for ourselves something of that which we hope for, that the sons will be better than the fathers, and as the natural consequence of that, will be more prosperous than they.

You remember that impressive scene in the life of the patriarch Jacob, when though in a strange country, yet confident in the divine promise, he regarded the land as the possession of his descendants; and, seeing in his sons, now grown to manhood, all the generations that were to follow, pronounced on each of them, by the spirit of prophecy, a blessing specially adapted to the peculiar characteristics of him who received it. We could desire nothing better than to find ourselves in a similar position when we feel that the time of our work on earth is drawing to its close. A man could hardly have a more enriching and comforting feeling in leaving this earthly scene than that of being able to indicate to each of those whom he leaves behind what is to be his special place in the work of God's kingdom, and what his own personal share in its blessings. And if this would be a comfort to us at the time of our death, so, even now, nothing could be more cheering to us, when wearied with the business of life and out of heart with our work, than some such prospect of what our children may be able to accomplish and what will be their portion in life. But as this prophetic vision of Jacob's was not solely the fruit of his faith in the sure promise of God; his exact acquaintance with all the characters of his family contributing something to it; neither can we attain to a similar comforting anticipation, unless the hearts of our children are opened to us, so that we have penetrated to their depths and know their inmost recesses. And how can this be if we have not lived in gladsome harmony with them, if they have not been frank and ingenuous in their intercourse with us? And therefore we come back once more to the warning of our text. Parents ought, by the nature of things, to be able to form a more correct judgment about their children than can be done in any other human relation. But this only holds good when the relationship remains natural and pure. The more a feeling of constraint grows up between them and us, the more readily shall we be mistaken in their characters. If they have become distrustful by being embittered, they shut up against us the access to their inner nature; the young spirit is enclosed in a crust through which often even the eye of wisdom and love is unable to pierce. Then our judgment varies with our feelings. We are able to make no happy forecast of their future; and we lose what would be our most effectual means of comfort when cast down by the imperfection of present things.

You see the matter, then, on both sides. When we provoke and estrange our children, both they and we lose the best of our life together. And as they, on their side, can best guard against any growing bitterness by respectful obedience, according to the first commandment with promise; let us, on our part, be unremitting in that self-denying love to them, which seeks not our own pleasure and advantage, but theirs, and which has its direct reward in the brightness and peace which the companionship of the young so naturally brings when there are no jars and misunderstandings.

It would be beyond the limits and the proper scope of our present meditation to go on to specify in what ways more particularly the feeling of bitterness is produced in children, that so it might be watched against the more surely. Therefore I can only repeat this general caution: be watchful; notice the very first appearances, and turn round at once if you find yourself entering on a wrong course. For however excellent a plan it might be to have exact and certain rules about this, who could depend on his being able to keep them all? Who could boast of being so entirely master of all his emotions that he could be sure of keeping clear of everything that went against the precepts he had himself laid down? No; even with the most thorough knowledge we cannot make sure that there shall not be now and then moments in which we both feel and give expression to something that we must acknowledge to be a cause of provocation. But let me not, in saying this, be thought to put any discouragement in the way of Christian people. If we only turn at once and earnestly exercise self-control, no real harm will be done. The evil in such cases is averted through the working of two gifts with which God has endowed the human soul; a capacity of forgetting, and clear-sightedness. The young, ingenuous mind easily forgets, especially impressions that are unpleasant; because it is intended to be nourished by love, not by fear. It is only the recurrence of the harsh or painful ways that gradually sharpens the memory of the children in that direction. Therefore we may take comfort in thinking of this gift of God in connection with what are only our occasional and infrequent failures in this respect. And it also tells in our favour in such cases, that the human soul is, from childhood upwards, abundantly clear-sighted. Children learn very early to distinguish between what we may say or do in the mere heat and agitation of the moment, and what is our real and habitual feeling. And therefore while, on the one hand, we may try in vain to bribe their confidence by a few occasional indulgences or marks of favour while the ruling tone of our intercourse with them is harshness or half-contemptuous indifference; on the other hand, we may be equally sure that if only we are truly and lovingly devoted to them, if we earnestly seek their real welfare, if we attach to our intercourse with them the importance and interest it deserves, they will not fail—even if our human infirmities should sometimes make trouble—to take the exact and true measure of our real and prevailing feeling towards them, and to cling to us in childlike confidence and affection. Only let our whole life be pure in their sight, and our inmost heart before God; let it be our constant concern to keep far away whatever may weaken love or be hurtful to frank simplicity; then we shall never have the sad experience of our children growing distrustful through bitter feeling, and the blessing of God shall direct the whole sacred work of training in the midst of us.

IX.

THE CHRISTIAN TRAINING OF CHILDREN.

(*Second Sermon.*)

TEXT: EPH. vi. 4.

IN making special mention of our children in our prayers, as we have done to-day, what we have chiefly in our thoughts is not merely to commend their earthly life and welfare, with all that affects it, to God's gracious care; we are much more concerned to obtain a blessing on the unfolding of their spiritual faculties, that it may be carried on in a right way, well-pleasing to God. This prayer is prompted in the first place by the humble conviction that if our manifold cares and painstaking for our children, which fill up so large a part of our life, are to prosper according to our heart's desire, the Holy Spirit must work in them; and further, we are encouraged to offer the prayer by the devout confidence that this is so. It is just in this confidence that we present our children in their tender infancy to be received by the heavenly Father into the Christian Church, that is, into the fellowship of His Spirit, by the sacrament of baptism; and as often as we take part in such an act we anew acknowledge this conviction and profess this confidence. It is reasonable, therefore, to suppose that we should be agreed as to the kind of influence we exercise on the young, and that in the hands of all Christians this important work should take one and the same direction. For if the Spirit of God is at work in the hearts of our children, what can we desire but to be His instruments? For Him alone, and in His name, not for ourselves, can we expend our cares on them. To try to make out of the rising generation either a profit to their elders or an exact copy of them, is an aim which we must leave to those who think first and most of themselves, because they lack this glorious faith in a divine Spirit who works in man, and with that, necessarily, the faith that there can be any progress in all that makes man's true dignity. But for us, let our one aim in the training of our children be the honour of God; they are the fairest portion of the vineyard which He has set us to cultivate. The essential point in all Christian training of children is to make them susceptible to the influence of the Spirit who is promised to them as well as to ourselves. We are to aim at this by trying to check the earliest symptoms of whatever might afterwards interfere with or oppose that influence, and striving by word and deed to awaken in them longings for what they can attain to only by the Spirit's help · we are to do it by helping them to judge clearly of every human model that appears to them worthy of imitation, and making them quick to see what is to be rejected. Thus they will be prepared for receiving and retaining the image of the Saviour; and this is the aim and spirit that should characterize both our general intercourse with the young, and all the special loving cares that we bestow on them. And the less of selfishness there is in this love, the less these efforts depend merely on natural feeling and impulse, the more possible and right it is for the whole of us as a community to participate in both. We can receive all the little ones without distinction, as the Lord said, in His name, for they are all represented to us by that child whom He set before the disciples; and while it is a most precious blessing from God to be directly entrusted with the care of a portion of the younger generation, there can be no object more worthy of the exertions of those who have not been thus privileged, than the furthering of this great work by every means in their power, despising no part of it that may fall to their share. In this sense of brotherly and common interest, therefore, let us pursue our meditation on this subject to-day, and may God grant us His blessing.

In this passage we find another precept added to that which I lately took as our subject of discourse from another epistle. That first exhortation was meant to set before us that which, according to the mind of the apostle, we ought most carefully to avoid in the training of children; this further counsel is meant, I might say, to include everything that ought to find a place in our intercourse with them, in order to their being brought up in the discipline and admonition of the Lord. It may indeed seem at first sight as if the apostle's direction were partial and insufficient. When we remember on how many different things we expend labour and pains in the education of the young, and how we all, without exception, have it in view not merely that they should turn out pious and Christian people, but that they should be thoroughly fitted for every worldly business they may engage in, and should develop every pleasing and estimable quality of mind and heart, this thought may very naturally arise. But the apostle's own feeling was certainly not that he was speaking of some single part of the work, incidentally selected, but that he had hit on a counsel which included everything. Let us then see if we cannot find in these words the basis of all training such as God approves. And to this end we must inquire what is implied in doing everything for the young, first with a view to discipline, and secondly for a purpose of admonition.

I. What then is included in, and what is meant by, all our dealings with the young who are growing up among us tending to their *discipline;* all that we teach them or enjoin on them, or give or deny them. We must first of all clearly ascertain the meaning of the expression, on which everything depends in the question before us.

Discipline is by no means synonymous with punishment, though in common conversation we are accustomed often to use it so; but something entirely different. For punishment is incurred by disobedience; discipline takes obedience for granted: punishment gives children merely something to suffer; discipline, something to do: punishment adds something of a disagreeable and bitter feeling, more or less voluntary on the child's part, to what is already wrong and deserving of blame in him; while discipline rather calls forth a commendable exertion of his powers to accomplish something or to do without something; an effort which is in itself sufficient to produce a feeling of inward joy. And just as the law never effects anything better than the knowledge of sin, and gives no strength to do right; as little can punishment, which derives its power from fear or from bitter experience, produce anything but an outward avoiding of sin, without any turning away of the heart from evil. For the heart can be disposed towards good only by love, which drives out fear, and with fear all the power of punishment. But discipline, which aims by steady exercise to control and regulate every emotion, and to subdue all the lower instincts of nature under the rule of the higher, imparts a salutary knowledge of the power of will, and gives an earnest of liberty and internal order. Such is discipline: and so very different is it from punishment that, as all will readily admit, the more we find ourselves obliged still to have recourse to punishment after our children have become capable of a conscious effort of will and of being stirred to shame, the more undeniable witness do we bear against ourselves that we have erred and have done too little in the way of discipline. For if we felt that we were teaching our children the right use of discipline, so that they had begun to exercise a habitual command over themselves and to be wrought upon by the nobler emotion of shame, we should have no need to call fear to our aid in order to quell one mere external manifestation by means of another. And thus, too, we should experience that the larger a place we have given to discipline in our method, the more must punishment lose its effect; because the young mind is already practised in refusing to have its decisions influenced by considerations either of pleasure or the reverse.

But while discipline is on the one hand an entirely different thing from punishment, it is just as far, on the other hand, from that indolent quiescence in which unhappily so many think they may watch the development of their children. Such persons forget that while God the Lord has, it is true, set heaven before us as a state in which we may satisfy ourselves with simply beholding, and with enjoying the blessings that flow to us through the exercise of heavenly energies, it is far from being so among men on earth. God has placed us here, not as spectators, but as rulers in His name; as His instruments through whom He means to carry out all His gracious purposes towards man; the strong and those of riper years guiding and bestowing care on the weak and the young. The right form for this rule and this painstaking as regards the young is discipline; but if we take no pains we impede the fulfilment of the divine promises. And if, where the system of punishment prevails, it might seem as if all hope of the Spirit of God being able to take possession of the young minds had been given up, the only endeavour being to keep each part of the natural disposition in check by means of some other part; it is equally true that the hope which predominates where the system of easy-going, indolent looking-on at the development of our children is followed is a delusive hope, which is only too likely to be put to shame. For if it is expected that admonition alone is to take the place of discipline, this hope is grounded on the illusive idea that everything can be effected by words, and that action is unnecessary: or if the non-interference extends to speech as well as to more active efforts, there is in that case a more mischievous delusion; whether it be the idea that a work of the Divine Spirit may begin in the children without God making use of the parents and others as His instruments; or even that they may naturally develop good dispositions and habits without that Spirit who is the life of the Christian Church, and who, in these words of our text, calls on us to train our children by discipline. And the further we are, on the one side, from that miserable condition, as slavish as it is tyrannical, of being satisfied with what can be accomplished by punishment; and the more free we keep, on the other side, from the dangerous error of flattering ourselves that in those respects which depend chiefly on us, our children can of themselves turn out well; just so much the more must we feel and acknowledge the great value and importance of discipline. But we must practise it not only now and then on special occasions, when we are struck by some quality or disposition in excess that seems to call for repression, or by some deficiency that indicates a need for stimulus; but seeing that discipline is the one thing besides admonition which the apostle commends to us in the training of our children, that training will only be of the right kind when all our dealings with our children and all the occupations we prescribe or allow to them become to them means of discipline, and are prescribed or allowed only in that light. This perhaps sounds strange and too severe; but it is just as true as it will prove, on closer consideration, to be kind and loving.

For where could Christian parents be found who would not try, so far as their position enabled them, to have their children instructed in all kinds of useful knowledge, and taught by practice to acquire skill in all desirable arts? Do we not in fact hold all those who neglect this guilty of a grievous wrong against their children and against the Lord who has committed them to their care? But are all, even of those who fulfil these duties, deserving of unqualified commendation? I think not. For if we see that parents, or those who occupy their place, do these things in an unreflecting way, just as the fancy may strike them, then, even if their operations turn out well, we do not give them the credit of the success, but ascribe it to the generally prevalent good customs and methods which they have followed without knowing why they did so. Or when we see that parents do act with consideration, and have reasons for what they decide on, are they, even in that case, sure always to be worthy of praise, and is it all the same, in our opinion, what their reasons may be? If parents, instead of waiting to see what their children may show an inclination or a natural turn for, or taking into account any such tendency that may already have shown itself, selfishly insist on keeping them to the parents' own special line of life, and wish only to have the children initiated into that, in order to make them as like themselves as possible, have we not here bitter cause to complain of an un-Christian exercise of authority over the young? And must it not be a source of both pain and indignation to the young themselves, when they are old enough to understand the conduct of those who brought them up, to feel how much selfishness was mixed with the love of their parents and guardians? Or, again, if a direction towards some definite line of life is given to the young by the kind and character of the instructions and training given to them, from such motives as these: that this special course seems to offer tempting worldly prospects; that patronage and support of various kinds make it easier and pleasanter than other paths might be; that wealth and honour seem to beckon from its goal more distinctly than from other directions:—is there not cause of reproach in this case also, that an utterly blind despotism is guilty of the grievous wrong of daring, for the sake of uncertain worldly advantage, to turn aside the young nature from that for which God has created it, and so to cripple its actings by a sense of constraint? And what can be the effect on the young themselves, but that either they will be misled into treating the things about which we exhort them as matters of indifference in themselves and holding them lightly, while they esteem worldly gain the really highest thing; or that, not less to the damage of their souls, their reverence towards those whose example they ought to follow must suffer shipwreck.

Or, to take another case: parents may take careful note of any indications their children give of natural gifts, and then, as if it were only a question of winning a race, strain every nerve to the utmost—often at the cost of a lifetime's happiness to their children, and at the risk of all permanent success—only that they may have the gratification of seeing their children surpass others, so that the excellence of their training may be admired, whether in the strictly correct conduct of their young people, or in the stores which they have acquired in the line of art and science. How this grieves us to the heart, to see even the noblest gifts of the young under such guidance made to subserve only vain and sordid ends!

In view, then, of all these ways in which we are liable to go wrong, we cannot but feel how difficult it is to keep a clear conscience in this important business. How alone shall we keep it void of offence? Certainly in no other way than this: we must neither set before ourselves any worldly aim in the education and training of our children, nor teach them to think of anything merely worldly and external as the object to be attained by it; but rather, putting out of view all other results, we must try to have them made distinctly conscious of what powers and capacities they possess which may, by and by, be used in carrying on the work of God on earth; and to have those powers brought under the control of their will, by their learning both to overcome indolence and dissipation, and to guard against being passionately engrossed in any single object. And this is just what the apostle means. For instruction and training of all kinds, so directed, will only serve as discipline to the young; and only by such discipline will they acquire a real possession in the shape of a thorough fitness for every work of God that, in the course of their life, they may find occasion to do.

But see still further how far the province of discipline extends. Even in the intercourse with their equals, and the pleasures suitable to their age which we permit our children to enjoy, our first consideration must be that these things are such as will tend to their discipline. This may, I admit, seem specially hard, that the very things that are meant for recreation and unfettered amusement should be used as means of discipline. But children receive quite as much of their education by companionship and in their plays as by direct instruction and regular work; and therefore when the apostle insists on their being trained by discipline, he refuses to look at even this part of their training in any other light. And as we cannot but acknowledge that, even with the best will, much is overlooked in the companionships and amusements of our children, so that they do receive spiritual injury; would it not be well for us to consider whether this may not result from neglecting this view of the subject, and regulating this important part of our children's lives on some other principle? I do not wish to speak of those parents and guides who have regard solely to worldly and external considerations in directing the companionships of the young. We know how ill such arrangements usually turn out; how the children sometimes become hard and obdurate, and sometimes deplorably pliant and easily led; and how, for the most part, their bright childhood passes joylessly away. I wish rather to think only of those who select so anxiously and cautiously the company in which they allow their children to mix, that they have only desirable examples before them, while all quarrelling and passionate excitement are as much as possible avoided. For even care such as this is often far from being successful; some of the children turning out vain and puffed up with conceit, others peevish and discontented, and none perhaps attaining to a salutary self-knowledge. Whereas, if we look at it simply in this light, that our children's intercourse with others is to be to them, as ours is to us, a means of discipline; teaching them to hold fellowship even with characters very different from their own, and each to make a happy life for himself by being ready to help others and willing to give way to them, and learning to suppress all disturbing and unfriendly feelings; then even in this position they are taken care of in the best way, if only at the same time we maintain rule and order, and keep away from them temptations that might be too strong for them. And it is the same as to their amusements, if we look at them in the light of discipline. In their games they learn to use and control all the powers that are least called forth in their work; in this way they will have the greatest benefit and the greatest enjoyment from them, and there will be the less danger of their becoming devoted to pleasure, or lazy and averse to work, liking mere pleasure as opposed to exertion; or even perhaps, if there is anything of sloth and idleness in their recreation, becoming ungodly and giving place to the devil.

Thus, then, it appears to me that the apostle was entirely right in laying down no other rule as to all the doings of the young of which we have the regulation and control, than that they should all serve in the way of discipline. And the more perfect we try to make our training, the less must there be which we have not been able to direct on that principle. And the more such training grows out of the circumstances of everyday life, without any need of altering or interrupting its natural course, so much the more pleasing to God, we may be sure, and the more certain of a prosperous issue, is the work of our love and wisdom on behalf of the young.

II. But, my friends, however excellent a thing it is to train our children by discipline, what is, after all, the highest thing that can be effected by this means? The preparing of the way for the Lord, that He may be able to enter; the adorning of the temple, that He may be able to dwell in it: but towards the actual entering and indwelling of the Lord, discipline can contribute *nothing*. To have all the human powers, in so far as they are capable of serving the purposes of the Spirit, trained and brought under control, so that they are accustomed only to act at the bidding or permission of a higher power that warns and commands through parents and teachers,—this is the work of discipline; and an admirable and excellent work it assuredly is. But even if our children learn ever so well in loyal obedience, to set aside their own pleasure and conform to the wishes of their elders, what profit is it, if a time does not come when the joy of the Spirit arises in their hearts to fill the place of the repressed pleasures of the flesh; when they, of their own accord, make a habit of following the good ways into which previously our will has drawn them; that is to say, what have we gained, if the Spirit of God does not actually come and make His abode in their hearts? For, until this takes place, the care and pains of our training have not attained their end; not until then have the faculties which we have drawn out and trained found their true Master; not till then can we comfort ourselves with the thought of one day seeing our children working alongside of us as independent members of the Christian community. And this, we are all well aware, no discipline is capable of bringing about. But, it may be asked, is this not as really beyond the province of all human influence as it is beyond that of discipline? Can we in any way whatever contribute to this end? Does not the Lord Himself say, that the Spirit moves where He will, and that we cannot so much as know, much less command, where He is to go? Yes, we recognise the truth of that word of Christ in this connection also, and therefore willingly confess our inability; both that God alone may have all the glory, and for the mournful comfort of all Christian parents to whom God has appointed the pain of seeing that their children do not come direct from their training hands as temples of the Divine Spirit, and to whose sorrow we have no right to add bitterness by assuming the place of judges, and charging them with the blame of their children not yet having received the Spirit of God. But while acknowledging our helplessness, let us not forget that the same Saviour who spoke of the Spirit acting where He will, yet charged His disciples to go and teach all nations; and that it was just by this free movement of the Divine Spirit that the mouths of those on whom He descended were opened to declare the mighty works of God; that is, above all, His works wrought on the soul of man, for there are none mightier. This, then, is what we are capable of doing, and what we are even commanded to do; in our daily intercourse with the young to commend the mighty works of God, that we may stir up in their minds aspirations after a happier condition, in which the Divine Spirit is won to enter the heart of man; and this is what the apostle, in the part of our text which we have still to consider, calls the *admonition of the Lord.*

And here I must begin by examining an opinion very common even among well-disposed people, which might seem to find some sanction in these words of the apostle. It is said that as he speaks first of bringing up our children by discipline, and then mentions the admonition of the Lord as the second thing, he must agree with those who think it is right to guard against speaking too early of divine things to the young and directing them to the Saviour, and that not till those riper years, when discipline shall have completed its work, will the young be capable of receiving the admonition of the Lord. But we must certainly acquit the apostle of holding any such opinion, and that all the more confidently because we are sure that no one in his days would have taken this view, not even those who now defend it. For in those early days of Christianity,—when Christians were not only closely surrounded everywhere with heathen or Jewish life, but were also exposed to their adverse influence and opposition,—if parents had deferred the admonition of the Lord to such a time, it must often have happened that, before it arrived, the young spirit was already deeply involved in un-Christian ways. But does this not apply to every time, only in other forms, so long as there is still a struggle between light and darkness? Does not ungodliness of every kind surround us only too closely on every hand, seeking to obtain a footing, and to disturb the holy regulations of Christian society? Has the enemy fallen asleep, who, while *we* sleep, is wakeful enough to sow tares among our wheat? And if he is sure to do this always, what will he not do, if we till the field indeed, but neglect to sow the wheat? will he not in that case completely fill it with tares, so that there will be no room left for the good seed? Therefore the admonition of the Lord, which the apostle enjoins, must be found side by side with discipline, as soon as we perceive that ungodliness is beginning insidiously to approach the young minds. And with good reason; for we cannot permit it to have scope, and we know of nothing else to oppose to it but the one power in which we know safety is to be found—the power of redemption. Therefore as soon as the age of innocence is past, as soon as sin becomes active and the law has brought some knowledge of sin, it is a fitting time for us to make the erring soul conscious of the need of a higher help, to bring it into contact with God, and seek to arouse in it love to the Saviour who is the fountain of life and blessedness, and love to God who has given us His Son. And this is the admonition of the Lord.

But what are the grounds on which it is possible for even well-meaning and pious Christians to fear that the young may be too early and to their injury admonished concerning the Lord? They evidently consider that the young cannot yet understand what we tell them about God and the Saviour, and therefore will either take up some wrong and merely natural and external idea, the effect of which will be, partly, to degrade the holiest things, and partly, to prepare the way for unbelief when they see, as they grow older, how poor and vain their conceptions were, and yet suppose that this is really what was taught them in childhood; or our instructions will become to them a dead letter, which they retain and repeat without thought; which will cause sacred things to lose their power with them, and will blunt and deaden beforehand the desire after those things that would otherwise have awakened when they were older. But let us ask, do we ourselves, then, comprehend God? are we capable of fathoming and measuring the Saviour? are we able to express in precise, universally applicable and universally intelligible language His mysterious influence on us? and do we, because of our inability to do this, refrain from dealings with our God and Saviour, or from conversation and teaching concerning Him? And again, how could we begin and carry on the education of our children at all—how strictly should we not have to shun all their questions—if we wished to avoid everything in teaching and conversation that they could not understand? Is anything that they meet with for the first time, and from which we have no power to divert their attention, more comprehensible to them than the Eternal? Is it to be supposed that their first ideas even of the things of this world can be exact and right, and not, rather, all formed according to their own childish fashion? And yet as their characters gradually develop it becomes evident that even in this childish way they have got hold of the germ of the truth, which goes on unfolding with growing power, and in due time casts away the husk that protected without disfiguring it. Therefore we may hope that this will still more be the case when we talk with them about Him who is Himself the Truth; that a living seed, though hidden in a poor husk, will gain a firm hold in their souls; and hence there is here no reason for withholding from them the knowledge of God and of the Saviour. But even supposing that we wished to do so, should we be able? And do we not feel constrained to say, God be praised that it is not in our power! for if it were, the indications in our domestic and social life of our belonging to a people of God and forming a community of believers would be far more rare than unhappily they already are. No; this cannot in any way be so kept concealed that the children should not very early hear something of God and their Redeemer.

And as to the fear that too early teaching about God and divine things might become to the children only a dead letter; it would, no doubt, be well grounded, if our instructions were only meant to satisfy a mere curiosity which had arisen in their minds about this as about other and mere outward subjects. But that would be no admonition of the Lord; for admonition has always a reference to something that the person has to do and to alter, especially in himself. Therefore it is especially when we wish to affect the inmost feelings of our children that the apostle would have us turn their thoughts towards the Lord. If we see them indulging in emotions either of joy or vexation, that border on sin, we are to point out to them the difference between godly and ungodly modes of feeling. And does it not seem to you that this difference will be best understood by a mind which has already felt the stirring of better things? If we see them presumptuously uplifted, though it may be only in half-childish over-confidence, or depressed and disheartened, —and this still more if they are old enough for greater and graver concerns to have a place in their lives—we can tell them of man's dependence on God. We can tell them of the blessedness of him who, making it his one endeavour to fulfil the will of God, holds fast, amidst all earthly reverses, the comfort that, without the will of the Father, from whom come none but good gifts, not a hair of his head can perish; and who uses all earthly possessions as entrusted to him by God for the furtherance of His work. And do you think they cannot understand this as soon as a sense of duty has been awakened in them, and they have noticed something of the difficulties of life? When we see that in their awakening minds conflicting thoughts 'accuse and excuse one another,' we are to point them to that law which God has written in men's hearts and made manifest in His Son, and teach them to distinguish its voice. And do you think they are not capable of fixing their eyes on that guiding star as soon as uncertainty and conflicting judgment has begun in themselves?

And it is not simply to God that we are to lead them in this way, but equally and at the same time to the Saviour, out of whose fulness they, like ourselves, must from the very beginning receive all knowledge of God and all enjoyment of fellowship with Him. This is indeed the direct meaning of the apostolic words; for it is Christ who is the Lord, and the admonition towards God is only included in the admonition towards Christ; as the Son presupposes the

Father. And as the Saviour Himself commanded His disciples not to forbid the little ones to come, and thereby made it plain that even for them there was to be a blessing in His presence; we may neither doubt of our having the right nor of its being our duty to bring our children early to Him who came for their salvation also, that He may bless them. Did not He Himself thank His Father that He had revealed the mystery which the wise and mature of His time would not receive, to the little ones who greeted Him with songs of praise as the Saviour who was to come. Why should it not be specially fitting, at that tender age when the mind draws so much of its food from pictures, to seek God also in a picture,—Him of whom we are permitted to make no image for ourselves, in that picture which He has Himself given to us; why should it not be fitting that the little ones should see and honour the Father in the Son, and direct their earliest pious aspirations to the express image of the divine nature, the brightness of the heavenly glory in earthly and human form? Why should not the young, as soon as they begin to distinguish between good and evil in themselves, to require perfection of themselves, and to have some misgivings of its being unattainable, be capable of receiving into their hearts Him who knew no sin? Why should not they, who owe their birth and their sustained life to human love, be both able and willing to hear and to obey the voice of divine love in Christ? Why, as soon as they begin to feel the burden of the law and to dread the bondage of sin, should it not be possible to point them, for their comfort and encouragement, to Him who alone is able to make them free from both? And how can we but lead them to Him, as soon as their attention is sufficiently aroused by what they hear about Him to make them ask, Who is He? Indeed as soon as they become capable of observing ourselves and our whole manner of life, and begin to take note of the more inward and spiritual part of it, and to ask, Why is that? could we at such a time deny to our children the presence of Him whose life in us makes everything in us that they honour and love? Would it not be taking to ourselves the honour that is due to Him, if we did not direct them, for help in becoming such characters as they admire, to Him who gave Himself that He might sanctify to Himself a people fitted for good works. Let us then, in this direction also, lay aside every anxious fear, and train not only the growing-up young people, but also, as the apostle says, the children, in the admonition of the Lord, in the firm confidence that, as soon as sin can be recognised and felt, and the fruit of the Spirit desired, it can no longer be too early to tell the news of grace and salvation.

But just as we saw that everything that we teach our children and set them to do must tend to their *discipline*, if the apostle's first word is to be fully carried out; so we should very imperfectly fulfil the second if we limited its meaning to words of instruction, and to such words alone as bear directly on spiritual subjects. On the contrary, every admonition must be an admonition towards the Lord, for otherwise some of them would very soon contradict others; and every method by which we seek to influence and stir their hearts is an admonition. Therefore if we wish to excite in them love of what is good and right, let us not point out to them the earthly blessings that result from it; if we wish to warn them against the evil that is beginning to show itself in their hearts, let us not talk to them of the bad consequences which it brings; for that would be an admonition towards the things of this world, not an admonition towards the Lord; but let us teach them to discern what is like God and pleasing to Him, or not so; what is according to the covenant and command of the Saviour, or the reverse; and this also will be an admonition to the Lord. And if we cannot hinder the whole chequered drama of life unfolding ever more fully before them as time goes on, with all the follies and weaknesses of men as well as with everything good and noble; let us try rather to turn away their thoughts about it from the judgment of men, from the blame or the admiration of the world; lest we should be admonishing them to vanity and to eye-service before men. But on the one hand while we show them how difficult a thing it is to judge what is in man, let us exhort them to the sole fear of Him who alone understands how to judge. And while on the other hand we teach them to recognise the first appearances in their own hearts of all the wrong and evil that cannot fail to be there; and to seek out the hidden virtues of Christ's disciples, often very far from what makes the greatest show in the eyes of the world; let us by this also turn their thoughts to the Lord, who sees secret things, and tries the heart and the reins.

But more than all words, our most powerful admonition to the Lord must be our whole daily life, lived with our children in true and faithful love; and this just as certainly as that God is love, and love is the most universal and intelligible manifestation of the Eternal. If they feel our love pervading everything, not as a mere form of selfishness, that seeks only to be pleased and caressed; not as the whim of the moment, favouring and slighting without reason; nor yet a variable natural instinct, that may easily grow cold, or degenerate into weak indulgence; but as a reflection—feeble, it may be, yet not too dim to be always more or less recognisable—of the eternal love, and as having the closest connection with that service which we have vowed to the Saviour as our Head: this will be the most powerful of all admonitions to the Lord; and only through this will they learn to understand and practically to accept all the rest.

In this way, then, the apostle proves his point, that

everything that we can do with our children is summed up in this, that we bring them up in discipline and in the admonition of the Lord. But here we are constrained to say, Blessed are the pure in heart, for they shall see God! For if everything is to tend to discipline and the admonition of the Lord for our children, we must lay aside all vain and ungodly views that terminate on the transitory concerns of this world, and seek only that our houses may become temples of the Holy Spirit, and that the abundant blessing of God may abide among us; we must not cease to receive willingly and joyfully into believing and obedient hearts every admonition to the Lord which we ourselves still need, that we may go on growing in purer love and more thorough self-command, and so allow nothing to frustrate our great aim of having our children brought to the Lord. If we keep this aim steadily in view, we shall certainly become aware that God is with us, helping in the work; and so far from the most assiduous care for our children interfering with our own spiritual life, that life will, through this very work, open out to us in the most wonderful way. For in working for the training and sanctifying of others, we are ourselves sanctified and trained; and thus a building according to God's mind will rise on the foundation which He Himself has laid, and which none may remove with impunity. Amen.

X.

REJOICING BEFORE GOD.

(Preached on the Anniversary of the Battle of Leipsic, October 18th, 1818.)

TEXT: PSALM lxviii. 3, 4.

ANY one who had heard our last hymn without knowing the occasion of to-day's festival might suppose that we seemed more like entering on a day of supplication in regard to the future, than on what it really is, a day of thankful remembrance of the great and divine deliverance wrought for us in the immediate past. But can we, or ought we, to separate these? God's kindness and grace always anticipate our will and resolution; and therefore we can only ground each request to Him for blessing and prosperity in the future on our heartfelt sense of gratitude for what we have already received from Him, for the favours of the same kind with which He has loaded and satisfied us. And so, in taking a thoughtful view of the past, the more our eyes are turned to one important point and we feel stirred up to thankfulness towards God, must we not ask ourselves so much the more earnestly whether we are even worthy, by the use which we make of them, to offer thanks for His gifts; whether, by a life tending more to His honour, we deserve to bring into His courts our thanks and praise for His gracious help? Let this, then, be the direction that our common meditations take to-day.

Let us go down into the depths of our hearts, and examine ourselves before the Lord, and beseech Him for cleansing, that so our thanks may rise to Him well-pleasing and not in vain.

In those times which we unite with all our brethren of the Fatherland in commemorating to-day, we were firmly persuaded that, especially in order to put far from among us all godless habits which threatened to take root so firmly, to maintain the old foundations of piety and loyalty which were in danger of becoming insecure, and to strengthen anew the natural ties of love which were becoming relaxed by the intrusion of the stranger;—that for all these reasons it was necessary to wage that perilous warfare. Well then, the more we were convinced of this, the more must it concern us now, in commemorating the divine help given in that struggle, that we be not of those who must melt like wax before the fire at the presence of the Lord; the more careful must we be that our joy is a heartfelt joy before the Lord, and that our whole being, consecrated anew to Him in thankfulness, may be maintained before Him in truth and faithfulness. To ask what is meant by a joy before God, how it is distinguished from the transitory joy of the world or in oneself, would be, unless in so far as each of us is able to answer it or has already answered it for himself, a wide question, too wide for one meditation. I will therefore confine myself to showing what our joy must be free from, if it is to deserve the name of a joy before the Lord.

Three principal points here suggest themselves to me to which I wish to direct your attention: that every joy that is to hold its ground in God's presence must be free; first, from falsehood; secondly, from slothfulness; and thirdly, from vanity.

I. Our joy in the deliverance which God wrought for us is to be free from falsehood. We know that when the war was imminent, of which we are now celebrating the decisive day (though not that day alone), all those whom we hail as brothers and fellow-countrymen were not of one mind on the great matter. If some had for long been waiting and hoping for the moment when their desire to win back with the sword a natural and honourable position should be gratified; there were others who thought that the existing condition of things could be borne, and that it was wiser to put up with it than hastily to stake everything in an uncertain war. Now those who thought and spoke in this way, must always have a claim to our respect, in so far as, after the resolution was taken, though contrary to their opinion, they did all that the Fatherland and the law required of them; because they fairly contributed their share to the common cause. For the first thing at the forming of any great resolution is always that every one should seek to bring his own convictions to bear; the second, that he frankly join in what has finally become the common will. But if the events that followed have not changed the opinion of those our brethren, and yet they feel able to take part in the general joy of an anniversary such as this, we must point out to them that theirs is a different joy from that of the rest, and that it cannot be quite that which the joy before the Lord ought to be. For by himself, perhaps, and in an earthly way, one may rejoice when that which he has done with half conviction or without any conviction comes to a successful issue; but before God he can only be ashamed. For it is not over outward things that we are allowed to rejoice before God, who Himself has no outward part and who makes no account of anything outward, but only of that which is in the heart; we are not to rejoice over consequences and events, but only in the power and deed from which they proceeded. But those persons cannot rejoice in those things, who hold that the influential opinion at that time was not the right one, but count that man should have a still greater power of endurance to bear what exasperates him, and to bend still lower under what can only appear to him an external necessity; for such persons rejoice only in the results, not in the deed. But be there few or many such, can the rest of us who are met here to-day to thank God for inclining the hearts of men and nations at that time to refuse any longer to bear dishonourable chains, for inspiring them with courage and hope and loving enthusiasm; —can we say that ours is a truthful thanksgiving, and can our joy be a joy before the Lord, if those sentiments over which we rejoice have no longer the same power in our hearts? Can we claim this if we are now no longer inspired with the same zeal to restore a social life befitting us and pleasing to God; if we are not striving, with a perseverance worthy of that first enthusiasm, to keep safe and to improve what then through God's blessing came anew into our possession? Can we claim it if we have now become careless about the difference between what is worthy and what is unworthy of man; if we are now turning back, and after the old, evil manner, each seeking his own; each one seeking to gain, out of the treasure won for all, as much as possible for himself; and all no longer united with that first love, each denying himself to seek the common weal? No, in that case our joy is no joy before God, for He is a God of truth; in that case the false spirit must melt before Him like wax; and the empty joy, let it show itself as it will, and put on what pious appearance it will, can only be, for the most part, the pleasure of this world; while the shout of our text, Let the righteous be glad and rejoice before God, when it sounds in the untrue soul, sounds like the cry of the avenger, destroying its joy. Only if the old zeal has not been allowed to cool; only if that is still true with us which we then felt as the most sacred truth of our lives, that a man does not exist for himself, but for the common cause; that to risk life for the brethren is the call of God in the soul, and that not arbitrary power, but the well-knit bonds of justice are the surest supports of piety and spiritual prosperity; only if we feel those convictions as strongly as we then did, are our hearts really rejoicing before God. If it is so with us, we are in a position to think, if not without pain and mourning, at least with feelings purified from base mixture, of what this war has cost us, to remember those who watered the harvest of our joy with their precious blood, and set their seal, by their death, to the faith and strength that inspired us; while this remembrance especially must without doubt cause the untrue heart to melt like wax before God.

II. But our grateful joy before God must also be free from slothfulness. It seems really superfluous to say this; for slothfulness and joy can never harmonize. Joy arouses the spirit, so that it is nothing but strength and life and activity; and this is pre-eminently true of joy before God, for it is ever exciting, ever bringing into action whatever may be specially in our hearts at the same time. But man's perversity has found out how to separate what God has intimately joined, and to join things which according to natural law are opposed to each other. And so there is such a thing as a slothful joy over even so great events as those which we remember on days like this. For the man who only rejoices because we have happily surmounted our miseries, and because the source of manifold calamities is closed; who after this happy turn of affairs would like to repose on the results of those exertions, and now rejoices chiefly that the time of exertion is past, and that now, without the putting forth of such efforts, without interruption to industry (hindrances being successfully cleared away), the prosperity of all, or at least his own must go on as a matter of course; such a man rejoices, if he rejoices at all, with a slothful joy. And of this joy, whatever else we may or may not be able to think of it, we must certainly think and feel that it cannot be a joy before God. In presence of the Eternal we cannot rejoice on account of anything being past; that which is but a concern of the passing moment vanishes at the thought of Him and cannot be joined to that thought. Hence also it comes that we can by no means associate the thought of God with mere pleasures of the senses and rejoice in such pleasures before Him; because the pleasures of sense pass away with every moment, and must be renewed every moment if they are to last. And those who have no better rejoicing to-day than the poor joy that the former distress is past, what means have they of quickening their joy, what makes their condition still something like joy, but the hope of now enjoying the pleasures of life instead of bearing its miseries? And thus the pleasure-seekers, who are slothful as to spiritual concerns, can by no means rejoice before God.

But now we must inquire whether there may not be found some slothful ones even among those who are conscious of a genuine sympathy with the acts of that time, the remembrance of which kindles our joy to enthusiasm to-day. We shall all, at least, be able to distinguish between two different positions. Besides the many who, in taking part, each according to his circumstances, in the efforts of that time, were laid hold of in a natural way by the common ardour; there were others in whom this sympathy was only a transient impulse, and who showed themselves at that time capable of doing and bearing what they would not have thought possible before, nor perhaps would think possible now. But even then, how every fluctuation of events was mirrored in their uncertain feelings; so that whenever affairs took an unfavourable turn they were full of dread about what was to follow, and inclined beforehand to throw the blame of the misfortune on those who had urged them on; and how much more must a feeling produced in so superficial a way, being only the effect of one momentous hour and without force in itself, have become, since that time, thoroughly deadened! And from all who only participated in those great deeds in this way, we can certainly expect to-day only a faint and dull kind of joy, that is nothing more than the dreamy remembrance of an unwonted state of mind in which they found themselves for a time, about which they know neither whence it arose nor whither it has vanished; only they know right well that they could not now rise to it again. The very core of their hearts takes shape from the slothfulness and impotence of their own souls, and can neither now nor ever send forth a living shoot of joy. If they desire to rejoice with us, it is only from the contagion of our joy; so that theirs is only a pale reflection of the lively joy of those in whom that first zeal was a true and living sentiment, and in whom still abides, as a steady and unchanging principle, the strength by which they laid hold of the slothful souls and carried them along with them. To those steadfast souls alone belongs not only their own joy, but that of the others, and they alone can truly rejoice before God, the living God who controls our doings as well as animates and inspires us; but those slothful ones would attempt in vain to appear before God with their soulless joy, when the thought of Him is not even able to keep their cold hearts steadfast. We can rejoice before Him only when we feel in ourselves an ever active power for good; feel it as His gift, flowing out to us from Him, as the effect of His Spirit in us. Yes, only when we are going forward in the work which we then undertook; only when each of us is constantly presenting anew to those who wish to sink down in indolent repose, the picture of what is right in God's sight and pleasing to men, ever bringing before them what is still lacking in us, how many enemies there still are to be conquered by the power of faith and love; only when we are of this mind can we rejoice together before God for all His good gifts, and so also for that great day. And it is only such joy that can be called a joy from the heart, as the heart is the source of life and activity in man, and of all the feelings that move him and pass over from him to others. Hence if it is the wicked who melt like wax before the Lord, it seems as if we must say that the slothful are wicked; at least if they cannot stand even before us, without being constantly steeled anew by the pervading strength of others, still less will their joy be able to stand before the thought of God. For what is lifeless and slothful fears and shuns life, as falsehood fears and shuns the truth.

III. Finally, our joy must be free from all vanity. That is to say, there are two ways of looking at human affairs. On the one side we really feel that all earthly and perishable things are nothing in themselves, that all not only originate from the Eternal, but are continually and actually carried on and upheld by Him, and can only live and move and have their being in Him. If we thus consider and feel about anything that concerns us, then we think of it in God, and we cannot fail to have in our hearts true joy in the Lord. On the other hand, the Eternal does none of His works directly before our eyes, but does everything in connection with the affairs of men by means of men and the influence of external nature. Therefore individual men and individual events always justly attract our attention. And in studying them we are led on from each individual to another connected with him, from each later event to one that preceded it; but the more we allow ourselves to separate this way of looking at things from the former, and please and satisfy ourselves with thus arranging facts in a circle, the more does our whole mind and character become tainted with vanity, and it is only pleasure or pain about transitory things that stirs our spirit. If, therefore, the joy that we feel to-day is to be a joy that will stand before God, it must not be joy in what this or that individual has done; it must not go back on—I will not say, any merit of our own—but not even on the merit of other individuals. For if we are to rejoice before the Lord, we can only rejoice in the deed which He the Lord accomplished among us. And if we rejoice in our own work, we are no longer rejoicing before Him, and so our sense of the Eternal becomes weakened, and that which the Lord wrought is changed for us into a vain and unintelligible play of earthly powers and acts and sufferings; indeed, the more we look into it in this way the more we believe that we see in events only that sport of chance by which man is always punished when he forgets God. And how vain a thing is joy of this kind! how little power of lasting there is in it! and how every human merit, even that which we sought thus unselfishly to exalt, melts away, when we reflect how often it would not have been earned at all, if some outward circumstance, that no one could control, had turned out differently! But certainly, be it said for our comfort, if any set of events is fitted to cure us of the vanity of a false joy like this, those great events are so. He who wishes to rejoice in human judgment and intelligence, in perfect art and skilfully calculated plans, must seek for himself some other subject. For about this, the opposite feeling is much too general for such ideas; the feeling that there is no single person of whom it could be said that it was his doing; no single event, not even the special one we commemorate to-day, after the occurrence of which it could be said that now all was safe. Rather, if we look at details and study man's part in the matter, the heroes and directors of the war themselves will not deny, that even the most brilliant deeds were accompanied by mistakes, and that as God brought all about for the best, He caused even those mistakes to prove a blessing. So that here very specially it is clear to us all that the glory is due to God alone, and here we can most easily resist all vainglorious joy. And so we come back to what we began with.

If we choose to derive our joy rather from outward than inward causes, from results rather than from sentiments, vanity will inevitably come into play; each individual may then take credit for one thing or another, and follow out endlessly the traces of what he has contributed to the work, and each may seek out one among those who have done the largest share, and make an idol of him, and give him the glory; for if vanity is once aroused it can make everything take what form it pleases. But if in our joy our thoughts are turned to God and to the powers which He stirred up at that time, we are constrained to take an opposite view, and we have the clearest perception that not only the will but the accomplishment of it came from God. Then we understand that it was in His counsel that the events which took place were determined; and we also feel that we defraud ourselves of the purest joy, if, on a day like this, we give the slightest place to vainglorious boasting. No, let all empty show disappear from among us! It is only joy before God that endures; while the joy of vanity is disposed of with that godlessness of character that melts like wax before God. For gratitude and confidence are inseparable companions. If we take credit to ourselves and to each other for the great things God has done, we can also cherish no confidence but in human strength and human counsel. And let us only ask if things are now in such a position, through what then took place, that such a confidence would satisfy us? When we look fairly at our needs, our wishes, our hopes, must we not still acknowledge that human help is useless, and that it is the Lord alone on whom we can rely? And therefore it is only from joy before God, far from all self-applause, that the right confidence can proceed; a confidence, not that He will always in time of need again order events for our profit and glory; but that He will not withdraw His Spirit from us; that He who at that time drew out among us so much self-sacrificing love, so much pure loyalty and faith, will preserve to us this treasure, and be ever re-animating it in us by the power of His Spirit. It will not be a confidence that, after the outward enemies are conquered, we may let things take their course, until a time comes when there shall again be need to fight; but that the Lord will keep the hearts of His people together in a living unity; that He will keep their spiritual eyes clear to see what is right; that He will work as effectually among us in time of peace as He did, to His own glory, in time of danger. It will be the confidence that the Lord is with the humble hearts; that He never forsakes those who have no reliance on themselves; that He will never suffer His glory to perish among those who glory in nothing but His strength; and that a permanent and inexhaustible power of enjoyment is the portion of those who in all things rejoice in God alone.

Let us then cleanse our hearts from falsity, from slothfulness, from vanity! for we feel that if these are overcome a pure and imperishable joy before God will naturally spring up in our hearts. For this purpose the holy table of the Lord is spread among us to-day. Join all of you in spirit with those who will partake of it to-day. If we are one with Him, who alone among those born of woman could say, I am the way and the truth; if we are pervaded by the spirit of Him whose motto was, The Father worketh, and I work; if we are one with Him who was entirely possessed with the conviction that it became Him to do the Father's will, and that He lived in God and God in Him; then we shall be ever drawing closer to the eternal, imperishable life, to freedom from all vanity, and ever becoming more worthy of the great things which the Lord Jesus has done for us. Amen.

Prayer.

Yea, Lord, to Thee be brought praise and honour! Thou didst raise us up when we were crushed and had almost perished! It is Thy will to make us again a vessel unto honour, after we were despised and seemed like a vessel of wrath; Thou alone hast done it, to Thee let all our hearts be devoted! Rule Thou in our hearts as Thou hast outwardly ruled among us. Make us by Thy Spirit more and more a people to Thy praise, a royal and priestly nation; govern us by Thy word and Spirit that we may be ever becoming worthier of that highest name which we bear, the name that comes to us from Thy Son. Amen.

XI.

LOVE AND SERVICE.

TEXT: JOHN xxi. 16. "He saith to him again a second time, Simon, son of John, lovest thou Me? He saith unto Him, Yea, Lord; Thou knowest that I love Thee. He saith unto him, Tend my sheep."

THERE is no more important charge than that which the Lord gave to His apostle in these words. He calls Himself the Shepherd of His flock; therefore what He here committed to the charge of the apostle was to do the Lord's own work in His name, and under His oversight and ruling direction as Chief Shepherd. But this is a charge committed by no means exclusively to the Apostle Peter, nor exclusively to the rest of the apostles, nor to those alone who now in a special and official way serve the Lord as teachers and overseers in His Church: it is the duty of all Christians without exception; we are all to be labourers in His vineyard. But in this vineyard, the plants of which are none other than redeemed souls, its fruits none other than the fruits of the Spirit, what can any one find to do that would not be included in the expression, Tend My sheep? Co-operation and help in the work which the Lord has to do on the souls that God has given Him,—this and nothing else can we supply to Him, and He can make use of nothing else. If therefore we are to present our whole life to Him as a living thank-offering; if we are bound to show that He has sanctified our souls, by our making some use of the powers we owe to Him, then we must all certainly take part in the work which, in the words of our text, He commits to the apostle. But He connects this charge with Peter's answer to His question, Simon, son of John, lovest thou Me? And thus it appears to us that in an examination to which, as it were, the Lord subjects Peter, this love to Christ is the one thing He requires of him, with a view to his feeding Christ's sheep. But we find among Christians in all ages very different opinions about this. Some adhere strictly to this word of the Lord, and say that there is absolutely no other spiritual qualification for this duty; that a man has no need to acquire anything else beforehand in order to render to the Lord the service to which all are called; that he only needs to be growing ever stronger in love to the Saviour, and to be able ever more joyfully to answer with the apostle, Lord, Thou knowest that I love Thee. Others, on the contrary, maintain that of course the Lord knew everything else that was in the apostle; what spiritual faculties were awakened, what light of knowledge was kindled in him; but because Peter had fallen and denied Him, He may have stood in doubt about just this one point; or rather, though He, knowing what was in all hearts, could not doubt, the rest of the disciples might have doubted whether love to the Lord was still quite as lively in his heart as it had been. And therefore, they say, the Lord addressed this question to him, not as if there were nothing else required in order to tend His sheep, but because all the other disciples knew quite well the kind and measure of everything else in the soul of Peter, but on this one indispensable point it was necessary for him to come out clearly. In response to these different views, whether love to Christ is sufficient qualification for the fulfilment of the Christian's calling, or something more is required, let us consider more closely the words of our text. First, and most necessary, let us try rightly to understand the Saviour's words in this connection; and secondly, let us go further back and inquire together how those different views may be supposed to have arisen among Christians, in order still more fully to assure ourselves as to what has been the mind and will of the Lord.

I. First, then, if we wish to ascertain which of those two meanings the Saviour may be supposed really to have had, it will be necessary for us to begin by asking what, according to the nature of things, is implied in the commission with which the Lord here charges His disciple, Tend My sheep. Confining ourselves to the figurative expression which the Saviour uses, it unquestionably includes very specially two things: first, that the sheep of the flock must be protected; then, that they must be fed. The shepherd's care takes in both of these parts; therefore the Lord expects from His disciple and entrusts to him both kinds of work. Well, now let us next ask by what means and in what manner the souls of men are protected, so that they may not again withdraw or wander from the Lord's flock, and that in the flock no danger may approach or evil befall them? Certainly, we answer unanimously, love to Him is the first requisite; that love must call forth in each of us the strong desire to keep our own soul and the souls of others in living fellowship with Him; it must make us quick to notice whatever might be adverse to that fellowship. But now if we are asked to go a step further, and assert that this love to the Saviour is sufficient by itself for the work, then, it seems to me, we must say No. What a knowledge of the human heart in its obduracy and in its despondency is needful in order to protect the soul in spite of these; with what clear spiritual insight must we penetrate its most hidden recesses if we wish to note and trace out, before it be too late, anything in men's own souls that endangers their fellowship with the Saviour—if we are to detect the first stirrings of evil, and make those aware of it in whom we see it, so that if possible they may turn before they have fairly entered on a wrong course! What a knowledge we need to have of the ways of sin, and of the various snares that are prepared by those who are still sunk in earthly cares and sensual pleasures, for those who are just beginning to show a desire to struggle towards the higher, spiritual life! What experiences of the ways of the world are needful—experiences always dearly bought—to know how to bring flattery and dissimulation to light by the truth, and to distinguish them by their fruits; to be able to warn the inexperienced, and dispel for them the illusive semblance of kindness and goodness behind which those only too often conceal themselves who are trying to entice others into the way of ruin. When we think of all this, we must indeed admit that besides love to Christ, true wisdom also belongs to the work of tending His sheep. And now let us look at the second point—that the souls belonging to the Lord's flock are also to be fed. What other food for souls is there but the Word of God? None, certainly; for the Word that became flesh and came into the world is also the true bread of life that came down from heaven. And Christ Himself said that the flesh profits nothing, but that His words are spirit and life. He therefore who means to feed redeemed souls must know how to dispense and portion out to them the divine Word. Now it is certain that if we are to partake of this food ourselves and dispense it to others, in the first place, our love to Christ must be a well-founded love which recognises that He alone has the words of life. But, in the next place, how needful it is on the one hand that we be able to form a correct judgment on the various relations and conditions in which men are found, to decide in each case what kind of food is most necessary and suitable for the soul, and with true wisdom to select from the great abundance and the infinite fulness of the divine Word that which is best fitted to nourish each one and strengthen him for good in every emergency. But then, on the other hand, still more, what is needful in order to be able rightly to divide the Word of God, although we know how it *ought* to be distributed to every one? Well, certainly this, that we first clearly and fully understand it ourselves. But the interval of a long course of centuries lies between us and the first utterance of those words; they are written in a foreign and now dead language: and yet the true and perfect understanding of the divine Word can only be that which corresponds most nearly to the way in which all those who heard it from the living lips of the Lord and His apostles—those whose minds were most awake, most favourably disposed and best prepared—understood it and applied it to themselves. Therefore a power of transporting our thoughts to distant times and into conditions of society strange to us, a knowledge of foreign tongues and customs, is a part of the qualification for rightly dividing the Word of God. And so, if we are to approach our brethren with the divine words, and thus tend Christ's sheep, love to Him is, no doubt, the first condition; for this is the same thing as our own pleasure and joy in the divine Word, and it is love to Him alone that can constrain us to this whole work, for he who does not love Christ Himself, does not love His flock. But if it is asserted that love alone *suffices*, we shall again deny it, and certainly still more truly in our case than in that of His first disciples, and feel bound to say that, besides love, a right perception is also needful for the work. And thus when we consider the subject on this side, those persons seem to be right who think, that when the Saviour meant to commission His disciple to tend His sheep, He asked especially about his love to Him, because there might have been room to doubt whether that remained unchanged; but everything else that he needed for the work—the wisdom and knowledge—He took for granted in him as already known.

But that justice may be done to all parties, let us now study the subject from another side. Suppose that love to Christ is a living principle in us; must we not, in that case, necessarily take a deep interest in the whole great work of the Lord? Must we not burn with desire to become acquainted according to the full measure of our powers, both with the Lord Himself and with the whole great work of God which is committed to Him? The reverse of this would indeed betray evident indifference. But if we wish to be acquainted with the Saviour, with Him who alone is pure and good, the one perfect Man of God, must we not at the same time go on looking into the sinful heart of man, in order that we may be able exactly to distinguish in it that which is the work of the Saviour and bears the features of His likeness, from what proceeds from human corruption and has no part in His character; so that our idea of the object of our love may be kept pure and holy, and nothing extraneous be mixed with it. And thus we see that love to the Saviour really produces in us, as a matter of course, that knowledge of the human heart, with all its depths and errors, which is necessary in order to our tending the Lord's sheep with wisdom, and fulfilling our work in His kingdom. And in the same way, could we suppose it possible that we should love the Lord without listening most eagerly to every word from His own mouth, as well as to every word which the Spirit, who took of the fulness of Christ and glorified Him, has spoken by the lips of His disciples? Can there be that living love to the Saviour, without our occupying ourselves diligently with His Word? And though every part of it is not equally available, seeing that some parts need more and some less of those helps that depend on all kinds of human wisdom and historical knowledge; yet do we not feel that in the Christian community, where no one buries his talent, every one has sufficient means at command for attaining to a knowledge of the divine Word, such as will enable him, in so far as can be expected of him, to feed the souls of his brethren, and at the fitting time to offer them the bread of comfort and truth out of the abundance of this divine teaching?

Yes, I will even go further. In this world each of us has his own particular calling in the civil community, according to the place in which the Lord has set us; and in order to carry on that calling wisely and with good results on behalf of his family, each one needs to acquire by practice, skill and sagacity about various everyday concerns, as well as much knowledge of the world and of men. Now do we mean to say that all this business activity is a thing apart from love to the Saviour, so that all our pleasure and joy in it comes from a different source? Do we mean to say that when we expend our time and put forth the powers of our mind on this, it must be some other motive that inspires us; and that every one who is engaged in any earthly calling must necessarily have a heart divided between love to it and love to the Saviour, and must take away from the one what he gives to the other? By no means; on the contrary, everything that can justly make demands on the powers of Christians is closely connected with the great work of the Saviour on earth. And when His apostles recommended to their congregations that every one should work with his hands to some good purpose, and should seek after all things lovely and of good report, those exhortations were just suggested, like all others, by the love of Christ which constrained His apostles; and this same love is to be the motive power by which Christians are to carry out such directions. For he who truly loves the Lord will do Him honour in the presence of men; he will help to glorify the spiritual presence of the Lord to the utmost; he will show that his whole soul is thoroughly pervaded by love to Him; all its emotions will be sanctified by His presence; and love to Him will be a power that helps the believer more effectually in all the concerns of everyday life, and that is able more thoroughly to overcome obstacles than any other incentive that could be set before him.

But this is equally true; that all those various kinds of human knowledge and insight which, when directed by the love of Christ, are a help to us in every part of our work, if they proceed from any other source, can only be injurious. A knowledge of the world and of the human heart, if it is only, as it were, a surreptitious means of carrying out more successfully schemes of selfishness, or of indulging ambition, will not only effect nothing in the kingdom of God and help no human soul, but in the end it will cheat its very possessors of their foolish aims. If all knowledge of past times and of dead languages, and of everything that belongs to a deep and thorough understanding of the different parts of God's Word, is only acquired in order to make a show before the world, or because a man, having missed his highest end, seeks to satisfy the cravings of his spirit in another direction; and if one should nevertheless set himself to use it in investigating God's Word as he would in any ordinary matter; oh, be sure he will never thus attain to a correct and living understanding of it: and so far from one who enters on the work of dividing the Word of God with only this equipment being fit to feed the Lord's sheep; his doing so is much more likely to tend to his own ruin.

Therefore, my friends, after all, it *is* nothing but love to Christ alone! If we consider it in connection with all that it leads to, we see that it does suffice for the fulfilment of the great work which the Lord, in the words of our text entrusts to all His disciples, in the measure that He expects from each. If one has been thoughtlessly dreaming away his time and has cared little about seeking out and employing the treasures hidden in every soul; it is love which first awakens him and impels him to take up and gather about him, according to the position in which the Lord has placed him, everything that can make him more capable of fulfilling in the world the great calling of all the servants of the Lord. Or if a man, before he is brought into the living fellowship of faith and love with the Saviour, has been eagerly following some other course, and from some other motive has been enriching his mind with knowledge and cultivating its faculties; what a change is made on such a person by love to the Saviour, as soon as it takes possession of his soul! It pervades his whole being, transforms everything in him, gives a new direction to everything that has been used in the service of vanity, and sets it free to be a living power for good; so that he stands forth a new creature; all the powers of his soul united in active obedience to the motive that inspires him, and obeying no other. The first apostles of the Lord seem to us to resemble the first mentioned class. He found them plain men, longing and hoping in their honest piety for better times; but feebly furnished, and far from having any deep understanding of the word of God and therefore also far from knowing the human heart and the world in which they were placed. But they received everything from Him; love to Him and the joyful belief that in Him they had found the promised Saviour, and heartfelt gratitude that He had chosen them to be His instruments—these motives impelled and constrained them to receive and hold fast in their inmost hearts all the words of wisdom from His mouth; and thus they were able afterwards to come forward and teach differently and more efficiently than they who from their youth up had been instructed in the Scriptures and in the commandments of the fathers. And on the other hand, those who had previously been wandering in some opposite way are represented to us by that apostle whom the Lord won to Himself when he was in the very act of persecuting His Church. He had sat at the feet of great teachers, and was equipped with all the wisdom of his people which concerned itself especially with the earlier divine relation; and thus he was well practised in everything that could in any way be necessary to ensure success in the profession he had chosen of scribe and teacher of the law. But how was everything transformed from the moment when he perceived that the Way he was persecuting was God's way; when he was arrested by the voice, It is hard for thee to kick against the pricks! from the moment when the question, Saul, Saul, why persecutest thou Me? sank into his soul; when his heart recognised the Lord and received from Him the great vocation to go and proclaim the gospel among all nations. From that moment everything was made to serve the one end, everything in his soul subordinated to the love of Christ, controlled and pervaded by it, and thus fitted to contribute to the work of the Lord; so that however much use Paul might make of what he had been taught from his youth, he could nevertheless say with truth that he did not come with the wisdom of men; for everything in him was changed into a really divine wisdom, learning and skill.

But if we were inclined to suppose from this that, because love to Christ produces everything that really carries on the work of His kingdom, therefore each individual should be fit for every kind of work, in proportion as he is inspired and constrained by that love; and if therefore each one tried to take a part in everything that was to be done in the kingdom of God—this would be both a false representation of human affairs, and a vain delusion. If we think of ourselves apart from all that has most to do in determining our work in this world and giving it for the first time a fixed direction, we see that we have got no further, with all our love to Christ, than to resemble those of whom the Lord speaks in His parable, who stood waiting in the market-place for some one to hire them; and then the Master comes, and as often as He finds any, leads them into His vineyard, and appoints to each his work, according to his powers and circumstances. And so with us; if only we have love to Christ this will not fail to occur; the Master calls us, some in this direction, some in that; whither and when is decided by the circumstances in which each of us is placed, and which are more favourable to some and more adverse to others; but all of us will certainly have experience of both. But whatever lot has been cast for any one, he becomes a labourer in the Lord's vineyard only in so far as love to Christ constrains him and teaches him what it is fitting for him to do in the place where the Lord has set him. This is what each one must see to; but for everything else, let him build nothing on the skill of man, or what he may choose to do. For all the rest is the mysterious dealing of God, who certainly often directs things so wonderfully just that no man may fancy that he himself is able to manage events, but that all may acknowledge that the Lord has reserved it to Himself in the secret course of His counsel, to appoint to each the place in His vineyard in which he is to tend the sheep of the flock according to his knowledge and capacity.

Hence then, my friends, it appears as if there could really be no dispute among Christians as to how far love to Christ does or does not suffice for the fulfilling of the work which the Lord has committed to us.

II. Let us, therefore, inquire shortly, in the second place, whence this dispute has nevertheless arisen, and on what it is founded. On this, of course, that alongside of the highway of truth run two opposite byways, one on either side, such byways as men are apt to wander into, even in the kingdom of God. The person who teaches that love to Christ is sufficient and that a man needs nothing in addition, warns us against one of these byways, and the person who says that love to Christ is indeed the foundation, the first and indispensable thing, but that we need much besides if we are really to bring forth fruit and be useful in the Lord's work; this one, in his turn, sets himself in opposition to the other byway. The first error arises from this, that many, even devout men, do not sufficiently remember what the Lord means when He says, My kingdom is not of this world. The Lord's Church still lives in perpetual warfare with that which, in contrast with it, Scripture calls the world; the conflict of light with darkness is still going on. For clearly as the light shines in the darkness, there is still a portion of the darkness that has not admitted it; and so the long struggle goes on, the struggle of good against evil, of simple, heavenly truth against the perversity of the children of men, the struggle with which we are all acquainted. But because this struggle is not always easy, and the Church of God still often meets with hard usage here and there; many, out of an ill-advised though really living and hearty love to Christ and His kingdom, still hold the opinion that if the world oppresses the Church by the employment of outward means, by power and authority, the Church would, on her side, do well to provide herself with all kinds of means of defence similar to those with which she is attacked. They think that if the opponents of the gospel seek to take advantage of its simple-hearted professors by human wisdom and skill, we ought also to try by a judicious use of our knowledge and skill to intimidate and perplex those opponents. And thus we very easily lose sight of that great word of the Lord, If My kingdom were of this world, then My servants would fight for it with the weapons of this world; and so men do fight for the kingdom of God with the weapons of this world, and thereby only produce in it more confusion and uncertainty; they dim the light and increase the darkness. Now when such things occur it is time to remember that when Christ commissioned His disciple to tend His sheep, He questioned him about nothing but his love to Him. Whatever resulted from this love, therefore, was to be used for the profit of the Lord's flock, but everything else, not allied to it, could produce no beneficial effect in His kingdom, and could neither protect nor help His flock. But such things *have* occurred, and the Christian Church has many times strayed into this byway, since from being a persecuted and much-enduring Church she has become a ruling power; but above all since she was called in a distinctive sense, the Church of Rome. For now she was honoured and glorified by the powers of the world and herself invested with authority, and every powerful weapon was placed in her hands to be used for her own purposes. And as worldly power uses speech in various ways to attain its ends, so here also an art of speech was adopted and practised, often flattering and treacherous enough, in order to carry out designs which so much worldly effort made impure and base. And indeed it took much more than love to Christ to accustom His flock to the oppressive yoke under which they were to be held prisoners. And so it came that, instead of a true temple of the Spirit of God, there arose a building in which it must have become ever more impossible for those to dwell who had learned to know for themselves the spiritual union with the Saviour, and desired to find their salvation in that alone; until at last the Lord brought about the time for which we so often thank Him in our meetings in our morning prayer; the time when the clearer light of the gospel was able to shine for us anew. Then we returned to the Christian's living and profound conviction that the Lord's kingdom is not of this world; that no worldly power or skill can ever protect or defend it; that spiritual power alone can enable it to stand against all storms and attacks; and that in all the concerns of that kingdom, no power must bear rule but love to the Saviour, and all that it begets in the souls of men.

Now as to the other byway; what leads to it is this, that there are really a great many Christians who would like to turn their love to the Saviour into something that they enjoy quietly and all by themselves. They wish to be absorbed in the sense of His spiritual presence and nearness; they reverence and love Him as the source of every good and lovely emotion of their hearts, and as taking a lively pleasure in them all. Now this is all beautiful and right, and is certainly no byway. But if they desire to know nothing but this kind of enjoyment, and thus virtually forget the whole world around them; what can be the result but a life whose aims terminate on itself, and which is therefore utterly inefficient for the great aims of the Saviour? For it is evident that a man is selfish if he allows himself to be satisfied with merely his own salvation, and so becomes always more indifferent to the whole outward duty of a Christian, and to the great work of the Saviour in the world—of that Saviour to whom we owe deepest love and exclusive reverence very specially on this account, that He did not live for Himself, but came to serve, to seek and save the lost, and to invite the weary and heavy-laden to come to Him. Now if a man truly enough feels himself lost and gone astray, and is glad of the coming of Christ to save him; if he feels himself weary and heavy-laden, and follows, not in vain, the path that leads to Him who alone can refresh his soul; and if yet it never enters his mind that the refreshed soul ought to bring forth all good and beautiful fruits; that he is to set himself, in the strength of love to the Lord, to save and refresh others; and that each one is not only to be a sheep of the flock, but is called to take his own part in tending the Lord's sheep; then he has got into a byway. And the greater the number is of those who follow this course, even though each does not mean to be for himself alone, and though they rejoice together by hundreds, but still only in this self-centred enjoyment of love; just so much the more numerous are those who are withdrawing themselves from supporting the kingdom of God, and from carrying forward His work. And when things come to this state it is high time for a voice from the opposite side to make itself heard by those secluded souls, buried in slothful love to Christ, and to say to them, Such a love as that is not enough; more than that is needful for meeting rightly the call which Christ addresses to you as to others: if you really wish to live with Him you must also act for Him; if spiritual gifts have been developed in you, you must put them to use in the kingdom of God. In this sense, then, it may no doubt be said that something in addition to love to Christ is wanted for the tending of His sheep; and yet the full truth is this, that such a love is not true love, but an impure and selfish substitute for it. For the Lord did not come in order to dwell in souls in an isolated way, and to begin His life mysteriously and specially in each; the blessings of His presence are to reach to all by means of fellowship and communion; and this ought never to cease until all the sheep are gathered from every quarter of the world, till all have come to the maturity of a perfect man in Christ, till His Church stands before Him blameless in regard to the whole duty of man on earth. Now he who does not labour in this work of the Lord, does not love it; and he who does not love the Lord's work would boast in vain of loving the Lord Himself. And if it is a poor, pitiful love like this we are thinking of—a love that will certainly always be impure and false as long as it is confined to mere personal enjoyment—then we are right in saying that for the fulfilment of a Christian's whole duty, more than love is necessary. But if we mean the real and vigorous love to Christ, such as it was in the apostles, and such as it has always been in all faithful, actively-working Christians, whose hearts are set on the common weal; then we must say, we need nothing beyond that. That love will produce everything that can in any way be useful to us as labourers in the Lord's vineyard, it will develop every faculty that each of us needs in order to exercise an influence wherever the Lord has placed us; and thus we shall be able with our whole being to praise the Lord, when everything that is lovely and commendable and of good report among Christians proceeds from no other source than love to the Lord.

It is just the same here as with the dispute whether faith is sufficient to justify and save a man, or whether works must be added to faith. As this is always only an empty strife about words—for faith which is not active by works is no true faith, but dead, and the works that do not come from faith are only dead works—in the same way the dispute as to whether love is enough to fit us for tending the Lord's sheep, or whether something more is needed, is only a vain strife of words: for that is not real love to the Saviour which has not the effect of making us devote and sanctify all our powers to Him, and use them in the work of His kingdom. If it does this, then we need nothing more. All occupation about earthly affairs, to which Christians, as men, are called, all knowledge of what is needful for the furtherance of Christ's cause on earth—all these things come rightly to us if only, in every moment and every part of our life, we are inspired by the right kind of love to Christ, if we regard everything that comes to be done only in the light of its being something belonging to His holy kingdom.

If then, my friends, we have concluded that one thing alone is needful, let us seek to experience in its glorious fulness, and to keep clearly before our minds, what is included in this one thing. Let us put out to interest this talent committed to us, and by means of it obtain whatever tends to the glorifying of God's kingdom, so that if the Lord asks in our inmost hearts the question he put to Peter, we also may be able, with a good conscience, to answer,

"Lord, Thou knowest that I love Thee." Then shall we all, with joy, and with gladsome hope that the word has not been spoken in vain, hear from Him the call, Go, then, and tend My sheep. **Amen.**

XII.

GOD'S RESTRAINING POWER.

(*New Year's Day.*)

TEXT: JOB xxxviii. 11. "Hitherto shalt thou come, and no further: and here shall thy proud waves be stayed."

THESE words are taken from a sublime discourse, which is put by the writer in the mouth of the Highest Himself, the Creator and Preserver of the world. In it He answers Job out of the whirlwind, when he had complained, though reverently and humbly, that the Lord did not allow men to find Him; that, moreover, He gave no account of His matters to them, and that therefore nothing remained for them but silently to fear Him. Then the Lord came forth, it is said, out of the whirlwind, and talked with Job about his want of understanding; and from this discourse the words of our text are taken. And when, on a day such as this, we look back on the past, on so many unexpected disasters, so many hopes left unfulfilled, wishes disappointed, complications, as the results of which the Lord brought about something totally different from what we had anticipated and hoped, not always, perhaps, out of mere human selfishness, but out of genuine love to what is good, and from wise desires for the common welfare—when all this is gathered into one view before us, how ready are our thoughts to take the same direction as Job's! The Lord is not to be found out by men; we do not divine His counsel, either in our most aspiring hopes or our most moderate wishes. He renders no account to us; for as one year after another passes, none of them solves the problem of those that went before; His ways are ever unsearchable, and His thoughts beyond the comprehension of us poor children of men. But if the Lord had wished us to rest content in this state of apparent submission, He would not have answered Job out of the whirlwind, and—which signifies still more—His Son could not have said to us, "Ye are no longer servants, but friends, for ye know what your Lord doeth."

To this knowledge of the doings of the Lord we shall be helped by this sublime address, the kernel of whose whole contents is contained in the few words of our text. The Lord represents Himself, throughout this discourse, as He who has called into being and who sustains by His almighty word all things that are, and has also appointed to everything in the world its measure and rule; nothing can hold back from obeying His mighty word, nor may anything go beyond what He commands it. "Hitherto, . . . and no further: and here shall thy proud waves be stayed!"

Let us, then, consider more closely how the spirit and meaning of all the Divine counsels, the great secret of the Divine government of the world, is contained in this fact, that God the Lord has appointed to all things their fixed and definite limits. And in connection with this day, let us see, first, how we find in this truth our best comfort in turning our eyes from the past into the future; and, secondly, how these words also contain for us the most sacred and precious example, the great law, according to which we are to regulate our whole life in the service of God.

I. A great part of the discourse which is ascribed to God the Lord in this ancient and sacred book is occupied with the works of Nature, and sets forth how, even in the natural creation, God has appointed all things their measure. As when the world came into being, and took shape at His word, He set free the infinite variety of forces by whose active agency all things consist, He also held them in check. Each of those forces is in itself just as proud and ungovernable an agent as that element to which the words of our text directly refer, and tends to go on extending in all directions, and to overwhelm everything, far and wide. But the Lord calls forth an opposing force, and checks the one by means of the other. In this way, at the creation, He separated and united all things; thus He separated the light from the darkness, while He caused to remain, in fixed and definite degrees, the beneficent alternation of day and night; thus He separated the solid land from the waters, and yet, by means of the appointed proportion between them, each supports, preserves, and fertilizes the other.

But looking at the natural world as it lies before us in these days, we know even by our own eyesight, and still more from the well-grounded and harmonious testimony of those who have seriously and continuously occupied themselves in studying those natural facts, that there are to be found manifold traces, both on the surface and in the depths of the earth, of great and repeated disturbances. The hidden subterraneous fire has cast up vast masses from below, devastating and transforming the face of Nature; the sea, which the Lord seemed to have gathered together and shut up within impassable barriers, has yet often overflowed; but only thus, by the repeated mingling and dividing of the solid and the fluid, could the earth gain that perfect proportion by which it becomes capable of supporting and nourishing the whole mass of infinitely diversified life that moves upon it.

And even yet, though all these natural forces seem partly

to be brought into equilibrium through the often recurring alternation of agitation and repose, and partly to be turned into other directions and controlled in various ways by human intelligence, the Lord sometimes allows them—though mostly in small and isolated instances—to overpass their ordinary limits, so that men again become afraid that this force or that might work its way to uncontrollable power, and sweep away all the rest. Often still the fires of the abyss, released from their bonds, burst forth into the air, and cover the ground with flaming death; the waters still often pour down in torrents from above, and far overflow their accustomed shores, destroying the works of men, and laying waste great tracts of the laboriously cultivated land; but the Lord, in His own time, extinguishes the fire, and causes the waters to go down, and man gathers again the spoil they have left; and everywhere it is God who determines, and gradually develops more and more clearly and exactly, the right proportions; and everywhere we see arise out of the seeming destruction a new and better order of things. But where one natural force seems to rise uncontrollable after having been confined, and in its unmeasured power threatens the ruin of all that is calm and peaceful, the presence of the Eternal is more hidden from us; just as the prophet did not find Him in the whirlwind and in the fire. Our predominant impression at such times is that of a force of Nature which has, as it were, broken loose; and we are overpowered by a sense of our own helplessness, and of the insignificance of man in presence of those universal powers. But when the floodgates of heaven or the doors of the lower world are closed, when the destroying tempests are stilled, and that which had poured forth without control returns to the limits within which it can subsist alongside of all other forces, then we perceive the Lord; then He makes Himself known to us, where order arises and is exercised, where a kindly and benignant rule prevails. And when we have thus grasped the idea that it was the Lord who spoke, saying, "Hitherto, and no further: here shall thy proud waves be stayed," then we begin also to reflect that the two aspects of Nature are closely connected, and we no longer see in that apparent destruction a revolted power of mere Nature, but the governing will of Him who commanded that the waves should so far overflow, in order that the just proportions should be obtained for each new step in the order of things.

But all natural things are really for us either a feeble shadow of spiritual things or a specially significant emblem of them. Let us therefore consider in particular that part of His creation into which the Lord breathed the breath of life; let us consider man, whom He formed into a living soul. Oh! here it is above all, my friends, that we have so often to exclaim that the ways of the Lord are unsearchable and His thoughts past finding out. Those who, by natural relationship, are meant to be bound together in love, are severed by pride and selfish passion; those who should be of one heart, often scorn even the most superficial connection; those who should be serving each other as equals having mutual interests, aim only at lording it over others. Wild passions break out and distract men's minds, so that there is an end to all rule and unity, not only for each individual but even for society as a whole. Thus in this department also we see Nature, after being brought into some degree of order, ready to destroy itself and to perish in confusion. And it is not always self-interest alone that kindles this fire, nor is the fire itself always a strife only over the possession of earthly things. This state of things occurs very specially when opposite views are taken in consulting and arranging about ordinary affairs; or as to the deepest sources of the public and common weal and woe; or the most efficient means, in difficult given circumstances, for promoting one object and discouraging another. And when such views are no longer confined to discussion, but each party, believing himself obliged to take precautions against the damage that might result from the other view, sets himself to oppose his antagonist by force, then what ruinous disorders take place in human affairs! How eagerly do men toil in their fury, believing that they are only destroying in order to build up what is fairer, but only building what must in its turn be overthrown. What a horrible game is then carried on with this as its watchword, that it is better for a few to perish, and so the mass be preserved, than that all should be corrupted through weakly sparing some infected members! and into what an abyss of ruin do great portions of our race sometimes plunge in this manner! But be it arrogant self-seeking and criminal ambition, or wild passions and burning rage; be it sensual lusts and ignoble pleasures, or only the man's better will, aiming at what is really good, but misguided, and so inflamed into the resemblance of those evil motives; sooner or later a point is reached at which the Lord says, "Hitherto, and no further: here shall thy proud waves be stayed." If men are no longer willing to derive their knowledge of sin from the law, God allows all the horrors of lawlessness to break loose, that they may see what is hidden in their hearts. But yet the Lord does not permit the reign of reason and morality to be utterly subverted. He has laid their foundations in human nature with a power that can never be entirely overcome. So if the wild flood has overflowed those shores, God brings man back to his senses, matured by sorrowful experiences; if there have been fierce outbreaks of hatred, the counsel of the Lord brings about a heartfelt love, made stronger by sufferings endured in common.

But let us turn our eyes from this chequered and tumultuous scene of outward acts and circumstances, and look into the more silent depths of the human soul. Think of a reflecting man who studies the mysteries of man's mind, and seeks to understand the internal nature of the world in which he lives, and to search out the laws according to which everything in it goes on. In thus penetrating ever more deeply into his own nature and into the essential nature of all things, he may soon become aware how much nobler a pursuit such investigations are than those in which the greater number of our brethren, constrained by the cares of daily life, are obliged to toil. But if he then begins to imagine that they are too noble to be mixed up in any degree with common life, and therefore more and more withdraws from it, then the balance of the soul and of life is in danger. Actual life appears to him petty, or even contemptible, in comparison with the ideals with which his mind is occupied; then, in a very different spirit from the humility of those in this book of Job, who, in their debates and interchange of thought, sought to vindicate God's hiding of Himself, he imagines that he has fathomed the mystery of the world and its laws; nay, that even the Highest Himself is not hidden from him, but that he stands within that light which is inaccessible to all others. Thus he builds for himself a temple of pride and sets himself up in it as the object of worship. And from this temple flows forth an icy stream of loveless and unbelieving sophistry, chilling to death the tender life of the spirit, and often even making the wonderful life-giving fountains of the Divine word for long periods unavailable to many because of its sweeping flood. But this flood also can only rage for its appointed time; then, to those spiritual elements that have burst their bonds, the voice of the Lord calls, "Hitherto, and no further: here shall thy proud waves be stayed." New problems arise in the mysteries of Nature as well as in the human mind, and bring to nought the premature self-complacency of the wise of this world, who thought they had grasped and fathomed everything: they seek in vain the key to the riddle, and are obliged to acknowledge that they have unwisely spoken about what they did not understand, that which concerns them most nearly becoming indeed a witness to their ignorance. And when this spell of self-conceit is dissolved, then the killing frost also begins to yield, and a more genial atmosphere is spread over the spiritual life. That life absorbs only the more eagerly all the renewing and refreshment of childlike confidence; and the spirits that had grown afraid to trust accept all the more cordially the wholesome mysteries of faith, the longer they have been deprived of these comforts. And so these proud waves of the human mind not only subside, but leave a permanent blessing behind them, and thus God appoints measure and limits to everything that seems to rise against His rule, and even to that which appeared to intend to take heaven by violence.

But however comforting are the prospects for the future which the knowledge of these truths opens to us, we have one point more to consider in this respect; that is, the new creation of God which has only taken shape since the Word was made flesh, and appeared to us in the glory of the only-begotten Son of the Father, full of grace and truth. In this new creation which the Spirit of God establishes in the hearts of men, and from which we more and more expect, as time goes on, a new heaven and a new earth to result, it might be supposed that all would go on within right limits, and that the new earth would be distinguished mainly by this, that it should never again be the scene of ruin and devastation, though only in appearance; but that everything should progress in regular and successful order. But unhappily we nowhere see this. The praise of never swerving from the fairest and most perfect rule, and of maintaining the most perfect harmony of character, belongs exclusively to One, after whose measure we, indeed, are to become a perfect man, but only taken as a whole; and from whom, according to the measure that pleases Him, each of us, as a portion of the whole, receives manifold but variously diversified gifts of the Spirit, which manifest themselves in different ways according to differences of time and situation as well as of Nature. And already in the earliest times, when it was a still easier thing for all Christendom to agree, did there not arise under the very eyes of the apostles, as we see from Paul's epistles to the Corinthians, an emulous contention as to those separate gifts, which presents to us an idea of confusion, in the single member separating itself from the body and wishing to be something by itself, as if it could do without the rest. That was not the effect of the Spirit's guidance, it was the impulse of human nature that did not yet understand itself in these higher circumstances, and which in newly receiving the gifts of the Spirit, wished to break away from obedience to His control. God allowed this to occur that it might be seen how much this mysterious bond still needed to be strengthened, and then the authoritative voice of the apostle interposed, reconciling and laying down rules. And when the Spirit of God was no longer confined to the limits of the Jewish nation, but brought heathen also to the knowledge of the truth in Christ, and the Church rejoiced that out of every nation he that feareth God and worketh righteousness is accepted of Him, to be brought to the knowledge of the Gospel; how soon was that first joy disturbed by hot contentions that threatened to rend the Church of God even in its earliest infancy! But through the wisdom of the apostles and the earnestness and love of the primitive Church, God spoke a calming word of peace, and the waves stopped short at threatening, and were not permitted to overflow. And when the Divine word in its rapid course laid hold of widely different peoples, and the diversity of tongues refused to be brought into harmony; when the variety of dispositions in the Church of God was always becoming greater, and each one had something different to fear as being injurious to the new life in him, as well as some point in the doctrines of salvation that he felt peculiarly bound to maintain; when, as the result of this, doctrine was presented in various lights and the Christian life assumed various forms, according to the riches of the Divine wisdom, which provided that the Gospel should be all things to all men so that by any means some might be gained; how very far were the minds of men from recognising and entering into the purpose of this rich wisdom! What strife and misunderstandings arose! and how quickly in this sacred territory of the Christian Church and of the Divine Word sprang up all the overbearing arrogance of a fancied exclusive knowledge, all passionate desire to persecute and destroy, by which means it is falsely imagined that social relations are best protected, and the fruits of human wisdom most securely preserved and extended! It was difficult to believe that there yet lay in the inmost hearts of the excited disputants, as the cause of all this, a true zeal for the kingdom of God. These sad scenes of devastation within the Lord's vineyard have indeed always been the most dreadful of all the manifestations of human nature broken loose from restraint. The Most High, in permitting them, wished to appoint a sign by which Christians might discern in how small a degree that word of Christ, "My kingdom is not of this world," had yet become spirit and life in their hearts. Often has the bloody sign been repeated, but ever again came the command of the Lord, "No further!" to those waves also; and so strife was again turned into peace, estranged hearts were again bound together, and always new light and life were gained. But now? Has not a permanent separation taken place since the time when a part of Christendom came to the conclusion in regard to all the teaching that still inculcates the legal spirit of the Old Testament, making much of outward ceremonial and never allowing men to feel secure; in regard to all the worship that is borrowed from the glittering pomp of sensuous paganism, and everything that compromises the equality of all believers under the one Master—that these are nothing but a defiling of our holy temple? And what a distracted condition was that of the Christian world so long as the warfare on this matter went on!—a warfare that was only ended by a schism which still continues, and makes itself from time to time more sharply felt; and the end of which we cannot forecast! Yet even in this case the Lord has spoken the same word of power, "One Lord, one Spirit, one baptism, one God and Father of us all." At this watchword of the apostle, for unity in the Spirit by the bond of peace, a halt was bound to be made; this barrier could not be forced; before it even those waves of strife were compelled to subside.

Oh, what comfort for the future is warranted to us by such a retrospect! what comfort both in view of that which lies directly before us, and for the more distant future! All the forces that have ever been roused to strife and contention against each other, not only still exist among men, but are still far from being bound in an indissoluble union. On the contrary, as the summit of perfection has in no respect been reached, the same occasions still present themselves from time to time, now for one force, now for another, to break out, and with destructive power to overpass their boundaries, so that the Lord must again draw them within their lines, and prescribe bounds and limits. And even in the Church of Christ—nay, within the borders of our own Church—the thing that has been still is. Vanity still stirs up rivalry in connection with men's different gifts; and the great diversity of views and opinions, instead of throwing increasing light on each, and helping men towards the truth in mutual love, still stimulates them to passionate contention, through their narrow and partial reliance on their own investigations on the one side, or the traditions of the elders on the other. Be it so! Even with these things in prospect we will look forward cheerfully to the future. The Lord has hitherto appointed limits in the natural world; and in the time to come that world will not deviate from His rule, according to which temporary disturbances are ever becoming of less significance. He has hitherto set limits to every outbreak of human passions; to all the complications that have arisen from men's conflicting dispositions and wishes, up to the present time; He has thrown over the kingdom of grace the defence that He promised to Him whom He set on His right hand; and He will do so still in the future. And this is not all. Out of every apparent convulsion Nature has come forth into more fixed order, and more receptive to the formative influences of man. All the often-recurring ruptures and wars have brought the relations of the nations to each other, as well as the internal relations of each people, into such a form, that their brotherly connection comes out more distinctly, and peace and concord are gaining a firmer footing and more enduring power. After every display of the overweening extravagances of the human mind, the chasm between what is evolved out of its own depths, and what is produced in devoutly exercised spirits by the power of the divine Word, is gradually becoming less. Through all the sufferings of the Christian Church, she has fought her way to a blessed liberation from the bondage of human authority, and to a clearer light of truth. And so it will be with all the troubles that may be before us in the future. God the Lord will set bounds and limits to them with the same result as before, and not without an equal blessing; and we may indulge the special hope that the Church of God, although passing through many forms of strife and division, will, as the salt of the earth, be ever attaining a closer likeness to the perfection of Him in whom, as the express image of God, there can be nothing discordant, but all is holy unity and blessed peace.

II. But we are to find in the consideration of this truth,

not only our comfort for the future, but our direction and the law of our life, for this and for every year which the Lord is still pleased in His grace to grant us on earth.

But we need to be on our guard in this matter against two forms of error. Men are often inclined, with an only too easy indifference, to accept it as a settled thing that the ways of the Most High are unsearchable. Out of this easy acquiescence the Lord thundered Job by the power of His sublime discourse. When men's views on this point are in some degree corrected, and they allow themselves to be persuaded that though they cannot understand God's doings in detail, or all at once—in which sense we may say everything is unsearchable to us—yet that at least in the great, general course of human affairs, they do see, though but as in a glass darkly, something of the beneficent rule and glorious wisdom of the Most High, in connection with all the struggles and commotions in this world; when this point is reached, most men are apt to fall into error, which takes with some the form of a culpable carelessness in regard to their own conduct; with others, that of an entirely passive expectation of coming events.

The latter class, when they see excess and overbearing pride bearing sway in the circle in which they move, and outbreaks of hostile and excited passions—though they are not without anxiety and concern as to how far the evil may have power to go, and all that may be ruined or retarded by it—yet console themselves with the thought that the Lord holds the reins over all, and directs in such a way that they may hold themselves entirely aloof, and regard themselves as not at all called on to co-operate in those divine plans. But for this comforting thought they would probably have taken some action, but now they wish to be mere spectators of what the Lord may bring about, as if in regard to human things, He carried out His purposes otherwise than by means of human instruments. The former class are persons who, if they believed that human instrumentality alone came into play, would perhaps often be alarmed at the manner in which they yield to their depraved inclinations; but they cherish the thought that the Lord Himself appoints bounds and limits, and restores order after confusion; and therefore they hold themselves no longer bound to feel any anxiety about the consequences of their acts, but think that, for their part, they can all the more readily follow, without measure or rule, the desires of their own mind. For, according to their theory, even though they could do no otherwise than obey the impulse of inward inclination and external necessity, the Most High will no doubt see to it that the consequences are neither more nor less than what He has determined. But what can we call this but a criminal indifference as to whether the will of God is to be done through us with our own will, or against it? And yet this is just what makes the essential difference between those who are God's servants and friends, and those who are only His slaves—involuntary and unconscious instruments. What can we call it but criminal indifference as to whether the things we desire belong to what God will establish and maintain, or to what He can only suppress and destroy? And yet in the one case we belong, by our will, to the kingdom of God; in the other case, to the world.

And to return to that class of persons who—while recognising God as the upholder and mover of all, who out of everything can bring good—are yet pleased to wait in slothful inaction for what may happen, without caring to take a share in His work—have they not cause to charge themselves with knowing God and seeing Him, only apart from themselves?

So let it never be with us!—us who claim to be not far from God, but in Him to live and move and have our being; not so with us, who have not merely a God working apart from us, but to whom Christ has promised to come, and with the Father take up His abode in our hearts! And if it is this very Father in heaven who appoints to everything its just limits and appropriate law, and if He has given us of His Spirit, manifestly this cannot but have the effect of leading us also to endeavour to maintain and restore limits and law everywhere. First, in the kingdom of Nature; for when, in the beginning, the Most High made over the earth, with all that breathes and moves on it, to the first parents of our race, it was His design that man should subdue it, and have dominion over it. Thus we ourselves are to be the standard of all earthly things; their relation to us is to be brought out in all circumstances, and is to be the true law of their being, and to this we are to direct our efforts. And if the Lord should again, for the moment, set free the forces of Nature from this law which is ordinarily in operation, so that they overpass the bounds appointed to them, and lay in ruins, more or less of the works of men, then what is the only wise and fitting course? Not, surely, to sit calmly waiting to see what the issue may be; still less to allow ourselves foolishly to be seduced into irregularity and strife, throwing it over on the Lord to restore, as He may please, the old state of things out of the new disorders. No; all such events should be a new call to us to bring our measure and rule to bear more powerfully on external Nature, to establish more and more the dominion of mind over it, and to impress on it ever more deeply the stamp of that dominion; in short, to subdue it more and more, by every means, under the spiritual power of man, whom the Most High Himself has appointed as its ruler. The more we unite our powers on every such occasion, in this new year; the more faithfully we support each other in this work, each one with the gift that he has received, whether it be clear insight into affairs, or power over minds, or abundance of outward means; so much the more shall we glorify the Name of the Most High, by making progress in fulfilling the great vocation to which He has called us.

But this is no doubt only the outside view of the subject, that to which the better educated part of the community, who decide the action of the rest, are naturally prompted by the well-understood motive of personal advantage, or the most careful calculation as to the best means of securing what is required by their social life, which is constantly becoming more artificial and complex, as well as mutually dependent. Much more should we be concerned to keep rule and order in the spiritual world, and generally where man has to do with man. Nowhere should we be able to look on idly at men wandering away into error. Wherever the restless excitement and inflamed passions of the human soul have broken out in fury; where selfishness and lust of power have engaged in conflict with the right and good, and are reaching the point of tyranny; there we are to interpose: wherever arrogance and violence work hand in hand with cowardice and servility, in the most mischievous alliance that can be formed against right and truth, we must, as a matter of course, come openly and boldly forward. Only we are to do this, not at all in the way of bringing to bear a force equally lawless and out of bounds, though of an opposite kind; but in this way, that by our whole life, by our opinions and modes of action, we really and truly represent law and order. And not only so: the spirit of order, that is a vital principle in us, should make us quick to detect the very first indications of the approach of a condition of things that in its consummation annihilates safe boundaries, and threatens to endanger and destroy all that promotes and preserves social life. But even without such premonitions, and without a definite purpose on our part, every one of us ought, in the circle of his work and of his social relations, so to contribute to the maintaining and strengthening of rule and order, that efforts in the opposite direction are restrained beforehand. Well for that community—and for such a community alone—in every rank of which there is a goodly number of those who, by their manner of life and the whole tone of their daily conduct, serve as a mighty voice of God, sounding out on every side the cry, "Hitherto and no further: here shall the proud waves be broken!"

But, my friends, if we are in earnest in this matter—and what could more nearly concern us on such a day as this?—if we really long that in each new year of our lives these principles should come more powerfully into action, we must guard with special care against what happens only too easily, allowing ourselves to be carried away either by the violent or the more insidious evil ways of men; and so, perhaps with the best intentions, giving vent to our feelings in an extravagant way, which it becomes needful for the Lord to check. For nothing can have more disastrous results than our attempting to overcome evil, not with good, but with counter-evil, and, in contending for law and order, ourselves going beyond what is lawful. But how easily do many, even of the best people, fall into this mistake! Indeed, we may as well say plainly, we shall only be safe from such errors in so far as we live fully and heartily in the new creation to which, God be thanked, we all belong, and obey the Spirit who rules in that creation. For only through this Spirit has the Lord caused His eternal and holy laws to find an entirely natural soil in the human soul. The Spirit who in our hearts cries, "Abba, Father," the Spirit who is at once the Spirit of sonship and the Spirit of liberty, He alone it is who brings us thoroughly into accord with that inward character of the divine government in human affairs, by virtue of which everything passionate and ungoverned must be opposed, so that law and order may be everywhere restored. But where the power of this Spirit of Christianity is not yet felt, even the rational desire to extend knowledge is not pure love of truth, for many side issues find a place; and even the most zealous and self-sacrificing public spirit is, in that case, still a selfish feeling, seeing that it does not embrace the whole human family, and is therefore still liable to be swayed by passion or even by hostility. Nothing but the universal love and the pure truth taught by the Spirit of God can make men wholly free.

But how can we possibly count on maintaining rule and order, by means of a pure and vigorous life as new creatures, in the whole world of men, even among those whose hearts are, alas, still closed against the Spirit of God, who desires to dwell in all,—how, I say, can we do this, unless this Spirit in the first place demonstrates by actual fact, in the Christian Church itself, the blessed power of overcoming all inferior motives, that the Lord's beneficent rule and order may be upheld? How shall we do it unless the Church is more and more getting rid of the delusion that the profit and honour of one may be shame and loss to another; and all are becoming more and more united in one Spirit, with a common aim; unless each seeks the good of the rest without fearing to lose his own in doing so; unless there is the most joyful and confident seeking of the truth in love, so that love may have the glorious courage to be everywhere and always true and only true? For only thus, we are well assured, is that blessedness advanced, which the Lord came to bring, and in this way alone are men more and more freed from the influence of every meaner power, which makes them in reality weary and heavy laden.

For this end, my friends, the Lord opens to us all another year of forbearance and grace. If, during its course, the comforting truths that furnished the first part of our meditation constantly confirm us in the resolutions that have occupied our later thoughts, we shall employ this year according to the holy will of God. Let us, for this purpose, seek after all spiritual gifts, in so far as we are able to stir them up and cultivate them in ourselves; for all have the power, if they will use it rightly, to maintain and restore rule and order in their own minds. And as to those gifts that seem to be denied to ourselves, let us not only rejoice heartily when we find them in others, but hold such persons in honour, and protect and further them in their operations as we alone can; for a thorough co-operation of all faculties and gifts of the Spirit is necessary, if suitable resistance is to be made where there are proud waves to be broken. But only in the proportion in which we allow the one Spirit, from whom come at once the gifts and the knowledge to use them rightly, to have undisturbed control; only in so far shall we be, each for himself and for the community, a pure example of divine moderation and eternal order.

As the divine Spirit who moved on the face of the waters established law and order in the natural world, so that those conditions are only developed more fully through all disturbances and warring forces; so when Christ appeared and His Spirit was poured out on all flesh, the eternal foundations of law and order were laid for the disordered spiritual world. Here also they will go on developing; each period as it passes will bear witness to their growing power; and as often as a new period begins, all in whom this Spirit lives and works should have this in view. But this Spirit is none other than the Spirit of love. And therefore the apostle, after exhorting Christians, as I have just been doing, to seek after all spiritual gifts, and most earnestly after the best, said rightly, in reference to love, that he would show them a more excellent way; for without love all the rest is worthless. And as those gifts are certainly perfect gifts, and the more richly any community is endowed with them the better times they may expect, love is even in this case the only bond of perfectness, because by love alone are those perfect gifts so united and kept in union that each fills up its appropriate measure, but never goes beyond it. Think of what spiritual gift you will; without love, it will either lie dormant in the soul like a dead faculty, or, once awakened, it will need only some slight provocation to exalt itself beyond the bounds of friendly concord with the rest. But love is this bond because love is itself the power that calls forth divine law and order. For it was through law and order that God, in His love, meant to reveal Himself in the creation of the world; and it is to love we owe the law and order of the new creation. Rule and limits must be set to all things else, but love, that produces and includes both, has no need to be so restrained. Love needs no rule, for she is not unruly; she has no proud waves that must be broken, for she envies not, is not puffed up, but is long-suffering and meek; she seeks not her own, and is not easily provoked (and what could raise more wild and foaming waves than that ?), but beareth all things, because she hopeth all things. Therefore if, in the new year we are entering on to-day, love only dwells ever more richly among us, then the love of Christ, which is the source of all Christian brotherly love, will, on the one hand, constrain us to promote, by every means, thorough harmony and cheerful co-operation in every good work. And so it will come to pass more and more that, without great noise and battle drowning the voice of Christ; by a gentle but irresistible power—the power that belongs to the creating and upholding word of God alone—all threatening waves will be broken, and all hearts so bound together by this mysterious and yet unmistakable power, that wherever in the spiritual world anything still rises in rebellion, it may find no solid support; and the swollen streams in separate places may never again increase to a general and destroying flood. And on the other hand each of us will experience, in himself and in our whole community, fewer and fewer interruptions of the inward peace which the Lord left to His people; and there will more and more rarely occur such seasons of disturbance, that even to His own Church the Lord must address these words—words of healing, it is true, but still always the threatening words of a judge, "Hitherto, and no further; here shall thy proud waves be stayed."

Let us then, with such comfort and such purposes, enter with cheerful courage on this new year of our lives. This year, like the rest—let us not deceive ourselves—will bring to us many occasions on which we shall find it needful to say, remembering with hope and confidence the words of our text; these waves also will find their boundary, and the limit which the Lord has appointed them. And if we are far from seeing how this can be, let us only, in the strength of love which rejoices in the truth, not be found wanting in our service to God; let us bear witness to the Lord's will whenever a favourable door is opened to us, and seek to overcome evil with good, and to hush the tempest with words of peace: and thus shall we also be fellow-workers, and in a similar way, though it may be only in a small degree, with Him who commanded the winds and the sea. And so it will come about that all the storms will be only external to us, while in our spiritual house there will only be heard the rushing of the Spirit, bearing witness with our spirits, that we, who are faithful according to law and order, as the Son was faithful in all His house, are the children of God. And this house itself will prove to be like that one which, though the floods come and the winds blow, and beat upon it, stands immovable, being founded on the true rock. Amen.

Prayer.

Even so, Almighty God and Father, we humble ourselves before Thy throne at the beginning of a new year that Thou givest us to use in Thy service, and in advancing Thy kingdom. Thou who restrainest and measurest all things, and under whose government nothing can happen but according to Thy command, wilt reveal in this year also Thy power and Thy wisdom, by all Thy dealings, to those who take pleasure in Thy ways, and whose eyesight is clear to behold Thy works, and their ears open to hear Thy holy voice. Oh, let that voice speak to us ever more distinctly from Thy written Word, and from the depths of our hearts, where Thou hast given Thy Spirit to dwell. Oh, that we might hear it ever more clearly, and follow it in loyal obedience more than hitherto, so that we should find the right measure of things without contention, and should live without times of disturbance and disorder in the kingdom which Thy Son has founded. To this end we commend to Thee, for this new year, all Christians on earth, and especially our evangelical Church. Build her up more and more, through the operation of Thy Spirit, into a Church well-pleasing to Thee! Let the light of the gospel be by her means ever shining brighter and further, that many may be awakened and born again to the new life, who are still sitting in the darkness and shadow of death! Glorify Thy Son more and more in all those who profess His name, and let the Spirit of order and of peace rule everywhere in the Christian Church! To this end grant Thy blessing on the bond of love and fellowship which unites Thy people, on the preaching of Thy Word, and on the distribution of the memorials of Thy Son.

We specially commend to Thee also, for this year, our beloved Fatherland. Bless the king, the crown prince and his consort, and the whole royal House. May that House be in this year an equally blessed and beautiful example of Christian piety, so that all loyal subjects may rejoice in seeing its undisturbed and ever-increasing prosperity. Continue to the king the enlightening and the support of Thy Spirit, for the fulfilment of the great duty which Thou hast laid upon him. Surround him with faithful and zealous ministers, who understand how to help him and to carry out what is right and well-pleasing to Thee. Keep all his subjects loyal and obedient throughout the kingdom Thou hast given him; so that under his protection Christian churches may rise up everywhere, and that we may be always coming nearer to our common aim of likeness to our Saviour. We likewise, gracious God and Father, commend to Thy special care the training of the young, and the Christian households throughout our Fatherland, and in this city; that so every family that guides its affairs according to Thy will, may have the sense of Thy good pleasure within, and may shine as a helpful example to those without. Yea, do Thou bless each one in that calling to which Thou hast guided him; so that we all may have the happy experience that we also can contribute something to the advancement of Thy kingdom, by wise use of the talent which Thou hast entrusted to us; and that from one year to another each of us, as a faithful servant of Thine, may be able to be set over more. And for those to whom, in the course of this year, Thou hast appointed sorrow and adversities, take Thou a loving concern when they seek refuge with Thee; and let us all experience, more and more, that in the measure which Thou appointest to all things, the purpose of Thy fatherly love is that our souls, for which Thou hast so graciously cared, may be more and more attaining to the right stature, and that for this very reason all things must work for the best to those who trust in Thee and love Thee. Amen.

XIII.

THE LAST LOOK AT LIFE.

(*Passion Sermon.*)

TEXT: JOHN xix. 30. "When Jesus therefore had received the vinegar, He said, It is finished."

THESE greatest and most glorious of the last words of our Saviour on the cross come immediately after those which are apparently of the least significance and importance. The Lord said, "I thirst;" then the moistened sponge was handed to Him; and when He had received the soothing, though not pleasant draught, He cried, "It is finished." And we must not break the connection of these two sayings, for the apostle has joined them most closely by placing just before his report of them the words, "When Jesus saw that all things were now finished, that the Scripture might be accomplished." Now if the former is the least important of the Saviour's last words, seeing that, considered in itself, it concerns merely the satisfying of a bodily need; the latter is indisputably the greatest of all those words; it is the saying which has always been, as it were, the anchor for the faith of Christians; the word in which this truth is perfectly proved and made glorious to them; that according to the divine counsel, salvation could be won for men in no other way than this; that He who was sent into the world for their salvation should be obedient even to the death of the cross. But if we direct our attention to this great word alone, we are overpowered by the infinity of the subject, and we have reason to be glad that the very apostle who has preserved this word for us has also left us a key to it, which gives our thoughts a more definite direction. Such a key we find in those preceding words, "When Jesus saw that all things were finished, that the Scriptures might be fulfilled, He said, I thirst." John knew that the soul of the Saviour was engaged in thus comparing all that had so far befallen Him, with the divine promises, as they were uttered through the whole series of revelations in the written word of God; and as He thus set promise and fulfilment side by side, and so became conscious in a human way of the completion of the divine purpose, He cried, "It is finished."

Of course at that moment everything was not yet finished. As our redemption from sin and our justification before God must go together; so also it was necessary that He who needed to die there for our sin should be raised again for our justification. As the fact that the disciples saw the Father only in Him, was connected with this, that when He left the world He returned to the Father; so also the fact that He loved the disciples implied that He could not leave them orphans, but must send them another Comforter who should abide with them, and after them with us also; even the Spirit of truth. But the spiritual eye of the Saviour saw everything finished in the sacred moment of His death; and for this reason that moment is the central point of our faith. For by His obedience unto death He obtained for us the life-giving Spirit; in that He suffered, He has been crowned with glory and honour. Therefore if in the moment of His death He could say, in this sense, "It is finished," He must have regarded His death in that infinite connection which begins with the first promise given to fallen man concerning the seed of the woman, and reaches forward into that eternity in which

He will bring to the Father all those whom the Father has given Him, that they may share in the praise and glory with which He has been crowned. All this is no doubt perfectly true; but let us return to the definite direction that the apostle gives us, and confine ourselves to considering this word chiefly as the final look at a past life; and let us, especially in the first place, see in it as the Saviour did, the accomplishment of His destiny during this earthly life; and secondly, apply the great word of the Lord, as our heart constrains us to do, to ourselves.

I. As the Saviour said so often during His life that the Son of Man did nothing of Himself, but did the things that He saw with the Father, and spoke the words that He heard from Him; we must naturally suppose that He was constantly engaged in the profoundest meditation on the ways of God; and that, raised as He was above all human weakness of mind, it was so still, even in these last painful hours of His life; and thus all words relating to Himself in the Divine revelations of the Old Testament were present to His soul. We have already had an example of this in His earlier words on the cross; when even the pains and weakness that He had to endure recalled to His remembrance words of holy Scripture, and He applied one and another of them to His own circumstances. But certainly we should ill understand Him, if we believed that it was these personal details in which He found everything finished that the Scriptures might be fulfilled. That He was hanging there on the cross, surrounded by the powerful enemies who had brought about His death; that His bones were consumed and His tongue clave to His jaws; that He saw His clothes shared among the soldiers and lots cast for His coat;—the contemplation of separate incidents like these, and the comparing of them with the words of the Psalm, might indeed to a certain extent, and perhaps more than would have been the case with another, turn away the attention of the suffering Saviour from the torturing sense of physical pain; but to occupy entirely His soul, that was ever bent on greater things, was what those outward details could not do; nor was it those things on account of which He cried with such satisfaction, "It is finished."

If then we must seek for greater things, let us not give the reins to our own imaginations, which certainly would not succeed in understanding Christ; rather let us speak of such words of Scripture as His disciples, in speaking of the essential facts of His life, apply to Him with inspired unanimity, and which must now have come most naturally before His mind. Now where could we find His whole office and work in relation to the ruined and weakened human race more perfectly expressed than, in the first place, in those words of the prophet, in which one of the evangelists describes to us the Saviour's whole manner of dealing—I mean those words, as tender as they are strong, "He will not break the bruised reed, and the smoking flax will He not quench"? These are words which, through what He had done throughout His life of duty, and what He was now doing in dying, were now being fulfilled to the whole human race, which might well be regarded as only a bruised reed and an expiring taper; so that even in the hour of death, yes, dying there alone, He could yet feel called on to praise and glorify the name of His Father in the great congregation; like him whose words He used when He said; "My God, why hast Thou forsaken me." And thus He also found that other word perfectly fulfilled, which His disciples universally apply to Him; that He took upon Him our sicknesses and that through His pains we are healed;—it was this which now in the last look at His life He saw finished, that the Scriptures might be fulfilled.

But we cannot properly feel the full value of this last word of Christ's, unless we can transport ourselves in thought into that time, and into the state of mind of all those who clung to the Lord with a faith that was still weak and imperfect. When He made His entry into the capital of His nation, coming to the feast which was to be the feast of His own death and resurrection, and was hailed by thousands as He who came in the name of the Lord, the promised Son of David; when the palms, the emblem of the victorious king who with victory brought peace, were strewn before His feet; what kind of expectations were probably stirring in the minds of that joy-intoxicated multitude, that streamed in from all directions to share in this triumphal entry? For the most part, unhappily, expectations of an external glory and power; expectations which the Saviour had never encouraged, and which He had not come to fulfil. And even His disciples, though many words must have lived in their remembrance by which the Saviour had often, indeed on every occasion, sought to turn away their hopes and their love from the glory of this world, and had pointed them to that spiritual world which would be subject to Him as its Lord and Master;—even they were not yet quite sure whether in some way, though perhaps further off in the future, an outward power and authority might not be the means of setting up this kingdom in its full splendour; and even they were perhaps carried away by the enthusiasm of the people in those glorious days to share in such earthly expectations. But the palms that were then strewn before the Saviour's feet were now first wound into the true, glorious victor-wreath around His dying head, when all that was at that time said in human misunderstanding was fulfilled in its real, spiritual sense, according to the secret counsel and purpose of God. Thus, on the cross, in His death, Christ was altogether He who came in the name of the Lord, and thus and no otherwise was He to be magnified and blessed from that moment to all eternity. It was thus also that the apostle felt it, who has recorded this word for us; and therefore he says, When

Jesus saw that all was finished, that the Scripture might be fulfilled. So that the Scripture was now completely fulfilled in Him, and, erroneously as the great majority had always interpreted these glorious words of prophetic men, their true import would now be better apprehended by all; and therefore, in this sense also, all was finished, that the Scripture might be fulfilled; and then He bore testimony to Himself in that great word, which, uttered now and here, must have made His disciples abandon for ever all their false earthly expectations;—then He exclaimed, "It is finished"! And now they knew also that seeing they could not fare better than their Lord and Master, they too could fulfil their vocation only through suffering and tribulation, and so enter into the kingdom of His glory; now they knew that flesh and blood cannot inherit the kingdom of God; for the flesh and blood of Christ had fastened Him to the cross, and that therefore they were now to know no man according to the flesh; now they knew that His whole work was a purely spiritual work, and that His authority, for which they were to fight and which they were to extend, was no other than that which He, as the Crucified, sets up for Himself in the hearts of the children of men.

But there is one thing more that we must not overlook. When the Saviour, in this connection with the fulfilling of Scripture, uttered the words, "It is finished," we cannot but feel that the reference is not only, nor indeed even chiefly, to what He has *done;* that He is not merely looking back on what He might regard as His own work; but what He very specially points to is what has *been done* in and through Him. It was not His own work, and He could not mean in these words to represent it as such, that He had so early reached the goal of His great destiny; but it was the fulfilment of the divine decree, through the divine leading and foreknowledge. His death was the great moment for which all human things from the beginning of our race had been bound to work together; it was indicated long before through manifold pictures of the sufferings of God's servants in an evil world; and who could question that those pictures, wherever they are found, contained the expression of a knowledge that came from above, although as yet seen only in a very feeble and glimmering light? But those representations became more and more distinct in the sacred discourses of men who were filled with the divine Spirit; and now they were being realized; for the appearing of the Saviour was an offence and foolishness to the perversity of the human heart; and this perversity was increased to spite and malignity by the faith in the Saviour and love to Him that began to be manifested. It was what was done to Him He was now chiefly looking at. His life, as regarded work, He had closed already with that sublime prayer which this same evangelist has preserved for us, in which He gives account to His Father of how He had glorified Him, the Father, through His whole life, and at the same time declares His hope that now the Father will also glorify the Son. But confidently as He could at that time present Himself before God with those whom the Father had given Him and chosen out of the world, perfectly conscious as He was of duty fully and purely fulfilled, it was not then that He spoke the great word, "It is finished." But if, speaking exactly, He *did* nothing more after that, what are we to understand by His refraining until now from saying, "It is finished"? Most evidently this: that the divine counsel concerning a man is never accomplished through that alone which the man does; and this holds good even of Him, the one gracious Man, of Him, the only righteous One. The counsel of God is always fulfilled through the working together of all the forces which the Most High sets in operation; not only those of which we can say, in a restricted sense, that He gives both the will and the accomplishment, but those also of which we like best to think that He merely says to them, Hitherto, and no further. The Divine counsel is only fulfilled through that which is utterly hidden from us—the reciprocal influence of all times and all spaces; one day must tell it to another, the earth to the heavens, and the heavens again to the earth; from everything, taken together, that the individual man has power to do, and does, though never from that alone, there results that of which it can be said, "It is finished." This word of the Lord therefore indicates to us that, in His last great moments, He forgot, or set in the background, even His own work on the earth, which for this very reason He had previously wound up, in order again to direct His thoughts solely to the work of His Father in heaven. That which filled up the last moment of His human life was this—He was absorbed in contemplating the mystery of the divine counsels; so that even this great act of His departure, though, in another aspect, it was emphatically His own deed and His holiest service, He preferred to regard as what had been not only foretold but prepared, as what was now directly accomplished only through the divine wisdom and its leadings, working together to this end.

II. Now if this is the right idea of the state of mind in which the Saviour spoke the words of our text; if we recognise even in this greatest and most important of His last words the profound humility of Him who, though He was in the form of God and thought it no robbery to be equal with God, yet in the last hour of His life, putting in the shade His own deed and service, rested and rejoiced only in this, that the counsel of His Father was being fulfilled, how can we then think of applying this word to ourselves, and how shall I redeem the promise that I have given for the second part of our meditation? Were it a question merely of the active life, of the human influence of the Saviour, even then we might well ask, what are we in comparison with

Him, and how could any one of us think of comparing himself with Him? And yet in that case the application to ourselves might be an easier thing. For when Christ, as our High Priest, in that prayer to which I have already referred, closed His account with His heavenly Father, it was with Him just as with other children of men. Although God was in Him, reconciling the world to Himself, yet that world still lay before His eyes unreconciled, enveloped in the darkness and shadow of death; and He presented to His Father only some few who had attached themselves to Him in faith and love as the fruit of His life-work, as those who were chosen out of the world, so that He could say with a glad heart, "They are not of the world, even as I am not of the world; they have heard and believed Thy word that I have come forth from Thee." And even then He had to mourn over a lost sheep, so that even in His own immediate circle what He Himself had said was fulfilled, that all are not chosen who are called; and thus He also experienced that in direct influence on men there is no perfect and invariable success. Then He also needed to come with prayer to His heavenly Father for the work from which He was now, as to His human agency, to withdraw His hand; and He thus acknowledged that though in another and a higher sense He had done all, yet the direct results were only now beginning, and that it was needful for the Father to complete what the Son could only initiate. In all this, therefore, my friends, we should find a great deal that we could apply to ourselves, if the question concerned the last converse of the soul with God before quitting this earthly scene. Each of us has those whom the Lord has given us, whom we are to present to Him as chosen out of the world; and he who, though feeling his own weakness, has faithfully and wisely carried on the work of the Lord on earth, desiring nothing besides, will also be able to say in faith, "Here am I, Father, and those whom Thou hast given me." And to him who, like the Saviour, has to mourn over disappointed hopes, if one or another forcibly tears himself away from the loving and guiding hand, in spite of all guarding and upholding love, to him there will assuredly not be wanting such a comfort as this, "that the Scripture might be fulfilled."

But this is not exactly the question with which we are concerned here in this great word of the Lord; it is rather as to what befel Him so that all that was written of Him might be fulfilled, and nothing left undone. And what kind of a comparison can we institute here? Do the Scriptures—which, as He Himself said, testify of Him in every page, if the Spirit of God enlightens the eyes of the reader—those Scriptures in which He was promised, from the beginning, and which He had in view as fulfilled in Himself when He spoke the word, It is finished—do those Scriptures speak also of us, my friends? Can we also, at the close of our life, cast such a look into the past as to be able to rejoice that the Scriptures are fulfilled in us? Oh, doubtless, they speak of us all! Do they not say, the whole of you are sinners, and come short of the praise that you should have with God? That, you see, is the first Scripture which is fulfilled in us all; and if we imagine our eye directed, in the last hours of our life, to the time that will then be past, and to Him in whom glory to God and to the divine will is portrayed to us all, ah, then each of us will say, Now I am dying; this Scripture is fulfilled in me! But the Scriptures say also, Christ is become to us wisdom and righteousness and sanctification. Well, then, he who can glory in the grace of the Lord, who has not been deaf to the voice of His Spirit, who finds himself in that living fellowship with Christ in which all things are common to Christ and him, and in his last moments can look back on such a life, lived in faith on the Son of God, and Christ living in him,—to him this Scripture is the most genuine expression of his consciousness of what has formed the full and complete value of his life. For whatever cannot be included under this, forms no part of the value of his life; and in the glad assurance that this Scripture, this edifying, saving Scripture, is fulfilled even in him, he will then be able to say, It is finished.

But let us not stop short, my friends, at the most general point of our faith, at the consciousness of salvation which is involved in fellowship with the Saviour; for in that fellowship (though assuredly never but through and with Him) we can certainly follow out still further the analogy between this word from His lips, and our experience in the moment of our departure; or rather, in the last look at our past life that we may be permitted to take with as entire consciousness as the Saviour had. For the whole time of the Saviour's presence on earth, but very specially the great moment in which He completed, by His death, the work of reconciling the world to God, was, to an extent in which it can be said of no other time, the great point of transition, at which two different periods divided: the time of longing desire and hopeful anticipation, and the time of blessed fulfilment and of life-giving faith, creating men anew to works of love. But we also, as a whole, yea, every one of us, mean and obscure as our existence in the world may be, are in a similar way included in the great connected plan of the divine dealings. For the same thing is always occurring over again in the Church of the Lord, only in less degrees. When Christ said to His disciples that He had yet many things to say to them, but they could not bear them now, and referred them to the Spirit whom He would send to them, He in fact introduced even for them a time of longing and anticipation, the fulfilment of which was not to come until later. And everything in the present time which we recognise as deficiency and imperfection stirs us to longing and anticipation, and these are followed by fulfilment. Now if this goes on until we have attained to the fulness of a perfect man in Christ—and until then we cannot cease to wish and hope—we are all so situated that longing and fulfilment alternate; and no sooner is one desire fulfilled, though always in only an imperfect way, than we long after something else. But to this still imperfect state of fulfilment something connected with the good pleasure and will of God is to be added by each living generation, leaving to the young only its unfulfilled aims; and to this work of the men of his time, every one who accounts himself a living member of this God-sanctified body is to contribute his share. Now as all that was to take place had not yet actually occurred when the Saviour cried, "It is finished," so in our case, also, we may, with the same faith which we see in Him who is the Author and Perfecter of ours, regard that which we have still to meet as included in what has already taken place. And just in the same way, when we come to our last look at the life we have spent, our thoughts may rest with heartfelt thankfulness to God, on what has been done, not certainly through our own merit, for that is the Lord's alone, nor by our work exclusively, for our outward position and a great deal that does not depend on us has always some part in it; but still, on what has been brought, through our presence, our agency, our indirect influence in many and divers ways, to its sole completion; or has, at least, gone on from being a wish and anticipation to the beginning of fulfilment. And we are to regard all this taken together, and indeed estimate it, as that which our natural characteristics, as well as the circumstances in which God has placed us, indicated from the first as our work; and in our last look at life we shall praise God with equal humility and gratitude that what He apportioned to us, according to His wisdom, as our day's work, is actually accomplished. We shall acknowledge humbly how much we have found it needful to avail ourselves of from without, in order to accomplish even the little that we have actually done; how many obstacles there were that could only have been removed through favourable circumstances or by the help of others; so that we may seek in vain anywhere for work that is exclusively our own. But if God will, we shall then also have to acknowledge thankfully how even in us, though it may be but in small measure, the beautiful word of Scripture has been fulfilled, that all the gifts of the Spirit in the Church are manifested for the common good; and that as the Scripture sets before us the fruits of the Spirit in the delightful group of love, joy, peace, long-suffering, gentleness, goodness, faith, meekness, purity; some of those fruits, though not perhaps perfectly ripened, nor of the choicest beauty, have grown up in the garden of our heart. It was no doubt Christ alone in whom everything belonging to the image of God in this human nature developed ever increasingly and without interruption, in the fairest symmetry; and the time at which He appeared, the circumstances amidst which He lived, contributed nothing to this; they only helped to make it possible for this glory of the only-begotten Son to take effect in the way and measure which the divine wisdom had determined from all eternity. And it was just that divine decree that He counted as accomplished, when, while He was yet on the cross, this glory appeared to Him in its full splendour. With us the case is certainly very different; for none of us will be able to look back on his life without becoming aware of the fluctuating and unsteady progress of his soul. Falls and risings again; the hand bravely laid on the plough and then dubiously withdrawn; the work of God eagerly entered on, and then again the hands hanging feebly down; this and no other is the manner of our spiritual life, only taking different forms in its early bloom and in its gradual coming to maturity; and different also in each according to his natural disposition and his outward circumstances. But however saddening this may be, yet, in another aspect, if at the end of our life we, like Christ, look less at what we ourselves have done, and rather at what, according to God's gracious counsel and foreknowledge has been done in and through us; then we shall be like Him, even in this, that everything at the close of our life will still harmonize in a joyful, "It is finished." For if once the Word of God has been held up before us as the pure mirror of the truth, in which each of us may recognise himself, and we have really looked into it; then we shall feel constrained to testify that though we have once and often forgotten what manner of men we were, yet we have been always drawn to return and look into that mirror anew; and that even our vacillations and falls, our negligence and our evil desires, have served to give us a deeper and clearer self-knowledge, which is one of the greatest possessions that can be granted to us with which to depart hence. If we have once turned away from the universal restlessness of the human race to the true Shepherd and Overseer of our souls, and have experienced that in Him we find rest and refreshing;—if then we have at any time, through the cowardice of the human heart, sought, when something painful threatened us, some other shelter that seemed to lie nearer to us;—or if, in the self-will of our heart, we have ventured alone into seductive pastures; yet our Shepherd has followed and sought us in various ways: and through these changes in our experience we have become the more firmly convinced that protection and safety, as well as comfort and refreshing, are only to be found in union with Him. Have we often, it may be, under the pressure of the world and amidst its obstinate opposition, admitted the thought that the Lord, whose pound, entrusted to us, we are to put out to usury, is a hard Master, who wishes to reap where He has not sown? yet we have been hindered, sometimes in one way, sometimes in another, from utterly burying it, and shall have something, little as it may be, to show, that has been gained by it. Now if through the gracious over-ruling of God, who glorifies him whom He has justified, even our weaknesses and mistakes have not only tended to confirm our own character, but have also been useful to our brethren in the way of doctrine, and warning, and instruction in righteousness,—as indeed we have often ourselves experienced this effect from the weaknesses of others,—then we shall be constrained to acknowledge that true as that other word of Scripture remains, which we shall each of us separately apply to himself, regarding the praise that we ought to have with God; yet to each individual member of the Church of Christ, as well as to the body in which we are united as a whole, that word is also fulfilled, and will always go on being fulfilled, as to our whole life, sufferings and work, that to those who love God, all things must work for good. If we thus some day look back on the life we have spent, when we have reached its close, we shall thankfully and gladly acknowledge that it has been the eternally wise kindness and the compassionate love of the heavenly Father towards all who are called His children, which, through errors and weakness, through joys and sufferings, has bound us ever more closely and at last inseparably to Him, whom indeed we cannot let go if the Scripture is to be fulfilled in us, and in fellowship with whom, and comforted as He himself was, we shall be able to cry, "It is finished." Amen.

XIV.

THE DEATH OF THE SAVIOUR THE END OF ALL SACRIFICES.

(*Good Friday.*)

TEXT: HEB. x. 8–12.

DEEPLY as our feelings may be moved on a day such as this, deeply as our hearts may be affected with a sense of sin, and at the same time filled with thankfulness for the mercy from on high, that planned to save us by God not sparing His own Son, we can only be sure of having found the right and true use of the day, when we bring our thoughts and feelings to the test of Scripture.

We find there a twofold treatment of the supremely important event which we commemorate to-day. The gospel narratives unfold to us the facts of Christ's life and death, setting them before us, each with its own accompanying circumstances; and in every line of their history we see, closely side by side, the clearest light of heavenly love and purity, and the darkest shadow of sin and perversity. Which of us would not gladly linger over this history during this time set apart specially for meditation on the sufferings of Christ? Who would not expect once more to experience the purifying and elevating power of those sacred narratives? And the more we kept in view, in such meditations, the spiritual aspect of the facts, not allowing it to be pushed aside by what is only external, the purer would be the blessing that we derived from such a contemplation of the life of Christ. But the apostles, in their letters to individual brethren as well as to Christian congregations, take this acquaintance with outward facts as a thing for granted; while they seize every opportunity of directing the attention of Christians to the deep, mysterious significance of the death of Christ for our salvation, and to its connection with the great end and purpose of redemption, with the whole of our hopes and our faith. And the more suitable such meditations on the historical facts are for the days preceding this great day, during which no doubt all the pious members of our congregations have been constantly so engaged, not only during our meetings, but in the quiet of private devotion; the more natural it seems to me to turn in this sacred hour to one of those apostolic utterances, and to devote our attention to the deep significance of Christ's death for the salvation of men.

It is very clear, from the whole context of these words, that the sacred writer regards the Saviour's death as the real transition point at which the old covenant terminated and the new covenant of God with man began. While he represents the death of the Saviour as an offering for sin, he at the same time sets it forth, in the words, "through one offering are perfected," as the end of all offerings and all sacrificial services, which, in the times before Christ, formed the essential element both in the worship of the Jewish people, and in the sacred rites, mixed with much delusion and error, of other nations. And we have here set in the sharpest contrast the inadequacy of all former offerings, and that eternal, divine power through which the offering of the Saviour transcends them all, and in so doing has made an end of all offerings. Let us then consider the death of the Saviour in contrast with all other offerings, and as the end of them.

In the earlier part of this chapter the writer had said

that the offerings would have ceased if those who offered them had had no more conscience of sin, but had been cleansed once for all; but through the offerings there was only a remembrance made of sins year by year; the sins themselves, he says in our text, can never, by the repetition of the offerings, be taken away. We shall, therefore, not only get hold of the real meaning of his discourse, but exhaust it as to its essential bearing, if we regard the death of Christ as the termination of all offerings in these two respects: first, because there is no longer need of any other remembrance of sin, to be renewed from day to day and from year to year; secondly, because, sin being really taken away, there is no longer need of any such insufficient offerings.

I. Offerings, then, served at first as a remembrance of sin; but now, since Christ became a sacrifice for sin, there is no longer need for any other remembrance of it.

How was it, then, that all the offerings under the old covenant were a remembrance of sin? In this way—that while the offering was supposed to make satisfaction for individual acts that transgressed the law of the Highest, so that there was no longer cause to fear being reproached or punished for them; at the same time the presenting of the offering was a confession of the guilty act; and by this public presentation each offerer made a remembrance of his sins, of everything in which he had come short of the law. We may only notice here, in passing, what an imperfect system this was. For what, after all, are the single outward acts, in which sin manifests itself, in comparison with sin itself? Nothing but occasional outbreakings of the inward corruption, dependent, in a thousand ways, on external circumstances. If we compare two persons, of whom, on the same day, one has a multitude of such outward offences to repent of and to expiate, while the other can boast of not having committed one, is the latter, on that account, better than the former? By no means! Only he has fallen on a favouring hour, the other on an evil one; and corruption may have just as deep and firm a hold in the soul of the one as in that of the other. For just look at it in this way! How do we suppose a man can single out particular acts that he commits as those which are to be attributed to himself alone? That man may indeed be always right who in his inmost heart ascribes to himself, without reflecting on any one else, a culpable and criminal deed committed by him; but it would be unjust in others to let him settle his account in this manner, and think themselves cleared from all blame of his act, because he imputes it to himself alone; and therefore that man will never be quite wrong who includes others as connected more or less remotely, and often at who can tell what distance of time, with his fault. No, my friends, if we are only in any measure seeking the truth, if we look intelligently into the manifold ways in which the concerns of society are woven into each other, and become aware of all the open and hidden influences that people exercise on each other, we shall be ready to admit that each of us has his share, directly or indirectly, in the sins that appear in others; and that we can by no means consider that our reckoning ends with those which we personally commit. Oh, in very manifold ways,—not only by misleading example and inconsiderate speech, but by easy, lenient judgments, by neglecting to express disapproval, and in many ways besides, we all help to cause sin in others; and we can hardly say that any sin is the sin of one alone. For this reason, then, all remembrance of sin made by the offerings was imperfect and unsatisfactory, because it depended on this division of human responsibility, because it only dealt with sin when it became outwardly manifest, so that there was no true remembrance of inward sin impressed on the mind of the worshipper. And when the apostle says elsewhere that "by the law is the knowledge of sin," he is perfectly right; for this is, in fact, the highest merit that can be ascribed to an external law, although it possesses no power for real amendment; but he could certainly never have meant that the remembrance of sin, provided for by the offerings prescribed in the law, could ever have produced a complete consciousness of sin or a true knowledge of it. No, this is only effected fully by the contemplation of the suffering and dying Saviour. There we have presented to us in one view, in the authors of this death, the full depth of human depravity, and in Him who suffered it, the full glory of the only-begotten Son of the Father; so that we may say with perfect truth that there is no real remembrance of sin but the death of the Lord. In this, sin has accomplished its greatest work; here it shows itself in its full strength and completeness. The apostle John must also have taken this view when he summed up all sin in "the lust of the eyes, and the lust of the flesh, and the pride of life." It was the lust of the eyes, the mistaken tendency of man to be captivated by outward appearance, and by that to estimate character, which caused so many of our Lord's contemporaries to perplex themselves by superficial judgments. What good can come out of Nazareth? Of what consequence can this man be who has not learned the Scriptures in our way? The lust of the flesh, the delight that men take in the transitory blessings of the present life, the striving after distinction and honour in the world, after the securing and increasing of every outward possession, the joy of seeing others dependent on them and of being looked up to by them,—this was what caused the high priest and the elders of his people to agree in the decision. It is better that one man should perish than that the whole constitution, under which we can direct and restrain the people, should come to ruin. And the pride of life,—what is it? It is the pride built on man's presumptuous self-confidence when he imagines that, in his sagacity and experience of life, he has already possessed himself of what is best and most perfect, and therefore holds the powers unsurpassed to which he owes those possessions. Thus nothing better can gain entrance to his mind, and in the pleasant twilight of self-complacency all pure light is scorned and rejected. It was through this pride of life that the wise and powerful of those times did not believe John's announcement of the kingdom of God; and it was because of it that afterwards the secret of the divine counsels remained hidden from them, and could be revealed only to babes. But from this very cause, that the light was hidden from the wise and mighty because of their pride, they were able so to sin against Him who was the centre of all the promises, that they crucified Him. Hence we may truly say that we find, in that which was the cause of the Saviour's death, the most notable example of all that darkens the human soul and keeps men far from the way of truth and salvation: and a remembrance of sin, ineffaceable to all eternity, was recorded in the fact that in the one nation in which the knowledge of the only true God had been preserved, those very persons who should, above all others, have possessed and kept up this knowledge, were sinful and corrupt enough to slay on the cross the Prince of Life and the Lord of Glory. What more can we need as a remembrance of sin? There it stands, once for all, just as much for every individual, as for all times and for the whole human race. For whatever stirrings of sin we still have, whatever in us resists the will of God, of which He was the eternal embodiment, may always be traced to something of that which was the cause of the Lord's death; and thus we must regard all sins as having a share in crucifying Him. And hence every succeeding generation needed, just as little as we, any other remembrance of sin than that which was created by the death of the Lord: and He is thus the end of all offerings; because the sorrowful confession of single sins by means of such sacred observances, and the sorrow and repentance for separate outbreaks of sin, of whatever kind they may be, cannot by any means be compared with the sorrow with which we all, without distinction of better or worse, must be bowed down by this thought, that it was our kindred, men like ourselves, who, through the same corruption that we find in ourselves, crucified the Lord of Glory. A remembrance which thus bears upon everything evil in the human soul, makes every other for ever superfluous. And again, if in connection with distinct sinful acts that we have committed, we prescribe to ourselves, or have prescribed to us by others, certain performances, whether works of love or exercises of devotion; these can never make what is done as if it had not been, nor dry up the fountain of such acts, and therefore can be nothing but a remembrance of sin; so what would this be but to turn back to that imperfect system which has only the shadow instead of the reality? and what would be proved by our doing so, but that we fail to ascribe the due value to the remembrance of sin made by the death of Christ? Let us then use this day's solemn commemoration of that death, to establish ourselves anew on this article of our Church's faith; that even in this respect we have regard to nothing but the perfect sacrifice once finished by Christ on the cross. And let each one whose heart admonishes him to think of the corruption in his own breast, and every one who is still conscious of occasional symptoms of his old sin, cast himself down before the cross of Christ, and there, in the name of Him who was made the offering for sin, beseech the Father to preserve him from ever again, by his lust of the eyes and lust of the flesh and pride of life, crucifying afresh the Prince of Life and Lord of Glory.

II. And as those offerings, often as they were repeated, were always only this imperfect kind of remembrance of sin; so, in the second place, they were quite incapable of taking away sin. But inasmuch as, with the repeated confession of sin they could only renew and keep up the remembrance of it, while its life and strength in the soul remained unchanged, those offerings kept alive the longing for some better help, and the earnest desire that One should appear, even though He must come down from heaven, who should in very deed be able to take away both sin itself and its power. Therefore in saying that the death of the Saviour was the end of all offerings, the author of our epistle specially means that even the sin itself was taken away, and so there was no further need of offerings; as he goes on to say, "Let us draw near with true hearts, in full faith, free from all evil conscience, and made clean."

But how—in what manner and in what sense—sin is taken away through the death of the Saviour—that, my friends, is the great mystery of the fellowship of His death and His life as declared in the Scriptures. For these two positions, that we are buried with Christ in His death, and that we have risen with Him to a new life, cannot be separated from true faith in the Saviour. For what is believing in Him if it is not at least this—acknowledging Him as the promised Deliverer of men, as He who could direct the lost to the right way, and bring life to the dead, because He was Himself the Truth, and because sin had no place in Him. But if we acknowledge Him as all this, how would it be possible that we should not all, just through His death, die to that which caused it? Believers could not have been willing to put the Saviour to death; therefore their faith must constrain them—otherwise it is no faith—to renounce everything that brought Him to the cross. And thus the old man, everything that manifests the power of sin in us, is crucified with Christ.

And not only so; it is just as necessary an effort of our faith in Him, that we receive His *life* as our own, so that we can say with the apostle, "I live, yet not I, but Christ liveth in me." For it belongs to man's nature to desire communion with Him by whose breathing he became a reasonable soul. Even in times of the deepest darkness and corruption, men have not been able entirely to lose sight of the desire to be acquainted with the supreme Being, and to link their existence with His. Rather than leave unsatisfied this highest and most vital need, having once lost the right track, they associated their worship, as the apostle says, "with corruptible images of the creature, and served the creature instead of the Creator." And therefore if, in the foolish fables of paganism, in the gloomiest delusions of idol-worship, nay, even in the unnatural abominations that arose out of it, we cannot fail to recognise this striving and feeling after the divine Being; (although we freely admit there can be no greater pain or horror to an enlightened mind than to see the holiest things represented in so distorted and dishonouring a manner)—if this was so, was it not quite natural that those efforts, partly misguided and partly repressed, should be turned in the right direction when the Father revealed Himself in the Son; when the divine Word became flesh, and the teacher who points to the Father appeared in human form; when the divine Love became visible in the glory of the only-begotten Son, who knew nothing else and lived for nothing else than to labour to communicate to His brethren all that He had received, and to draw them all to Himself and into the one life which is His with the Father? For in truth there was nothing in the human soul beyond this sense of need and unsatisfied longing, that could take the side of the Saviour; there was no real perception of truth, no real inclination towards good. But as it was a part of His work both to communicate such a perception and directly to create such a desire, His mighty, divine influence required no other ally than this sense of need. And thus it came about that those who acknowledged Him by faith not only died with Him as to the old man, but also rose again with Him to a new life;

that is, to a life that was peculiarly His own, but which He gladly shared with them; a life that constantly drew fresh nourishment and strength from every word of wisdom that He spoke, and from every glance of divine compassion and love in His eyes. And these life-giving processes are now made permanent in the Christian Church by the preaching of the Word, and by the divine Spirit, who works by means of it. The works of creation, on the other hand, considered in themselves, although our knowledge of them has largely increased, have not become more efficacious, as experience sufficiently teaches, in making us acquainted with God and leading us to Him than they were long ago; and thus it still always comes to pass that the Father manifests Himself to us only in the Son; and that the mysteriously communicated life comes in the same way, by our rising again with the Saviour to the new life, but only after we have been buried with Him in His death, and therefore always in connection with that death.

Seeing then that in this sense we are crucified with Christ, and with Him have risen to a new life, sin is in truth taken away; for not only the consciousness of it, or as the writer of our text expresses it, the "conscience of sin" is destroyed, but also its guilt is cancelled.

For, as regards the first, we may surely say that he who has died to sin and the law—for both of these had a part in crucifying the Lord—has thereby lost the consciousness of sin thus far, that his will has thrown off its authority, and all participation in it. And he who has risen with the Saviour to a new life, so that Christ alone lives in him and is ever being more fully formed in him, while his former self lives no longer,—he has in so far lost the consciousness of sin, that he has gained the consciousness of something else, of this oneness of life with Christ, who never willed to do anything but the will of His heavenly Father. Now as in Christ Himself there was absolutely no sin, so no consciousness of sin can exist alongside of the consciousness of His life in us. Rather, as the life of Christ was a blessed life, so also our consciousness, in so far as we are united with Him, is only blessedness. For when our will is in thorough harmony with the whole will of God, so far as we can in any way know or conjecture what it is, there can be nothing to disturb or trouble us; while even the weakness that still remains in us, finding no encouragement from our will, is no longer a part of our real life, but rather belongs to the things apart from us against which we are to fight the good fight of faith; and in that fight we feel truly blessed, because we act as God's instruments and in His strength. It is true, therefore, that just in the measure in which Christ lives in us we are free from the "conscience of sin." This is indeed a doctrine of which, on the one hand, we may well say, "Not that I have already attained, but I follow after, if by any means I may attain"; but on the other hand we must admit—and praise God that it is so—it is the deepest, simplest, purest truth even now in the life and heart of the Christian. Union with Christ means for us nothing but blessedness, pure joy in the Lord, closest communion with His and our Father in heaven.

But, it might be said, all this being granted, How is it brought about? How is this new consciousness which expels the "conscience of sin" wrought in us exactly through the death of the Saviour? For manifestly His disciples had faith in Him as the Son of the living God, and took heartfelt delight in the words of life which were at His command alone; and thus, even before His death, had that participation in His life. That is true: but to Himself at least, even from the beginning of His public life and work, the knowledge and the prospect of His death,—of the very death He died, were always present, so that we must say He always acted under the power of His death. That which He could not make His disciples understand until after His resurrection,—that it behoved Christ to suffer these things and to enter into His glory,—was always alike deeply impressed on His own heart, and influenced His words and works throughout His public life. And thus His disciples, long before they distinctly knew about His death, were already living in the power of it. For it was only because He had been pointed out to them from the beginning as "the Lamb of God that taketh away the sin of the world," and because they saw Him, who alone was without sin, thus setting Himself to destroy the sin of the world, that this true and living faith in Him as the Saviour could spring up in the hearts of His disciples. And for us it is still less possible to separate the power of His death from that of His life.

But it is not only the conscience of sin that is taken away when we are crucified with the Lord and risen again with Him to newness of life; the guilt of it is also cancelled; God's verdict about us—the relation to the Highest in which sin had placed us—is reversed. This is the meaning of the words of our text, "Sacrifice and burnt-offerings Thou wouldest not, neither hadst pleasure therein; then hath He said, It is written of me in Thy book that I am come to do Thy will; He taketh away the first that He may establish the second." For that which is taken away is just the system of sacrifices, which could not justify from the guilt of sin. But its guilt consists in this, that "to be carnally minded is enmity against God." Now he who has died with Christ to sin and the law and risen to new life, still lives, it is true, in the flesh,—that he cannot deny, nor will be able to deny throughout his earthly life; but the mind of the flesh is no longer in him, the enmity against God is taken away, and God also loves in the Beloved those to whom the Son, because they believe on His name, has given "power to become the children of God." And when it is said in verse 16 "This is the covenant that I will make with them after those days, that I will put my will into their heart, and write it in their mind," that is just what we have described as the simple and natural effect of our oneness of life with the Saviour. And we desire that you should all note these words, so that no one may understand us as meaning that the guilt of sin can be taken away by any mere wish, however sincere, for amendment. For a wish, even though with no reservation, is still a mere empty and inefficacious thing, and leaves everything in the man as it was, so that God's verdict must also remain the same, and the guilt the same: he who wishes, turns to God with only the lips of his soul, if I may so speak, not with his inmost heart. But to have the will of God written on the heart and mind is something much more than this. In that case all the man's aims and efforts, all his works dictated by his inmost feelings, are directed to fulfilling the will of God; and in mixing with the world his mind will most readily concern itself with what has reference to this. Therefore even the weakness that may still remain in the man as the consequence of old sins, is there against his will, which is entirely at one with God's will in being set against all sin; and where the whole will is in this way opposed to all sin, there the guilt is taken away. For that is laid to no man's account which really takes place against his will. This will is just fellowship with Him who came to destroy the dominion of sin; and we only attain to such a will when we are united to Christ, and His will—the only pure will—is communicated to us. Love to Christ, and the good fight of the whole will against sin are one and the same thing. But every attempt to improve ourselves and others by our own power, and otherwise than in fellowship with the Saviour, is not only unsatisfactory, but comes so very far short of what we ought, at least, to wish, that it cannot be distinguished from the useless wish, which cannot determine the verdict of God.

If then we put forth our powers—repressed, it may be, hitherto, but ready to expand and grow by the power of Him who alone can make us strong—in building up the kingdom of God, and labouring to put down all sin within and around us, the guilt of sin is thus taken away; God no longer looks on us as each of us was in himself and might have remained, but only in the Beloved and as what we have become in Him. Nay, more; if, according to this new covenant, the will of God is put into our hearts and written in our minds, then even He can remember our unrighteousness and our sin no more; but only regards as ours the new life that we live in His Son.

Let us then fix in our minds what is the real meaning of the writer in the words of the text: that the death of Christ is a sacrifice which He offered for sin, because free obedience, even to the death of the cross, is the crowning act of all obedience. The Saviour's obedience, and the sacrifice which He offered, are not different, but one and the same. And the holy death of the Saviour is the end of all imperfection in the view and representation of our relation to God, of all outward ceremonial, of all other offerings and purifying observances. While we see in Him, most specially in His death, the glory of the only Son of the Father, and see, at the same time, by that death, the power to which sin had risen as enmity against God, by this very means, for all of us who have died with Him to that which is imperfect, old things are passed away, and a new life with Him is begun, which, in fellowship with the Saviour, seeks after righteousness and true holiness. And the more we desire to see this life extending on all sides and exercising an ever mightier influence, the more thankfully do we constantly come back to the Lord's death as to the everlasting remembrance of sin, ever anew calling on all to die to it in the death of the Lord, as the one offering by which "He hath perfected for ever them that are sanctified." Yes, my friends, those who are sanctified, all who hold on and grow and make progress in the life that the Saviour has kindled in them, and in deed and truth go on renouncing all participation in sin, and all trust in the law and its works, building themselves up together more and more in the spiritual love of Christ,—all those who are thus sanctified are perfected once for all by the offering that He presented; their obedience, although to outward view always imperfect, being yet an outcome of the perfect obedience of Christ and of a piece with it. They are perfected for ever for this very end, that they may really be able to be sanctified in a new life, after the conscience of sin and the guilt of sin are taken away from them, and they have become partakers in the liberty of the children of God; the only position in which there can be progress in what is truly good. Therefore, as the apostle Paul says, there is now no condemnation to them that are in Christ Jesus; and we may thank God who has delivered us from this body of death, and given us the victory through our Lord Jesus Christ. We owe it to His sacrifice, which He once offered for sin, that the guilt and the consciousness of sin are taken away from us, so that we can no longer live in fellowship with sin, which crucified Him, but in glorious and blessed fellowship with Himself.

How, then, can we but bring deeply moved and thankful hearts to commemorate the death of Jesus? And in meditating on His eternally efficacious sacrifice, how can we but ever more fully yield ourselves as a living sacrifice, holy and acceptable to God? How can we but become, through this eternal and ineffaceable remembrance of sin, ever more confirmed in a holy hatred against all that is enmity against God and opposes His will? And moreover, how can we but clothe ourselves more and more in the righteousness and the love of Him who, even when we were yet enemies and sinners, gave His life for us all, in order that with a love like His we may embrace those who are still held in enmity against God, and may win them to share with us the happiness of reconciliation. How can we but invite all who are wearing themselves out in delusive and fruitless service to come, weary and heavy-laden, to Him, in whom they will find rest and refreshing for their souls; if in a right spirit they allow us to direct them to the only and eternally availing sacrifice, through which all may be made perfect! And thus let us in deed and in truth praise Him who, equally by His life and His death, has become to us redemption as well as holiness, wisdom as well as righteousness. Amen.

Prayer.

Yes, merciful God and Father, who didst not turn away from the sinful world, but in Thine eternal love didst conclude all under sin that Thou mightest have mercy on all, praise and thanks be to Thee that Thou hast been mindful of us in Thy Son, and didst reconcile us unto Thyself in Him, to open to us the way to that blessed communion with Thee, which we enjoy in Him. Oh, let Thy power be felt more widely in the kingdom of Thy Son on earth, that He may gain many more as the reward of His life and His death; that the number of those who find life and blessedness in Him may go on increasing; and establish all those who have already come to the saving knowledge of Christ ever more firmly in the holy bond of faith and love, so that it may be ever becoming more true that we are dead with Him to sin and to outward law, and that the life of God, which He alone could bring, may be more and more gloriously manifested in us. We beseech Thee, in the humility of children, that Thou wilt give us to enjoy these fruits of His death. Be pleased to cause them to increase more and more abundantly on earth, so that the renown of the Crucified may ever become more glorious, until all shall bow the knee before Him to receive from His hand what Thy fatherly love and compassion have wrought through Him. Amen.

XV.

CHRIST'S RESURRECTION AN IMAGE OF OUR NEW LIFE.

(*Easter Sunday.*)

Praise and glory be to God, and peace with all who with joyful hearts greet one another with the cry, The Lord is risen! Amen.

TEXT: ROM. vi. 4–8.

IT is natural, my friends, that the glorious festival of our Saviour's resurrection should attract the thoughts of believers to a far remote time, and that it should make them rejoice to think of the time when they shall be with Him who, after He had risen from the dead, returned to His and our Father,—a joyful prospect, expressed in the hymn we have sung together. But the apostle, in the words of our text, recalls us from what is far off to what is close to us—to the immediate present of our life here. He takes hold of what is the most immediate concern, of what we are at once to share in and which is to form us, even here, into the likeness of Christ's resurrection. We are buried with Him, he says, unto death, that as He was raised from the dead through the glory of the Father, we also might walk in newness of life. And this new life is that which, as the Lord Himself says, all who believe in Him possess even now as having passed through death to life. The apostle compares this with those glorious days of our Lord's resurrection; and how could we more appropriately keep this feast—a feast in which, above all others, many Christians draw renewed strength for this new life from the most intimate union with our heavenly Head—how could we better celebrate it than by endeavouring to receive this directly for ourselves from the words of the apostle? Let us then, according to the teaching of these words, consider the resurrection life of our Lord, as the apostle presents it to us, as a glorious, though it may be unattainable, model of the new life in which we are all to walk through Him.

I. This new life is like that of our risen Saviour, first, *in the manner of His resurrection.* In order to appear to His disciples in that glorified form, which already bore in it the indications of the eternal and immortal glory, it was necessary that the Saviour should pass through the pains of death. It was not an easy transformation; it was necessary for Him, though not to see corruption, yet to have the shadow of death pass over Him; and friends and enemies vied with each other in trying to retain Him in the power of the grave; the friends rolling a stone before it, to keep the beloved corpse in safety, the enemies setting a watch lest it should be taken away. But when the hour came which the Father had reserved in His own power, the angel of the Lord appeared and rolled away the stone from the tomb, and the watch fled, and at the summons of Omnipotence life came back into the dead form.

Thus, my friends, we know what is the new life that is to be like the resurrection life of the Lord. A previous life must die; the apostle calls it the body of sin, the law of sin in our members, and this needs no lengthened discussion. We all know and feel that this life, which Scripture calls a being dead in sins, pleasant and splendid as may be the form it often assumes, is yet nothing but what the mortal body of the Saviour also was, an expression and evidence of the power of death, because even the fairest and strongest presentation of this kind lacks the element of being imperishable. Thus with the mortal body of the Saviour, and thus also with the natural life of man, which is as yet not a life from God.

And this our old man must die a violent death in the name of the law, such as the Saviour died, not without severe suffering and painful wounds. For if the body of sin dies out in a man of itself, through satiety of earthly things, and because no excitement can any longer affect his exhausted powers, that is a death from which we see no new life proceed. The power of sin must be slain in a man by violence; a man must go through the torture of self-knowledge, showing him the contrast between his wretched condition and the higher life to which he is called; he must hear the cry, and accept it as an irrevocable sentence, that an end is to be put to this life; he must groan and almost sink under the preparations for the execution of that sentence; all his accustomed habits of life must cease; he must be conscious of the wish that he were safely through it all, and it were at an end.

And when he has yielded up the old life to a welcome death, and the old man is crucified with Christ, then the world, which knows nothing better than that previous life, if it only goes on well and easily, uses all kinds of efforts to hinder the rising up of the new life, some of them well-meaning, others self-interested and therefore hostile. Some, with good intentions, like those friends of the Saviour, consult together, and try all in their power, keeping away all extraneous influences, to preserve at least the appearance of their friend from being defaced, and though no joyful movement can ever again be awakened, to preserve the form of the old life. Others, seeking their own interest and pleasure in a way by which they almost certainly accuse themselves, try to prevent an abuse being practised in this state of things, and also to guard against the gay, merry life which they lead, and into which they like so much to lead others, being brought into contempt by a question of a new life arising after this dying off of the old man, when, as they think, there is really nothing else and nothing better here on earth, and when it is a vain pretence for some to assert that they know this new life, and a mischievous delusion for others to attempt attaining it. Therefore wherever they perceive such a state of things, they have their spies to watch against every deception that might be practised about such a new life, or at least at once to discover and publish what kind of delusions prevail in connection with it.

But when the hour has come which the Father has kept in His own power, then in one form or another His life-bringing angel appears to such a soul. Yet how little do we know about what part the angel had in the Saviour's resurrection! We do not know if the Saviour saw him or not; we cannot determine the moment at which he rolled away the stone from the tomb and the re-animated Saviour came forth; no one witnessed it, and the only persons of whom we are told that they might have been able to see it with their bodily eyes were smitten with blindness. And in like manner, neither do we know how the soul lying, so to speak, in the tomb of self-destruction, is wrought upon by the angel of the Lord in order to call forth the life of God in it. It arises unseen in that grave-like silence, and cannot be perceived until it is actually present; what is properly the beginning of it is hidden, as every beginning usually is, even from him to whom the life is imparted. But this is certain, as the apostle says, that the Lord was raised from the dead by the glory of the Father, and thus also, according to the words of the Saviour, no man comes to the Son except the Father draw him; that same glory of the Father, which then called forth the Saviour from the tomb, and which still awakens in the soul that has died to sin the new life, like the resurrection life of the Lord. Indeed, among all the proofs of the Father's glory in heaven and earth, there is none greater than this, that he has no pleasure in the death-like condition of the sinner, but that at some time or another the almighty, mysterious, life-giving call sounds in his ears—Arise and live.

II. And, secondly, this new life resembles its type and ideal, the resurrection life of Christ, not only in being risen from death, but also *in its whole nature, way and manner.* First, in this respect, that though a new life, it is, nevertheless, the life of the same man, and in the closest connection with his former life. Thus, with our Saviour; He was the same, and was recognised by His disciples as the same, to their great joy; His whole appearance was the very same; even in the glory of His resurrection He bore the marks of His wounds as a remembrance of His sufferings and as the tokens of His death; and the remembrance of His former state was most closely and constantly present with Him. And just so it is with the new life of the Spirit. If the old man has died to sin, and we now live in Christ, and with Him in God, yet we are the same persons that we were before. As the resurrection of the Lord was no new creation, but the same Man, Jesus, who had gone down into the grave, come forth again from it; so in the soul before it died the death which leads to life in God, there must have lain the capability of receiving that life when the body of sin should die and perish; and that life is developed in the same human soul amidst the same outward circumstances as before, and with its other powers and faculties remaining unchanged. We are entirely the same persons, only that the fire of the higher life is kindled in us, and also that we all bear the signs of death, and that the remembrance of our former state is present with us. Yes, in manifold ways we are often reminded of what we were and what we did before the call to new life sounded in our hearts; and it is not so easy to efface the scars of the wounds, and the numberless traces of the pains under which the old man had to die that the new man might live. And as the glad faith of the disciples rested on the very fact that they recognised the Lord as being, in the glory of His resurrection, the same person that He was before; so also in us, the confidence in this new life, as a permanent and now natural state with us, rests only on this—that we recognise ourselves in it as the same persons that we were before; that there are the same faculties, lower and higher, of the human soul, which formerly served sin, but are now created anew as instruments of righteousness. Indeed, all the traces of that death, as well as of the former life, make us more vividly conscious of the great change that the life-giving call of God has produced in us, and call for the most heartfelt gratitude.

And as the Saviour was the same person in the days of His resurrection, so His life was also again of course a vigorous and active life; indeed, we might almost say it bore the traces of humanity, without which it could be no image of our new life, even in this, that it gradually grew stronger and acquired new powers. When the Saviour first appeared to Mary, He said, as if His new life had been, as it were, timid and sensitive, "Touch Me not, for I am not yet ascended to my God and your God." But after a few days He showed Himself to Thomas, and bade him boldly touch Him, put his hand in the Master's side, and his fingers into the marks left by the nails of the cross, so that He did not shrink from being touched even on the most sensitive spots. And also even in the earliest days, and as if the new life were to be fully strengthened by doing so, we find Him walking from Jerusalem to Emmaus, and from Emmaus back to Jerusalem, as well as going before His disciples into Galilee, and leading them back to Jerusalem, where He then ascended to heaven in their sight. And as He thus walked among them, living a life with them, human in every part, and exercising a human influence on them; so also His most important business was to talk with them of the kingdom of God, to reprove and rouse them up from their slowness of heart, and to open the eyes of their minds. Now so it is, my friends, with our new life,—that is like the resurrection life of the Lord. Oh, how very gradually it gains its faculties in us, grows and becomes strong, only bearing still more than the new life of the Lord the traces of earthly imperfection. I can appeal on this point to the feeling of us all, for assuredly it is the same in all. How intermittent at first are the manifestations of this new life, and how limited the sphere of its action! How long does it retain its sensitive spots, which cannot be touched without pain, or even without injurious consequences, and those are always the places in which the old man has been most deeply wounded in his dying hours! But in proportion as it becomes stronger, this new life ought the less to give the impression of being a mere phantom life,—the impression the Lord's disciples had when in the first moments they thought in their fear that they saw a spirit, so that He was obliged to appeal to the testimony of all their senses, that they might perceive He was no spirit, but had flesh and bones. And thus if our new life in God consisted in mere states of feeling and emotions, which were not in the least capable of passing into action, or perhaps did not even aim at doing so; which were too peculiar and special to ourselves to be actually communicated to others or to move them with good effect, but rather might touch them with a chill sense of awe; what would such a life be but a ghost-like apparition that would no doubt excite attention, but would find no credence, and would make men uneasy in their accustomed course, but without producing any improvement in it? No, it is a life of action, and ought to be ever becoming more so; not only being nourished and growing stronger and stronger through the word of the Lord and through heart-communion with Him, to which He calls us, giving Himself to us as the meat and drink of eternal life, but every one striving to make his new life intelligible to others about him, and to influence them by it. Oh, that we had our eyes more and more steadily fixed on the risen Saviour! Oh, that we could ever be learning more and more from Him to breathe out blessing, as He did when He imparted His Spirit to the disciples! Oh, that we were more and more learning like Him to encourage the foolish and slow of heart to joyful faith in the divine promises, to active obedience to the divine will of their Lord and Master, to the glad enjoyment and use of all the heavenly treasures that He has thrown open to us! Oh, that we were ever speaking more effectively to all connected with us, of the kingdom of God and of our inheritance in it, so that they might see why it was necessary for Christ to suffer, but also into what glory He has gone! These are our desires, and they are not vain desires. The life-giving Spirit, whom He has obtained for us, effects all this in each in the measure that pleases Him; and if once the life of God is kindled in the human soul, if we have once, as the apostle says, become like Him in His resurrection, then His powers are also more and more abundantly and gloriously manifested in us, through the efficacy of His spirit for the common good.

But along with all this activity and strength, the life of the risen Saviour was yet, in another sense, a secluded and hidden life. It is probable that when, in order to show Himself to His disciples, He went here and there from one part of the land to another, He was seen by many besides them, who had known Him in His previous life. How could it be otherwise? But the eyes of men were holden, that they did not recognise Him; and He made Himself known only to those who belonged to Him in faithful love. At the same time, however, He said to them, Blessed are they who do not see, yet believe! And what was the little number of those who were counted worthy of seeing Him, even if we add to them the five hundred whom Paul mentions, compared with the number of those who afterwards believed in their testimony to the Lord's resurrection? And thus it is also, my friends, with the new life in which we walk, even if it is, as it ought to be, strong and vigorous, and ever at work for the kingdom of God; yet it is at the same time an unknown and hidden life, unrecognised by and hidden from the world, whose eyes are holden; and he who should set himself to force the knowledge of it upon them, who should hit upon extraordinary proceedings in order to attract their attention to the difference between the life of sin and the resurrection life, would not be walking in the likeness of the Lord's resurrection. As the people in the time of Christ had opportunity enough to inquire about His resurrection, in seeing how His disciples continued to hold together, so our neighbours also see our close alliance, which has nothing to do with the affairs of this world; and if they, because of this, inquire about what unites us, the answer will not be lacking to them. But our inner history we will as little thrust upon them as the risen Christ thrust His presence on those who had slain Him, and who had therefore no desire to see Him. Instead of this, as He showed Himself only to His own, we also will make known our inner life only to those who are just in the same way our own; who, glowing with the same love, and cheered by the same faith, can tell us in return how the Lord has revealed Himself to them. Not by any means as if we followed some mysterious course, and that those only whose experiences had been entirely alike should separate themselves into little exclusive groups; for even the days of the Lord's resurrection present examples of various kinds of experience, and of one common inner fellowship connected with them all. And not only so, but even those who as yet have experienced nothing at all are not sent empty away. Only they must first become aware, by what they see without our thrusting it upon them, that here a spirit is breathing to which they are strangers, that here is manifested a life as yet unknown to them. Then will we, as was done then, lead them by the word of our testimony to the foundation of this new life; and as, when the word of preaching pierced men's hearts, when to some of them the old man began to appear as he really is, and they felt the first pangs that precede the death of the sinful man, there also sprang up faith in the resurrection of Him whom they had themselves crucified; so will it always be with the knowledge of the new life proceeding from Him who has risen. Therefore let us have no anxiety; the circle of those who recognise this life will always be widening, just because they are beginning to share in it. And as soon as even the slightest premonition of it arises in a man's soul, as soon as he has come only so far as to be no longer pleased and satisfied with the perishing and evil things of the world, as soon as his soul absorbs even the first ray of heavenly light; then his eyes are opened, so that he recognises this life, and becomes aware what a different life it is to serve righteousness, from living in the service of sin.

III. And lastly, my friends, we cannot feel all these comforting and glorious things in which our new life resembles the resurrection life of our Lord, without being at the same time, on another side, moved to sorrow by this resemblance. For if we put together all that the evangelists and the apostles of the Lord have preserved for us about His resurrection life, we still cannot out of it all form an entirely consecutive history. There are separate moments and hours, separate conversations and actions, and then the risen One vanishes again from the eyes that look for Him; in vain we ask where He can have tarried, we must wait till He appears again. Not that in Himself there was anything of this broken or uncertain life, but as to our view of it, it is and cannot but be so; and we try in vain to penetrate into the intervals between those detached moments and hours.

Well, and is it not, to our sorrow, the same with the new life that is like Christ's resurrection life? I do not mean that this life is limited to the few hours of social worship and prayer, glorious and profitable as they are; for in that case there would be cause to fear that it was a mere pretence; nor to the services, always but small and desultory, that each of us, actively working through the gifts of the Spirit, accomplishes, as it were, visibly and tangibly according to his measure, for the kingdom of God. In manifold ways besides these we become conscious of this new life; there are many quieter and secret moments in which it is strongly felt, though only deep in our inmost heart. But notwithstanding this, I think all without exception must confess that we are by no means conscious of this new life as an entirely continuous state; on the contrary, each of us loses sight of it only too often, not only among friends, among disturbances and cares, but amidst the commendable occupations of this world. But this experience, my dear friends, humbling as it is, ought not to make us unbelieving, as if perhaps our consciousness of being a new creature in Christ were a delusion, and what we had regarded as indications of this life were only morbid and overstrained emotions. As the Lord convinced His disciples that He had flesh and bones, so we may all convince ourselves and each other that this is an actual life; but in that case we must believe that, though in a hidden way and not always present to our consciousness, yet it is always in existence, just as the Lord was still in existence even at the times when He did not appear to His disciples; and had neither returned to the grave, nor as yet ascended to heaven. Only let us not overlook this difference. In the case of Christ we do not apprehend it as a natural and necessary thing that during those forty days He led a life apparently so interrupted; but each of us must easily understand how, as the influence of this new life on our outward ways can only gradually become perceptible, it should often and for a long time be quite hidden from us, especially when we are very busy with outward work, and our attention is taken up with it. But this is an imperfection from which as time goes on we should be always becoming more free. Therefore always back, my friends, to Him who is the only fountain of this spiritual life! If, ever and anon, we cannot find it in ourselves, we always find it in Him, and it is always pouring forth afresh from Him the Head to us His members. If every moment in which we do not perceive it is a moment of longing, as soon as we become conscious of the void; then it is also a moment in which the risen One appears to our spirit, and breathes on us anew with His life-giving power. And thus drawing only from Him, we shall attain to having His heavenly gifts becoming in us more and more an inexhaustible, continually flowing fountain of spiritual and eternal life. For this He rose from the dead by the glory of the Father, that we should be made into the likeness of His resurrection. That was finished in His return to the Father; our new life is to become more and more His and the Father's return into the depths of our souls; there they desire to make their abode; and the life of God is to be ever assuming a more continuous, active and powerful form in us, that our life in the service of righteousness may become, and continue even here, according to the Lord's promise, an eternal life.

Prayer.

Oh, for this end, Thou exalted Saviour, help us more and more by the contemplation of Thy glory! As Thou art exalted from the earth, draw us more and more towards Thee! As Thou didst walk in the days of Thy resurrection, so let us more and more live and walk in the bond of love and faith which Thou didst form among Thy people, and be ever receiving more abundantly from Thee nourishment and strength for our spiritual life! And as Thy resurrection was blessed to Thy disciples for the establishing of Thy kingdom on earth, for the encouraging of the faint-hearted, for banishing despondency from men's hearts, and for making known the deepest mysteries of the Scriptures; oh, thus may our new life be more and more, through the power of Thy Spirit, a proclamation of Thy word and of all the mysteries of Thy grace, a loving support to all that is weak, an effectual call to life for all that is still dead, a quiet, undisturbed enjoyment of Thy love and of the blessed fellowship with Thee in which Thy people stand. Amen.

XVI.

JESUS BORN THE SON OF GOD.

(*Christmas Sermon.*)

"Glory to God in the Highest, on earth peace; goodwill towards men. Amen."

TEXT: LUKE i. 31, 32. "Behold, . . . thou shalt bring forth a Son, and shalt call his name Jesus. He shall be great, and shall be called the Son of the Most High."

THESE were the words of promise spoken by the angel to Mary, that He whom she should bear should be called the Son of the Highest; and as this promise is afterwards brought into direct connection with the statement that the power of the Highest should overshadow her, Mary had no room to suppose that her son was only to become the Son of God at some future time through some specially great deeds of His own, or by the outpouring of God's grace upon Him. She was made to understand that from His very birth He was to be the Son of God, for from that time she was to call His name Jesus. And it is only in this fact that we grasp the full meaning of our solemn Christmas joy, to-day and always. For if the Saviour of the world had not been different from others at His birth, if the divine nature which we adore in Him had only come down upon Him afterwards, then our special connection with Him would not have begun with His birth; and our joy in His appearing would make less account of His birth (seeing that He was not yet, in that case, the Saviour) than of that moment of His life in which He became filled in a special manner with the power of the Highest. This, then, is the central thought in all that stirs our hearts on these days of solemn festival; that the Saviour was born the Son of God; that the divine power by which He was able to redeem the world dwelt in Him from the beginning of His life; and let this be to-day the subject of our devout meditation. Let us consider the necessary connection of this truth on the one hand with our common Christian faith; on the other, with that love through which faith works.

I. We assert first then, that it belongs to the deepest foundations of our Christian faith, (as this very festival bears witness), that we regard Christ as endowed, from the moment of His appearing in this world, with all that was necessary for Him as the Saviour of the world. We are to believe that He was already in Himself the eternal Word, though as yet silent; the Light sent to shine in the darkness, though as yet concealed; distinguished from all sinners by that saving power that dwelt in Him; and separated from the fellowship of sin. This, I admit, is a hard saying. It is so because of the difficulty we find in doing in connection with spiritual things what we are constantly doing in material and natural things—fully believing in what we cannot clearly imagine and picture to ourselves in all its bearings; and that is what is required of us here. Our own experience contributes to this difficulty. For while there is no question that we know something of an inward union of a divine power with the human soul, because all of us who can glory in belonging to Christ know that in becoming partakers of the Holy Spirit, we become partakers of a divine Being, thus being made one with God; we know also that we could not actually receive this divine gift until full human consciousness had begun in us, and all the mental powers which the Spirit of God should directly and specially control were awakened, so that He could begin this control, and with it His sanctifying work; and otherwise than thus we have never become conscious of Him. But in the case of the Saviour, if we are to think of the divine power being in Him while He was still in man's most imperfect state,—that of the newborn babe, in whom all the faculties, through which the presence of the higher divine power could be manifested and proved, were still dormant,—we must conceive of it as having been present without being in any way brought into exercise; and it is just this that we find it difficult to imagine, and therefore hard to believe.

Hence it comes that there have always been Christians who hold an opinion such as I have referred to,—that not only in the years of the Saviour's childhood, but up to the time when His human faculties attained maturity, He was in no way different and bore within Him nothing different from other children; and that not until He was to enter on the great work to which He was appointed, did the power of God come upon Him and pervade His whole being. And hence it is also that many Christians, though they do not hold this opinion, yet cannot quite heartily join in the child-like devotion which, going back to the very beginning of Christ's life, with the full reverence which binds the grateful soul to the Saviour, recognises in the new-born Babe, even in His unconsciousness, the Son of God, in such a sense that He needed to receive nothing new from above, but would become, by the ordinary development of His human soul, the Saviour who, by word and deed, by His life and by His death would both merit and produce that faith which those doubtful Christians themselves cherish; that He was, in short, the Son of the living God, He through whom God would in these last days speak for the last time to men, and after whom we need expect no other. But if these fellow-Christians will only look at things clearly; if they are really in earnest in that faith which brings us here together, then must they not grant that it would be at least as hard for us to give up this faith, on which the festival of to-day is founded, merely because we can no more understand the beginning of the second creation than that of the first or any other beginning? For if in Christ the divine Word did not become flesh so soon as His human eyes opened, what follows? This much is certain, that it is the experience of all without exception that in every one who has appeared on earth, endowed only as the children of men, sin has sooner or later developed. There will be differences; but these, great as they may seem to us, are really slight when we take into account the differences in mental capacity and strength of will; but that the development of sin should ever be wholly wanting, is entirely contradicted by the testimony of our consciousness. And therefore we cannot but believe that so it would have been with the Redeemer Himself if he had been from His birth like other children. Whatever promise the angel had left laid up in the humble soul of Mary, however thoughtfully she might have prepared herself, in childlike and fervent fear of God, to be the mother and nurse of One who was to be called the Son of the Highest; still, if He was only to become this in the future, however faithfully and wisely she might have watched over the tender mind, and kept far from Him the wide-spread poison which, alas, is breathed by every child of man, she would not have been able entirely to guard Him from it; for here we recognise the limit of all, even the most perfect human love and faithfulness and wisdom. And if Christ had been a sinner even in the least degree, could He have been our Saviour? God might have spoken through Him, as through the prophets of the old covenant, who were, like ourselves, sinful men. But would we call ourselves after the name of a prophet—would we gather together in the name of a prophet, whose work was only a continuation of what had gone before? And indeed, as there can never be *little* sin anywhere, however little it were thought to be in Him, we could never be sure that this continuation of the old way was the last. And though God might speak more fully by Him, and manifest Himself more clearly through His life than ever before, still all this would come only under the head of law. And whether an external law, written on tables of stone or brass, comes directly down from heaven, or is a human law and given through a man, such a law can never redeem the human race. Even when spoken by the holiest lips, and written with the finger of God, it can only produce a consciousness of sin, from which it provides no deliverance,—a consciousness which, the more fully we recognise our sin, constrains us the more to cry, "Who shall deliver me from the body of this death?" Salvation must consist, before everything, just in this, that we are freed from the consciousness of sin. We must have sinlessness clearly set forth to us; and the Redeemer is this living sinlessness; and only as we make this our own by the most intimate friendship and fellowship with Him, (as all things are common with friends), only so can we partake of the peace and blessedness which are the fruits of redemption.

Could this sinlessness, then, have been manifested to us in the Saviour and have claimed so entire a self-devotion on our part, if He was only at some future time to be filled, in some mysterious way, with the Holy Spirit and with divine power, even though it should be without measure and quite differently from those former prophets? If after this change He was still a man, and the very same man, and had not become a weird, spectral vision, whose history would constantly give us a feeling of repulsion, in spite of our reverence for His nature, still the remembrance of His former life and position could not be effaced, even supposing that after this wonderful, sanctifying change, He were incapable of ever again committing sin. And if He retained the memory of His former sinful state,—well, let us see, from our own and the most common experience of men, what would follow from that. We feel that it is a sorrowful experience, one which in many respects we would rather leave hidden in silence than communicate, that even the most remote remembrance of former sin which our soul retains, never remains there only as a dead letter, a mere piece of knowledge, as of things that exist and go on apart from us. It remains as something alive, and often casts a stain on our holiest thoughts and actions, even on those in the beginnings of which we were most distinctly conscious of the power of the Holy Spirit; it lives in us to teach us that so long as man walks as sinful man on earth, richly as the grace of God may be poured out on him, his soul can never become so perfectly pure a mirror for that grace as it might have been if its depths had never been penetrated by anything of that poison. Then, if the Saviour was like us in having such memories, His after experience must also have been similar to ours. And do we not know that every sin of which even the slightest stirring remains in the soul will inevitably have the effect, in particular instances, which a besetting sin has habitually, of darkening our understanding, blinding our judgment and swaying it to false conclusions, and making dim and impure our view of the divine will? If, then, the Saviour had retained in His soul the faintest shadow of sin, how could we hope that the words in which He declares to us the will of His and our Father and unfolds our whole relation to Him, were such perfect truth, and rested on so clear and complete an understanding, that men might safely be guided by them for ever? How could we suppose that His whole being was in harmony, His human nature being entirely pervaded by and made one with the Spirit, so that He is the model after which all are to form themselves, the guide in whose footsteps all are to walk; without feeling at the same time that we could never exhaust His truth, even by our most earnest appropriation of it; never, even by the truest obedience, quite attain to His likeness? And yet it was just such a Saviour we needed if we were to feel entirely satisfied, and have no wish for any other to come after Him.

Let us look in this connection at the great and weighty words of the Saviour Himself—words that so essentially distinguish Him from all the sons of earth: "I and my Father are one"; "He that hath seen Me, hath seen the Father." Let us reflect that these words contain, at the same time, the measure of our own union with Him; which, though we are brought into it by faith, is, as an effective reality, only to be attained to by degrees, according to His prayer for us, that we should be one with Him; from which it necessarily follows, that He who sees us sees Him. How can we take these words but in their full sense, as they stand? And how, in the case we have supposed, could the Saviour have used such words, without thereby appearing, as one who was either deluding himself with a vain fancy, or who, lest his hearers should apprehend his words too slightly, had, even with the best intentions, chosen expressions stronger than was consistent with truth, and so deluded with false hopes those who took His words in their exact meaning? Certainly, He must have given this impression, if, while He thus spoke, there had been about Him even the slightest taint of sin. For how could he, in whom remained the very faintest trace of sin, say that he was one with the Father, with Him who is the Father of Lights, Him who alone is good and pure, and to whom each one comes near only in proportion as he becomes a partaker in His goodness and purity? If those words of His are true,—if there is a fellowship between Him and us which is an outcome of His oneness with the Father, the Word of God must have been in Him from the very beginning of His life, and have protected Him from all that had even the most distant likeness to sin: it must have guarded every development of His natural human powers,—so guarded them that His very senses remained pure; waiting, as it were, till that indwelling divine power should gradually come into visible action, and seeking to be nothing but instruments of that power. Only if it was thus with Him from the beginning of His life could He justly say this of Himself.

And, finally, let us think of the holiness of Him before whom we come short, through sin, of all the approval that we should have had from Him; and that therefore we needed a helper, for whose sake this holy God could count and declare pure the whole human family; and who should, in His perfect purity, represent us all before His Father. Oh, even the faintest breath of corruption and sin cannot be hidden from this holy God; and if anything is impure in His sight, even in the smallest point, that may escape all other eyes, then the whole is impure. And thus our faith in the Saviour's mediation with the Father,—our faith that we see in Him the image of the heavenly Father and the brightness of His glory, our faith in the completeness and perfection of His teaching, and its perpetual application, as well as in the sufficiency and unquestionable character of His commandments,—our faith in all these respects depends on the fact that He came into this world as already the eternal Word, who was made flesh,—as the light from above that shone into the darkness.

II. Let us consider, secondly, that if we do not take this view of the Saviour, the pure and unfeigned love of which He is the source, lacks its true motive. For both the spotless purity of true Christian love, and its breadth, in which it embraces the whole human race, depends on this; that He, for whose sake we thus love, and apart from whom such a love would certainly not be striven after, is such as He is here described to us.

Undeniably one of the strangest phenomena of the human soul is the conflict between two feelings, both lying deep in the noblest part of our nature, and yet constantly opposed to each other: our love to our fellows on the one side, and our pure sense of right and wrong, of good and evil, on the other. We may hate and oppose some fault ever so strongly, and yet if we find that fault in one to whom we have already become bound in love, how much we are inclined to excuse it, and to take a more lenient view even of what is most odious.

Does some human form or character attract our love? then, the more devoted our soul is to good and truth, the more readily is it seized with repulsion when we perceive the stirrings of sin or the breaking out of sensual corruption and foolish conceits,—a repulsion that only too easily passes over into passion, and checks our love. Now, if we always mixed only with each other, having no other object of love than those who were sinners like ourselves, should we be capable of any other than this troubled kind of love—a love always disturbing our noblest instincts? And could we, even in that case, be willing that our moral sense should be incapable of such emotions?—emotions that cause us, even in a passing way, to pronounce harsh and cutting judgments on those we love, or actually to oppose them with something like enmity. No; we could not give up our noble and vigorous indignation against all that is opposed to the divine will. And hence, it follows that we could just as little love ourselves rightly as our brethren. For even the allowable and necessary love that we bear to ourselves is modified in the same way. The more strict a man is with himself, the more clearly the voice of the divine will speaks in him; just so much the oftener is he found in a state of transition and wavering between undisturbed satisfaction in the progress of which he is conscious, and the noblest scorn of himself. And it cannot be required of us to love even those nearest to us more than ourselves, or in quite another sense and manner. Indeed, to a man who loves and judges himself after this strict fashion, there can be but few, even among those who are most highly esteemed, and who seem the best and noblest, about whom his opinion and feeling will not have to vary as often as about himself, that is, if he is closely enough associated with them to have their inner life clearly revealed to him. This trial, then, is common to all! For we cannot but feel that a dark shadow thus broods over all human love, by which the pure light is clouded and broken, and the blessedness of our love is marred.

But, must we not as Christians refuse to accept such a position? Is it not unfeigned love to which the Bible calls us? Could the disciples of the Lord be known by their love to each other, if that love were only more or less different, in some indefinite way, from that natural, but, alas, so unsatisfying love which is found in all sound-hearted men? Well, then, how are we to attain to a different kind of love to others, and, therefore, also to ourselves? If we acknowledge Christ as having had the divine nature united in Him with the human from the beginning, so that, in our love to Him, love to our neighbour and love to the will of the heavenly Father are most perfectly the same thing; then we have at least One to whom our hearts can cling in entirely pure and unalloyed love. And only on the same assumption can His love to us be pure and unsullied. For the fact that He does not find the divine will living and reigning in us, forms no impediment to His love; it only stamps it with the special impress of helpful sympathy. And as we, remembering the voice from heaven, "This is My beloved Son, in whom I am well pleased," live in the firm confidence that if we can in real truth say, by faith, "I live, yet not I, but Christ liveth in me," God regards us not as we are in ourselves, but only in this union with Christ, making us sharers in the good pleasure which He has in His Son; so, just as the result of this faith, the circle of our pure and unfeigned love becomes enlarged, and embraces all whom we know to be in union with Christ. Then whatever of human corruption we still find in our brethren appears to us to be taken away and annulled in Christ, and can only excite in us such a love as that with which He has loved us,—a love that seeks to promote the life of Christ in them, so that it may become strong enough entirely to overcome the sin, whose occasional appearances will only remind us that the happiness we find in unalloyed love is a gift which we have received from above, and which could become ours through One alone. Here then, is a love very different from that natural kind! We may say of it, "Old things are passed away; behold, all is become new." But only through Christ, and for His sake, can we thus love. That uncertain, imperfect love can do nothing towards purifying itself. One must be given to us, who directly both claims and creates pure love. Only so could the imperfect put on perfection; our love to others is only a truly sanctified love when it is a result of our love to Him, and a reflection of His love to us.

But if Christ was not One who gave us the impression of perfectly pure love, without the slightest suspicion of an imperfection in the beloved object, then we must always have remained in the old incomplete condition, and nothing better would have fallen to our lot. For if what we explained before is true, that even Christ, if at any time whatever in His human life there were motions of sin in Him, was not in a position to obliterate the remembrance and the living traces of them, then what follows? Glorious as He might appear to us afterwards in His public life, in His holy proclamation of the kingdom of God, in the courage and the certainty with which He invited men to Him and promised them refreshment and rest, as the greatest of the children of men, the choicest and greatest instrument of God; yet how could we restrain ourselves from striving to detect the traces of sin that we knew must exist? Indeed, the less we succeeded in finding out any definite imperfections or defects in His life, just the more surely would we assume that there were hidden defects under all that excellence that we are accustomed especially to laud and praise. And whether we were always obliged to do no more than assume, or had actually discovered individual instances, it would be all the same so far as love is concerned. We might love Him infinitely more than we love all others, we might cling to Him with a reverence to which nothing else could be compared, but still it would be an impure, a tainted love; it would not be different from our love towards other men, and therefore could not change and sanctify that love.

We have thus seen how this view of the Saviour affects the *purity* of true Christian love; let us next consider how on this it also necessarily depends that this love shall be *universal*; embracing, like Christ's salvation, the whole human race. It is true we usually regard it as an instinct of human nature, quite independent of the appearing of Christ, and as a precept dictated by human reason, that wherever we see a human being we should enter into relations of giving and receiving love. But we do not always remember that this only came to us first through Christ, and that it is one of the sad and ruinous results of sin that it confines and limits love in the human heart. And where, before the Son of God appeared, were the men —where does history refer to any such?—who so much as thought of requiring universal and unrestricted love either from themselves or others—not to speak of really feeling it and acting on it? Such a conception could hardly take shape even in a few of the souls who devoted themselves to quiet meditation, and it passed away without becoming a living impulse in any direction; nor would it have shown itself more powerfully even in themselves if they had gone back to active life. For was not love everywhere confined to those who were related in language and race, so that to all beyond those limits there was a feeling, if not of hostility, at least of indifference? And indeed this was quite natural. Because reason itself, which demanded a universal fellowship of love, declared by that very demand that such a love ought to be natural to the human race, and that there would also be natural dissimilarities of all kinds in all the greater sections of the race, in virtue of which some would be more able to give and others be obliged to receive. But it was easier for every one to carry on this interchange of giving and receiving with those who spoke his own language. And therefore it seemed most fitting that every one should remain among his own people, and so it came to pass that out of this separation grew strife and hatred whenever the separate districts became embroiled either through the faults of individuals or by the pressure of human needs. And seeing that this state of things still exists everywhere in some degree, men not having yet fully embraced in heart the one Shepherd of the one flock, we know by experience that no human wisdom, wherever it might appear, no softening of manners that might be brought about in the course of time, could set us free from this limitation of love. But if men ceased to think that each community could find in itself all that was needful for its well-being,—imperfection still existing everywhere, though everywhere also some germ of goodness and truth,—and if the news were announced that the Dayspring from on high had somewhere appeared, a pure light that could and would dispel all darkness;—if, on the one hand, men's hearts, wearied with imperfection, turned to that perfect light; and on the other, the Saviour, equal with the Father in love to the whole human race, inspired those who believed in Him as the Son of God with the conviction that in bringing Him and His peace to men they gave them something that could be obtained nowhere else; and if the love of Christ constrained them to carry the good news ever further and further, then the partition wall would fall, and hearts would be filled with a universal love, a love of which we catch glimmerings through the darkness of earthly strife that, alas! still surrounds us; a love that, working outward from the heart, is ever becoming more victorious over that strife. And where indeed was that narrowing and isolating race-prejudice keener and stronger than just where our Lord was born? The nation who regarded all other nations as unclean, and avoided intercourse with them; who interpreted the Word of God as laying down the precept, Thou shalt love thy brother, and hate thine enemy; a people who, utterly failing to recognise that the narrowing laws under which they lived were only meant to keep them together till the light of the world should appear, imagined that God was their peculiar property,—such a people could not of themselves have produced, nurtured, and instructed Him who is the Fountain of universal love. Had the Word of God not dwelt in Him from the beginning, guarding and protecting Him, how could He have escaped sharing in those narrowing ideas, rooted as they were in the whole life of the nation, and hallowed by all their traditions from the most ancient times?

Or are we to believe that He did not escape? that His disciples were the first to get above those prejudices—they who had nothing but what they received from Him, and who so often failed to understand what He wished to communicate to them; they who afterwards only spoke and acted by the Spirit, who could not do otherwise than take of the things of Christ and show them to them? No, this we cannot believe; for the disciple was not above his Master, and they were constrained almost against their will, by the Lord's command, to preach the gospel to

Samaritans and heathen, and to hold fellowship with them. But He, through the divine Word that dwelt in Him from the beginning, was safe from the influence of all those narrowing habits of thought; He was through His oneness with the Father the Author of a universal love, which, founded on the eternally planned union of all men, indicates the incarnation, in His person, of the divine power which can effect that union.

And now, in conclusion: without that faith which we have briefly defined, without that love which we have faintly pictured, what would redemption be worth to us? where would be the sanctification, where the righteousness which Christ was to be made, and has been made to us? If there is to be through Him glory to God in heaven; if through Him is to be glorified the spiritual creative power of the universal Creator, who has called the human race to something very different from their present imperfect state; if peace is to be established on earth through Him before whom all discord and hatred are constantly giving way, that all may become one in love; if an unmixed goodwill is to be possible to us—and without that no salvation is to be thought of,—then there must be a truly divine person as a Saviour, on whom our eyes can rest; One of whom it is true, from the beginning of His life, that in Him the Word was made flesh. And we have a sacred right to greet Him, even in the infant form in which He first appeared on earth, with holy reverence, not as He who was only to become the Saviour of men, but as being then actually such; not as He in whom the Father was afterwards to be glorified, but as already, though not manifestly, glorifying Him, and as He who was one with Him from the beginning.

This festival of the Saviour's infancy, which we all celebrate, is very specially the beautiful and joyful festival of the children. When we think of Him who for their sakes also took flesh and blood like them, our eyes rest on them with tender interest, while we lovingly promise them the blessedness that is to be found in faith and loyalty towards the Saviour. Let us then hold fast this truth, that, while He did indeed become a child like others, because He was to be like us in all things except sin; the divine power through which He was able to be the Saviour of the world must have been in Him, living and active, though concealed, from the beginning. Let us maintain that only in connection with this faith can that word which He spoke out of a loving heart towards the young have its complete fulfilment: "Of such is the kingdom of heaven." Amen.

XVII.

CHRIST BRINGING A SWORD.

(*Christmas Sermon.*)

"Glory to God in the highest, peace on earth, and goodwill towards men!"

TEXT: MATT. x. 34. "Think not that I came to send peace on earth: I came not to send peace, but a sword."

HOW wonderfully out of harmony these words sound with the angelic greeting that we have just heard; threatening to rob us of all the joy and blessedness of this holy season! For is the sword pre-eminently the glory of God? and if it rages anew, is that a special delight to men? When the message has come down from heaven, Let there be peace on earth, how can the Lord Himself say, "Think not that I came to send peace, but a sword"? and even though this is true, should we not, on this very day of rejoicing over His coming, try our utmost to conceal from ourselves the sorrowful truth and to put it far from our souls? No, this will not do. It has long been the custom in a great part of the Christian Church to commemorate, on this second day of the Christmas festival, that first martyr who died for the name of the Lord. It was in that death that this Word of the Lord began to be fulfilled. And why then do we thus connect the two events? Does it not seem just to express this thought, that the birth of martyrdom is, as it were, the first and most direct glorification of the birth of Christ Himself? Yes; and as at other times we think of what it cost Him to redeem us at so great a price, so now, in these our days, we ought to know and lay specially to heart what kind of crowns of victory are thereby procured for us—I mean for the whole race of believing men since Christ's first appearing. All the suffering that men have endured for His name's sake, all the misery that has come upon His believing disciples, all the disquiet that has been caused on earth by strife about His name—all these things we should keep in view when we celebrate His appearing; and thus we shall recognise Him as the Dayspring from on high who hath visited us, as the Prince of peace, who guides our feet into the way of peace. Well then, in this way we shall not be afraid to join the thought of this earnest and weighty word of the Lord with our Christmas joy; rather, let us use the consideration that the Lord came to bring a sword, in the way of exalting and purifying our joy on account of His coming. It is to this thought, then, that I beg your devout Christian attention for this sacred hour. And the points to be considered are these; first, the fact that the Lord came to bring a sword on the earth affords us the strongest security for the truth that He became really our Brother; even to the extent of His whole life and work being subject to all the conditions of really human work; secondly, we find in it the best guarantee that the fulness of the Godhead truly dwelt in Him; and, finally, it gives us the most comforting assurance of the immovable firmness of the covenant between Him and us. Let us try to look at these more clearly in their order.

I. I say, in the first place, the fact that the Lord could not but bring a sword on earth gives us the strongest security that His life and work were, from the very first, truly human.

For how do men act in relation to every human influence

that acts on them? They inherit, as the indelible mark of their frailty, the liability to *mistake*, to which, however well-intentioned they may be, and however earnestly striving towards good, they are still unhappily so subject that it may even steal on them unawares. Hence a man may blind himself about everything that is offered to him by others; that which is most beneficent may appear to him dangerous; what is most salutary he may think hurtful; even what is divine may seem to him wrong and unpleasant. Now if the influence of the Lord Himself was to be a really human influence, with no secret power modifying the usual way of communication between the minds of men, then He also must have been subject to having His work received and judged in the same way as that of other men. When the evil spirits fled before Him, it could not fail to happen that some of those who witnessed His deeds should be so blinded about Him and what He was, as to imagine that He cast out devils only through the prince of the devils. When the rumour of Him began to spread abroad, and men softly and, as it were, stealthily whispered to each other the surmise whether this Jesus of Nazareth might not be He who was to come, the Helper, the Saviour, the Messiah; it could not but be that even among His own people, acquainted though they were with the divine promises given to that nation through many generations, there would be some so blinded about Him that even the proofs and indications of Scripture confirmed them in their blindness. And thus it came about that some said, When Christ comes, we shall not know whence He is; but we know whence this Man is, we are acquainted with His father and mother, his brothers and sisters. Others again held to another prejudice, and said, Is He not from Nazareth? and did you ever hear that a prophet had arisen, or should arise, out of Galilee? It was inevitable that this should be the lot of the Saviour if His influence was to be genuinely and purely human; and it was just this blindness of men who wished to find salvation in some other way than that in which alone it is to be securely and abidingly found, that was the cause, in the first place, of His bringing a sword on earth, by parents taking up arms against children, and children against parents, brothers and sisters and friends against each other, on His account.

How, we ask again, do men act in relation to every human influence that acts on them? We are like each other, we know, so far as it concerns the deepest and most essential parts of human nature; and yet the same event that occurs to several persons, that touches many at once, affects them in very different ways according to the different general attitude of each, or to something that may determine their feelings at the moment. And so it could not but be that as it was in the case of the Lord Himself, as long as He lived on earth, so, now that He is here no longer, the preaching of the Word which He has appointed in His Church should affect men in various ways. When it was proclaimed that this Jesus, whom they had delivered up and slain, was made of God both Lord and Christ, and that salvation and forgiveness of sins could be found only in His name, some were cut to the heart, and asked, What shall we do to be saved? But how many others heard it with indifference, shook their heads, and went away just as they had come? Now when men are so differently affected, is it not quite according to human nature that he who has remained indifferent counts as only a foe to his repose his neighbour who has been moved to the depths of his heart, and who would fain have all others to share his feeling? And it is just thus that things have gone on from the beginning until now. Ever since the word of reconciliation began to be proclaimed, there have been men who refused to be disturbed out of the rest in which they were in reality only sitting in the darkness and shadow of death, though they probably thought themselves safe and well-advised, till at last the divine impulse reaches their perhaps already hardened heart.

Hence it could not be otherwise than that He who occasioned such a stirring of men's minds as the Saviour did, must in doing so bring a sword on the earth. For, my friends, if once men are at variance, and yet they restrain themselves and keep within certain limits, so that their difference never reaches such scenes of violence, such conflict and destruction as are indicated by the word "sword," what is the reason of this but that they do not hold the subject to be of sufficient importance? But although the life and influence of the Lord was subject to all those limitations which told on the influence of other men; yet this, at least, always necessarily belonged to it, that the movement which He awakened on earth must have always, as time went on, appeared to every one a greater movement than any other to which they had ever been prompted; otherwise the kingdom of God could never have proceeded from it. Hence the variance between men of different minds, produced by His appearing, and afterwards by the tidings of Him, was generally keen enough to justify the expression that He had come to bring a sword on the earth; and hence it is also that we see this sword raging, now more now less bloodily and destructively, everywhere without exception where the word of peace is proclaimed. Now if it had been otherwise than this, how would the matter have stood? In that case this word of the apostle could not have been true, "When the fulness of the time was come, God sent forth His Son, born of a woman, made under the law." For the absence of the sword would imply that men's minds were not yet prepared to be sufficiently interested in the object of His mission to be very strongly moved by it, or stirred either to eager approval or vehement dislike. But when the human race had reached such a stage of progress that wherever the Saviour appeared He brought the devouring sword, then the fulness of the time was come,—then it was time for the Saviour to appear. And well for us, my friends, that He came at that time! Or would it have been better, perhaps, that His appearing had been delayed until it would have been no longer necessary that with the promise of peace He should bring the sword—until all the blessings of His appearing could have been brought in gently and peaceably, with no disturbing movement in opposition? Nay, verily. If men had been able of themselves to make so much progress that they would at once, without variance or division, have ranged themselves on the side of the divine life and the heavenly light as soon as it appeared to them, then they might also have found it out for themselves, and there would no longer have been any need for the Saviour's appearing. But if it is not and cannot be so, then we might still be sitting in darkness and the shadow of death, thousands of generations might still perish, but never would salvation come. Therefore either no real redemption could have been found at all, or it was inevitable that the Deliverer of the world must first have brought a sword, before the peace which He left to His people could extend its blessings over them. Thus the stern and sharp word of the Saviour, that He came to bring a sword, coincides exactly in this respect with the milder saying of the apostle which we have quoted, that He should be born of a woman and made under the law. For in the law of His nation, everything that had any resemblance to magic, every use of any secret power, was most strictly forbidden. And therefore the Saviour, just because He was made under the law, was limited to the mode of acting on the minds of men that was in accordance with Nature. If it could have been otherwise—if He had drawn hearts to Himself in any other way than by genuine, human influence, then He could not have been our Brother; because the divine power in Him still made use of other instruments and means than His human nature, and set it aside as useless. We could not then glory, in the sense in which we so gladly do so, that in Christ the Dayspring from on high has visited us. For this beautiful and precious word means nothing less than this, that when the Dayspring from on high appeared in this world, which is our dwelling-place, He took part in the whole order of our life and wrought in no other way than as one of ourselves, in this world; where everything, as we have just been showing, is what is natural, and can only cease to be natural and in order when His work is completed at the end of the day. Therefore while we rejoice in Him and in His appearing, we will rejoice also in this, that He so came, born of a woman and made under the law, that His redeeming, saving work could not fail to bring a sword on the earth.

II. But this is also, secondly, a sure guarantee to us that in Him dwelt the fulness of the Godhead, and that He who visited us was truly the Dayspring from on high.

For, as we know from the words of our text and from so many other utterances of the Lord, this result of His coming was not hidden from Him; He knew it well and most clearly foresaw it. He who had seen so deeply into human nature and the human heart, as well as into the special circumstances of His own times, knew that He was bringing a sword on the earth; and yet He came; and yet, because no other way was possible, He could not forbear from saving the human race in this way, and freeing those who sat in darkness and the shadow of death!

My friends, just call to mind that account which the Lord gave to the disciples of how He was tempted in the wilderness; consider how, in His so purely and simply rejecting every seductive suggestion, we find the clearest proof of the Divine strength that lived in Him; and then say what, nevertheless, are those temptations, as there related, in comparison with what we can imagine they might have been. Let us suppose that the tempter had come to

Him, and instead of showing Him, from the top of the mountain, the kingdoms of the world and their glory, had shown Him the rivers of blood which would flow on earth because of Him; that he had not merely shown Him His own cross, but how it would be endlessly multiplied for the whole host of His believing confessors and disciples,—had shown Him how the devouring sword would sweep away thousands on thousands, the bonds of slavery in which His witnesses would have to groan, all the insult and scorn of the world, all the pains and privations of love: suppose that he had showed Him the full fury of the persecution that would come upon His people, far more bitter than the bondage out of which Moses had by a strong hand freed the people of the old covenant; and, finally, the heart-rending breaking up of the holiest human relationships for the sake of His Name,—that he had showed Him all this in one dark picture embracing hundreds and thousands of years, and had then earnestly put it to Him, whether, having thoroughly considered all this, He was yet firmly resolved to bring upon men this incalculable amount of woe and misery, in addition to all the sufferings which, apart from this, by their own fault or innocently, they had to bear,—whether He were even sure that the salvation He hoped to introduce on earth would outweigh all this misery. Suppose further that the tempter reminded Him how men, through their ancient and inveterate tendency to follow delusions and error, would pervert His teaching,—and here again what a terrible picture he might have drawn,—what multitudes of wretched figures in hair shirts, reduced by fanatical mortifications to feeble shadows, their minds darkened by a system of genuflexions and prayers in which heart and thought have no part, vainly wearing themselves out in a narrow round of dead works, yet all this without the old man being slain in them, and a new glad life created. Let us suppose that he showed Him all this also, and then pressed the question whether He really meant to risk the undertaking at this cost,—whether it did not seem to Him more prudent to return to the secluded life from which He was just in the act of coming forth, and in quiet prayer to avail Himself of the Father's regard for Him, in inducing Him to alleviate the lot of those brethren of His in some other way; or even whether He should not leave the human race to themselves, if perchance they might find without Him a less costly way out of the darkness that encompassed them. Now think of a man, the very bravest, who so far as he himself alone is concerned goes firmly on in the way of faith, though devils should threaten him from every roof; think of the most cheerfully willing-hearted man, who does not shrink from demanding both from himself and from others all kinds of self-sacrifice for the good cause; and then reflect whether in view of all this, with such a prospect for the future, even such men would not faint in spirit, and withdraw their hand from the plough. But, you perhaps ask, did the Lord actually encounter this temptation, or were not those still far distant events and conditions rather at that time unknown to Him, as indeed He said Himself that the Father had reserved many things in His own power? But then we have sufficiently clear evidence in His own words how distinctly these things were before His mind, not only from the words of our text, but still more from what follows, where He speaks of setting the son against the father and the daughter against the mother, as well as from other warning and encouraging discourses. And with what unshaken tranquillity, with what heroic calmness He says all this, seeming indeed hardly able to wait for the first blazing up of the fire which He had come to kindle! Yes, without a doubt He knew that He was very different from other benefactors of His race,—that He had something more to bestow than what had until then been counted the best human possessions; and as He had no external possessions whatever, but on the contrary was in this respect the poorest of all men, He must have had within Himself something more than human; He must have been aware of an inexhaustible source of spiritual blessings, and indeed have known that He was the sole possessor of those good things, and that through Him alone men could attain to the possession of them. And all this just means that He must have been conscious of a Divine power and fulness in Himself; so that in dealing with this temptation, about which He kept silence to His disciples, because they were not yet able to bear it, He did not so much as put all those terrible things into the balance, but let them pass Him by ineffectual, that He might worthily pursue the path of His duty.

Now, if a man could foresee in spirit even the smallest part of such troubles and scenes of destruction as the result of his efforts, supposing those efforts to be merely selfish, aiming only at his own security and repose, at personal fame or dominion; and yet were capable of going on in cold blood, with tranquil mind and undisturbed self-possession, should we not say—nay, why do I put the question, have we not said it a thousand times—that there was something more than human,—that such a man was driven on by some dark power, stronger than himself? But even when a man's labours are directed to the reviving and blessing of others, to furthering the common salvation and the common welfare,—when he who in this way brings a sword, yields himself, and that not without consideration, as the first victim to the power of the sword, desiring nothing but to awaken and to establish permanently among men the higher life which is in his own heart; even in such a case we may well say that not only would such a purpose and plan be mere empty delusion without a higher than human strength; but also, unless there were a higher strength dwelling in him, no man could bear the picture of the misery that would precede and accompany what he meant to bring about. The Saviour must indeed have been divinely certain of this, that, after all the troubles caused by the sword, and in the midst of them, He could not fail to guide the feet of the children of men into the way of peace,—a peace higher than any that the world had known before; He must have known certainly that, after all those scenes of destruction, and in the midst of them, He would draw men out of the darkness and shadow of death, and transplant them into the glorious kingdom of light and love; He must have been certain that all those hostile demonstrations were only the last struggles of that ancient power of death, from which He was just redeeming men, the decisive birth-pangs of that new and eternal life which was just being received into human nature. But such a confidence implies nothing less than this—the consciousness that in Him dwelt the fulness of the Godhead, that it was the Father's words that He spoke, the Father's works that He did, and that what He was going forth to accomplish was the eternal counsel and will of the Father, which could be carried out through Him alone. The confidence that this Divine purpose, holding steadily on through all those horrors, could not possibly fail of its fulfilment; this confidence, it must certainly be evident to us all, is one and the same thing with the certainty that He Himself was divinely moved to this work; and that this will of God was so thoroughly His own that even in the moments of life most fitted to suggest doubt the two wills could never be separated. We can have no Saviour who brings a sword in such a way, unless that Saviour is the only begotten Son of the Father, and as such, even in all this, full of grace and truth.

But, my friends, this is still not all; we have not yet fully examined these words, "I am come to bring a sword," even in this one aspect. Can we think it enough to remember what the Lord's witnesses and disciples have suffered from those who are the *enemies* of His word? No; in these days, when we desire so specially to rejoice in His appearing on earth, and therefore in His whole work, we dare not close our eyes to the inner history of the Christian Church! Ah, the sword has raged even there! Even there we see fathers and children, brothers and sisters opposed to each other in bitter strife as to what is the real and true meaning of salvation in Christ, what are the necessary means, the essential and indispensable conditions for becoming partakers of it. Did He know and foresee this also? We certainly cannot doubt it. For although His gentleness did not give it such distinct expression, yet let us remember how fervently, in His last solemn prayer, He besought His Father for this very thing, that they whom the Father had given Him during His life on earth, as well as those who should believe on Him through their word, might be perfectly one, even as He and His Father are one;—a petition that suggests to us a sorrowful, but only too sure foreboding of His divine mind, that it would not always be so. And when they are not entirely one in spirit,—and they are so and can be so no longer when they seek after some other unity than the unity of the Spirit in the bond of peace;—then they are exposed to all those troubles which continually arise from all kinds of schism, and from the manifold delusions produced by the magic power of the letter and the law. This sad page of Christian history, which has so often been repeated in various forms,—this also the Saviour was aware of! Did He know that He must bring, instead of peace, even this sword? And yet what could be more fitted to weaken and darken the pure impression which otherwise His work might make on men? Could we imagine a greater hindrance to faith for those who are not yet believers, than to see that even there, where love is set forth as the law which is to govern all, where internal peace could be the only sure compensation for all outward adversities,—that even there discord reigns, that even there enmity breaks out, that even there the sword rages? And yet so it is. But when the Lord on the cross prayed to His Father for His enemies and persecutors, and even spoke of them to Him only as men who knew not what they did, He was even then regarding in the same light the great host of souls who, since His appearing and the completion of His work, have fallen into deplorable dissension over His word, His doctrine, and the constitution of His Church. All the mistakes of love, and the turning aside into the path of strife by those who yet desired to walk in the way of peace;—all this He recognised beforehand, as ignorance of what they did. Now we know that none of these things kept Him back nor arrested His steps; that He was able, with all this clearly in view, to retain His tranquillity and calmness. For He knew that though His people might be at variance among themselves, and to outward view excited to so bitter a hostility against each other that no common eye could distinguish it from an outbreak of selfish passions; yet they were certainly delivered out of the darkness and shadow of death, with which these clouds of division, through which the light was really shining, had no longer anything in common. He knew that their feet were really turned into the way of peace; because, although human blindness made them wage this noble spiritual warfare for the truth with unseemly and prohibited weapons, they were yet seeking to become one flock under one and the same Shepherd. And while His judging of these things in this way and no otherwise affords, on the one hand, the clearest proof that He saw human affairs exactly as they are seen by the Father in heaven, to whom He commends His people; on the other hand, we must admit that to be able, with such a view of the future, to enter on this path and continue in it in effecting the work of salvation, demanded a consciousness of divinity in Himself; and that human strength was incapable of either planning or carrying out such a work. He alone could thus act, with the knowledge of all these things before His mind, who had come down from above, and was conscious of possessing an eternal dominion and a firmly established authority, by which all those difficulties would be adjusted and smoothed away; nay, more;—changed into peace and happiness.

III. And because of all this, my friends, the fact that the Lord could not but bring a sword is to us the surest measure of the immovable steadfastness of the union between the Saviour and His people.

How little His work had advanced when He had so suddenly to leave this earthly scene, so that even His own human soul desired that the cup which He was to drink might pass away from Him, though only for a time,—all this we know. But even then it did not come upon Him unexpectedly: it was really that when He meant to begin the work which His Father had committed to Him, He was obliged,—He who knew what was in man,—to resign Himself to the necessity of doing the greatest work by means of weak instruments. And,—without recalling the fact that not only was he who betrayed Him among the twelve, but that the others also asked, "Lord, is it I?"—weak indeed the whole of those whom He had gathered round Him as His dearest and most trusted friends still were when He was obliged to leave them. This is evident, whether as regards the pure fulfilling of His precepts; for they had only a short time before disputed about which of them should be next the Master in the kingdom of heaven; or as regards a correct conception of His aims and a mature understanding of His teachings;—for they were still thinking of an outward glory in which He would sooner or later reveal Himself; and even later, many of them countenanced those Christians who still clung to the ceremonial of Judaism. In every respect, therefore, they were still children as to their faith; like those Christians of whom the apostle says that they were not yet able to bear strong meat, but needed still to be fed with the first milk of the gospel. And yet they were to begin at once themselves to feed others; indeed, on their testimony and their preaching depended from that time forward the whole result of the Saviour's mission. For while most assuredly the work of reconciliation and of justifying the human race in the sight of God was accomplished by Christ alone, who not only needed help from no one in that work, but could have made use of no one in it; yet if men were to reap the benefit of that work, it was necessary not only that He Himself should actually appear, but that after His departure the gospel should be preached and the association of Christians instituted. And so the Apostle Paul places these two things in direct connection, praising God that God was in Christ, reconciling the world to Himself, and then that He had appointed the office which proclaimed among men the message of reconciliation. But what kind of apostles for such a message, what kind of instruments for such a purpose, if they had continued such as they then were! How would it have been possible that everything which, although mixed with innumerable defects, has been developed during succeeding ages in the Christian Church,—all the strength of faith, the purity of discernment, the confidence amidst dangers, the steadfastness before temptations, the power of love, the gladness of hope,—that all this should have emanated from such teachers! And yet, from the time when the Saviour Himself was withdrawn from this earthly life, there was no other means of influencing men than through those disciples, who, however, could call forth nothing in others but what they had in themselves.

But hear what those men became,—hear it from the mouth of one of those very apostles. We suffer persecution, but we are not forsaken; we are troubled, but not distressed; we are cast down, but not destroyed; we bear about always in our body the dying of Christ, that the life of the Lord may be manifested in us. Therefore, what can separate us from the love of God? Shall tribulation, or anguish, or persecution, or famine, or nakedness, or peril, or sword? In all these we are more than conquerors, for we know that no power, either earthly or more than earthly, no separation between life and death, can ever separate us from the love of God, which is in Christ Jesus. But what more does he say here? We are more than conquerors, *because of Him who loved us.* And what does he set in the forefront of all this? That the excellency of the power may be of God, and not of us. It came from Christ, who was of God; and it was the life of Christ that was in this way made manifest. And this the Lord must have known when He came to bring a sword, and to yield His own earthly life as the first sacrifice to it. He must have known that when once, through His appearing on earth, the Divine power that dwelt in Him had begun to act on men, it would, of necessity, continue to act, and would do ever greater works. He must have known that He would abide constantly in His people; that their understanding of Him would become ever clearer, their love to Him ever purer; and that so, without His bodily presence, though still only by reason of His presence in Spirit, they would become fit to carry His message. Through all temporary denial, all unstable turning back, He must have seen that He was able to kindle in all believing hearts a love and loyalty like those of that first martyr whom we hold in sacred memory to-day; who, in the face of death, bore his testimony that in Jesus of Nazareth all the promises given to the fathers were fulfilled, and that in Him alone salvation was to be found. He saw not the rage of the excited crowd, not the stones already lifted to crush that radiant and heaven-lighted head, nothing of all the wrathful tumult: he saw only heaven (in which even here he had lived his life) opened, and the Son of Man standing on the right hand of God; and thus made plain to outward view the firm inward conviction to which he had just given utterance; and for the sake of which he now counted his life so little dear to him that he laid it down as a fruitful corn of wheat, which, when it dies, does not remain alone, but is preserved to eternal life and brings forth much fruit.

Yes, my friends, the Lord must have had in His heart this confidence; that He would, in this way, and ever, more gloriously, live on in His people; and this confidence reaches even to us, as certainly as that He still goes on working, and that He works only through us, the whole body of living Christians in all times. Thus the first of our principal festivals is connected with the last. How could we even rejoice truly in the appearing of the Saviour, unless we could also rejoice that this same strength of love and loyalty, and all that the apostle designates as the fruit of the Spirit, was poured out on us also by the same Spirit? Do we hail Christ in these days of solemn festival as our Lord? we can do so only through the Holy Spirit, who is the fountain of all these gifts. Do we hail Him as the Saviour who frees us from all other bonds? then that can only be, and continue to be, truth, if at the same time He holds us firmly united in one life with Himself by the indissoluble bonds of love, according to His promise, that when He should be lifted up from the earth, He would draw all men unto Him. Now if we are objects of this confidence of Christ, that all human life is to become one with His; then as surely as this confidence belongs to the divinity of His nature, we must share in it and work in the strength of it. Therefore if we, though living neither in the earliest times of the Christian Church, nor on its frontiers, yet experience in many ways that we must bring a sword;—only let us see that, like Him, we only *bring* it, but by no means ourselves take it and draw it, lest we perish by it; but if bring it we *must*—then let us be of good courage, ever keeping fast hold, like Him, of the love that makes free, which is always able to regard even those who oppose His truth as persons who know not what they do. Let us so much the more, constrained by love, gladly unite all our powers in the beneficent service of making Him known to those who, through ignorance, are in any way against the Lord; in such a way, certainly, as that on our side we follow after peace with all men; but also in such a way as not to be false to the Word of God which is committed to us; lest in this way the office of preaching reconciliation, which is the common duty of us all, should, through us, be accused of cowardice, and fall into contempt. And if, in doing this, we cannot avoid contention, whether with those who fight against the kingdom of God through want of understanding, or with those who, while acknowledging the doctrines of salvation, yet, out of the obstinacy of a foolish heart, refuse to be disciplined by them to godliness; well, let us reflect that at the festival of the Lord's birth, and therefore, from the beginning of His life, we greet Him as the Prince of Peace, and that this always continued to be His character in the midst of all the strife that He Himself brought, so that in this sense also His life is carried on in us. And thus, both in the midst of the internal dissension, which, alas! not unfrequently exists among the professors of His name; and in the outward conflict with the world; we also preserve the cheerful calmness, which with Him was never disturbed; and go on in the way of peace; so that, notwithstanding the sword, peace still rules on earth, for it has fixed its seat in the inmost heart of believers. And notwithstanding all apparent vicissitudes, a hearty good-will is found among all men to whom the grace of God in Christ has appeared; and who have had a glimpse into the depth of the riches of the wisdom and knowledge of God; for they know that, often as it threatens to grow dark again around us, the kingdom of Light is firmly established, and that all things must work for the best in the fellowship of those whom God loves in His Son. And so, through Him whose birth we are celebrating, peace and good-will have in truth, in spite of the sword, turned in to dwell with us, for which glory be to God in the highest now and evermore. Amen.

XVIII.

THE SAVIOUR'S PEACE.

(*Second Sunday after Trinity*, 1831.)

TEXT: JOHN xiv. 27. "Peace I leave with you; My peace I give unto you."

THE word which the Saviour here makes use of in speaking to His disciples has with us a twofold meaning. It suggests to our minds a condition of human society which, when it has been interrupted, we all long to recall; a state in which alone we look for universal contentment, and all things going on prosperously. But it has also another meaning; for we all know by our own experience the inward strife that goes on in the heart of man, and as its opposite, a peace—often interrupted, it is true, and seldom perfect—but still, the peace of the Lord. The Saviour could not promise peace of the first kind to His disciples. Referring to that, He said, I came not to send peace on earth, but a sword. He had told them before, and could tell them nothing different, that they would be hated and persecuted as He was, that like Him they would have to fight with spiritual weapons in the cause of His kingdom. But now that His work in the souls of His disciples was so far accomplished, He could promise them that which He had lovingly announced from the beginning, the rest that He invited troubled souls to come and find in Him; He could assure them of that inward peace even now, when He was just about to leave them. This word of the Saviour directs our thoughts, then, to the inmost depths of each individual soul, and shows us what is and ought to be wrought there by the Saviour, who claims this as His own work in our souls. Let us, therefore, in connection with these words, take this thought as the subject of our consideration—how each individual soul who is a partaker in Christ's redemption discerns, in the peace which He leaves to His people, in *His* peace, a fulness of divine wisdom such as no imagination can surpass. Let us first inquire what the Saviour's peace really is; and then reflect, and ask whether there does not lie in that, and in that alone, the whole fulness of the divine wisdom that can be revealed to a human being.

I. First, then, what is the Saviour's peace, which He left to His people? Is it the peace which He Himself had, or is it a feeble image, a dim shadow of it, a slight approach to it? What was the peace of the Saviour? His peace was grounded on this—that He was eternally, and in all respects, one with His Father; that whatever His eye rested on around Him, His spirit considered as a work of God; that He suffered His will to be determined by no emotion of His own mind, without having first recognised the will of God in what was required of Him; and that thus the one effect constantly kept pace with the other. He studied the works of His Father, and the Father showed Him greater and yet greater works; He did the will of the Father, and was ever more vehemently impelled to the fulfilling of that will, until He could say that all was finished. And as the divine will is nothing but almighty love, this oneness of will with God, by which the Father's will, and no other, was always His, could be in Him also nothing but an eternal fulness of love welling up from His heart. It was a love that was ever offering to men, sunk in the misery of sin, the greatest gift it could bestow, the gift of fellowship with His own life, so that they should be able to draw from His fulness, peace and truth and oneness with God; but it was also an indulgent and compassionate love, which did not refuse to men even the meaner things they craved, but with tender hand provided help for their bodily need. And this love, with the greatest gift always in store, but ready, at the same time, to bestow the lesser blessings—this love, making itself felt on all sides—this was the peace the Saviour had. And nothing whatever could disturb this peace, just because He had no plans, and took no step in His life that could have been out of harmony with the will of His and our Father,—just because He knew nothing whatever of an inward strife, but all within Him was, and remained, agreed in harmony, as it had been from the beginning. But certainly He would not have been able to carry in His heart this fulness of a love so moving, ever reaching forth to others, and offering itself to them; indeed, He would not even have seen the works of God which His Father showed Him, and no purpose of God would have ripened in His soul into a definite act; unless, sinless as He was, He had had the keenest and most thorough sympathy with the misery of sin. He saw men who were capable of being like Himself, for that was what they were meant to become—men whom, for that very reason, He did not scorn to call His brethren—sunk in that state of bondage from which the law had not been able to save them, for the law only brought them the knowledge of sin; and in this sympathy with sinful men the sinless One passed His life on earth; yet this had never power to disturb His peace, but rather was a living and essential element of it. How strongly does this compassion for the misery of sin come out in all His discourses, in which he sought to awaken a true conviction of sin in men who carried it in their hearts, and yet had so little sense of it! How deeply did this very sympathy enable Him to see into the human heart, even with regard to that which could have no place in His own pure heart! And the further He proceeded in His great work, the war of the divine Word against the sin of the world, so much the greater became this compassionate sympathy. If He could have thought it a possible thing that the power of sin, and His power to overcome sin, could exist together without sin being utterly vanquished by Him, He might have used, as the utterance of His own feeling, the words which could only be the expression of this sympathy with the sin of the world, "My God, why hast Thou forsaken Me?" But even then there was in His soul the same peace in which, a few moments later, He commended His spirit into the hands of His Father.

This, my friends, this is the peace that the Saviour had. Now when He says, "My peace give I unto you," is it this same peace, or is it something else? It is the same; and it becomes the same just in proportion as we can say with His true disciples and apostles, "The life that I live in the flesh . . . I live, yet not I, but Christ liveth in me": in this same sense and manner His peace becomes our peace. The Saviour could not say those words until He had given His disciples the promise that goes immediately before,—the promise of the Spirit, the Comforter, whom the Father would send in His stead, and who would bring all things to their remembrance that He had said to them. And He has left the remembrance of those things not only to them but to us; and it is the very beginning, the deepest and holiest foundation of our peace. That peace rests, not on the letter of Scripture, which relates to us certain incidents of His life and preserves for us some of His discourses; but on the power of the Spirit, without which the letter would be dead; and which could always, even apart from the written letter, have called forth the word that has carried the image of the Saviour down through all the ages. It is in this remembrance that peace is given to us; the more His image fills our souls, the nearer do we come to His peace; the more our life is pervaded by His, we feel ourselves drawn the more into agreement with God, and into such repose of spirit as He had, about what the Lord has ordained for us, and what He brings to pass among us.

But our position, it must be admitted, is different from that of the Saviour in this respect, that we know sin, not merely by sympathy with the condition of our brethren, but as what we are abidingly conscious of in ourselves. His soul was ever tranquil and unruffled: in ours there are continually storms to be subdued. If the Christ in our heart is asleep, the storms rage the more fiercely, the waves of passion swell the more mightily, until in the agitation and conflict we might often despair; but when we call on Him to awake, He hushes the storm, and rebukes us as fainthearted to be able to think we could perish, when He was in the ship with us. And in the subduing of this storm we feel the more strongly the power of the Divine life which He imparts to us. That might indeed be so, perhaps some one may say, if the storm only arose to be stilled by the awakened Saviour, if we had only to fight to be always sure of victory! But who can undertake to say this of himself? Which of us is not often worsted in the conflict of the flesh against the Spirit? And yet, my friends, let us hold fast the persuasion, that if only we never come to think that we were obliged to sin, or that, at least, it was allowable for us to do so, in order that the power of grace might be the more manifest; if we never cease to condemn sin; then out of every conflict, even if we have been defeated, we shall draw new gain in the way of self-knowledge and watchfulness; and with the consciousness of this, if the soul comes back to the Saviour, we may at once feel again His peace in our hearts. We struggle amid the waves, but He stretches out His hand and keeps us from perishing; he who rises from a fall is held up by Him with the same love that leads Him to leave the ninety-and-nine sheep in the wilderness, and go after the one that has gone astray until He find it. And because He thus goes after the lost, we too feel the drawing of His love in our hearts when we have fallen, and thus His peace comes back to us. And as eternally springing love establishes its throne in our hearts; as He, being one with His Father, comes to make His abode with the Father in our hearts; as we become more able in all we do to say, The love of Christ constraineth us; we gradually attain to a position in which our feeling toward sin, against which we fight with the whole armour of the Spirit, is only compassion in regard to something that has become alien to us. For as His soldiers we feel ourselves set in opposition to all sin, even to that which is in ourselves; and if it is the power of His love that influences us, it must be also His life which we live—a life in which we find ourselves utterly opposed to sin, as those who desire to have no part in it. And in thus regarding the Saviour, and in ever seeking to have Him live anew in our hearts, how can we help contemplating the picture of His peace, and receiving it into our hearts? If we thus go on growing richer in the experience which He has promised us, obeying His teachings and seeking to act in His strength, we become conscious that the power is from God, and that by it we are drawn more and more closely into fellowship with Him.

This, then, is the peace that the Saviour gives to us; a peace which belongs entirely and undividedly to Him, for He alone is its source,—a peace which, as Christ came to overcome the world, will certainly more and more overcome everything in us that still belongs to the world,—a peace which, because all things work together for good to them that love God, enables us to see in the whole chain of the divine procedure what the Saviour Himself saw in it—nothing but the almighty love of the Father in heaven.

II. Now, my friends, the more nearly this peace which the Saviour imparts to us approaches the perfection of that which He Himself experienced; the more free we become, through our life in Him, from the power of anything to disturb or perplex us; the more, we may be sure, shall we feel our hearts lifted up to give spontaneous utterance to the feeling that truly there is no higher good for the human soul, no more satisfying position that man can imagine, than that which is his when he can say that the Lord gives and leaves to him His peace. But it belongs to the nature of our present existence, and our having constantly to deal with the contrast between the great and the little in all the concerns of our lives, that if we wish to convince ourselves that the gift of peace is, in fact, the complete bestowal of the inexhaustible riches of God, we must compare the condition which it produces with something different. But with what shall we compare it? Not with the wavering condition of a soul which has, it is true, entered into some relation with Christ, but fails to maintain it. And just as little with the conditions which we regard, in the Christian world in which we live, as not depending on Christ. Neither of these comparisons would meet the case. If we wish to institute a comparison to convince ourselves that the peace which the individual soul obtains in Christ is the most perfect thing that can be imagined, we must compare what Christ has effected with what might be if there were no Christ. It is always, indeed, a dubious proceeding to try to look at what does not exist; but this view of the subject is so closely connected with the true, full, and cordial recognition of the divine counsels of salvation in Christ, that we cannot avoid it.

If we wish thoroughly to examine this subject, we must, in the first place, keep this clearly in view, that we have all along to deal only with man, and that we cannot imagine man without at least the capability of sin, even if possibly free from actual transgression. In this connection, our thoughts naturally turn to the picture presented to us in various lights, yet difficult or impossible to fill up, of the first parents of our race,—a period in whose lives is laid before us, in which, while sin was certainly possible to them, it had not come to actual life. And when we think of that happy state of human life, in which as yet no want or sense of need had awakened any sinful desire in man's heart, and in which an easy life called forth only a slight exertion of his faculties, we are ready to ask whether it would not have been better to continue in that condition. But let us consider the subject as a whole. Imagine the whole human race in a condition like that, and the whole habitable earth as just such a scene of innocent existence as we are accustomed to picture that garden of God at the beginning of our race; compare that with the form which our earthly life has assumed since sin appeared; see how everything, from the memorials that remain of all past ages down to the present day, bears witness to the alliance or the strife of human powers; how everywhere are to be seen the traces of art and science; and we must see clearly that all this could not have been without the incitement of pleasure, or the struggle caused by man's sin. If we compare these two conditions; will they not appear to us, the one like the pure, guileless countenance of an innocent child, on which there lies as yet, it is true, no shade of dark memories, but on which also no definite characters are written; and the other as the face of a man, deeply furrowed with the lines of many cares;—the face of one who has had experience of the world, and has battled with it both in his own heart and without? Which is the higher position? Which is the richer? in which is the higher manifestation of power, and therefore the greater glory to God? There can be no doubt as to your verdict. But I do not intend at present to go back on the great features of man's history; rather let us confine our inquiry to one point in regard to these two phases of his life, and say to which of the two we would really give the preference. And certainly we do not wish to picture man before sin began, as leading an idle life. No, he might be anxious to acquire knowledge, and disposed to work; he might obey the call to have dominion over the earth; but life would be for him without allurement, and without conflict; for wherever there is conflict, there has already been sin. Hence he would know nothing of the strength that comes only from conflict sustained; and the consciousness of his powers, which is only acquired in struggling to the utmost against temptation, would also be lacking to him. For if sin has once found a place in our nature, it becomes so closely connected with everything else, that our consciousness can only be complete when the sin has become actually manifest.

And the second condition? Well, let us suppose sin to have actually appeared, and that man has found himself engaged in the continuous warfare of spirit against flesh, but that he is to carry on this warfare by his own powers, and that no such Saviour as ours has been made known to him. If we compare even this position with our own, we must admit that, judging of men only according to outward appearance, so to speak, there will be no great difference. Our whole present life is maintained, as it were, out of the stores and at the expense of nations before us who knew nothing of the Saviour, because He had not yet come, and who therefore certainly sustained this warfare of spirit against flesh in their own strength. The Apostle Paul bears this testimony to them, that so little had the revelation of God, originally written on their hearts, been capable of being effaced, that having no law given to them as to the Jews, they had become a law to themselves. This law was in every heart, and every one recognised the demand and the power of conscience in regard to that which, as right and good, it set in opposition to evil. And how should we still so frequently linger over the works of those long extinct peoples in their dead languages, if it were not that we find in them shining examples of all human virtues? There is no sacrifice, no manly energy, no self-devotion of the individual for the common weal, of which instances could not be found among them; the names of the virtues—the names by which we still designate everything good and noble in human conduct—come down to us from those times. But shall we therefore give the preference to their position? There were two things lacking to them, and which would always have been lacking to every man so long as we had been left to ourselves in this warfare. The first is just that eternally outflowing love of the Saviour, which embraces the whole human race; that going out of His heart to all His brethren on earth; the supreme satisfaction that came to Him from the assurance that although by the will and counsel of God His work on earth was confined to a very narrow space, yet He should, after His departure, move all mankind. At first no eye had seen this love, no ear had heard of it, nor had the thought of it entered into the heart of any man; neither would it have done so if the Word had not become flesh. A darkness rested on the earth that kept the nations apart, so that each saw and loved only its own people. It was necessary that a light should shine from above to illumine them for each other; they needed to behold the glory of the only-begotten Son of the Father, and in Him to see God as a Father, in order to recognise and love one another. Only through Him could we be brought to look for a kingdom of God that should embrace all men; and what would everything else be in comparison to this? But still more! Let us suppose that the constantly extending commerce of men, the increasing intercourse of the nations, the ever-advancing maturity of mind in the whole human race, should have in course of time subdued the enmity among men, and checked the selfishness that stood in the way of universal love; and that just by these means a love at least similar to that which we have spoken of could have been produced towards all men; yet how entirely different a form would this have taken! and it could always only have been in this way, that we had become a law to ourselves, though possibly a better law than all former ones.

And in the second place, the pure image of the man who walked the earth without sin, the idea of a soul constantly one with God,—whence should that have come to us? The crowning point of our knowledge would have been lacking had He not been! What has more elevating power than this, that the Word was made flesh and dwelt among us; that He who was thus one with God gave us the right to call ourselves His brethren, to become children of God. No, without this fulness of vital power and joy which we receive through the Saviour, I do not care to live!

There is a fable that has long been current among men, and which is often heard even in these days. Unbelief invented it, and little-faith accepts it. It speaks of a time that is to come, or that may perhaps be already come, in which the case of this Jesus of Nazareth will be fairly concluded. Every human influence, it is said, is effective only for a certain time: the human race may have much to thank Him for; God may have done great things through Him; but He was only, after all, one of ourselves, and His time to be forgotten must come. If He was in earnest in wishing to make the world entirely free, it must also have been His wish to make it free from Himself, that God might be all in all. Then men would not only perceive that they had power enough in themselves to fulfil the divine will; but in the right perception of this they would be able even to go beyond the measure He laid down, if they only chose to do so. In short, it is not to be until the name of Christian is forgotten, that a universal kingdom of love and peace will be established, in which there shall be no longer any seed of enmity, such as has been sown from the beginning between those who believe in this Jesus, and the rest of the children of men. But never will this fable become fact. Since the days of His flesh the Saviour's image is indelibly impressed on the human race; and even if the written word should perish, which is only sacred because it preserves that image for us, the image itself will remain for ever; it is too deeply engraven ever to be effaced; and the words of the disciple will always be true, "Lord, to whom shall we go? Thou hast the words of eternal life!"

XIX.

WHY THE DIVINE INVITATION IS REFUSED.

(*Twentieth Sunday after Trinity*, 1831.)

TEXT: LUKE xiv. 18–20. "And they all with one consent began to make excuse; . . . I pray thee have me excused."

WE need no more than these few words to recall to us the whole parable from which they are taken. From the different accounts of this parable in the gospels we must conclude that the Saviour often repeated it. Its substance is that an invitation was issued to a great supper, and the guests at first promised to appear; but when the appointed hour was come, and they were required to present themselves, one made a pretext of this, and another of that piece of business, and said, "I pray thee have me excused."

The first thing to be noticed about this parable is the frequent occasion which the Saviour had to repeat it. He lived, as we know, entirely among His own people, saying that He had come only to the lost sheep of the house of Israel. Them He did not cease to call to Himself, and proclaimed to them that the kingdom of God had come nigh to them, that they might enter it, and to that end might gather around Him; He told them He would take care of them, protect them against all danger, and conduct them safely into that blessed kingdom of God. And there were many who gave ear to His first invitation. Where His voice was heard, men gathered around Him by hundreds and thousands, and their eagerness to hear the words of wisdom from His lips seemed more and more to increase, as if they could never have enough. But when they were required to take a decisive step, to show that they wished really to take their place in this kingdom of God, such as He represented it to them; when He, for that purpose, gave them clearer indications of the nature of that supper to which they were invited,—then they drew back and turned away.

That which led me to take these words as the subject of our meditation to-day was my having occasion to remember our recent harvest-thanksgiving. For this was my thought. It is bad, no doubt very bad, if a man invites himself to the enjoyment only of earthly comforts and possessions, forgetting the word, "Thou fool, this night thy soul shall be required of thee;" but far worse if a man in this short and fleeting earthly life misses hearing the divine invitation, and so little heeds this significant warning voice, that when the message comes to him, Come, for all things are ready, he brings forward this or that as an excuse. The higher the position of him who invites us into his society, even for fleeting moments, which are therefore all the more memorable; the less would we venture to offer an excuse, even when we ought to do so on account of some duty that hindered us. But when those who bring to us the invitation to the great feast receive so often the answer, "I pray thee have me excused"; when we are still constantly hearing this around us, and note the consequences; what a crowd of sorrowful reflections must stir the hearts of those who have themselves accepted this divine invitation, and who know the glory and beauty of the feast! To what class, then, do we belong? I can only ask in order to give an answer which all take for granted. We who meet here to remember Him who has called us into the kingdom of God, to nourish and strengthen ourselves with His words, certainly present ourselves as those who have not only heard but accepted His invitation; otherwise we should not be here at all. Whether there may not be here and there among us individuals who are in the position of saying, "I pray thee have me excused," is another question which may remain for the present undecided. But if we have indeed given ear to the invitation of the Lord, then we are all without exception what He called His disciples from the beginning, His servants; sent by Him, as He was sent by the Father, to invite men in the Father's name and in His. And this duty of inviting men into the kingdom of God is a work which may be done well and skilfully, or quite otherwise. Many a one who is called to this great work is urgent with souls, and constrains even those to heed and accept his invitation who, perhaps, if they had been addressed and called on in a different way, would only have said, "I pray thee have me excused." And if it is an experience too frequent to be disregarded, that still excuses are constantly being made, not only by those to whom the gospel is brought as something new from afar; but not less, and in various ways, by those who live among us and are familiar with the name of the Lord and His Word; we may depend on it that there has been something amiss in the manner of the invitation. Let us therefore consider these two points as they stand connected here: how it is that so many refuse the divine invitation, and then some of the mistakes into which we may fall in conveying that invitation to them.

I. In hearing of the invitation of the Lord to this great feast, which is meant to figure to us the kingdom of God, we think first, and quite rightly, of the universal call that comes in the name of the Saviour to all men without distinction, to turn their backs on the transitory things with which, unhappily, most people are taken up, and to enter on a higher life by turning to eternal things. This is the great, all-embracing invitation which had certainly been issued before in, as it were, a preliminary way, and often repeated; but that all things were ready for the enjoyment of this life in God could not be announced to the race of men till the fulness of the time had come, and the Son of God had appeared on earth. And even now among ourselves we distinguish between that preparatory news of all being invited, as we make it known from their youth up to those who grow up among us, and that decisive and urgent invitation, which we delay until, having made them acquainted with the Saviour, we count them capable of distinguishing for themselves what is mean and what is noble, what is perishable and what is divine in human nature. What is it then that hinders so many, even if they do not flatly and openly refuse this invitation, from accepting it as it is meant? If we adapt the call which we address to them to the sympathy with the spiritual life which Christ imparts to us, there would not easily be found among us any one who would utterly and once for all excuse himself, entirely renouncing his portion in the blessed life to which we are invited from above; and if he did, we should take no notice of it, but again and again renew the invitation. But many excuse themselves for the present, and would like to put off to an indefinite time. And why is this? Why do they think that they could not be ready yet, and could not resolve to comply with the divine invitation? With many it is certainly nothing but the indolence and inertia so natural to men. They prefer to go on in the way that they have hitherto followed; and if any kind of change is to be effected with them or in them, they do not care to calculate on what is unknown and uncertain, and would rather have everything happen to them without their needing to take any resolution or exert their own will in the matter. With others again the predominant feeling is a love for their present manner of life and for the things they possess and enjoy, in proportion to the satisfaction they find in them; and what keeps them back from obeying the call into the kingdom of God is the idea that in doing so they must give up everything in which they have found pleasure; that the kind of work which has easily and comfortably sufficed them must be set in the background, or be entirely abandoned; and for what? Only, in the first place, to enter on a hard and painful struggle. But if we ask what kind of enjoyment it is which a man must renounce in order to comply with God's invitation, is it anything but what the apostle meant when, speaking to the Christians in Rome of their former life, he said, "What fruit had ye then in the things whereof ye are now ashamed? for the end of these things is death." It is only the pleasure that is steeped in sin, only the work that ministers to selfish passions that must be given up; for these cannot but deaden the capacity for true life; and then shall the fruit be unto holiness, and the end everlasting life. For let it be remembered that we cannot say of any kind of work in which it is worth while for a human being to occupy his time in this world, that it will be repudiated or held in contempt in the kingdom of God. That kingdom is wide enough to give scope for every right exercise of the human faculties.

Now, this being the case, when the difference is so undeniably great and obvious between the unsatisfying pleasures and vain toil which men are to give up, and the blessedness of the divine life which is offered to them; have we not cause to suspect, when so many, instead of accepting the Lord's invitation to His great and blessed feast, still draw back and put it off, that the fault must lie, in great measure, with our manner of giving the invitation? There are, indeed, manifold errors which we may commit in this work; but the one which is most hurtful, and which is very common among us is this: that instead of showing men the happiness of the life to which they are called, we first set before them a death through which they must pass; we tell them of an anguish of soul over their past condition, which they cannot be allowed to escape; we demand of them a sense of utter loss and ruin, as that from which alone the new life can begin. But in so doing we go beyond our commission, and thus we must miss our aim with many. For such is the nature of man (a nature that we cannot change), that if we hold up to him the greatest and most glorious objects only very far off, and as nearer facts nothing but struggle and toil, sorrow and tears, self-sacrifice and abnegation, he holds back; he does not wish to make his way through all these to the higher things, great and excellent as they may appear in themselves. And therefore the Saviour Himself did not act on this plan. It was not at all His way to proclaim to men that they must, as the first thing, endure agonies of repentance, or to lead them to despair as to their own position. When He calls Himself the Physician who has come for the good of the sick, can you say that He presents Himself to them with the red-hot iron in His hand to cauterize their wounds? or are the medicaments which He employs internally of such a kind as to produce, though only as their first effects, pain and terror? And when He makes Himself known as He who has come to seek that which was lost, does He speak of using measures of terror and intimidation towards the lost sheep, that they may be driven back to His arms? Does He not tell only of going after them in faithful love into the wilderness, alluring and drawing them back to Him, and then rejoicing over them? But it by no means follows from this, that we are to make light of the difference between the higher life to which man can attain only by the Holy Spirit being given to him, and the earthly life as it appears in any well-ordered community. The effect of that might be that men would not be invited at all to the great and glorious feast to which we are to call them. But as regards the vanity of their life beforehand, oh, they will feel *that* of themselves all the more keenly, the more clearly we show them, as we are bound to do, the glory of that state to which we invite them; the warfare which they must maintain against all the memories and habits that would hold them still in captivity under the law of sin in their members will not fail to begin, if we have only first awakened in them a love for the blessed communion of the Spirit. Hence we shall most fully execute our commission as His messengers if we enter into the closest possible social intercourse with those to whom we are sent, and so be able to show them in ourselves the happiness to which they are invited. In this way we shall both attract those who have been kept back by indolence from complying with the Lord's invitation, and win over those who are absorbed in other pleasures or pursuits. Even in other connections we see men drawn to a new forth-putting of their faculties by coming into association with more highly cultivated powers with which they can ally themselves. Therefore, if we are to invite others successfully to share with us the abundance of the new life, we must ourselves be cheerful—not full of fretting anxiety, as if we might easily lose our share of this treasure. And we shall do this still more by gladsome deeds than by joyful expressions of faith—deeds that furnish them with ample proofs of the power of our own spiritual life, and awaken in them the desire for such a life. Then, when they are deeply impressed with the peace and happiness of the children of God, some will be helped to overcome their slothfulness, others their evil desires; and when once they have their eye fixed on the aim which we have pointed out to them by word and example, then will power be given them from above to carry on the conflict which, it is indeed true, none can escape.

II. But we must not confine our attention to this very general view of the subject. It is not only the call in a general way to the heavenly life in God, which is addressed to men under this figure of an invitation to a great and solemn feast; let us also consider this feast in its full abundance, in its great, inexhaustible variety. Once when the disciples of the Lord had left Him alone while they went to buy food during a journey, and He had meanwhile had an opportunity of preaching the kingdom of God to a lost soul, He said to them, when they returned and invited Him to eat, "I have meat to eat that ye know not of . . . to do the will of My Father in heaven that sent Me, and to finish His work." That was His meat, that is ours, to accomplish the will of our Father in heaven, and in this view, to what a rich and varied feast, to what an abundant table are we set down! Who can overlook the great mutual relations of human affairs in which we are all called to do the will of God? Who can overlook the great, divine work which is to be accomplished by the Saviour and those who are his faithful servants and fellow-workers? And whatever part we take in this important work—whether it seem great or small, it is a part of the great whole; it is one of the meats at this divine feast to which we are invited. And as in such feasts the wealth and affluence of him who gives them are made known; so, in the inexhaustible abundance and variety of the spiritual viands, all rich with the savour of the blessed fellowship into which we are brought with God, we recognise the unutterable riches of the blessedness of God, who has invited us to this spiritual feast. If, then, everything to which any of us feels called for the furthering of the Saviour's work is at the same time that which forms our enjoyment in this royal feast, let us be ever inviting others to every work of God as to the highest kind of pleasure. The opposition between work or duty and enjoyment, which makes so much difficulty for us in our earthly affairs, is not found in the kingdom of God: for every work that we accomplish is to the consecrated soul at once nourishment and pleasure. And to such a soul there is no pleasure that cannot be turned to practical effect; all the refreshment found in quiet meditation on the grace of God either leads to active work for others, or it becomes operative in the inner life, rooting us more firmly in the common soil of the divine kingdom, so that we may produce new flowers and fruits. In what rich abundance, in what inexhaustible variety, does this union of spiritual work and pleasure in the strength and blessed fellowship of the love of God lie before us! And in truth, when we see how, from one age to another, the kingdom of God has extended without losing its divine power, in the midst of all conflicts with the world—of all the conflicts that each man must carry on with himself, which indeed are just his conflict with the world, which has still some part in him—we are constrained to say that this is all the effect of successful invitation. And therefore we must believe that our invitation will still succeed in accomplishing a work of God, if we only make sure that it bears about it the spiritual savour and offers the spiritual nourishment that are found at this divine feast. How much friendly readiness do we find even in the great Christian communities to unite their efforts, when the Divine Spirit has awakened in hearts here and there a new resolution to take out of the way what is dangerous, to bring together all that is profitable, and here and there to produce some new thing that is still wanting to the beauty of the whole! And if every single purpose suggested by the Spirit of God finds friends and supporters, how sure we may be of not inviting in vain where a new ideal of life is demanding help against difficulties, and fresh exercise of newly-awakened powers that new work may be accomplished! But it must be admitted this is not always the case. When we address calls of this kind to men in the name of the Lord, and claim their help for some work of God, we sometimes find that, like those in our text, they say, "I pray thee have me excused." What can it be, then, that keeps back our brethren from responding to the call to a work of God? The chief mistake seems to me to be that there is still a distinction made between earthly and spiritual, between our duty in social and business aspects and our duty in the kingdom of God. But these ought never to be separated. For if a man is moderately busy in his worldly calling, and thinks his energies should all be expended on what it requires of him; if he is entirely taken up with his business, and considers, seeing that earthly business has its distinct claims, that he will be able to render a good account of the use he has made of his powers, although he has been able to give no help in anything, however beautiful or excellent, for the futhering of the kingdom of God—how are we to answer such an excuse? As long as our invitation takes for granted this opposition between the duties that are binding on us as members of society and those to which we are called by the voice of the Holy Spirit, in the name of the kingdom of God; just so long shall we have no certainty that our invitation is right, and it will always depend on a peradventure if it is to be complied with. For it is not easy to find a rule of universal application by which to accommodate to each other things of different kinds not already connected: every one has his own plan of how much he will give to the one or limit the other, and no one can assert that another has laid down an unfair rule, where each has his own. Therefore if there is to be a ready compliance with our invitations to an active interest in the works that concern the furtherance of the kingdom of God, we must set aside this distinction by regarding everything incumbent on each of us in our social position, as a part of our duty in the kingdom of God. We must, in fact, regard that position, as the place appointed for each at this great feast, and therefore expect from each in the first place that he fulfil all those duties as for that kingdom. There is certainly no earthly condition that more entirely claims all men's powers for the earthly life than did that of servants at the time when Christianity began. Yet what does the apostle say to those who, as slaves, were utterly subject to the sole will of their masters, and spent all their strength in ministering only to their earthly comfort? He bids them remain in the calling in which the Divine Spirit had found them; but to do what they did in that calling not as unto men, but unto God. And just so it may be and ought to be with each of us in our earthly calling. What we do in it, let us do as the work of the Lord; for everything that calls forth and strengthens the mental faculties, all that gives man mastery over human things and the forms of nature, may be of service in the kingdom of God, and is therefore connected with the Lord's work, which we are all to forward; and in the same way, whatever we may fairly expect others to do, must be what can be accomplished in this connection. And hence what a difference it makes whether we do a thing merely with a view to the outward life, or for some one person, or do it as to the Lord! I do not only mean that in the latter case the thing is better and more thoroughly done; but that what is done in a mere earthly way depresses our spirit, while in the other way it is lifted up and elevated; the consciousness of having done our work for the Lord will cheer and support us against all depression and amid all suffering. And will not he who has once gained this consciousness, be always finding that he has a surplus of strength to take part, beyond the narrow circle of his own business, in all kinds of work for the kingdom of God, and to do something more than his regular work when it is a question of helping to build the temple of the Lord! This employment of surplus strength and helpfulness will be seen wherever there is not a lack of hearty love of work; and where it is so, we may be sure that the difference will come out very clearly between those who, while doing everything to the Lord, are also obeying this invitation of His by always finding some new work to do for Him and strength in themselves to help in it; and those who, besides their ordinary business, aim only at perishing pleasures, and find their life in works of vanity, and therefore are always falling back into anxiety about trifling and transitory things.

Let us see, then, that we always take this right way of inviting—confirming our words by our actions; and we may be sure of always finding a friendly and favourable hearing, and that there will always be many to join with us in a thoroughly efficient way in all kinds of Christian work. And thus the circle will be ever widening of those who share in the glorious enjoyment of the spiritual feast to which the Lord invites us all.

III. Let us now notice shortly a third particular. We have seen that in this universal call we are invited to take part in all kinds of Christian work, by means of which life as a whole is to assume an aspect worthy of the Christian name, and to expand into fairer bloom; in which spiritual fellowship will thrive and increase, while the one thing needful will more and more hold its due place. But does this include all that is conveyed in the Lord's invitation to His divine feast? If I was right in saying at the beginning that we who assemble here implied by so doing that we had not only heard but accepted His invitation, then a call to assemble ourselves thus for the pure worship of God must be included in that invitation. It is true, we know that though the Christian says, "A day in Thy courts is better than a thousand," he does not refer exclusively to the Lord's day and to seasons of public means of grace; for wherever we are doing anything to the Lord, we are in His courts and in His temple. Nevertheless, these our Christian assemblies are a special point in the invitation; for remember how the apostles charged the Christians not to forsake them, but diligently to gather together. But in saying this, you are well aware that I do not here speak of an invitation to the presence of those who are appointed to dispense the word of God to souls. You know well it is not my view of the purpose of our meeting that I come to instruct you, and you come to be instructed by me; but that I only desire to be edified together with you by the divine word of our Lord and Master, as we meditate on it together. And let us not conceal from ourselves, but recognise the fact, that this is indeed a beautiful and glorious portion of that great spiritual feast to which we are all called. This passing from active life to quiet, united meditation on the word of God on an appointed day, is an arrangement so fraught with blessing, that we cannot dispense with it if we are in earnest fully to appropriate and rightly to enjoy the abundance of the Lord's spiritual benefits which are here offered to us. And I must say it is the case among ourselves that Christian people are diligent in assembling together, so that our gatherings are not thin and poor. But if we go no further than our near neighbourhood, there are many among the inhabitants of this great city to whom the pleasure of uniting with others for the animating of their hearts from the word of God is a more unusual thing than it ought to be; indeed, it is an ordinary remark among us that whole sections of the community are indifferent and deaf to this invitation. What is the cause of this?

There is one cause, certainly, which ought not to be found standing in the way of this invitation; that is, the pressing cares for the outward life, which so fret the soul that it has no power left for spiritual enjoyment; longing only for physical rest, when one more week of the toilsome life is past. And it is one great part of the problem which, looking from the standpoint of doing all to the Lord, we must ever be striving with united strength to solve; how the too great discrepancies in outward position, between those who are called to sit at the same feast may be more equalized, so that none may be obliged to be unduly engrossed in worldly business; that every one may have some time and capacity left for spiritual occupations and enjoyments, by which in turn, fresh vigour will be gained for every right kind of common work.

Another obstacle to the acceptance of this invitation is, no doubt, in many persons, their overweening self-sufficiency. What we hear at public worship, they say, we can say better for ourselves; there we are bound to a fixed time, but we can choose for our own meditation the time that suits us best; whatever we may do for our edification, whether from our own thoughts or in connection with the divine Word, will be more useful to us than what is not intended alone or even chiefly for us. But such ideas reveal a serious misconception; and if we are really concerned to gain a hearing for this part of the invitation, and to be always helping more of our brethren to this spiritual enjoyment, we must, if possible, correct those false ideas. How can this be done, do you ask? I think in this way. When we separate here, and each of us returns among his own circle, let the conversation be less about him who has been called on that day to explain the Word of God, than on the subjects themselves on which he has spoken; let the preacher disappear and the divine Word become the point of interest; let there be more said about the effect of such blessed Christian fellowship,—how each has been strengthened by the consciousness of a common interest in prayer, and by the fresh stimulus we have received together on our way to the goal set before us, and what joy we have had in seeing so many with their faces directed thither. In this way others will see how much value we attach to Christian fellowship, and that this is the chief thing in our assemblies; and in this way they will lose their mistaken ideas. For no one can believe that he is, or can accomplish for himself alone, all that offers itself to him in the full united power and kindly contact of a spiritual community. That a man should think he is able to do himself as much good as the voice of one other man can do, is natural enough in these days; but how great would be the vanity that should feel able to dispense with the Communion of Saints!

And now, would that it were not necessary to mention another hindrance! And yet I am constrained, and cannot but do so! The great difference in the ideas of Christians, when they come to express the great gospel call more minutely, one laying down its essential conditions in this way, another in that;—ah! this interferes only too effectually with the agreement and harmony of mind in our assemblies. You invite one or another, and he says, I do not hear there that which alone I count to be true Christianity; there the mystery of faith is not spoken of so as to edify me; there the words that most help me to communion with the Saviour are wanting; there certain expressions are used that disturb me in my devotion; the whole effect produced has a suspicion of scepticism, says one; it savours of superstition, says another. It is this unhappy narrowness that makes such divisions among us, and deprives us of so many spiritual blessings. And how are we to meet this difficulty? How weighty a question! This at least is certain, that if our invitation bears traces of this party spirit, it will have very little influence. Even natural things hold up an example to us here. The same forces in the soil produce a thousand different plants; but look at the proudest ornament of the garden, and the meanest flower of the field; the bee plunges humming into the one and into the other, gathering the same precious honey from all. Oh! that we showed ourselves as such bees, knowing how to draw honey from everything that contains any of the true spiritual sustenance! If we show in this way that we are bound by no such narrow views, but are able to draw strength for the spiritual life wherever only Christ is preached, in whatever manner; then in our invitations to our brethren we shall more and more get the better of this miserable party spirit.

Let us, then, not be weary of inviting others in every way to the Lord's great spiritual feast; for we are sent forth to do this. Our Saviour, though He devoted His whole public life to this mission, had but little outward and visible result to rejoice in; but He had in His heart the certainty that He was doing His Father's work, and was able to say when He left this world that He had finished that work. And therefore, in the midst of all the opposition that He met with from men, He held fast the same courage, the same serenity of spirit, the same unquenchable love to those whom He was to invite. And this is the pattern which we must follow. Then will our message be blessed at least in secret, even if we see but little outward result. The present is a time, specially favourable for this work—a time in which each of us cannot but hear a voice, which says that any night his soul may be required of him. How clearly at such a time does the difference show itself between those who, because they have as yet given no heed to the divine invitation, have fled from the sound of that alarming voice into the tumult of life, so that it dies ineffective on their ear, instead of drawing them away from the emptiness of earth to higher things; and those who hear that voice with tranquil hearts, because they have obeyed the call of the Lord and already, through faith, have won their way to eternal life, and conquered death. We have a fine example of how to invite under such circumstances in Ephesians v. 16, 19, 20. The apostle is telling the Christians how to suit their conduct to the evil days in which they were living; and what does He say to them? He bids them give thanks, and amidst the trouble of those evil days to sing and make melody in their hearts to the Lord.

Oh, friends, if our brethren see that we are able to do this in the present, and every evil day, *that* will be to them the most powerful invitation. If they see in us, in all circumstances, the same calmness and assurance, they cannot doubt that it is God's power that works in us, a power to which all have only to yield themselves, in order to enter the blessed kingdom of God; and thus will the number be ever increasing of those who join us in praising Him who has brought us from death to life. Amen.

XX.

LOVED IN THE BELOVED.

(*Third Sunday in Advent*, 1831.)

TEXT: JOHN xvi. 27. "For the Father Himself loveth you, because ye have loved Me, and have believed that I came forth from the Father."

THAT was a great word of the Saviour about Himself on which we lately spoke together, in which He represented Himself as from of old the one object of desire and longing to all the best part of mankind, to those who were nearest to God and had received most teaching from Him: but this is a still greater saying, in which He sets Himself before us as the real cause of the love of God towards us,—as He for whose sake alone, by virtue of our relation to Him, that is to say, on account of our faith in Him and love to Him, we became objects of the love of God, His and our Father. But it is He who can say of Himself what one would have been disposed to dispute in the mouth of any other, "If I bear witness of myself, yet my witness is true; for it was eternally clear to His own consciousness what He was to be to the human race to whom He had come. In all others this knowledge could only be gradually unfolded by experience; that is, by their obeying His word and actually fulfilling the will of God which He declared to them, that they should "believe on Him whom the Father had sent." Therefore, as we count ourselves among those who have learned to love Him, and have attained to the faith that He came forth from God, let us examine His word by the light of our own experience and make it clear to ourselves, in talking over it, how the Saviour is He for whose sake, if we love Him and believe in Him, we also are loved by God.

I. In the first place, every one will no doubt say to himself in contradiction of this, that if God is love, His love must reach as far as His omnipotence, and there must be a universal love of God. And certainly we shall feel bound to admit that this special love of which the Saviour speaks in our text is only an outcome of that universal love. As surely as the highest knowledge which we have reached through the Son of God is this, that God is love, so surely must we believe that every work of God's hands is also an object of His love. Only, of course, dead things could not be objects of His love; nor could that which, though certainly alive, yet was incapable of any perception of Him, be such an object; but the spiritual eye of those who know Him soon becomes so clear as to all outward things, that they perceive that anything which we can only regard as inanimate and dead is really in itself nothing at all. That which we could imagine as having no kind of connection with that life which alone among created things is the image of God, would have no proper existence. But there is nothing that is not in some way allied to it. Everything endowed with mind, everything that can, even in a very imperfect and distant way, become conscious of God, everything that according to its nature can be reached by the beams of His love,—all these are certainly in themselves objects of that love. And so the ancient accounts in the Old Testament of the creation of the world are closed with the words, "And God saw everything that He had made, and behold it was very good." That was the breathing of love, the look of divine delight over all His works; and it reached as far as His almighty power had done in calling into being that which was not; but still all was good only as connected with that part of this created, finite being which could be the reflection of His own being; which was capable of knowing Him and of feeling after Him in His works. And yet when we reflect that the principal subject of that old story is this earth alone, the scene of our life and work,—that it notices only in so far as they affect this world, all the rest of God's works, which our present knowledge shows us as being so much greater and of so much wider range; when we reflect further, that in this world man is the only intelligent being; with reference to whom everything is arranged, for whom everything is made that belongs to this world, or that has any bearing on it in other worlds;—with these things before our minds, oh, how can we understand the statement that God the Lord pronounced it all very good, when He saw not only man as the noblest work of His hands, appointed to have dominion over the earth; but just as clearly the fall of man, and all the loss to his spiritual life and work which sin would bring to this man and to the whole human race? We may surely say that if at that time God the Lord said of man and of the earth which was to be his possession, that all was good, it must have been because He had in view not only sin and the fall; but further,—and that not merely as included in His satisfaction, but as being the essential ground of it,—Him who was appointed to restore all things. Indeed it was only in reference to Him,—only because human nature was capable of receiving into union with it the Word who was to become flesh, therefore only because through Him man was to be brought back to God, into a closer and more intimate relation than had been possible before,—it was only in view of all this that God the Lord pronounced all good. And therefore already in this Word He made Himself known as the God who would have compassion on sinners, and who would overlook the times of ignorance, if only in those times He in whom God was already well pleased, should find in men the adherence, the faith, the love without which He could neither impart His thoughts to them nor bring them into perfect union with God. And thus this universal love of God is everywhere shown to man as to the creature made in His own image, in all his various conditions; this is the way in which the Scriptures throughout explain and make intelligible that love and compassion of God; that He has included all under sin and unbelief, that the promise might come through faith in Him in whom alone it would be made plain to all for what a glorious destiny God had created man. Therefore all that we are told of the special love of God and His delight in individuals concerns those who, according to His unsearchable plan, were appointed to stand in a closer earthly connection with Him who was to come. And so the nation from which the Saviour was to arise was His chosen nation; for this reason it was preserved and kept separate and again and again delivered from the distress into which it had brought itself by sin, in order that the revelation of God should be kept safe, and that from this nation should come the only-begotten Son of the Highest. And thus we must say that all mankind was from the beginning the object of the divine good-pleasure and love: nothing that was created in His likeness, nothing connected in any way with this created image of Himself, was excluded from His fatherly care; but no one was an object of God's love and solicitude in himself and for his own sake.

II. This brings us, then, to the second point to be considered; namely, what is the distinctive nature of that special love of God to us on account of our faith in Christ and love to Him? But this special and that universal love are so joined that even what the Saviour here spoke of specially to His disciples signifies nothing different from that universal love. It was not His disciples in themselves, as they had been and as they would have continued to be without Him, who were the objects of the divine love He speaks of; but only, He says, for this reason does the Father love you, because you have learned to love Me, because you have attained to the faith that I came forth from God. For as the Saviour of the world was, even from the beginning, as the only-begotten Son of God the one immediate object of divine satisfaction in this whole world of men; God chose and drew to Himself in a special manner, (as we lately saw in the case of Abraham,) only those who were connected with Christ's future; although they received, in the greatest moments of their lives, only a far-off prevision of that future, which, faint as it was, became their greatest possession and the most precious treasure of their lives. And just in the same way He chose the disciples of His Son, only because of their closer connection with Him; as indeed it was natural that their love to the Beloved of God should attract the love of God to them. How like man the Most High seems to speak in these words! And yet how directly obvious must their divine truth be to us as well as their human character! This is just what we all feel; he who loves those whom we love, becomes thereby the object of our love. And if he was already such in some degree, he becomes now the object of a different, a new and more fervent affection. It cannot be otherwise. If the Saviour was the direct object of the divine delight, how should not God have taken delight in those who recognised in that Saviour the glory of the only-begotten Son of the Father? If He was the object of the Father's delight because through Him the whole human race was to be brought to God and to glory; how should not those also have become objects of God's delight, and have been, as it were, flooded with a reflection of His glory, who not only recognised that in Him all the divine promises were actually fulfilled, and knew Him as the source from which alone flowed the words of life, but who, moreover, could not but serve Him with their whole being in the accomplishment of all the divine purposes for the salvation of the world.

And how does the Saviour Himself represent to us this love of God, of which we become the objects for His sake? He said to His disciples, I will not say that when you have need of anything, when you wish to ask anything from the Father, I will pray for you to the Father; for the Father Himself loveth you, because ye love Me and believe that I have come forth from God. Now is not this the highest relation in which man can stand towards God—that he should make requests and God grant them, that he should ask and God should answer? For each question is really a petition, and every answer is a gift. Nowhere among the human family, indeed, has this relation been regarded or expressed otherwise than just in this way. If in any place there was a sanctuary specially consecrated to higher beings or to the Highest, it was in order that prayer might thus be presented before God, and that thence might flow forth the blessings granted; that doubting spirits might there propound their questions, and receive an answer out of some mysterious depth of the divine nature. And this is the peculiarity of our relationship to Him, the Father—that He is only called on to give us such things as the heart purified by the word of His Son desires, only to answer such questions as are connected with our love and faith, because just by reason of our love to the Saviour and our faith that He came forth from God, no other questions arise in our hearts. Oh, what grander imagination can we have of our relation to God than this? Is the highest Being the source of all happiness and of all good? Well, then, all must be good that comes from Him. And if His gifts are granted in answer to our requests, that is a sign that we ask what it was in His mind to grant us, that our souls are in harmony with the principles on which He rules and arranges the world of intelligent beings whom He has created in His likeness—a sign that we are only desiring that which He has Himself appointed as best for us. For if we asked anything else than this, He would not grant what we asked. And the Saviour therefore regards this as the fruit of our love to Him; for how can those who love Him and believe that He came forth from God ask for anything but what belongs to the work for which He came from God and came into the world, and after it was accomplished left the world and returned to the Father? What can they ask but what belongs to the work of saving the world through Him? And if our prayers have no other object than what is suggested by our love and faith towards the Saviour,—well, He says, I need not even say that I will pray the Father for you, for the Father Himself loveth you; that is, the thing you ask will come directly from Himself. But in fact these two ideas are essentially connected, and are the real ground of the relation which the Saviour means to establish between God and us; the fact that we have really learned to love Him as He was, in view of what He came for, what He lived for, what He laid down His life for; and further, that we have arrived at the conviction that He came forth from God, given by God to men for their salvation, to fulfil His purposes of blessing towards them. And so the Saviour says also to His disciples a little earlier, "Hitherto have ye asked nothing in My name." For that alone is a prayer in His name, which is prompted by this faith in Him and love to Him; and it is only what is asked in His name that He promises His disciples will be granted. And therefore, He says, when I am no longer among you, you will ask in My name; for not till then will your souls be quite purified from the misconceptions which before were still mixed with your love and faith; and then you will only wish to obtain by your prayers that which from the beginning has been the real object of your doings and efforts; that is to say, only what belongs to the great work which the Father has appointed Me to accomplish. So far, then, as we no longer ask anything but what can be asked for in Christ's name, the Father loves us, so that He grants us what we ask; and such love to the Saviour is inseparably connected with the faith that He came forth from God. How otherwise could we so utterly bind ourselves to the work and will of a single man?

Yet, my friends, let us still linger a moment to look particularly at these words. How long they have given occasion to ever-renewed keen dispute and painful dissension among Christians! How have believers longed and striven to penetrate more and more deeply the mystery of this doctrine of the Saviour's proceeding from God! and how often has some particular way or another of thinking about it been the cause of utterly dividing Christians, and of rending apart their loving fellowship! If such mysterious doctrines, if any such exact definitions of the manner in which the Saviour proceeded from God were a part of the faith on which God's special love to us depends, oh, how was it possible that He who was the very brightness of that love should have been so careless of His own as not to have given them the plainest and most definite explanation of this in the most impressive way! How could He have left it, as it were, to chance, whether they should attain to this knowledge or not, if yet their share in this special love of the Father depended on it? How easily has now one, now another, been always falling on some new interpretation of the doctrine, how difficult Christians have always found it to agree on one and the same view, while yet each supported his own from Scripture! But how ruinous is this apparently so unavoidable difference of opinion, if it is not enough to believe that the Saviour came forth from God;—if the love of God does not rest on him who holds that it is to be understood in this particular way and not in that other way. But, my friends, just because the Saviour brings our love to Him and our faith into so immediate connection, we may be sure that what only affects our belief that He came forth from God, in such a way that it has no influence on our love to Him, can just as little affect God's love to us; and we may tranquilly allow all such differences to take their course, so that this subject may always be coming up anew for Christian investigation. But that which cannot contribute to the growth of our love to the Saviour, for that very reason, does not determine God's love to us; and oh, still less let it mar our love to each other, still less let it break the bond of unity in which we show our love to the Saviour by helping forward His work. So we may let all that rest; if we are only sure of this, that to the question John sent to ask the Lord, "Art thou He that should come, or look we for another," there can be no answer but this: yes, truly, in Him all the promises of God are yea and amen; there is no other to be looked for after Him; in Him the whole fulness of divine love and grace is revealed to us, and the true life communicated to us through Him; yea, all saving truth is set before us in Him. And if we know this, that is believing that He came forth from God. For the fulfilment of the divine decrees can only proceed from God, and He must have come forth from God, who was to solve the mystery of man's so chequered and intricate and often so dark destiny;—so to solve it that the issue of all shall be that very peace that comes from above, and that very eternal life to which all who believe in Him have made their way through death.

III. But let us propose and answer yet a third inquiry. We have seen that because we love the Saviour and believe that He came forth from God, therefore the Father loves us, and that we thus stand in a certain direct relation of love to God. Now, from the moment in which we take possession of this relationship to the Father,—when it actually becomes our property, does not our separate relation to the Saviour become something superfluous? is it not from that time cancelled? And so would it not be most correct to say that the first and original love is still that universal love of God to everything that lives and is capable of taking knowledge of Him in His works? but because men kept back the truth in unrighteousness, because they refused to see and praise Him in His works, and so must have gone on sinking ever deeper into ruin, therefore God had resolved from eternity to send His Son, on whom their love and faith might in the first instance take hold. In this way they would be made capable of perceiving God's plan, and understanding His will; they would not only become conscious of His omnipotence, but would infer His fatherly love. But when the ruling consciousness of this relation between God and man is re-established, and they are thus brought back to the position of children of God; then the knowledge of His love calls forth answering love, and there is no longer need of any special medium through which to use and enjoy this relationship. Does the Father love us? then we no longer need any intercession, not even that of Him whom the Father sent for our salvation, as indeed this is just what Christ says! Why then should we not be able to continue in this direct relation to God, and the mediation of Christ be just as well forgotten in time, as it was out of sight before? Now here, you see, is the difference between Christians. There are those who wish only to *learn* from Christ, who believe that He was sent to open men's spiritual eyes anew to necessary and saving truth; but that if a man has again found his way to the truth, and is enlightened by it, that light is kindled in himself and goes on burning; and that his mind would not be at one with itself unless the power increased in him to follow the truth he knew. And thus each of us must count on his own efforts to help himself on after the truth has been given us by Christ: He must ever be held in blessed and grateful remembrance among men, and His teaching must be always the first step on which they take their stand: but now men's relation of childlike obedience to God, as well as their confidence in the blessings of His fatherly love, is a direct relation, based on their own knowledge. Very different from this is the language of those who not only wish to learn from the Saviour, and who do not merely believe that it was necessary for Him to come into the world in order, as the Light, to pierce through the darkness; but who regard Him as the Life of the world, in whom alone we have life. Such persons never believe it possible to do without the Saviour, even if they have come to the Father; even if they feel it to be true that the Father loves them because of their love and their faith, ah, they cannot depend on being able to maintain this relation, if they forsake the Saviour. Towards which of these views do the Lord's own words in general point, and more especially those which have been the subject of our present meditation? If the Father loves us for this reason, that we love the Son, would not the Father's love necessarily cease if we could ever cease to love the Son, for whose very sake He loves us, as the effect always ceases with the cessation of the cause? If the Father loves us because we believe and are confident that Christ came forth from Him, would not the Father's love necessarily cease if this faith and confidence became of less value to ourselves? But the words of the Saviour say even too plainly that this is impossible! Just as He was aware of the weakness of His disciples, and knew beforehand that when they should be tempted, after the Shepherd was smitten, to scatter every man to his own, yet His prayer must be fulfilled, that they should continue in His truth; so by the very act of expressing this assurance, He declared that their love to Him could not cease. What kind of a love would it be that could ever let go the beloved object? Such a love could only be a fleeting emotion, that had no spring in the calm depths of one's being. If we have really learned to love the Saviour, we cannot forsake Him; nor can we entertain the question whether, if we forsook

Him, we should continue in the Father's love. We feel the truth of what He says, Because you love Me, without Me you can do nothing; our very existence is involved in the question of whether we persevere in love to Him or forsake Him. If we have once acquired the confidence that He came forth from God, must we not then feel unsafe in every step that we should take on our way to salvation, if we consciously had less desire to follow Him than to seek out some path for ourselves? No, the thing is impossible; we love Him, and therefore we cannot cease to love Him: we believe that He came forth from God, and therefore we cannot wish to live apart from Him. And therefore we continue sure of the love of God to us, because love to the Son is never extinguished in us. And it will always remain true, that there is no way for us to see the Father but in the Son; He will ever be to us the nearest and most complete revelation of the Highest; we shall always, in our union with Him, be conscious of the fatherly love of God, and continue in it. He who abides in love, abides in God, and God in him; but this is the love that came from God, that we love the Son whom He has sent, that we cleave in firm confidence to Him, out of whom no salvation is to be found for the human race.

And so, my friends, let us anew welcome the Saviour, through whom we are brought into fellowship of God's fatherly love; let us acknowledge it as the greatest benefit that God could pour forth on us, that He sent Him to bring us into such a union of love with Himself; but let us not proudly trust in ourselves, as if we could go forward in the way of life without Him. Rather let us keep faithful to that word of the disciples which has always been the watchword of all who loved and believed in Him: Lord, to whom shall we go if we leave Thee? Thou hast the words of eternal life! Amen.

XXI.

THANKSGIVING AFTER CHASTISEMENT.

(*Preached on the Cessation of Cholera, Feb.* 1832).

TEXT: HEB. xii. 11, 12.

MY devout friends, the terrific form of the devastating disease which has so long been raging in this great city has now left us, though we cannot feel entire confidence that it will not return; for it would not be the first instance if it appeared a second time, in a place so densely populated, to repeat its devastations. But are we right in availing ourselves of the apparent cessation which has been granted to us through God's kind providence, merely for the purpose of offering Him our thanks that the chastisement is past? Not so! that would not exhaust the meaning of the sacred words which we have just heard. Although this disease has been a chastisement which has brought forth the peaceable fruits of righteousness only in so far as we have allowed ourselves to be exercised by it; yet it assuredly befits us to give thanks not only that it is past, but also that it has been here. In a preceding verse, the writer speaks thus of the divine chastenings, saying, if we were left entirely without chastening, of which all the children of God are partakers, we should have no right to consider ourselves sons, but only bastards. Therefore it is most fitting on an occasion like this that we should consider

God's providential dealings, which are the cause of our meeting, in their whole connection.

I do not, of course, wish to be here understood to mean that we must be able to discern and comprehend why exactly this or any other chastisement of the same or of a different kind has been needful. But as soon as the chastisement is so far past that we are able to breathe more freely, and to raise our thoughts to calm meditation, our minds should be disposed to give thanks to God by such considerations as these. We feel that we must not remain without chastisement; and even a small amount of self-knowledge suffices, in general, to convince us that the manifold forms of chastisement that we meet with in the course of our life are arranged for us all by the Father of spirits in His fatherly love, in order to exercise us now in this, now in that lesson of Christian piety.

Regarded in this way, my dear friends, the words of our text form, as it were, an explanation and application of those words of the Apostle Paul which we so often weave into our united prayer, to which also reference is not unfrequently made in our meditations, that to those who love God—and they are assuredly only those who not only regard all that comes from Him as sent for their exercising and training, but who use it to that end—that to them all things must work together for good. And our text has a similar relation to those other words of the same apostle, in which he calls on Christians in all things to give thanks to God, whether they seem at the time to be joyful or sorrowful things. And it is to be thanksgiving with prayer and supplication, proceeding from the consciousness that we shall always need new chastisements as means of training, as well as new tokens of favour. In order, then, that we may present our present thanksgiving to God, as it becomes His children, let us see what the words of our text represent to us as the good which our chastisement is to effect for us. It mentions two things: in the first place it is said there grows out of it a peaceable fruit of righteousness; and then, secondly, we are encouraged—and who would not count this just as great a blessing—after having endured chastisement, to lift up again the hands that hang down and the feeble knees; that is, to rise again to undiminished courage and to cheerful activity.

I. As to the first point, then—the statement of the writer of our epistle that chastisement when it is present seems not to be joyous, but grievous; but that afterwards it brings forth the peaceable fruit of righteousness—let us, first, for a moment turn our attention to this point, which of course he believes and by no means denies, that chastisement seems to us grievous. If now and then strong-minded people claim that a man should always stand unshaken, not bowed down by the heaviest trouble; that the sharpest and bitterest trial is to leave no trace on his features; the Scriptures make no such demand on us. If a severe, unwonted calamity interrupts the peaceful course of human life; if we make unexpected and disastrous experiences of the powerlessness of all art and science when opposed to the inscrutable forces of Nature; if it seems to us that, as it were, every sinew of the noble power over the earth, to which God has appointed us, were cut, and as if our mind could only slowly recover from a great defeat which it has suffered in its struggle with Nature;—Scripture does not require us to think that joyful; it must rather, according to human nature, be grievous to us. Only we must not understand the words of our text in so limited a sense as to suppose that the peaceable fruit of righteousness may not appear until the affliction is entirely past. That could only apply in the case of sufferings that pass quickly over, such as do no doubt often fall on individuals, but not as to those which press for a length of time on the same community, though, it may be, passing from one to another, and thus daily renewing the affliction. And so it has been with us in the past months. When we read in the public papers the daily number of the sick and the dead; and the list of those who had recovered, beginning from a very small number and only very slowly increasing, the great disproportion was grievous to us; if a faint hope had begun to dawn upon us that the force of the disease was broken, and it spread afresh with increased virulence, that bowed us down in deeper affliction; but the peaceable fruit of righteousness was already springing up between these alternations of sorrow, and was nourished by them. I am not speaking especially of those members of the Christian congregations in this city who have made sad acquaintance with this frightful disease at close quarters: from whom members of their domestic circle have been snatched away by death—and how often have the dead in one house been many! Even so early as the end of the year, when we kept our usual day of remembrance, this terrible form stood in painful distinctness before us; even then, we were all most profoundly sharing this sorrow with those on whom the stroke fell, while, full of the deepest sympathy, we looked round over the circle of its devastations. Now let us rather, so far as we can, fix our eyes on the whole compass of our common life, which, however, is hardly to be taken in at one view; let us look at the form which it has gradually assumed; then shall we become conscious what is pre-eminently the peaceable fruit of righteousness which proceeds from such affliction; which indeed must go on showing itself during a longer continuance of public and general suffering, and must grow and ripen in proportion as we are compelled to struggle with that which is pressing on us.

All great divine chastisements, my devout hearers, whether it be a desolating disease or a destructive war; whether it be that Nature has for once shown herself unusually niggardly, and refuses to bring forth fruits enough for the sustenance of great masses of men crowded together into narrow space; or whatever else it may be; all similar calamities, which become actually oppressive, appear to us in a natural and close connection with the state of human society. We feel that partly they would take a milder form, partly they would be more easily borne, if they did not always anew, yes, and always even more strongly produce out of the present so complicated course of our life so great an inequality of outward circumstances. This is what we are most deeply impressed with in such circumstances; the great difference between those who not only have ready everything in the way of remedy that specially depends on man and lies in his power; but are also able to afford help to many others, if they no more than cut off here and there something superfluous, and are willing to make a slight retrenchment;—the difference between such persons and those who, being obliged in the ordinary course of life to put forth all their powers to meet the principal and most urgent needs, cannot be able to cope with such times of unusual distress and suffering. In such times we become aware of this difference in a specially painful way; for it is with good reason that we pity our brethren less on account of not being able in ordinary times to enjoy the same high and refined kind of life as ourselves, than because of being unable in unusual times to protect themselves against the pressure of distress. And the greater share we have in the benefits of our social position, and the more conscious we become how even the spiritual helps which we have at command are connected with those outward advantages, so much the more painfully do we feel oppressed by this inequality. But in that case there results to us so much the more certainly the fruit of suffering and of chastisement, which is righteousness.

That is to say, my beloved friends, this virtue finds a place only in man's social condition; if that condition did not exist, there would be no righteousness. If each of us depended only on his own ways and doings, and had only to care for himself and the narrowest circle of those belonging to him, we should know next to nothing at all of such a virtue and of the manifold discharge of obligations that arise from it. What then is righteousness? Assuredly nothing else than the justly guiding sense of the relation of each individual to the community to which he belongs. It is the endeavour to meet the requirements of this connection at every point; and the making, with our own free will, a suitable appropriation to what circumstances demand, of all the blessings for which we are indebted to this position of united human energies; thus directing the stream of prosperity into places where things are least prosperous. It is the coming forward with active help where there is most manifest inadequacy; so that the benevolent eye may rest rather with pleasure than with pain on the still remaining inequality, and that everything in its own place may appear worthy of the whole and express its spirit. Times of repose, whether we regard them more from the side of work or from that of enjoyment, rather bring with them various temptations to unrighteousness, and, as experience teaches, are not specially fitted to favour a correct estimate of our relations towards others and of our duties towards the whole. As long as all around us are at least in a tolerable state, each of those who are in more favoured circumstances believes only too easily that he has a perfect right to all that he possesses and enjoys, and that he may dispose of it as seems best to him for the carrying out of his own wishes, without being in the least under any obligation as to others. That is the beginning of unrighteousness; and how easily, if nothing intervenes, can it grow from this beginning to a threatening and dangerous height. Therefore from time to time, by unknown and ungoverned forces of Nature, or by means of the seeds of discord that are always present in human society, or through some general blazing up of passions, the Most High brings about sharp chastisements that affect wide districts; and there is indeed good reason then to say that whom He loveth He chasteneth. Then those possessions often flee away suddenly in vapour and smoke; then the firmest edifice falls to ruins in a moment; and then each one learns by experience that what he possesses and enjoys is not his own work, but dependent in every way on much that is not in his own power; and above all on the security and protection of public spirit and good-will. And in this way every one learns also to regard himself more as an administrator of a common property; and in this conviction gives up his false idea that he is a proprietor sufficient to himself, and so entirely rightful a possessor that he would have a claim to compensation if he ever sustained any damage. And the same holds true even of the bitterest loss which such times of chastisement may bring to an individual. For if love has lost a beloved object, there lies even in the sorrow which we feel, the consciousness of a power which is not broken, but only quiescent; and even amidst and through the sorrow a longing is stirred, and reminds us that this power of loving is a talent entrusted to us, a common property; and we thankfully acknowledge that if the chastisement does not offer us exactly a compensation for what we have lost, yet that it satisfies our impulse to be working by love. Now if every one not only considers himself as a steward of common property as to his outward possessions, but also lives in the consciousness of how he himself is indebted to the whole, that becomes a new beginning, a fresh seed of righteousness among a people.

And this, my beloved, is called in our text a peaceable fruit. This expression of the sacred writer stands in the closest connection with what goes immediately before; that every chastisement, at the time when it lays hold of us, seems not joyous, but grievous. Joy and sadness—the alternations of these opposite states of mind—are most closely connected with our natural temperament. Where joy is so strongly and vehemently expressed that it almost overpasses the bounds of a certain moderation that we have in our mind's eye; and, in the same way, when we see men going along oppressed and bowed down by sorrow; there we have a foreboding that for the moment, at least, things are going ill; indeed that the power of the spirit over the flesh is almost endangered; then we see how easily the soul can be shaken from its true balance, which yet is necessary to it if the spirit is to keep a firm hold of the reins and assert its ruling position over the flesh. But all the vicissitudes of life, whether they may plunge us suddenly from joy into sorrow or the reverse, are meant, just through exercise, through the wise encountering of danger, to raise us more and more above this vacillation; so that we may guard against excess, and equanimity may be the prevailing habit of our life. But we only encounter danger thus when the consciousness of spiritual well-being, which does not depend on the changes in our natural life, has become really our own feeling, the true substance and strength of our life. Then those varying emotions of the mind will more and more be repressed, and the uniform higher life will predominate; the oil of peace will more and more smooth and level the troubled surface; and the summons by the divine will will make us as secure amidst all storms as in the most sheltered haven. But above all, is it this very righteousness to which we are called by the divine chastisements, which produces and confirms this peace in us. For how can we still be keenly moved by the acquisition or the loss of outward possessions, if we regard ourselves only as stewards of those things, who will have no further account to render for what is taken from them? And if in suffering and in joy we equally feel the need to keep faith and to show love to those among whom God has placed us, how can it but be that in a soul thus exercised God's peace should prevail even during His fatherly chastenings.

That, my friends, is indeed the blessed experience which we have already made in the time now past, when that bitter chastisement assuredly lay heavily and oppressively enough upon us. Indeed what I have just been expressing was the view and the disposition which on the whole was prevalent; and how did we rejoice to see this seed of righteousness not only spring up everywhere, but make such increase that, with the exception of a few easily forgotten moments of transient tumult which perhaps took place here and there, we were preserved throughout our land from all kinds of violent deeds which often enough result from great general calamities. And many undoubtedly have become aware of this to their comfort; that it is only the sentiment of piety and of submission to the divine will, deeply impressed by the grace of God on our people, and well sustained and fostered in their character and spirit, although often concealed in ordinary life and not at all making an outward appearance everywhere,—that it is this alone which, in this time of trouble and anxiety, has kept us free from everything that would hinder us now from looking back, with a pure feeling of thankfulness, on the chastisement which God has removed from us. Oh, if to all the misery that we have seen and borne together, crime had been added! if disobedience to the laws, whether to those which always rule our life, or to the regulations which in that trying time were judged necessary to check the destructive spreading of the disease,—if this disobedience had broken out into acts of violence, so that internal peace and security had been destroyed; how heavily should we have been bowed down by the reproach which in that case would have lain on our commonwealth, that we were not capable of offering prayer and supplication in a way pleasing to God! and moreover how little should we be fit to lift up the hands that hang down and the feeble knees! Well for us, therefore, and let us thank God specially for this, that in the midst of the sorrow and suffering of this painful time, the peaceable fruit of righteousness has grown up among us; that a disposition to Christian gentleness and benevolence was so actively manifested that even those who are most at a disadvantage in our complicated social condition must yet admit, with joy and gratitude, that their fellow-citizens are not unworthy stewards of temporal blessings, and that they have faithfully come to their help in the time of need. And thus also, through this trial, every fair bond of harmony and confidence has been more firmly knit. Only let us not, through being too strongly moved by anything that the moment brings, thoughtlessly forget the chastisement which God brought upon us and which He has now removed; and so we may hope that from one period to another the tree of righteousness will bear still richer and fairer fruit; that we shall be more and more richly adorned with all social and Christian virtues, and that by public spirit and regard to law, by integrity and pure goodwill, we shall show ourselves worthy of the divine chastisement. For the Father chastens those whom He loves, and means by His chastening to exercise them in godliness.

II. And now let us lay to heart the second part of our text: "Lift up," says the sacred writer, "the hands that hang down, and the feeble knees."

You will feel bound to admit that it is the nature of all chastisements like this, that in more ways than one they impede men in their usual work. We have to rejoice over many beneficent works of brotherly love, which this time has brought to light among us; but let us not forget, at the same time, how urgently these were required; and then we shall certainly be obliged to confess, that however laudably sympathy was expressed during this distress, that is still no proof that our hands had not become weary and our knees feeble; only this effect is often not felt until afterwards! Were we not all filled far more than ordinarily with the sense of the insecurity of all human things? and it is the universal experience that this feeling cannot but weaken in many ways the inclination for and ardour in all the social movements and operations working into each other, from which, nevertheless, the common well-being must always, as it were, proceed anew; so that only too often, during such general troubles and after them, a great many ruin themselves in the most criminal and hazardous play with earthly possessions. But if it is only the more thoughtless who do this, yet we notice similar changes in almost all; and there are only a few who distinguish themselves by continuing quite the same. And if we go back to the cause that produces such effects, it is evident that the appeal in our text directly points to it. As soon as this pestilence began to devastate our part of the world, so rich in arts and sciences, how keenly did we feel that all our acquaintance with the forces of Nature, our skill in setting one over against another and overcoming one by another, yet always again proved insufficient as soon as an unknown evil broke out; so that this shape of terror has swept over one country after another without being unmasked or arrested! And when it came into the midst of us, how fully we all felt, even apart from the way in which efforts were made to arrest and suppress the evil, that the ordinary course ot life and of business was forcibly broken up! Now if that was what met us everywhere when we swept our eye over the great field of most multifarious work in our social life, how natural it is that, as the result of this, when the evil has passed away, every one should ask himself, What then is to be the fruit of all the toils and anxieties on which I am now about to enter anew? This is certain, that if I make use of my faculties in the accustomed way, I shall soon again approach the position in which in the former free and happy times it was well with me. My works will again go on in my hands, and the reward of them will again come to me as before; industry and faithfulness, knowledge and skill, will again, though not alone, yet for the most part, determine the measure in which, in my own sphere, I shall share in the good things of this life. But how poor a thing is this whole mode of action! how does this great fabric of human operations still lack a stable foundation! Were there indeed no other danger than that of falling into the hands of men, no other troubles than those arising from the conflict of human passions or the complications of human circumstances, then we could still count on probabilities, there could still be something favourable drawn forth from what was unpropitious. But when Nature pours out on us from her own bosom entirely new and fearful calamities; so that in spite of all precautions and all the skill of the physicians, human beings perish in great masses, is it worth while in such an uncertain state of human affairs,—an uncertainty that we thought ourselves out of reach of long ago—to plunge anew into a life that is nothing but labour and toil? What pleasure could there be in carrying on even the simplest undertaking, when death may so suddenly come between the beginning and the end? To what end do we sow and plant and water, when we know so little, ah! not merely if we ourselves, but if any one distantly related to us shall escape this plague that snatches away its victims so suddenly, and reap what we have sown? Why not return to the simplest possible life without so many appliances, which yet are so often in vain, without so many exertions which yet may so easily be brought to mockery? Such thoughts betray the paralysed activity which is unhappily with too many the result of the divine chastisement. Are not all the sinews of courage cut where such words are heard? have not the hands there truly become weary and the knees feeble?

But where the peaceable fruit of righteousness has really

ripened under the heat of chastisement, there more lively voices are heard instead of such talk. We whose aim is not enjoyment, and who have no desire to strive after possessions in order to enjoy them—why should we stop and turn back? Shall we do so because we have certainly been convinced in the most impressive way of the insecurity of enjoyment and the deceitfulness of possession? Possession is not the spur of our zeal, enjoyment is not the reward of our labour! Our reward is with our Father in heaven, who sees in secret; and the secret thing that He sees is the spirit in which and the faithfulness with which we share in the whole duty of men on earth. If we are to have dominion over the earth, and more and more cultivate it and bring it to perfection, then let us do our best! How much of our works shall remain, lies with Him who knows how He means everywhere to adorn and beautify, even externally, the spiritual body of Christ. Whatever of it is destroyed, let us begin diligently anew, so that the damage may soon be repaired. If through chastisement we become conscious how much we still come short of perfection in this earthly calling, let us the more faithfully see to it that everything salutary may turn to the greatest possible good, that no profitable experience be lost, so that the spiritual eye may be always becoming more keen, and the action of the faculties accelerated, and so the fabric of the commonweal rest on ever firmer foundations. If death has snatched away an unusual number of the friends who should have worked with us, let us each according to our ability take up their work and bear their burden; and above all, let us also, on the other hand, limit the power of this death wherever and so far as we can by temperance and moderation, and by pious cheerfulness. And why should the chastisement that has come upon us make the manner of life which we have inherited and continuously cultivated, in any way distasteful to us? Have we really experienced in this time of suffering—experienced perhaps more than ever before—what happiness it is even amidst sorrow and tears to show love and do deeds of kindness? And does not a life like ours, with these complicated relations, which can only be regulated by love and faithfulness,—with these manifold difficulties, which only love and faithfulness can overcome,—does not such a life afford us most opportunities for doing this, and, in the facility with which powers can be united for good work, the most abundant means for the purpose? Let us then keep our common duty steadily in view; thus let us listen to the voice of the divine chastening; and so shall we be already beginning, even before the sound of that voice dies away, to lift up the hands that hang down and the feeble knees, in order, as what follows our text implies, to take sure and vigorous steps without stumbling. To this, my beloved friends, may this time conduce for us, and for all whom the Lord has visited!

And even to those among whose relatives some have fallen victims to this desolating disease—for even this sorrowful page must not remain unnoticed in our solemn meditation—even to such there will open, in that case, a special source of comfort. After all, the children of men are always dying and being torn away from the midst of their families! nay, the ordinary proportion of death, looking at least at such an extent as that of our own country, will only have been increased to a trifling amount by this pestilence. They are really always dying, at all ages, sometimes suddenly, sometimes slowly, after more or less suffering; and after the first pictures of memory are somewhat faded, the one manner of death or the other makes but a trifling difference to the survivors as to the reality of their loss. Let us therefore set aside this difference as of minor importance, and in its place bring forward another. Every case of death is meant at least to make an instructive and elevating impression on a portion of our community, and to lead us back from the outward appearance to the inward mystery and the deeper significance of life; and this is the last service that each one can render to the society in which he himself has become a partaker of the divine Word. But the separate deaths of men in the ordinary way produce this salutary effect in a much slighter degree, and extend it only over a smaller circle, which, having been in general more or less prepared for the event, receives the impression only very gradually. And when relatives and friends accompany to the place of rest the cast-off vesture of a beloved one departed, is it easy for them, in the sense of their loss, to rise above the thought of the individual? Can we suppose that one readily thinks how many such mournful processions daily traverse our city? Does one reflect at such times that the rule of being severed from life is, when considered as a whole, as settled and regular as that of coming into it? But this great harvest of death, how universally has it awakened and heightened the sense of the uncertainty of this earthly pilgrimage! How has it, by the unwonted form of the disease, which truly had always the seeming of a very death, by the inconceivable rapidity with which life gave way,—how has it in these ways brought closer to us all the mystery of this transition! How has it impressed this on the hearts of all, that we can only walk worthily and cheerfully in this presence of death by keeping our minds at all times well regulated, and preserving the peace of God unbroken, so that we are conscious of being prepared for any kind of season, and for going on in peace with whatever the Lord may have appointed, as His servants. And this last and important service has been rendered in a very notable manner by the victims of this disease, even by those who have breathed their last far from their own people, tended by public servants; and who rest apart from their fathers, among those who shared the same lot.

And now, though doubtless this increase in wisdom, (as

well as the peaceable fruit of righteousness and the re-awakening of energy and courage,) is shared only by those, who, as our text says, have allowed themselves to be exercised by chastisement, yet we may all be supposed to have had a part in this exercise. For those alone have excluded themselves from it who have either sought in the whirl of dissipation to deaden the consciousness of what was going on around them; or who, not without at the same time evading their proper duty, escaped, by going to a distance, the sight of the common distress. But every one who, faithful to his ordinary rule of life, has gone forward in the way of his duty, has continued busy while conscious of the danger equally near to all, and has served the common cause according to his ability, has also been exercised in a way for which such a time has an advantage above all others. Only let us by no means confine this exercise to the chastisement now happily past, and so bring it to an end with this day's solemnity. No; as surely as every one of us will remember this time, may the remembrance be as indelibly fixed in all our hearts that in such immediate contact with death we can only be firm and undismayed because we have the prevailing consciousness of being citizens of a higher world, in which what is uncertain and transitory has no part; and because the eternal life which we owe to Him, who brought with it true immortality to light, far surmounts all adverse contingencies, and does not allow the heart's gladness in God to be lost even amidst His chastenings. If these naturally seemed to us at the time to be sorrowful; yet it was not the sorrow of this world; but that divine kindred feeling, which not only leads to salvation, but includes it. With such sentiments let us hold fast the remembrance of this time, that it may become a permanent blessing to us, as a salutary token from our own life, that though here we walk amid transitory things and in the presence of death, yet even here our manner of life is in heaven. Amen.

Prayer.

Yea, gracious Father in heaven! we know Thou chastenest whom Thou lovest! Therefore in Thy chastisement we have discerned Thy fatherly love, according to which Thou didst seek to make us riper in Christian godliness, to unite us more heartily together, and to give us a new and precious pledge that to those who love Thee, the most crushing and painful things must work together for good. Let then Thy dealings be honoured by us, in that Thy chastening is not lost on any of us, and that we always rejoice in the peaceable fruit of righteousness that grows out of it. Then will our course become ever more secure and our steps firmer; and thus exercised in the understanding of what tends to our peace, we shall be ever becoming worthier of the glorious title of a royal priesthood, the people of Thy choice, whom Thou, according to Thy gracious good-pleasure, art leading even through earthly sufferings to unclouded peace. Amen.

XXII.

GOD'S LOVE MAGNIFIED IN CHRIST'S DEATH.

(*Good Friday*, 1832.)

TEXT: ROM. v. 7, 8.

IN the whole passage from which these words are taken the apostle is trying to convince his readers that it is only through Christ that we come into right relations with God. He begins by saying, Let us have peace with God, through our Lord Jesus Christ; and so let us rejoice in the glory that God is to give; nay, more, let us rejoice in tribulation also. He goes on to say that the love of God is shed abroad in our hearts by the Holy Spirit; and then he continues with the words of our text, "for God commendeth His love towards us, in that, while we were yet sinners Christ died for us." He thus represents the death of Christ as the most glorious manifestation of the love of God to us. Let us then take this thought as the subject of our meditation to-day. There are two points in it, which Paul goes on to explain in the following verses; first, that God appointed Christ to death as the uttermost proof of obedience; and secondly, that now, through this obedience, as he says, many are made righteous. Taking these two ideas together, we recognise the completeness of the divine love in the death of the Saviour.

I. In considering together how God appointed our Lord and Saviour to suffering and death as the most perfect proof of obedience, it seems necessary to begin by removing a difficulty, which will certainly occur to every one. That is, that the death of the Saviour seems by no means so obvious an evidence of the love of God, His and our heavenly Father, as of the Saviour's own love to His brethren; and that it is only, as it were, on the ground of this love of His to us that we have any right to see in His death the love of God towards us. And yet the case stands as I have stated it. It is indeed difficult to separate things that are in the very closest connection; and who could wish to make a division between the Saviour's love to us and His obedience to His and our heavenly Father? And yet the two are so related, that His love to us is shown most directly in His life, and His obedience to the Father in His sufferings and death. His love to men is seen in His labouring to seek and to save that which was lost, to show Himself as the ever-ready Physician of the sick, to communicate His own life to men, and instil it into them through His words and His works, to offer Himself to them, that in Him they might find rest and refreshing to their souls. On the other hand, when He speaks of His death, representing Himself under the figure of the good Shepherd who gives his life for the sheep, He contrasts Himself with the hireling, who flees when he sees the wolf coming. The hireling flees because the sheep are not his property; therefore the reason of the good Shepherd's giving His life for them must be that they are His own. But which of us is able to distinguish between love of his property and love of himself? Everything that is our property, in the strictest sense of the word, is also a portion of our power and our life; and love to it is connected essentially and inseparably with love to ourselves. The Saviour says in another place to His disciples, Greater love hath no man than this, that a man lay down his life for his friends; ye are My friends, if ye do the things which I command you. But it was not for them as His friends, not for them in a special and exclusive and distinctive sense, that He laid down His life; for He gave His life for the salvation of the world, and the world was not His friend. And when we remember the Saviour's one command which He gave to His disciples, "that ye love one another even as I have loved you," we rejoice indeed that, in so far as this love consisted in striving to bring salvation to all around Him by sustaining and filling them with His divine strength, we can love each other with a similar love; for that finds expression in the beautiful interchange of loving service, which is the very essence of Christian fellowship; but how could we love each other with such a love as that of the alone holy and pure One when He gave His life for the world of sinners? Therefore if He Himself regarded His death as the necessary and direct result of His love, as its highest and most essential expression, this command of His would be futile; we should have to set aside just the best and highest part of His example before we thought of beginning to follow it. But He always spoke of His death as the will of the Father. "If it be possible," He says, "let this cup pass from Me;" which He could not have said if it had been the work of His love—the choice of His love—to drain it; "but," He continues, "not My will, but Thine be done." It is true He speaks always of His obedience to the Father through His whole life, and therefore we cannot separate it from His love; His love was, in fact, the very work which the Father gave Him to do, and which He did continually. But if we wish to speak separately of His giving Himself up to suffering and death, we must say that in this, above all, is shown forth His obedience to the will of the Father. And we shall see this the more plainly if we consider what is so clearly implied in the words I have just quoted, that His obedience was (to speak after the manner of men) in conflict with His love. Not for Himself could He pray, "Father, if it be possible, let this cup pass from Me," but only for the sake of those whom the Father had already given Him. Love would have liked to live still longer with them and for them, love would have liked to impart still more to them out of the fulness of His divine nature; but He left it to the decision of the Father, when the time and the hour should be come. He first said, "If it be possible, let this cup pass"; that was the expression of His heartfelt, unalterable love to His people; "yet, not as I will, but as Thou wilt"; that was the expression of His perfect obedience, and of His utter submission to the will of His Father.

And now let us consider more closely how the death of the Saviour was really the most perfect act of obedience to which God could call Him. Scripture elsewhere represents it as being so. Thus the author of the epistle to the Hebrews says that as He suffered and practised obedience, He was made perfect through obedience. Now if His perfection was to be shown forth in His obedience, it was necessary that this obedience itself should be of the highest and most perfect kind. But here again we are met by a crowd of examples and considerations that would seem to diminish the value of this obedience of the Saviour, in showing that there have been, and will always be, many similar cases in the history of human life. How many are there, even without taking into account this holy and divine work of redemption, and those who have witnessed to this faith with their blood—how many have there been in all ages who have laid down their lives for their convictions! Whether these were true or false, whether they presented a distinct or an obscure view of divine truth, does not affect the argument. And it is certainly true that many men have shown, by the readiness with which they have gone to death, that they would rather give up their life altogether than make it into a self contradiction. To profess from conviction, and then to retract with convictions unchanged, is what no one can do in whom there is the living love of the truth, to whom there is anything greater than the vain and passing things of this life; but the case of the Saviour was by no means so simple as all those apparently similar instances. In the narrative of His life we find frequently a variation, difficult to explain when we look at isolated instances, and yet most plainly discernible, between open avowal and cautious silence. At one time He teaches men that the only will of God which they have to do is to believe on Him whom God has sent, thus clearly pointing them to Himself; and again, when hailed as the promised Son of David, the object of all men's hopes and longings, He forbids them even to speak of it, charging even His disciples to tell no man that He is the Christ. We must, therefore, admit that this concealment was a part of His plan, and had its motive in the circumstances of His life as a whole. There was then no necessity for Him to avow Himself on all occasions—to come forward with His testimony, and most especially with His testimony concerning Himself, when it was only those who were capable of receiving it for whom it could be anything or effect anything. But the avowal which He made before the High Priest, Thou sayest it, I am the Son of God; nevertheless, I say unto thee, Henceforth ye shall see the Son of Man sitting at the right hand of power and coming on the clouds of heaven—this avowal He regarded as on the one hand the cause of His death and on the other the founding of His kingdom; and He made it as an act of obedience. It was a part of His being made under the law. He could not keep silence before the High Priest, unless He meant to evade this universal lot, to which He was called by the will of His heavenly Father. It is true this very confession of the Saviour's has drawn many others to similar sufferings and death. What numberless Christian martyrdoms there were in those earliest times in which the faith in the Son of God had to struggle against the enmity of the whole world, of all those to whom His cross was foolishness, all to whom it was an offence. But in what light are we to regard this? A part of it was the work of Christ's obedience in the souls of those who believed in Him; it was the effect of His life in them, and just on that account had a connection with His death, as the Apostle Paul speaks of filling up by his sufferings that which, so to speak, was lacking in the sufferings of Christ. But how much also was the effect of human fanaticism and weakness—how much intentional and needless seeking after such a death—how many prejudices and misconceptions were mixed with the self-sacrifice of otherwise noble spirits! and in such cases it was not the pure obedience of the Saviour. And now let us remember how His obedience was in conflict with His heartfelt and true love to His own, for whom He would gladly have lived longer to establish them more firmly in their life in Him. Let us remember that He died in obedience to a law of which He plainly said that it should soon altogether lose its authority and power—a law which He knew that men had misunderstood from the beginning, regarding as the means by which they could please God and make sure of a future reward from Him, that which had only been given to include all the world under the consciousness of sin. And thus we shall see that it was no direct impulse of the Saviour's own soul, humanly speaking, but only pure acquiescence in the will of God, that led Him to suffering and death.

And now do we ask the reason of this? The answer brings us back to the first part of our text. Scarcely, says Paul, will one die for a righteous, an upright man; for every one considers that this character may belong to himself just as well as to any other. Yet, he continues, for a good man, peradventure, some would even dare to die. That is, he supposes that if a man saw in another a fervent love to all that tends to the welfare and happiness of others, with a great power of effecting good not only for himself but for all about him; then, in order that the work of such a one should not be cut short, that he might go on using his splendid powers in noble deeds, he might even be willing to lay down his own life, counting it, though not worthless, yet of less value than the other. And yet how nature would resist,—how many questionings would arise in such a case! Will he for whom such a sacrifice is made continue even to be what he has been? Can any one answer for the constancy of his will, for his faithful discharge of duty, for his self-devotion in the cause of good? Or, if it is more a question of the success of a single work, or of all his works together, who will make sure how much will turn out for the good of men? Who knows how much of it will be counteracted by the power of evil? And therefore, says Paul, one would hardly die even for a good man, and yet it is certainly a possible thing. And the Saviour says, "Greater love hath no man than this, that a man lay down his life for his friends." Those are always really our friends whom we chiefly regard as the good, with whom we believe, according to the inmost bent of our nature, that we can work most in harmony. To sacrifice one's individual existence for the sake of such powers in union is a love, says the Saviour, than which there is none greater. But God shows forth His love to us in this, says Paul, that, according to His command and will, Christ died for us while we were yet sinners; not for the sake of the righteous, not for a good man nor for a circle of friends, but for the whole world of sinners. And so we cannot doubt that this was the most perfect act of obedience, and that God called Christ to it for our sakes; for it was necessary that He should endure this death, not for His own sake, nor with any other good object but that of effecting the salvation of sinners.

II. This brings us to consider in the second place what was meant to be accomplished and therefore *was* accomplished—for when we speak of a divine purpose, we cannot separate design from fulfilment—by this death of the Saviour; that we may see how it was the full glorification of the divine love.

The greatest love is that which effects the most good to the person who is the object of it. We should try in vain to give another definition of it. Now the apostle says, As by one man's disobedience many were made sinners, so by the obedience of the One, the many are made righteous. This then, this is what was to result from the Saviour's obedience unto death on the cross. He needed to die for us, Paul says, when we were yet sinners. *Were* sinners! Are we such no longer? Do we not always continue sinners? No, he says; through the obedience of the One, many are made righteous; the justification of life comes upon all who believe on Him. But what is meant by many becoming righteous in Him? We could not easily find a word which is susceptible of more various shades of meaning. Righteousness is in one sense the least that we think we have a right to require from every man; in another it implies an idea of the highest perfection; and this is the sense in which it is so often used in Scripture, and even in merely human writings. And whence comes this great distinction? The inquiry into this leads us into the innermost depths of our being, and gives us the key to the whole history of man and to the connection of the divine counsels. Which of us has not, at least in the earlier part of his life, had in his mind the picture of a paradise condition, such as, from the few hints given us, we suppose that of the first man to have been before sin came into the world? Do we ask ourselves, Was there righteousness there? We shall be obliged to answer, No! Was there a comparison that the man could have made between that which he actually was and something else which he was meant to be and to become? Again we must answer, No! And if we ask ourselves if we can regard this as a condition which it would really be worth striving and longing after, which we should be right in wishing back or recalling; certainly we must say No. This kind of peace with himself and harmony with external Nature around him, this kind of enjoyment and possession of life without difficulties, without struggles, with no greater development of his faculties, is not what man is made for. What is meant, then, by being righteous—on what does it depend? On this, that something is set before us which we are to attain to, after which we are to strive, and which therefore we as yet are not and have not. Only under such conditions is there any righteousness; and under these it is in one aspect the smallest and most trivial thing, and in another the highest and greatest,—a condition to which, strictly and literally speaking, we can never attain. It is the most trivial if the object to be attained is the keeping of an external law which is given to regulate the relations of men. Not only must every one measure himself by this rule, but every one also is bound to fulfil it. If he does not do so, he becomes a hindrance to social life, and instead of forming a constitutional part of society is rather something which must be removed from it that it may safely subsist. This is the righteousness which we have spoken of as being the least that we can require of every man. And now if we ask what kind of righteousness was man capable of attaining to before the Son of God appeared on earth—ah, how paltry seem the aims and efforts of even the noblest, the most cultivated, the most gifted nation among men! For what was the aim they had in view? Merely the welfare of a small number of people; and to secure this they were ready at any moment to take up a position of hostility towards all others. What was the standard with which they compared themselves? It was one particular aspect of human life, such as they found it in their own community, and as it had been transmitted from one generation to another. Well for us that we have a High Priest "without father, without mother, without descent," and in Him a standard not limited to one time or place; but the express image of the divine nature in human form, the brightness of the divine glory, embodying in Himself the whole human race, and yet standing above it as the ideal which all must strive to reach. And it was necessary that He should be thus made perfect by obedience unto death, in order that no doubt should ever be possible as to whether He would have resisted this or that temptation, whether He would have maintained His character in this or that position, whether something might not have occurred that would have been too much even for Him, and in which He would have shown something of human weakness. It was necessary that we should see in Him this perfect obedience, even to the death of the cross; and through this obedience we become righteous, if we receive Him into our inmost hearts as the standard on which we are to form ourselves. Therefore He himself says, "He that believeth on the Son is not judged," because he is at every moment judging himself, having found the true rule by which to do so.

But was I not directly contradicting the apostle, in saying that righteousness, in another view, is something that we can never attain to, seeing that he says, Through the obedience of One many are made righteous? We become righteous, only it is not because and so far as we have set Him before our eyes as our ideal, for thus we shall never reach it, but really because and in so far as we have received Him into our hearts as the fountain of life. We become righteous if we no longer live in the flesh, but Christ the Son of God lives in us,—if we are fully identified with that common life of which He is the centre. For then each of us can say of himself, Who is there that can condemn? It is Christ that justifies! We are in Him, He is in us, inseparably united with those who believe on the

Son of God; and in this fellowship with Him we are truly righteous. But if we come back to ourselves and consider our individual life just in itself, then we are glad to forget what is behind and to reach forth towards that which is before. Then we know well that we must ever anew take refuge in Him, ever be looking to Him and to His obedience on the cross, ever be filled with the power of His life and His presence; and thus we shall attain to that growth in righteousness and holiness and wisdom, in which truly consists our redemption through Him, through His life and His love, His obedience and His death.

Well then, my dear friends, how shall we most suitably commemorate this death? Certainly in no better way than by accepting Him in every form in which He offers Himself to us—and in His feast of remembrance He does this in the most cordial though mystical manner; accepting Him in accepting the words of life which we receive from Him and which abide imperishably among men; in never ceasing to keep His image before us; in loving each other with the love with which He has loved us. If we do this, He will be in the midst of us in all the manifold circumstances of our lives, in the quiet of solitary meditation, and where two or three are gathered together in His name, and in the great assemblies of His people. He will be with us in the busy stir of the world, ever in all our doing and suffering, Christ in us, Christ among us, Christ the strength of our life, His death the power of our obedience to the divine will, while, like Him, we desire no other meat than to do the will of our Father in heaven. Let us together pledge ourselves anew to this beneath His cross! let this be the allegiance that we swear to Him, who was faithful to us even in death; thus let us follow His example of that obedience unto death through which He was made perfect, through which we also shall be made perfect and brought nearer to His life. Then shall we understand these words, It became Him who would bring many children to salvation, to make the Captain of their salvation perfect through the suffering of death. Amen.

Prayer.

Yes, holy and merciful God and Father, praised be Thy name for Thy holy and wise guidance of the family of man. No blessedness could there be for us but in seeking Thy kingdom and its righteousness. To reveal this to us, it was needful for Thee to send Thy Son into the world, who raised again towards heaven the downcast glance of our spirits, lifted up our hearts and purified them to love Thee truly; who showed us how thine image can live in man, and what that holiness is which we are to aim at. Oh, give to Him, then, an ever-increasing multitude as His spoil! let the story of the cross of Christ be blessed now, and to all future generations! Spread abroad the joyful sound more and more among all nations on earth, till there remains not one where Thy name is not praised—where we shall not see more and more the glorious effects of this divine proclamation of Thy love and Thy grace, in those who are now sitting in the deepest darkness and the shadow of death. Let us all know by our own experience that our only wisdom is in becoming ever more closely united with Him,—our only blessedness that which comes from our consciousness of our life being one with His, our only peace in coming before Thee as those whom Thy Son has reconciled through the suffering of death; love to Thee being shed abroad in our hearts again through this, that Thou gavest Thy Son to die for us when we were yet sinners. And then it will be Thy work, the work of Thy Spirit, that we cease to be sinners, even though we are still sinful men; that the habit and practice of sin gives place to the habit of obedience to Thy holy will; that we more and more hate everything that is contrary to His example and unlike Him; that so, all being united in following this rule, all more and more filled with this power, the image of Christ may be fully formed in us, and His spiritual body may be presented to Thee as the witness of His sufferings and death, while ever becoming more free from all imperfection, that so He Himself may be the first-born, the first-fruits among many brethren. **Amen.**

XXIII.

THE PRAYER OF STEPHEN.

(*Fifth Sunday after Trinity*, 1832.)

TEXT: ACTS vii. 60. "And Stephen kneeled down and cried with a loud voice, Lord, lay not this sin to their charge. And when he had said this, he fell asleep."

FREE and unrestricted as we are in our church as to our choice of subjects for meditation from the treasuries of the divine Word, many of you may still perhaps wonder why I have selected this passage. For you are aware that I have often lately taken occasion to express the opinion that the state of things brought before us in this narrative no longer exists in our times: that when people boast of having had to bear sufferings for Christ's sake, it has usually been only a self-deception on their part; for when the thing has been more closely looked into, either it has been found to be no suffering at all, judged by the ordinary measure of human life; or, if it was real suffering, then it was not for Christ's sake, but for the sake of some man's system or opinion. But all Scripture given by God is profitable for doctrine and instruction in righteousness; and there is no part of it, however slight its direct bearing on our circumstances may be, about which that statement does not always hold good; and that, without our having to wander into applications of the words widely different from the direct meaning of the writers. Therefore, with this belief, we will take to-day, as the subject of our devout meditations, this prayer of Stephen in its various aspects.

I. I shall call your attention first to the thought that most deeply touches and stirs our feelings, that we may then be able to take a calmer view of other points,—the thought, namely, that these words are the prayer of a dying man. And it is the utterance, not of one who was merely experiencing the common lot of men, but of one who was dying for the Saviour's sake, and for the confession of His name,—the prayer of him who was, after the Saviour Himself, the first martyr in the Christian Church.

What a joyful thing it is to think of these words in their original connection! how immediately and vividly they recall to us those words which they so closely resemble, the words of the Saviour on the cross; Father, forgive them, for they know not what they do! And yet we do not even know if he who uttered them had ever heard of those words of the Saviour; for it was not until later that the plan so rich in blessing to believers was systematically set about, of collecting and handing down the sayings of the Lord, so that every one might easily acquire a knowledge of the most important of them. But if Stephen had not heard them, it only proves the more certainly that the same Spirit who had spoken in the Master was speaking in the disciple. And because this Spirit has never since that time been withdrawn from the Christian Church, because it is He who is the source of all good gifts, of all words and deeds that tend to the advancement of the kingdom of God, we may all claim this utterance as our own. For remember the words of the apostle, that "all things are ours,"—each individual with his gifts and his works,—so that in the Church of God every deed pleasing to Him is not only a common benefit, but something that all, as members of one body, may appropriate as their own. And how often may similar prayers have gone up inaudibly from the hearts of those who followed the first preachers of the gospel on this thorny path! For how much precious blood was poured out in later times through this same animosity of men against the greatest proof of goodwill that God had ever shown them! And how could it but be that in those who were impelled by the same feeling to brave such dangers and sufferings, the same Spirit should stir their hearts and speak through their lips in a similar way?

But now that the Christian faith is enthroned in so many nations; now that, ready as the heart of man would still be to rise against the name of the Lord and to fight against it with the sword of earthly power, none are tempted to do so, because there would be no chance of success; now that through the increase of intellectual gifts and the manifold outward blessings produced by the beneficent spirit of Christianity wherever it has reached, the Christian nations maintain so clear a supremacy over all others;—whence now should come any such sufferings for the Saviour's sake? The more remote from us those times become, the more rare become such instances of persecution. Christians themselves have indeed sometimes been found in fierce antagonism against each other, each party sure that truth and pure love to the Saviour are on his own side; while their party feeling makes all real knowledge and perception of His teaching impossible. But seeing that this has only occurred on passing occasions and in times of unusual excitement, we gladly throw over it a veil of loving oblivion. And yet we cannot but say that though the trial may not perhaps come in exactly the same form, yet times of a similar nature may be before us. For just because the spread of the Christian faith brings in its train so rich an enlargement of all human faculties, of all mental endowments, of all the comforts of common life; because, at the same time, on its doing so depends the possibility of making known the word of the Lord ever more widely among men, till it gradually fills the whole earth,—for these very reasons everything that concerns the true prosperity of men in all their affairs stands in close connection with the kingdom of God. And if differing opinions arise as to what does advance the well-being of men; if men engage in hot controversy,—each seeing in him who differs from him an enemy of all good, whether as hindering human development, or as an enemy to repose and peace and to the secure enjoyment of what God has given us; if from feelings they go on to action, each believing that he has a right, or that, in fact, it is his duty to crush the other by all lawful means; and so cripples him in his work, and prejudices others against him and alienates them from him so far as he can; then indeed there is suffering for the sake of convictions and for the sake of what is good. And the more really such disputants are Christians according to the Spirit, and not merely desiring to be called so; and the more they therefore connect all the good that they might wish or effect for men with the Fountain of all good, desiring that it should conduce to the advancement of God's kingdom; just so much the more sure are they to see, in everything that opposes them in their efforts, sin that is specially sinful as rising in hostility against the Lord.

Only there is one thing that we must not forget. Even in such cases, if we regard what befalls us only in its bearing on ourselves; if he who suffers in this way—granting that he has been the means of doing good in the way of his calling and duty—is thinking only of himself, then there cannot arise from his heart a prayer such as this that we hear from the heart of Stephen. For in that case it is not sin, specially as sin, that he desires the Lord may not lay to men's charge, it is only that he is willing to forgive the wrong done to himself. But if one is strong enough to look away from himself at all in his last moments—and we imagine such a one, after having been, perhaps for the best part of his life and up to its close, the object of enmity and persecution—one who has experienced all that can be poured from that fountain of bitterness into a human life;—if we think of him looking back as one whose only thought about himself concerns the well-being of his soul, how must the past appear to him? If the sufferings which the Lord has appointed to him have not served to purify his nature and to eradicate from his heart the last root of bitterness against his brethren; if they have not cleansed his heart and ripened his spirit by compelling him unceasingly to labour that he might, amidst those distracting troubles, keep steadily in view the aim set before him: if they have not worked to these ends, then, oh, far from thinking of others and having wishes for them, what can be his nearest concern but to repent and seek mercy for himself, because he has not used according to God's will those things which, bitter though they were, were gifts from Him? But if his trials *have* produced such fruits,—if he has been ripened in the school of suffering and persecution, and so grown in the true wisdom of God's children,—if the image of the Saviour's gentleness has been so formed in him that the malice of his enemies could never call forth answering hatred in him, but that he ever met with love those who opposed him; oh, then he has indeed cause to praise God for what He has done for him. And what kind of a prayer will he offer for those whom God has used as His instruments? What but that God will bless them for the salvation that has come to him through them, for the good they have been the means of doing for him? And far from thinking of the wrong which he has suffered, bitter as it has been, he will, in his last moments, bless his enemies as the channels of God's grace and love.

II. Let us therefore mark, as our second thought, that this prayer, "Lord, lay not this sin to their charge," in any circumstances similar to those in which that servant of the Lord was placed, can be the prayer only of one who entirely loses sight of himself. By this I mean that we, as Christians, should not at all be taken up with the weighing and considering of our own position, as to what, according to the customary and prevalent notions of men, it may contain of happiness and prosperity. He who cannot rise above this, but is always taking an estimate of his life, comparing himself, in this respect, with others, and asking, on every favourable or unfavourable turn of his affairs, who has been the cause of it; he who thus never loses sight of himself cannot but regard those whose influence has proved so adverse as in the case before us, as his enemies and adversaries. And if any one, while full of such feelings, could yet rise to such a prayer as this, and say, Lord, lay not this sin to their charge, nothing could be less like the prayer of Stephen. It would rather be a vain and false generosity; it would be what men so often, though erroneously, call noble, and take much credit to themselves for, as something great and difficult of attainment; counting it, though I must call them mistaken, as the highest point of Christian virtue, to be able sincerely to forgive our enemies. I, at least, am so far from holding this to be the height of Christian love, that I do not believe it would enter the mind of a real Christian at all! For he who loses sight of himself in the way I have spoken of, so that his only thoughts about himself are as to what he is bound to do, what is committed to him, what he has to render account of; who, whatever befalls him, whether joyous or grievous according to the world's view, only seeks to turn it to account, and asks what use he is to make of it; he who feels and acts in this way,—for him there are never enemies,—never any over whom he vaingloriously exalts himself, and then magnanimously asks forgiveness for them, as it were, for his sake. If, then, we detect in ourselves any such feelings, let us at once search our hearts for the hidden selfishness which is there, that we may rise out of it to the self-forgetfulness in which we shall simply regard ourselves as instruments in God's hand for the work of His kingdom. No, let us never turn back to striving for earthly possessions and advantages, even for good ends. Let us never measure by so mean a rule an existence which, if it has really become one with the Saviour, can have no other aim than, like Him, to do the will of God. If we have taken up such a position towards men that for us there exist no circumstances in which we could call any man our enemy; then, in whatever way they may act towards us, they are always and only our brethren, whom we are to care for, to warn and instruct, when we are in a position to do so, to draw away from danger, so far as they are willing to grasp our offered hand, and in whom, even should they reject all our advances, we can never see enemies or antagonists. And the more justly we can claim to have dedicated our life to the Saviour, and as His servants, to whom His word is addressed, to have recognised in it the will of our heavenly Father; just the more certainly is it some remnant of that dangerous spiritual pride through which we are so ready to exalt ourselves above others, which leads us, in any case, to take such a view of our relations towards others as to suppose we need to ask forgiveness for them for sins committed against us. We are anxious that they should honour us as persons whose lives are devoted to the kingdom of God; we think that on this account they should give way to the violent outbursts of their passions much less against us than against others. Thus we set ourselves up over them, and then we are willing to ask pardon for them from above. But that cannot really be called prayer, to ask that the Lord will not lay to their charge the sins which, in fact, they cannot have committed against us. For nothing can properly be called sin but that which is sin against God. And beside such sins, be they laid to men's charge or not, any wrong which we may have suffered from them must utterly disappear. Men may, no doubt, do us wrong, and we ourselves may forgive them for it, and we do well in so doing; but *sin* they commit only against God; that is, against His holy laws, against His will, made known to us through His Son. Hence he only who has one sole aim in view, who is concerned about nothing and wishes for nothing in this life but to see the kingdom of God ever more firmly established, more widely extended, more gloriously built up;—he alone, when men, by their sin, oppose this purpose of God, can say, in deed and in truth, without the slightest reference to himself, "Lord, lay not this sin to their charge."

III. Let this then be our last lesson from this subject, that these words can express the thoughts and feelings only of a man who seeks after nothing but the kingdom of God and His righteousness. Such a man, without doubt, was he whose last words are here reported to us. For, consider, he was one of those whom the assembly of believers had selected from among others, in the confidence that they would manage the temporal affairs of the Church with perfect integrity and most impartial and careful fidelity, and would themselves do works of love in distributing the gifts of love among those who needed them. This office, to which he and the others were ordained by the apostles of the Lord, opened to him a wide field of work, and yet he did not feel that this was enough. He felt that this special work must not hinder him from fulfilling that great duty which was then binding on all Christians—the confessing everywhere of their faith in Jesus of Nazareth as the Christ. Therefore Stephen did not forsake the place where he had been accustomed to meet with others on appointed days for prayer, and to hear and meditate on the Scriptures together; but after his appointment, as before, he went to this gathering of devout men who still adhered to the old covenant. But now he did so especially for the purpose of giving an account of the faith that gladdened his heart, if perhaps he might win some into the blessed fellowship of the Son of God; and it was this course of conduct that brought him into the position in which we see him in our text. And what ardent zeal for the progress of God's kingdom appears in his whole discourse! He was a stranger in the land of the covenant people, one of the descendants of Abraham who belonged to the Dispersion. The most devout among these always aimed, above everything else, at returning to live in Jerusalem, where they would be near their holy temple, and be able there to join in the worship they loved, and to celebrate the glorious feasts of their people. Stephen had succeeded in doing this; and therefore in his speech he rapidly reviews the past history of the nation, in order to show that though for long he had been, as to his place of abode, a stranger, yet, while far away, he had been no stranger to the progress of events among his own people. He shows himself well acquainted, not only with their external, but with their inner history; he reminds them, for their warning, how persecution had always fallen on the prophets who had sought to press the claims of God's will on the people; and he shows his hearers that all the prophets had spoken of that Just One whose name he now declared. And so utterly was his whole mind bent on the one object, that though he might easily have foreseen what he was bringing upon himself (for already the people had gnashed at him with their teeth), yet he so lost sight of himself that in the fervour of his speech and exhortation, looking up to heaven, he felt constrained to say that he saw the Lord standing on the right hand of God: so fully assured was he that the way which he proclaimed was the one way by which alone men could gain access to God, and that, in due time, all should bow to Him whom now in the Spirit he saw at the right hand of the Majesty on high. Such was the character of Stephen; and therefore he had no thought to give to the injustice done to himself,—none to the wild storms of passion that raged against his life. He heeded only his people's resistance to all the testimonies from history and from the word of God, their persistence in the sin against which he had warned them from the example of their fathers, their stubborn opposition to the counsel of God; and, with the thought of these things weighing on his heart, he prayed, "Lord, lay not this sin to their charge."

It is not improbable that we may find occasion to use this prayer, not merely at the close of our life, but throughout its whole course in this world, where it has not ceased to be true that the flesh lusts against the Spirit. Let us therefore use every such occasion as a means of maturing in ourselves a state of mind like Stephen's. Let us especially use in this way every occasion on which we can show that while we estimate the actions of men only as to what may be their bearing on the beneficent will of God, we also see in all wrong-doing only opposition to the good that God has intended towards men; and that when we say, "Lord, lay not this sin to their charge," we use the prayer in the sense in which Stephen used it, and with no thought of ourselves. For what, my friends, does it mean, this laying of sin to a man's charge? It is laid to his charge if he holds fast to it; it is laid to his charge if he is successful in it; it is laid to his charge in the surest and saddest way of all when he reaches, even for a passing moment, the goal at which he aims; it is laid to his charge when he persistently disregards all exhortations to enter the kingdom of God, and turns a deaf ear to the solemn voice that invites all to come. When Stephen uttered these words, was not this what he meant—that God would be pleased not utterly to exclude them, on account of their sin, from that kingdom of His into which Stephen as a faithful servant had sought to draw them, and invited them even with his last breath—that He would not lay sin to their charge by closing that kingdom too early against them, so that even yet, during their life on earth, they might begin to share in its blessings,—that He would bend to the keeping of His commands those powers which were now arrayed in hostility against the kingdom of His Son? That was what Stephen had in his mind when he said, "Lord, lay not this sin to their charge," and that alone is the meaning it should always have for us. When opposition to the progress of God's kingdom abates; when minds that have been at variance draw ever closer together in seeking salvation at the same living fountain; when the spiritual eye becomes clearer to distinguish truth from error and turns towards the heavenly light; then sins are forgotten and forgiven; then indeed they have vanished, for their power has ceased. When, on the contrary, men harden themselves in opposition to God's way of salvation; when they stop their ears more and more closely against the call, 'Arise from the dead and Christ shall give thee light"; then, too truly, their sins are laid to their charge. And how nobly Stephen's prayer was fulfilled at least in one case! But how notable a case that one was! For the convert was Saul, at whose feet were laid the garments of those who assembled in wild fury to stone Stephen. He was thus not merely a witness of the deed, but took part in it, and approved of it. And though we know nothing of others who joined in it, what a blessed result of this prayer is seen in the life-work of the great apostle! And who can tell what influence the remembrance of this memorable scene may have had, when the Saviour called to him in this way, "Saul, Saul, it is hard for thee to kick against the pricks." And for those who are able in the same pure way to plead with God that He may not lay the sins of their brethren to their charge, there will always be such blessings to rejoice over.

But the more we have occasion to use this prayer, the less must we let it remain only a petition. If we use it in the spirit in which it was used by Stephen, then, as long as life and strength continue, our desire must not rest satisfied with rising to heaven; it will return, as it were, with blessing to our own hearts, and become a fountain of deeds well-pleasing to God, of love that cannot be wearied, of zeal that never grows cold in leading men to Him in whom alone they can find salvation. We must not tire of trying to draw men to Him, and we must continue steadfast in the duty of being always ready to give a reason of the hope that is in us, and to direct every one into the right way; till at last, when the Master calls us from the scene of our active service, and our life on earth is closing, to the prayer that the Lord will advance His kingdom and dwell in His grace wherever faithful souls already fear and love Him, we shall join, as an inseparable part of our last benediction, this other petition, that the sins of those who still strive against the kingdom of the Saviour may not be laid to their charge. And this longing for blessing to others which characterized the prayer of Stephen as it had characterized that of the Saviour, which alone has always set the stamp of consecration on those who were martyrs for the faith—for those who were not capable of such a petition were no true martyrs—this spirit is still in operation, and its effects may be clearly traced. Therefore however much disunion we see in the Christian community and in regard to all spiritual matters; however often evil passions may mingle with those things, and wrath and hatred be stirred up; let us only, as long as we live, oppose to all this the power of love, striving after this one thing, to overcome evil with good. Then shall we be sure of having, even in our last moments, none but loving feelings towards those who have been most hostile to us; and on prayers breathed in this spirit there will always rest the blessing of Him whose prayer, "Father, forgive them, for they know not what they do," we are to use as our pattern,—of Him who could regard even the sin of resisting Him, the Son of God, as ignorance—as darkness to move compassion, and that only lacked the light. Let us resolve to rise by the help of the divine Word to the spirit of this prayer, and more steadfastly to consecrate our whole lives to the work of bringing hearts into union, that there may be less and less sin, and therefore less cause to pray that it may not be laid to men's charge.

XXIV.

PROVOKING EACH OTHER TO LOVE AND GOOD WORKS.

(*New Year's Sermon.*)

TEXT: HEB. x. 24. "Let us consider one another, to provoke unto love and to good works."

THIS day is usually regarded more as a secular and social than a religious holiday, and given up to the enjoyment of family and external relationships. But when we assemble here on this day, we surely do so in the belief that everything pleasant and joyful in our working and social life during the past year, for which we have had to thank God, had its source in nothing but the spiritual good wrought by the grace of God in the hearts of men, through the word and teaching of Christ and the gifts of His Spirit. And not less do we believe that all the progress and improvement in the future, for which we pray, as well as the remedying of all the shortcomings and faults that rise before us in the retrospect of the past year, amount just to this, that all the good that ought to be found in the disciples of the Lord should be ever assuming larger proportions in us all. And in reference to this we find in the words we have read a rule which, though always binding, we do well to lay to heart specially at the beginning of a new year. We are called to notice in these words, first, what is our true need for the year now opening; and second, the way in which this need can be met.

I. First, then, let us be sure of this, that on whatever side we consider our life, whether its busy, working side, or that of social enjoyment, we can have no other universal need in any future than just this—that love and good works may be ever more abundant among us. Perhaps some of you think that though there is certainly a great deal in this, it does not yet include everything; it does not contain all that we might think desirable in our domestic and social concerns; it does not depend entirely on this how much prosperity or trial each of us may meet with: and yet if we reflect on everything in a really Christian light, it will soon become evident that everything does ultimately depend on this.

Yesterday we all surely looked back once more over the year that is gone,—for I hope that the innocent gaiety with which many are accustomed to close the year would form no hindrance to this serious work,—and I cannot but believe that all of us, in looking at our whole circumstances, found much cause for thankfulness to God. But I might just as confidently assert, on the other hand, that if we could recall all our different states of mind during the year, we should find that there has been much complaining and dissatisfaction among us. Now if this is to be remedied, so that in each new year there shall be less to vex and make us dissatisfied, how can we better attain this object than just by increasing in love and good works? And again, in looking forward to-day into the future, and picturing to ourselves what may with more or less probability be marked out in the life-path of any one of us in the year we are entering on, we shall certainly find there various disturbing and saddening things, for those are never wanting in any year of a human life. And if we ask ourselves what is the very best that each of us can do to soften and mitigate those things, what should we wish for ourselves in order to bear them the more easily; no doubt it would be, first of all, to have a heart still more filled with love. For this is most certain, that nothing more gladdens a man, nothing makes him at once so happy in himself and so able to bear difficulties from without, as having his heart overflowing with love. To be thoroughly convinced of this, we need only call to mind the Apostle Paul's splendid eulogy on love. "Love suffers long and is kind; love envieth not, boasteth not herself, is not puffed up; beareth all things, believeth all things, hopeth all things, endureth all things." The apostle teaches us here how a man feels who has given love full play in his soul; and we must admit that there can be no richer fountain of joy and blessedness; for such a man is independent of all external advantages, and whatever he may meet with from without, he will find no cause of complaint. For, whence come most of the ills of life to a man? In so far as, in our various relations, they are caused by the faults of others and their wrong ways of acting, which cross our legitimate efforts and spoil our well-begun work, the natural result is that in such a case love feels less trouble at its own loss than compassion for the faults of another; so that vexation is kept down by sympathy, and there is hardly need of special meekness to keep all harshness in check. In this way, indeed, a heart full of love is less susceptible to all troubles that are caused by the defects and faults of others, or even, if there can be such a thing among Christians, by their intentional ill-treatment. And in all such cases are not those who cause evil to others by their faults just the very people who most need help? And what, then, is the help that he needs who, because he follows ungodly pleasure and tries to seize on the fleeting things of this world, works harm to his brother? or he who spoils his neighbour's work because he is too much taken up with himself to inquire how he may be affecting another's concerns? All that either of them needs is that he be "provoked to love." For why does a man shut himself up within himself and love no one but himself, when we are called to a common inheritance? Why does he cling to earthly joy which is followed only too soon by earthly sorrow, when he should take everything at its spiritual and heavenly value, seeing that even here our citizenship is to be in heaven? Earthly joy is a fleeting thing which we can never keep fast hold of; he who knows no higher joy has a mere passing gleam of pleasure; and selfishness sets such narrow bounds to our enjoyment that no one will remain within them to whom a wider circle is open. But love opens such a circle; where love is, everything selfish appears so empty and poor that the heart will no longer be bound by it; it is love that changes things transitory in themselves into something eternal and heavenly, and stamps them with her own divine impress. Therefore for all such erring people the only real help is that we seek to incite them to love; to kindle that divine spark in their souls, so that they may emerge from the fogs of earth, and their efforts take a higher flight.

But we may have adverse experiences with which the conduct of others has nothing to do, which we may regard as coming to us through the hidden purpose of God and directly from His hand. Must we not admit, then, even as regards these, that the more pure and tranquil a man's heart is by the power of love, the more it is filled with grace and peace, just the more easily will he bear all that thus comes to him from without, and to surmount it; because the sufferings of this present time cannot be compared with the blessedness that is in a loving heart? And if we find that any one lacks the real strength to overcome what he has already encountered, or calmly to meet what may still threaten him, no doubt the first thing that we desire and recommend for him is trust in God. But how can we have living trust in God if He is not near and present in our soul; that is, if we do not in the depth of our hearts see His divine nature as that of the strong and beneficent God? But God is love, and therefore we can only be near Him in the living strength of love. And so it will only be the loving man who truly trusts in God; and if, in whatever circumstances our consciousness of God has another stamp than that of child-like confidence, the cause of that can only be that the heart is still closed against love, and its hard crust has not yet been softened by that penetrating power that can fill every part of it with its divine fire, and draw forth and cherish everything fair and good.

But now, passing from the thought of individuals and what concerns their welfare, let us turn our attention to that which is more important—our life as a community in its various aspects; a subject which on such a day as this is of deepest interest to every right-thinking man. Here also we must as truly acknowledge that we should not have had so much to complain of as undeniably there has been in the past year, if there had been found among us that of which our text speaks—a greater abundance of good works. This is surely made plain to us by the fact that in this connection we do not easily hear a complaint without attaching blame somewhere. And though the blame may often be unjust and groundless, yet there is implied in this the general admission that in the nature of things there is some blame connected with every such complaint; because in these matters everything depends as much on integrity and goodwill as on sense and judgment. Therefore if each one, as he could and ought, sought not his own, but the things of others; that is, whatever might conduce to the common good; if each kept clearly in view what it depends on, in all his relations, that justice be done and good promoted among men, and all imperfections and inequalities more and more smoothed away, so that we are always making life easier to each other; then there would be no cause to complain. And what tends most to this is just such good works as the apostle describes, "If there be any virtue, and if there be any praise . . . whatsoever things are lovely and of good report, strive after these things." And this applies by no means only to so very imperfect a state as our own justly appears to us; for even if we were much further advanced than at present, and in consequence had much less among us to be regretted, yet if there were any real cause of complaint, we should still be obliged to say that there had been a lack of good works. For had these not been wanting at the proper time and place, nothing evil would have happened of which we should have cause to complain. How could there be a better rule and a greater blessing for the social life of men than that evil be overcome with good? But overcoming presupposes action and effort; therefore if evil is to be overcome with good it can only be done by earnest diligence in good works. And thus we can truly say that this is all we need for our life in common.

If these two things, love and good works, dwell richly among us, not only should we all be cheerful and content, because each one would exert a beneficent and cheering influence in all his relationships, but everything praiseworthy and of good report before God and man would blossom out among us in richest abundance. And therefore if in passing over into a new year we still see something gloomy and forbidding, we cannot deny to ourselves that there has been a lack of the true power of love and of true diligence in good works. Love is the balm with which we are to refresh every wounded spirit,—the wine which we are to hand to every sorrowful one. And diligence in good works is the perpetual offering, indeed the only one, which we have to make to the commonweal in order to clear ourselves from the reproach that we make such slow progress towards the aim which we all set before us. Let us only unite those two, and soon all that we have to complain of will be removed, and all attained to that we wish and hope for. Not only is each of these by itself a real need, but the two together are in fact the only means by which everything is put to rights; and they are so closely connected that each promotes the increase of the other. How could the abundance of love fail to increase everywhere the wealth of good works? and if we were everywhere surrounded by good works flowing from a pure heart, how could love fail to have ever freer course in every breast, and so everything unite in making us rejoice more and more in the Lord?

II. We are taught secondly, in the words of our text, how we are to satisfy this need, which is common to us all. We are each of us ever more strongly and urgently to call on ourselves and others for good works, and this incitement is to proceed from our considering one another; that is to say, this expression that we are to consider one another certainly aims ultimately at this, that we are to care for each other in regard to those specified points; but it also declares very distinctly that our care is to begin with each of us well considering others in order that we may concern ourselves about them, and gain an intuitive knowledge how things are with them, taking note of their condition, and rightly recognising their needs. See here how the writer of our epistle in this beautiful exhortation presents us to each other, if I may so express it, at the new year, as a possession entrusted to us, of which we have to take care. We are to consider one another; that is the work of the Christian community; we are to care for each other in the true Christian sense; that is, in reference to the kingdom of God and its advancement; and that is to be the light in which we always regard each other. Now if we ask in the first place how we are to set about stirring up others to love, most people will certainly consider the thing demanded impracticable, if it is made so universal. But in these days we make far too great a distinction between the more distant and the nearer relationships in which we stand to others,—much greater than the Christian ought to make it. For this does not admit of a doubt, that the more our Christian feeling increases, the less does this distinction become; the more distant draw nearer to us, and the distance seems to us not nearly so great as is taken for granted in the usages of our ordinary life. Because to the true disciple of the Lord there is absolutely no man who is nothing to him; on the contrary, every man who at any time crosses our path is either one who already enjoys with us the benefits of redemption, and confesses and praises the same Lord, or he is one whom we should feel called on to seek to make a partaker in those benefits. Therefore we should regard no one as a stranger; but all and always, though in different ways and degrees, as our brethren. And so we must say, on the other hand, that no one belongs exclusively to one or to another among us; but that we are all the common property of each other. Inasmuch as we are all called to a great partnership, each one has rights of love over each, and demands to make on each, in so far as the life of one touches the other, or anything can be transmitted from the spirit of the one to the other. And yet there does always remain this difference, that we have many opportunities of fulfilling this duty towards some, few of doing so towards others; that with some it is made easy for us to consider them, with others not so. We need go into no further detail to explain how it is that in the closer relations of life we consider each other, and how the true Christian life in each should so find expression, that each point of contact with another should be to that other a stimulus to love. But is it not possible also with more remote connections, if we only carry everywhere the tender solicitude of a loving spirit? Can we not, if only our will is earnestly bent to it, consider in the same way those who are not immediately around us, so as to note what each is in want of? And shall any one, whose need we have discerned, go from us without having received a spiritual gift according to the measure of our powers? Oh, how we limit our noblest influence to a small section of our life, and therefore how empty is all the rest, if we neglect this duty!

And now there only remains to us the question, If we are to stir up others to love, how is it to be done? Only in one way. Does it seem to you that if love is to begin for the first time in a human breast, if there is no living spring of love there, then, in order that this spring may break forth, he must first receive love from without, and be, as it were, inoculated with it? But this can only be effected by the presence of another love, to which the new love may spring up as a response. How can we but admit this from the depths of our hearts, when this principle is the foundation of our common faith? For what was the need of the human race but fellowship with God, that is, love to Him? The natural disposition to this was fast asleep in men; and what other way could God have taken to awaken it than by manifesting His love in his Son? Then sprang up in man's heart a love responsive to that which had appeared in the Son,—to that original love which kindles the true spiritual life in man,—an answering love, flowing heavenwards from man's heart. And just so it is with the first awakening of love in each individual life. And even where love does not altogether need to spring up for the first time, but exists already, as it must in every Christian heart, it may yet not be sufficiently operative, and may need to be strengthened. In this case also a love is to be produced that is not yet there; and this must be effected just in the same way as that first awakening. Do you ask again, then, how can we stir up one another to love? In no other way than this, that we ourselves show love to him in whom we wish to excite it. If it is hearty, brotherly love with which we consider another, and try to understand him without giving way to any unfavourable prejudice, so that we cast no look upon any brother but one of love that seeks to serve him; it cannot fail that he will become aware of that love and its considerate efforts to do something for him suitable to his circumstances; and when he does so, our love will not return to us empty but will produce some fruit in his heart. When the Lord sent out His disciples for the first time to declare His Word and to preach the Kingdom of God, He prepared them for the case in which their word might not take root in men's minds, and told them that their blessing would return to themselves. But in all the workings of love, simply as love, we have not that to fear; it is not possible that it should ever be quite unfruitful. The heart of man may be hardened against the divine Word and against the voice of truth; but that it should ever be able to harden itself against pure love is not to be imagined. If love is only there, alive and active in the soul, and expressing itself in word and deed, it must find entrance, it must take hold and move, it must work a change in some way. And as the effect of love can be nothing but good, seeing that love is gentle and patient even when it punishes and afflicts, it cannot but move the human heart to love in return. And if only we do not relax in the expression of our love, we shall have to rejoice in its taking captive our brother's heart, and our provoking him to love will not be in vain. But otherwise than thus it cannot be done. Perhaps we can only say for ourselves as to the past, that we have rather sought to move men to stronger manifestations of love by severe words and harsh judgments, or by representing the advantage they would derive from doing so, or the harm they would avoid. Let this be past with other mistakes. It may be that those counsels, if they were well intended, brought back at least a blessing to ourselves; but in the future we are going to do better. For nothing creates love but love itself. If we wish to stir others to love, let us ourselves be filled with love, so that every word and act may show it. Then there will assuredly be abundant fruit, and the incitements to love which proceed from love will not be in vain.

But further, according to the direction of our text, we are to consider one another to provoke to good works. Indeed, if faith works by love; if this active faith means that the Spirit of God has, through the preaching of the Word, taken a settled place in the heart; then all virtues and all that is lovely and of good report, and therefore also all good works, are nothing but the fruit of the Spirit; and thus it appears as if love and good works were inseparable. Only we may say that love is more the inward side of a right state of mind, and good works its outward and active side. And if we question experience, we are constrained to confess that they do not always keep pace together. Why is this, and whence also the need, in addition to provoking to love, of special incitements to good works? From this reason; that love, in order to produce its proper abundance of good works, must first, if I may so speak, come to years of discretion. For if we see that there is really love somewhere, but miss the good works, what can be the reason, but that the right perception is wanting, partly of what is, for each occasion, good and well-pleasing to God, and partly of how to accomplish it. How otherwise should it be that often, with the best will and the most entire honesty, there are so many blunders and wrong-doings? And how then are we to stir each other up to good works? Just by seeking, according to our ability, to bring our brother to a clear understanding of what is right, and to throw light for him on the just and true connection of things. And this can be done without any self-sufficiency. For we are bound to assume that there is love in the heart of every Christian, until the want of it is forced on our notice; and therefore if we find one lacking in good works, we must not ascribe this beforehand to anything contrary to love; for this judgment would itself be at variance with love. Rather let us remember how the Lord Himself spoke of that which was pre-eminently a work of darkness, when His enemies vented their malice on Him and delivered

Him up, guiltless, to death,—how, with full and true knowledge of all, He said to His heavenly Father, "They know not what they do." And in like manner we are to account for all deficiency of good works and all wrongdoing that may still appear in the Christian community, by the supposition that in some way those concerned know not what they do. And then, if we understand better than they the matters in which they fail, we are bound to communicate our knowledge to them; and if otherwise, we can at least try to make them aware of their lack of knowledge, and then help them to seek it where it is to be found. There is no other real stirring up to good works, than that each one strives to increase the amount of true knowledge and correct judgment, wherever and however he can. For if there is the will to do good, then the knowledge which directs this inward desire, and presents the good aimed at in its full worth and beauty, is the most powerful incitement, which no one can withstand. And if this effect does not appear, then undoubtedly something else is wanting, and that can be nothing but love, which we must therefore seek to stir up in order that it may produce good works. But again, if we find that there is a disproportion between the love which we know actually exists in the heart of our neighbour, and his good works—the latter lagging behind the former—we may be sure the only reason for this is the want of correct knowledge, which he will gladly receive from any one who has it to communicate.

And now, my dear friends, let us be thoroughly honest with ourselves in this matter and ask ourselves how faithful we have really been as to these things in the past year. I fear we have been greatly wanting in this way; that even when we have made advances to others with inducements to love, we have yet not considered them to provoke them to good works. For I think, if this were not the case, we should be able to show among us a much greater abundance of deeds well-pleasing to God. Only do not suppose that I mean at the new year to blame you for that commendable modesty which is not in a hurry to judge of a neighbour, and still less is inclined to take for granted beforehand that another does not know how to help himself in what is his duty; for this is only a pretext that vanity takes for displaying its own wisdom. No; we honour this commendable modesty; but, if we will really be honest, we must confess that behind this modesty is very often hidden an unbrotherly mistrust that the other might not admit that we had the right, even so far as every Christian must joyfully allow it to another, to look so nearly at the more intimate concerns of his life as to be able to consider him with a view to his good works. There is concealed under it a lazy indifference, as if we were not called on to kindle for others the light of truth, and, by communicating to them correct knowledge, to show them what beautiful and good work they could do for God;—an indifference which is so much the more culpable, if we are afterwards only too ready to blame where we were not willing beforehand to enlighten. Yes, I fear that we cannot carry over from the past year into the new one a clear conscience in this matter. It is difficult, there is no doubt, to lay down an exact rule here; and yet, if our own knowledge is clear and active, and we feel honestly sure on some point; if we remember how our brother's work and duty are connected with our own, of which we must render an account; then we may be very certain that if we neglect to compare our views with his, to bring light into his dark places, and to try whether he may not also have something to communicate to us, so that we may, if possible, attain to agreement in opinion and to working in concert; then real modesty was not the cause of our holding back; and by doing so we defraud our brother and ourselves of a common good, and also directly or indirectly endanger our own sphere of work. Genuine modesty sets to work humbly, giving no cause for supposing that we only wish to show off our own wisdom and to set ourselves up over others; and we shall certainly fulfil in the best way this duty of stirring up to good works, and be most happily successful in it, when this modesty is united with the natural ardour and enthusiasm for all that each of us has discerned to be true and right. And then the love for truth which we have in our hearts, and our evident zeal for good cannot fail to be a stimulus to good works; while active co-operation, with frank interchange of benefits and mutual support, must produce such works in ever-increasing abundance.

And if we thus more and more consider one another to provoke to love and to good works, oh, what a beautiful year shall we then spend! how much will then more quickly and easily assume a better appearance, how much will then disappear, over which we have now to lament! And in a fulness of contentment and joy how much fairer and more blameless will the Church of the Lord appear! how much steadfastness and security shall we have gained, each in his own calling, and with how much greater gladness of heart shall we then look back on the year now opening, when it, too, has passed away!

Let us then lay to heart these words of Scripture, and may we all be agreed in resolving that, as the Lord has cast our lot together, we will all of us consider each other to provoke unto love and to good works. Then shall we be ever more worthy followers of Him who, throughout His life supplied the first and strongest stimulus to love and good works; awakening in us, by the fulness of His divine love, the purest responsive love, that of gratitude; while by His knowledge, the living knowledge of the Father, with whom He is one, He becomes to us the Truth, teaching us the works which we are to do, and towards which we are to encourage each other. And thus it must always be by His power that we stir up each other. It is only the grace of God in Him that we must always go on understanding better and making known more diligently among men, that through it the man of God may be made capable of good works, and rich in them to prepare for Him the dominion which is His due. And so will our whole life be a truly Christian life; that is a life that is blessed of God and really heavenly.

XXV.

THE SAVIOUR'S LAST HOURS.

(*Preached on Good Friday.*)

"Praise and thanks be to Him who lifted up the Saviour on the cross as the bringer of salvation, that thereby He might glorify Him with heavenly glory! Praise and honour be to Him who by His obedience even unto death has become the Author of our faith, that so He may be able, as a faithful high-priest, to represent before God those whom He is not ashamed to call His brethren. Amen."

TEXT: LUKE xxiii. 44–49.

THE habit of expecting to find great events accompanied by strange portents is so old and so universal, that, though it might not shake our faith, we should miss a certain feeling of satisfaction, and should also be inclined to wonder, if all that took place in connection with the great event that we commemorate to-day had not been full of significance regarding the work of Christ, and the great end which the heavenly Father purposed to bring about by His death. But we find that it really was so. Looking at the sad and mournful spectacle of the death of Christ, surrounded as He was by unfeeling enemies to the last moment, the watchful eye sees greatness and sublimity shining through all, and the believing heart is calmed and refreshed by clear tokens from above. Let us then in this light meditate together on the circumstances that accompanied the Saviour's last hours; that our comfort and hope through

His death may receive new strength, and that we may take a broader and more confident view of its blessed results. We will consider first the outward signs that accompanied the Saviour's death, and then the effects which, according to the gospel narrative, those signs produced on the feelings of men.

I. When we look at the outward signs that accompanied our Lord's death, we cannot resist a feeling that there must be some great and mysterious connection between the kingdom of nature and the kingdom of the Spirit and of grace. We take note of such a connection in all the great events that take place in the world. The endeavour to trace relations of this kind is indeed a somewhat dangerous practice for those who are only slightly acquainted with natural processes, and who, on every unusual natural occurrence, set themselves anxiously to wonder what it may indicate in the spiritual world. But right as it is to warn people against this, it is very different with those who are awake to all that pertains to the spiritual life, and who look at things from the other direction. In that case the finest feelings are called into play when we search into the natural signs that may accompany and correspond with the value of spiritual events. The discovery of this connection in the great course of the world's government is the utmost, highest aim of the profoundest human wisdom and knowledge. But even in single instances, when anything great, either good or evil, occurs in the domain of the spirit, it is only the tenderest conscience that can teach us how to seek out significant signs in nature. Was it not just the consciousness of the divine in Christ that, as it were, compelled so many to discern, in the wonderful works that He accomplished, an evidence of His high dignity and mission? This connection appears at the time of His death full of significance, first in the darkening of the sun, and then in the rending of the temple veil.

It was about the sixth hour, says the evangelist, and there was a darkness over all the earth until the ninth hour, and the sun was darkened. This darkness was not one of those eclipses which result, according to ascertained law, from the natural course of our earth and her attendant planet; it was a phenomenon out of the regular order of Nature, which covered the whole land with darkness, while the sun concealed or lost his light until the ninth hour, when the Saviour gave up His spirit. And then also,—and this is just the most significant point,—then the darkness ceased, and the extinguished sun beamed forth again in his brightness and spread abroad his beneficent light. Oh, my dear friends, that which made it necessary for the Saviour to appear on earth was the universal, mournful darkness of the human spirit through error, delusion, and sin; but still it was a special darkening of men's spirits, not so easily to be explained by the laws of human nature, or appearing in a general way,—an abnormal darkening,—that could make them put to death, and that under pretext of God's law, the man mighty in word and deed, whose teaching was in the Spirit and with power, who went about freeing those whose spirits were bound, and miraculously healing their sick; and it was to such a darkness that nature called attention when the sun was darkened in an unusual way. But inasmuch as it shone out at the moment of the Saviour's death, oh, let that be truly a token to us, a more glorious token than the bow of peace that Noah saw on the cloud after the waters of the flood had subsided! As then the Lord said, "Let this be a sign between me and thee, that I will not again destroy the race of man," so here, by the shining forth again of the darkened sun after the death of the Saviour, the Eternal says to us, Let this be a sign between Me and you that the darkening of the human soul is withdrawn and past. The light had come from heaven and shone into the darkness; and though the darkness had not yet welcomed it, though the cross was surrounded by a crowd of the very most darkened spirits, yet the light was now to hold a permanent place in human nature; its kingdom was founded, and in the gracious counsel of God it was decreed that this heavenly light, proceeding from a point which at that time appeared so insignificant, should go on spreading ever more widely, and the power of the faith kindled and cherished by this light should triumph over the world and all its darkness. It is true that in the history of the gospel and of the kingdom of God there have often been times of darkness; it is true that the followers of the light that appeared in Christ Jesus have often, like Him, been put to death by the children of darkness; but the servant cannot expect to fare better than his Lord, and the darkness which made such treatment possible towards the servants of the Most High,—weak and sinful, though truly chosen men,—must be regarded as less deep than that in which men could so act towards the anointed of the Lord Himself. Therefore the assertion still holds good, that the cessation of that darkness was the great turning point in the history of men, and in the development of their spiritual nature. From Adam downwards the Spirit was working with growing power through the revelation of God written on the hearts of men; but the darkness could not thus be entirely dispelled. For from the beginning the flesh lusted against the Spirit, and took pleasure in the darkness, and kept back truth in unrighteousness. In this continually renewed struggle divine voices were ever coming to aid the hearts of men; but the victory of the light over the darkness became decisive only in the death of the Lord, when the kingdom of light was established, and the Lord's work accomplished. Those who are buried with Him in His death rise with Him to a new life; those who renounce the darkness of sin which the Prince of Life vanquished on the cross shall have His life manifested in them from glory to glory.

"And the veil of the temple was rent in the midst." This veil concealed the mysteries of the old covenant from the eyes of all, one man excepted, who was allowed to enter the holy of holies only once a year, to sprinkle there the blood of the covenant. As the outer curtain separated the priests of the Lord from the congregation of the people, so this inner veil separated the high priest from all his brethren in the priesthood. The rending of this veil signified in the first place that now all the mysteries of God were revealed, all hidden things to be disclosed, and that special purposes of God and declarations of His will were no longer to be announced to men in some mysterious way from one hidden spot, but that one purpose of salvation was to be openly proclaimed everywhere. And it signified further that there were no longer to be separations and distinctions among those who worshipped God in and through His Son, but that the time was come in which all should have free access to God in Christ, when all believers should be priests of the Most High, all taught of God, and each mutually serving the others in the Lord. These two truths, that all separate priesthood has ceased, and that now the whole will of God has been declared to us, cannot be separated; and only when these are taken together can we take the full comfort that there is in the power of the gospel of redemption. Before Christ fell into the hands of His enemies He testified of Himself that He had made known to His disciples all the words which He had received from the Father. What clearer testimony could there be to His having, as the Son in whom the Father was well-pleased, received the whole fulness of divine communication, securing to the human spirit a blessed fellowship with God, than just the rending of this veil; indicating that God would no longer dwell among men in one secret place, that faith need no longer, as it had hitherto done, seek His presence exclusively over the ark of the covenant which was concealed from all eyes. It meant that as Christ, when He had finished

His work by the pouring out of His blood on the cross, entered into the true holy of holies; His kingdom is now the unlimited spiritual house of God, in which He is Himself the true mercy-seat, the place in which God most fully manifests His presence among men. And although during His life on earth it seemed a strange saying to the disciples that they should see the Father in the Son, yet after He was perfected and glorified by His obedience to death on the cross we recognise in Him the true image of the divine nature and the brightness of eternal love. What need, then, of any further human mediation or intercession? Here there is nothing which one alone is permitted to behold; to this mercy-seat all are free to approach. And as Christ became our Brother by coming down to us and taking on Him our flesh and blood, so we now become His brethren by His lifting us up into spiritual union with the Father, so that through Him we are all members of the household of God, all equally through Christ the children of Him to whom He has reconciled us, all members of His spiritual body, through His Spirit whom He sends into the hearts of believers. Thus then every veil is rent, and all may fix their eyes in confident faith on the Saviour on the cross, while from the exalted Saviour we receive directly the spiritual gifts and blessings which the priests under the old covenant might certainly desire for the people, but could not bestow.

These, then, are the comforting signs which our faith sees accompanying our Lord's death. But that which these tokens of grace and peace signified could only be realized through the saving power of the gospel in the hearts of men. And when we review the history of the Christian Church down to the present day, we see with joy and comfort how that power has gone on extending since that eternally significant hour. The extension of this blessed kingdom still proceeds too slowly for our devout wishes; we still see on the earth too much darkness, into which the light has not yet penetrated. But even in regard to this slow progress we see something to comfort and gladden us when we consider what took place in the minds of men at the Saviour's death, to which let us now direct our attention.

II. "And the centurion who kept watch beside the cross, when he saw what was done, cried out, Certainly this was a righteous man!" What was it then that took place before his eyes and called forth this exclamation? He saw how the darkness fell and the light of the sun was quenched; he saw with what unexpected suddenness He died, who seemed still to have long agonies before Him; he saw and heard how He, charged with such crime as would make peace and calmness impossible to most men, yet could with perfect tranquility commit His spirit into the hands of the heavenly Father;—then he spoke, and said, "Certainly this was a righteous man!" How little had the rough soldier up to this time concerned himself about the excitement caused by the appearing of the Lord among this strange and despised people of the Jews!

We see here, then, an effect of the death of the Saviour, even if it were but a passing impression, in the stirring of this man's mind out of utter indifference to a recognition of Christ's dignity. Another of the evangelists reports the man as saying, "Truly this was the Son of God!" that is, that what He had been accused before the Roman governor as claiming, He had proved Himself to be. As the centurion had now become fully assured of this, we may well suppose, taking the two sayings together, that since, in the fulfilment of his office, he had led Christ forth to death, his mind had been fluctuating between the impression made by the high position of the accusers and that produced by the person of the Saviour. And in proportion as this latter impression became the stronger, he must also have debated in himself the question whether He had been a righteous man given up, guiltless, to death by His enemies, or whether, seeing that

He quitted this earthly life amidst such portentous signs and in so kingly a manner, He were not in truth the Son of God. Oh, blessed question, that arose in an utterly darkened soul! Oh, sudden awakening of the spirit out of the deepest darkness, to drink in the heavenly light that comes with the faith that the Word has been made flesh, and that the Son of the Highest has appeared in human form! And just so, thanks be to God, does the preaching of the death of our Lord still go on producing effects peculiarly its own. When thoroughly blinded souls are to be initiated into the mysteries of the kingdom of God, when the kingdom of heaven is to be opened to those who are still walking in the shadow of death, then nothing will avail but making known the dying Saviour to men. The story of His death has ever been the mightiest word of life; and when the scene is described by one whose own spirit is inspired by faith, even careless souls are often awakened. And if at first they say no more than, Certainly this was a righteous man; let them but hear afterwards His own words about the glory which He has always had with the Father; let them hear the history of His life and the results of His resurrection; then they will join in saying, "Surely this was the Son of God!"

And "All the people that stood by, when they saw what was done, smote on their breasts and returned." These were the same people who had cried, "Crucify Him, crucify Him!" who had laid a curse on themselves with the words, "His blood be on us and on our children!" And now, when they saw what had taken place, they smote on their breasts and turned away. Was it only because the spectacle of the Lord's death, with which they had come to amuse themselves, was finished? No; for the evangelist says they smote on their breasts; so he must have seen, by this and similar signs, that something more was going on in their minds; that the death of the one righteous man had staggered them in their contempt and hatred; that they had begun to be doubtful if it was for their own good that they had slain the Prince of life. And even if it cannot be denied that with the greater number this was only a transient emotion, yet many of these same people were afterwards present on the day of Pentecost, and heard Peter bear public testimony to the Prince of life; and then many among them smote on their breasts a second time, and with very different feelings, and cried, "Men and brethren, what shall we do?" My dear friends, may this day on which we commemorate the death of Christ be every year blessed with like blessings in every Christian community, in every land where the Christian name holds a place! And we know that it is so indeed. For the kind of people have not yet died out from among Christians, who stumble at the offence of the cross, who are even bold enough to scorn the Crucified One, though they do not disdain outwardly to bear His name. Indeed, it may be said that many turn their minds so entirely against Him, that with all their power they resist being taken hold of either by the impressive signs that accompanied His life and His death, or by the Spirit and the power that work in His words, or by the effects that have followed the preaching of His name in the world. But even such people, when they see believers bending in the devotion of grateful hearts before the cross of the Redeemer—when they hear us renewing together our engagement to make known the blessings of His death till He comes—oh, then, many who have hardened themselves in opposition against the Saviour begin to feel troubled, and smite on their breasts. And if there comes another and yet another stirring of the Spirit; if the word of the Lord again and again sounds in their ears and knocks at their hearts, oh, then at last they turn thoroughly from the way of ruin and become His and ours.

"And His acquaintance, and the women who had followed Him from Galilee, stood afar off, beholding these things." Close to His cross stood only His mother and the disciple whom He loved. The rest had been scattered as He had foretold to them, and did not until later join those who were the immediate witnesses of His death. And these, His acquaintance, His faithful handmaids and friends, stood afar off, beholding it all. Just as it was in His own mother's heart that the influence of the Saviour was first felt on earth—when, after His presentation in the temple, she pondered, in quiet meditation, all the words that were spoken of Him there—so now His faithful handmaids stood silently watching from a distance the ebbing life of their beloved Master, comforting themselves in the thought of His passing to the Father, and laying up in the depths of their hearts all that they saw. But why did they stand afar off? Oh, may we not still put the same question to many Christians? Those who cling closely to the Saviour's cross, those who are there led by Him, like Mary and John, into the tenderest and closest union of heart, are always comparatively a small number. But let us not hold lightly those who stand farther off; let us rather look on those disciples of the Lord who also stood afar off as saying something in their favour. For many who do not seek after an assured personal union with Christ have yet salutary impressions made in their inmost hearts by His self-sacrificing death and the quiet greatness of His life—impressions of which they become more or less conscious, and which sooner or later come to bear fruit. We know also of those who do not gather so closely as others round the cross of the Redeemer,—we know it from manifold experience that the contemplation of His death has not been without a blessing to their hearts. And yet we will call to them, as we might have done to those disciples of the Lord, "Why stand ye so far off?" Draw nearer, that you may see still more clearly how the glory of the only-begotten Son is revealed in the Crucified. For the more closely you listen to His last words, the nearer you come, to catch, as it were, the parting glance of His eye, the more believingly you witness His death, just so much the more surely will you become joyful witnesses to His resurrection; and His whole nature will more promptly, effectively, and deeply take hold on you and bear you onward to eternal life. Yes, there is still always room there. All who have been already stirred up to faith, all who have been taken captive by the glory of this day, by this vanishing of the darkness before the shining forth of the light that shall be quenched no more, by the rending of the veil, throwing open for ever all the blessings of the spiritual sanctuary; all may now gather ever more closely around the cross of Him who came to this world for the salvation of men, and who died on this day that He might return to heaven. His cross is the sign under which alone we can all conquer. As He, the Captain of our salvation, overcame by His obedience unto death, so we can overcome only by taking up His cross and following Him; by not shrinking from going through tribulation into the kingdom of God, which He has prepared for us; or even from being made perfect, as He was, through suffering and the cross. Let us all vow anew such allegiance as this to Him, and never will He cease to bless us as from His cross. Amen.

XXVI.

THE PARTING PROMISES OF THE SAVIOUR.

(*On Ascension Day.*)

TEXT: ACTS i. 6–11.

THE great event that we commemorate to-day was no doubt something very different to the disciples at that time from what it is to us. They had hardly recovered from the stunned condition into which His death had thrown them; they had hardly come to realize calmly their pain at His separation from them; at least, they had certainly not yet learned to look at it in the right way, for they regarded it as the ruin of His whole work on earth—when His joyful resurrection took them by surprise, comforting them and setting them right. But now when He was withdrawn from their eyes while they gazed up to heaven, it was more tranquilly and wisely, and certainly with a greatly lightened sorrow, as one looks at the close of a full and completed life, that they regarded the end of the relations in which they had hitherto stood with their beloved Lord and Master. For us, on the contrary, this event stands as the beginning of that relation of Christ to His people which has continued ever since then—the only relation which we know by direct experience. Hence, while we can, it is true, sympathise with the sorrow of the disciples, we cannot feel it directly as our own; and it would be unnatural in us to try to work ourselves up into such a state of feeling, as if we missed something by the personal, visible presence of the Saviour being denied to us. But we may profitably inquire to-day whether we thoroughly appreciate all the good and beauty of the relation that has subsisted between the Saviour and His people since He ascended from the earth, and enjoy it, as He intended, in all its fulness. The Saviour certainly brought that good very thoroughly into view in the comforting promises that He gave to His disciples as often as He already in spirit saw Himself exalted to the right hand of the Father. If, in a general way, there is little or nothing, even of what Christ said to His disciples in their most intimate intercourse, that might not also be applied to us; if we share with them almost all the privileges that He bestowed on them, as well as all the duties He imposed on them; how much more may we apply to ourselves what He said for the purpose of preparing them for the position which we have in common with them. If we take all the utterances, ever becoming more clear and intelligible, concerning the spirit and manner of His kingdom; the tender outpourings of His glorious love in the presaging sense of His departure; the earnest warnings and exhortations addressed to their hearts not yet fortified against danger;—if we regard all this as said to us also, whom He embraces in the same love, and for whom He prayed, even as for those through whose word we believe;—how much more may we claim a share in the elevating promises by which He sought to comfort the disciples for their loss, and to make them fit for their new position.

These promises of the Saviour to His disciples in reference to His complete departure from them are scattered through His discourses, and it would be necessary to collect them from many passages if we wished to study them fully and in detail. But as custom requires us to take one connected portion of Scripture as the leading thread of our public expositions; the account of the ascension, which we have just read, will serve our purpose, in so far as it reminds us distinctly of those promises to which I wish chiefly to draw your attention, and which we may most directly take to ourselves. For certainly when the Saviour tells the apostles they are to wait till they are endued with power from on high, and then to be His witnesses; we cannot appropriate to ourselves what belonged specially and peculiarly to the gift at Pentecost, to which Christ here unquestionably alludes. And indeed that power from on high was not, after all, the Spirit of God, whom Jesus had already breathed into the apostles in the first days after His resurrection,—whom He had even earlier spoken of them as possessing, when, on their acknowledging Him as the Christ, He said that flesh and blood had not revealed it to them, but the Father in heaven; for when the Father reveals anything, He does it by the Holy Spirit, as it is said in another place, No man can say that Jesus is Lord but by the Holy Spirit. Now if we further reflect how, since then, many have become His witnesses who had no share in the extraordinary gift of Pentecost, as we ourselves are, each in his own way; how can this call to be His witnesses but remind us of that glorious promise, without which no one would be capable of fulfilling this commission—the promise which the Saviour linked with this very commission, saying, Go, and teach all nations, and then adding, And I am with you all the days, even to the end of the world. And the words of those who came to the apostles after the Lord was taken away,—to what could they refer but to the promise which, during the recent days, the Lord had often expressed in various forms, that the Son of man would return in all the glory of the Father, a Lord and King, a Judge of all living. If, then, we desire to reflect together on the promises of the departing Saviour, it is just those two on which we should fix our attention: first, that He will be with us even to the end of the days; and second, that He will come again to judgment. But, my friends, let us deal in the same way with these two promises; with the one as with the other!

If no time is too late for the one, so let us also believe that no time is too early for the other. If we enjoy the one as an immediate and precious possession, let us not regard the other only as a hardly discernible form, approaching with little show out of the dim distance; but let us appropriate both, not as something strange and far off, but as something present, forming the essence of His living relation to His Church, of His kingdom already set up,—something of which, just for this reason, He could say, It is not for you to know times and seasons, because it is not at all a matter of times and seasons, but has always existed, from that time onwards, and must from one period to another come ever nearer to completion. In this manner, then, let us talk together of these two promises.

I. In the first place let us think of the Saviour's promise, I am with you all the days, even to the end of the world. Yes, my friends, our own consciousness, our Christian experience must tell us this,—that He is ever with us, and in many different ways: He is with us in the Scriptures, He is with us in the holiest and most elevating emotions of our minds; finally, He is with us in the persons of those who bear His image, and justly and honourably bear His Name.

He is with us in the Scriptures. What He says Himself, even of the books of the Old Testament, "Ye search the Scriptures, because ye think that in them ye have eternal life, and it is they that testify of Me,"—how much more gloriously, and in how much larger a sense, has this been true since we have had the Scriptures of the New Testament; since the narratives of His deeds and sufferings were recorded by His disciples, since, the teachings and precepts collected in intercourse with Him, and presented and applied to the Christian Church by the apostles, have come down as a legacy to us! Whenever we search into those books, if we do it with a pure heart, everywhere He comes to meet us; everywhere He is pictured to us, everywhere we find a sacred bequest that He has left to us. And just as there are paintings in which all the light by which the rest of the objects become visible proceeds from Christ, so the Scriptures are such a painting, in which His image lights up everything else, that would otherwise be dark, with a heavenly radiance. For how much do we find in Scripture which, if regarded from the ordinary human point of view as general moral maxims or instructions, is unintelligible, doubtful in its consequences, or exaggerated and unnatural, but becomes quite clear when placed in connection with Him, with His work and His reign, as the reign of confidence in God, of the banishment of all care, of the power of prayer, of calm endurance. And much that, without Him, would be too high for us—of reconciliation to God, of the riches of His mercy and grace, of the intimate fellowship of men with God and God's dwelling among us;—how close all this comes to us! how powerfully that which in every point corresponds with the features of His likeness takes hold of us, so that His action makes it plain to us, and it, as it were, streams from His lips into our minds! And there may still be much in these books for thoughtful students of Scripture to investigate; but whatever they may discover, it can only tend to make the image of Christ clearer; never will it be obscured or altered. The need of having Christ near and present in this way began to be felt, it may be said, from the day on which He was taken away. Now that they could no longer see and hear Himself, the believers became eager to learn, from the accounts of others, what they had not themselves seen and heard; and every one wished to fix in his memory and to communicate what He possessed, and thus written memoirs began to be made, which grew into the histories of the life of Jesus as we have them in our sacred books. Who does not feel how important this holy possession is for our living relation to Him; how indispensable it was for all successive generations to have this compensation for His absence? Who does not feel what a hold faith and love gain by this many-sided revelation of the Lord? And therefore this treasure will remain with us, according to His promise; He is with us in the Scriptures, even to the end of the world. And much as the spirit that is hostile to Christianity has sought to deface and depreciate these books, they will in the future, as they have done hitherto, surmount all opposition.

"The word shall still unshaken stand,
In spite of all the scoffing band."

Again, the Saviour is with us in the holiest and most elevating emotions of our minds. Many, indeed, say doubtfully that it is only a fancy when one speaks of a special nearness and presence of the Saviour in this sense, and that His presence in the Scriptures would be perfectly sufficient for us. It is very possible that with some it is a mere fancy; and yet we could wish that even those dubious spirits might not lack the reality that we mean by this expression; and let us not forget that without such moments, even the Scriptures themselves, and therefore our way of having Jesus near in the Scriptures, would not exist. For we know how human feeling fluctuates, and how, even apart from any direct influence of external circumstances, one hour is not like another; in some, life is more dull and uninteresting, while others are filled with richer blessing from God. And assuredly it was not in their lowest and most listless moods that the Lord's disciples ventured to write anything about His life and work; but when they had a specially vivid view of Him in any connection, and the divine form stood out before their minds more and more glorious in light and splendour, then they sought to preserve, through the power of the Word, the substance of such richly blessed moments. It is just for this reason that the Scripture is such a treasure, because the blessing of the most highly favoured hours of believers is compressed into it. And can we suppose there are not still similar differences with us, perhaps only because having never seen the Saviour with our bodily eyes, a bodily image of Him could not present itself to our inner perception? We see in the first days of the Church how naturally and, as it were, imperceptibly, the physical passed over into the spiritual, and that therefore the two conceptions must be in their nature one and the same. Thus, long after His ascension, Christ appeared to Paul, when He meant to send him forth to enlighten the Gentiles; and Paul, who had perhaps never seen Him during His life on earth, or, at most, only in a passing and distant way, records this very appearance as the last on the list of the appearances of Jesus in the days of His resurrection. And thus Stephen, and assuredly many others afterwards, saw Him seated on the right hand of God, uncertain, amid the rapt and exalted feelings of martyrdom, whether it was with the bodily or the spiritual eye that they beheld Him. And thus also He often appears to us in unusual nearness and living presence, only, of course, in the spiritual splendour of His peace-bringing person; whether longed and prayed for in times of special heart need, or, as it were, spontaneously and unexpectedly, when our life has insensibly been raised and ripened anew to a higher enjoyment. And as, in the case of those we have spoken of, this assurance of Christ's presence was connected with the most important moments of their lives; as it changed Paul from being a persecutor of Christ and His people (though with the best intentions) into the most zealous preacher of His name; who could afterwards say justly of himself that he had laboured more than all the others; as Stephen's enraptured gaze rested on the Lord in His glory just when the crown of martyrdom was bestowed on him; even so with us, this immediate nearness of the Saviour will sometimes lead to the most momentous crises, and sometimes accompany them, lighting them with glory. If we have been long in doubt while honestly trying to find out what, in this case or that, is right and true; then in such an hour our doubt will be resolved, and Christ will be specially near to give us the assurance that it is in and through Him that our heart has become confirmed, that what we have found out or decided on is according to His mind and Spirit. When in the strength of faith and prayer we have successfully withstood any temptation, then Christ will be specially manifest to us, and will cry to us, Go in peace, thy faith hath helped thee; or while we are still in the midst of a hard struggle, His image suddenly rising before us will remind us that He died to deliver us from sin, and this will decide the issue for the good Spirit in us. When we feel in ourselves a calm that stills all earthly pain; when we feel drawn to all, or to individuals, with a higher power of love,—this also is from the special nearness of Christ, who is the bond of all love, and who is thus raising us above everything earthly, and drawing us to Himself. Or even when we have to groan over the feeling of being entangled in earthly things, it will be a longing look at Him that first lifts us up again to that purer, holy frame of mind. How otherwise could we say that a living relationship exists between Him and us? How could we say that we have a share in the blessing which yet He specially prayed for on our behalf, that we should live in Him and He in us? Those blessed moments are what give zest to life; it is those seasons that develop faith and love, and by which the rest of life is maintained and strengthened; they are indeed the force that holds together the whole Christian community, for it is only through them that any one is able to strengthen and animate others.

And hence, and just in this way, Christ is also near us in those who wear His likeness, and who honourably and worthily bear His name. That is to say, the more of such higher seasons as we have been describing each of us enjoys, the more will he recall Christ to the minds of those who live with him. For it is through such moments that the spiritual life makes progress; every pure disposition is strengthened by them, every virtue reanimated; and the more truly Christian we are, the more everything good in us has proceeded in this way from fellowship with Christ, it will bear the more clearly Christ's image and superscription; weak indeed, and in clouded brightness in comparison with Himself; and yet it helps to fix in our minds the true, unfalsified features of His likeness. Each individual, it is true, shows only certain separate features of the original, in whom all perfection is reflected; for our growth into His likeness only develops freely in certain directions, while in others it is checked or hindered by the power of our natural sinfulness, or by our blindness and indolence. But this is just how it comes that, as Christ Himself promised, He is most perfectly among us where two or three or several are gathered together in His name; where, impelled by our ardent desire to give Him the glory, and thankful for all that we have through Him, we mutually give frank expression to our feelings; where brotherly love gladly forgets everything else, and looks only at that in which Christ is glorified. Oh, assuredly, these manifestations of Christ in those who are most like Him are a very essential part of our relation to Him. In this way it is evidently given to us that He continuously lives and works among His people; and thus—whatever the world may say, whatever it may with scornful exultation cast in our teeth as to the decay of Christianity and the gradual dying out of its power—yet thus we are confirmed in the comforting conviction that His Church stands immovable, and that His covenant remains the same, however much may perhaps be changed in its outward forms. And this is the faith that overcomes the world, and that keeps us free from all anxiety, though in a bodily sense we are entirely separated from our protecting Lord and Master.

Thus, my friends, ever since His departure from the

earth, and without bodily appearance, Christ is near to His people. Every Christian feels this, and thus it will still be experienced, even to the end of the days.

II. In coming now to consider, secondly, the promise that the Saviour would come back to judgment, I have, it is true, already intimated that you should set this promise on a level with the former, and regard it just in the same way as a present thing, already in course of being fulfilled; but it will be only the smallest number of you who will be readily inclined to do so. It always seems to us as if the Lord had not yet set up His judgment-seat; and although we distinctly know that the kingdom of God comes not with outward show, yet as respects the judgment of God we are accustomed to expect that it *will* so come. But what right have we in reality to make this difference? As the kingdom of God is not yet completed, but there is always something more glorious to come, and it doth not yet appear what we shall be; even so, no doubt, the judgment of God is not yet completed. But are we therefore at liberty to regard it as very far off, and something that belongs only to the future? Scripture constantly connects the two things, God's kingdom and His judgment; what is true of the one is true of the other. The Saviour Himself represents it to us as present when He says, "He that believeth on Me hath eternal life, and cometh not into judgment; but he that believeth not is already judged. For I have not come to judge the world, but to save the world." Therefore, why do we think of waiting for the future? He who is liable to judgment is already judged. From that time this word holds good; He is present for judgment, although He Himself does not judge; and from that time the generations of men are being judged. This judgment consists in these particulars—first, that the good are distinguished from the wicked; second, that they each receive their due reward; and finally, that they go away each to his own place.

The Lord then comes already for judgment, inasmuch as it consists in distinguishing between the good and the wicked. There is a great deal said, indeed, about the skill with which the wicked are able to cloak themselves, to throw a fine appearance over all that they do, and in their talk to represent themselves as ardently and heartily honouring all that is good, and as haters of evil. But I believe I am not venturing too far when I assert that this art can only deceive those who have not goodness firmly established and active in themselves. For that which is true and good recognises itself everywhere, and so it also distinguishes its opposite. The Lord knew what was in man; so that, though many seemed to believe in Him, He did not commit Himself to them; and we also, the nearer we are to Him, and the more we have already received from Him, ought to have, and may have, the same knowledge. Not, indeed, instantly, or of what is at a distance from us: and he who takes upon him to pass hasty judgments, or to judge at all about people who are not near enough to him, or who have not influence enough on his own life to make it needful for him to judge about them, has himself to blame if he is mistaken, and if by spreading a false report he even helps the wicked to extend their operations and to increase their importance. But of the people who are near enough for us to be able to take note of their lives, so that a false judgment of them would necessarily be hurtful to us;—ought we not to be capable of knowing about them whether they are good or evil, whether for the Lord whom we follow, or against Him? Even if falsehood and dissimulation were successfully practised in all great matters, would not the real and inherent evil all the more surely betray itself in a multitude of unguarded expressions, which perhaps might seem to the persons themselves utterly trifling and insignificant, but which would give the surest indication of the state of their inmost hearts? Certainly if we walk in such darkness, we are not blameless in doing so;

every day must make us wiser in this respect, provided the word of the Lord is always producing its effects on us, and we are always more and more appropriating Him as our own. Besides, what would it signify that His light shines in us if it does not make us able to discern where there is light in men and where darkness? What would it signify that we hear and follow His voice if we cannot also see who does not follow it with us? And if thus each of us is able in his own circle to discriminate between the good and the evil; and if, at the same time, where it is needful, we rely on the well-considered judgment and the sure perception of our brethren, as it is right to do; then wherever the Lord has established His seat, is there not a distinction made, even now, between the good and the wicked?

And thus it comes that the Lord even now returns to judgment, in so far as it consists in a separation being made between the good and the bad. It is true that, as regards place, they are mingled together. We find ourselves surrounded on every side by the children of the world and of darkness, and we seem to ourselves to be so, even oftener than is actually the case; we feel oppressed by them; the sight of them saddens us; their neighbourhood is not unfrequently perilous to us, and our work is hindered by their active opposition. And on the other hand, how often do those who really belong to us keep at such a distance from us that it is hardly possible to extend a hand to one of them! How often do we miss their support, and how slowly the work of God seems to advance on earth, chiefly because they are not able sufficiently to unite their powers! All this is no doubt true. But then, on the other side, do we not always feel that every one who, like ourselves, belongs to the Lord is near us in a way in which no others are? If we have once really known such a one and taken him into our heart, then no change of place can ever again separate our spirits—no time can efface the beloved image, or carry away the blessing which association with him brought into our life. The invisible Church of Christ is, in reality, everywhere one; a living fellowship exists among all its members, into which nothing of an uncongenial nature can find its way. For what more can the wicked do than to give a different direction to our outward work than it might have taken without their intervention? Or could they really disturb our inner life? could they spoil for us the spiritual enjoyment which is afforded and made sure to us by Christ and the association of His people, the peace of God, the calm trust, the heartfelt love? Certainly no further than as there is still in us something of the same kind as in them; but if we are entirely Christ's, then anything opposed or hostile to Him has as little power over us as right in us; if He has conquered, He has certainly deprived evil of this power. But that which has no effect on me is separate from me. And how entirely it is so with us in everything! However near to us one may stand who is an utterly unthankful denier or enemy of Christ (though there are but few such), is there really anything about which we could take common ground with him? any undertaking whatever, unless something quite trivial and external, in which we could join him, or about which, if we did attempt to make common cause, we should not immediately be of different minds? Can he make use of us, just such as we are, in any way whatever, or we of him? Does he understand us, our joys and sorrows, our views and thoughts; or do we understand his? No; fellowship is not permitted to us; there is a gulf fixed between us, which no local separation could in reality increase; no word, in fact, comes across it from them to us, nor goes from us to them; we can receive no single thing from them, nor they from us, until they actually come over to us—until they have received from us the one great thing about which we are ever praying them in Christ's stead, that they will be reconciled to God.

And finally, as a part of this judgment, and, indeed, what

is regarded as the principal point; that is, that the righteous will enter the kingdom of their Father, and the wicked go away to the place assigned to them. This also let us not regard as a promise not to be fulfilled until that day. Rather let each one put himself to the test, and look around him to see that the Lord is even now judging, and how He is doing so. Many, it is true, think this lies very near, and is very easy to find. Virtue, they say, is its own reward; the good man alone has his happiness in himself; he feels himself safe under God's protection, and even in the storms of the world the peace of the Most High is not wanting to him; while the wicked man, on the contrary, is not made glad by his good fortune; the transitory nature of his enjoyment makes him uneasy; all his memories are poisoned by the sting of conscience; in short, at the heart of everything is the worm that dieth not. But if we look at the matter more closely, we often find that the children of darkness, being wise in their own way, are well able to take precautions against all disaster; that by natural or acquired thoughtlessness they escape the fear of the future; that becoming hardened in the habit of disobedience, they soon hear no longer in their inmost heart any voice that condemns them; so that they drink with untroubled gaiety from the cup of their worthless pleasures. And in the same way we see how, though the godly man has indeed the peace of God, yet this peace is often beyond human nature, and the heart longs for a day of manifestation of the Lord, in which it also may obtain its rights. And when we see how many tears the godly man sheds over unsuccessful attempts to extend and further what is good; how he is worn out by the scorn and derision of the adversaries in his often vain opposition to them; then we cannot deny that it has not yet appeared what we shall be, and that the Lord has not yet set up His throne for judgment. Therefore let us take yet another point of view, different from this ordinary one—a view to which the

Saviour Himself directs us when He says, Well done, faithful servant; enter thou into the joy of thy Lord; thou hast been faithful over a few things, I will set thee over many things; but take from the slothful servant that which he has, and cast him out into the outer darkness, where shall be wailing and gnashing of teeth. What is the condemnation of the ungodly, into which he is already entering even here? It is that he is more and more losing what was originally given to him of the divine image in man's nature; that the divine light is gradually quenched in him, and he is cast out of the kingdom of spiritual liberty, and left under the dominion of his own nature. Could we ask a heavier condemnation for him than this? And what, on the other hand, is the kingdom which we are appointed to inherit, and into which the faithful servant begins even here to be brought by his Lord? It is just that busy, active life in which we are already engaged, in which this promise of Jesus is being fulfilled. Amidst these tears and sighs we are yet always earning something for our Lord, and He sets us over more. Amidst opposition and conflict our spiritual strength increases, His image is formed more gloriously in us, and we are more and more seeing Him as He is, and becoming like Him. Do we with whom it is no question of any praise from without, which has nothing to do with the matter, but only of the satisfaction of our Lord and of gladsome fellowship with Him—do we desire anything more?

Thus rules the victorious Lord, who has sat down at the right hand of God! thus He blesses and prospers and guides—not from afar, but as near and present—all who hear His voice and follow Him; and thus He allows the unbelieving to pass judgment on themselves now and evermore! Let us then lay to heart the exhortation given by those men to the disciples, not to be looking up with impatient longing towards heaven; but let us turn from the contemplation of His ascension to earnest prayer in the Spirit and in the truth, being, like them, of one mind ; thus will He meet us also in His love and power; thus will be fulfilled in us also what He promised to the disciples. We shall taste and see how lovingly He is present with us, and we shall sit with Him, and, according to His mind and law, judge the generations of mankind. Amen.

XXVII.

TRUE HARVEST JOY.

TEXT: LUKE xii. 16–21.

TO-DAY the harvest thanksgiving is celebrated throughout the land, and it is most fitting that it should be with all of us a day of great and joyful giving of thanks. Although there are but few among the masses of people crowded together in this as in other great cities, who have any direct share in this great business of agriculture, yet we are all aware that it is the prime source of our common prosperity; indeed, I may say, the first condition of the development of our mental powers. So well do we know this, that whatever may be a man's special calling or business by which he seeks at once to advance the common good and to benefit himself, we speak of it in every-day language, and not inappropriately, or without good reason, as "his field and his plough." And so it is. All the different occupations of men that have to do with our existence and ordinary life in the world form a great inseparable whole; each is supported by the rest; failure in one direction spreads its effects far around; while every success, and, still more, every improvement, causes universal joy and gratitude among intelligent people, even among those who have no direct share in it. In the words of our text we find, it is true, a harvest joy,—the joy of a man over a year's rich and blessed produce of his fields; but it is joy of a kind that the Lord condemns as folly. Are we to suppose from this that He disapproved of and condemned joy altogether, and therefore wished also to repress the thanksgiving for any favour or blessing from God,—thanksgiving that flows only from joy? We cannot admit such a thought. It was the kind and manner of this joy that He blamed. And we find the key to the whole in the closing words of our text: "So is he that layeth up treasure for himself"—who rejoices over earthly riches—"and is not rich towards God." We find it also in the words that immediately precede these verses: "Take heed, and beware of covetousness." We cannot, indeed, say of the man in our text, that he was covetous in the strictest sense of the word, for he not only wished to gather up goods, but to enjoy what he had gathered. But because he thought only of himself in connection with what God had given him; because his joy was entirely on his own account, —utterly selfish,—this is why the Saviour charged him with folly. And let us not omit also to notice that though the Lord tells us nothing more of what passed in this man's mind, He brings clearly to light the folly of his soul, when He tells us that he was reminded by a voice from heaven (a voice which in these days is speaking so loudly to us)[1] of the uncertainty and transitoriness of earthly life: "This night thy soul shall be required of thee." Let us try to see, then, how the Saviour makes use of this the remembrance of the transitory nature of earthly life to warn us against selfishness in our joy and gratitude for God's earthly blessings, and to give to that joy and gratitude a higher direction.

I. The first point, then, that we have to consider in our text is the saying of this man to himself: "Soul, thou hast much goods laid up for many years; take thine ease, eat,

[1] Berlin was visited by the cholera at the time when this sermon was preached.

drink, be merry." These words, if we take them just as they stand, suggest a very primitive and crude state of things as compared with our present ways. The man who had reaped so rich a harvest is described to us as if he only thought of using and consuming in his own household what he had gained; although, of course, that would take a long series of years; he regarded it as his own provision, intended directly for his own use. The growth and increasing strength of association among men has brought us far beyond such a state of things. That which each one gains or produces, in whatever way or by whatever business, does not remain shut up with himself—it goes out into the general circle of commerce. But it does so because there is and must be something that we want above everything else,—above that thing itself which we have, and it is to the acquisition of this something that those among us who are like-minded with this man direct all their efforts. What will this bring to me? each one asks himself; that is, how much will it bring of that which will procure for you everything else? And if that is plentiful and abundant, he says in the same way, "Soul, thou hast great store of this much-praised representative of all things; now consider how thou wilt use thy treasure; use it entirely according to the desire of thy heart; eat, drink and be merry!"

Now here we have the two great motive powers,—human covetousness and self-indulgence,—and we see the conflict there is between them in each individual. To acquire and to enjoy, to gather up and to use,—how clearly each one reveals his character by the way in which he balances these against each other, and how long the greater number remain undecided as to which way they shall take! Some choose the plan of spending the greater part of their lives in continually accumulating, continually acquiring; but this with the hope of being able at last to rest and enjoy in comfort what they have gained; they are content in the meantime with rejoicing in their increasing gains, that at last, when they have enough, they may give way to and gratify every bent and desire of their souls. Others again—and it looks as if this word of the Lord were directed somewhat more specially to them—who hear already, at least afar off, the voice from heaven, "This night thy soul shall be required of thee!"—these others set acquiring and enjoying closer together, gathering and acquiring as much as they can according to the order of nature in the short space of a year, in order at once to take the good of it; the next year, they say, will bring new activity, and as its result, new enjoyment. But the one plan is no better than the other; for if it were said to these last, there is no question of the course of a year, this night thy soul shall be required of thee, their calculation would be as mistaken as the other.

But further, if a man has once taken measures for deciding this question, and laid down a rule for himself in the matter, then he will be deaf to all demands that interfere with his calculations. He has gathered and toiled, he has laboured and put forth all his powers for himself and for a circle that he has clearly defined to himself; and is he to be asked to turn his attention elsewhere? is he to have demands made on him for help to those who do not belong to this circle? is he to miss something of the enjoyment that he has set before him as the whole aim of his work? Rather he will try to turn away everything of this kind, that he may go on undisturbed in the course of life that he has laid out for himself. But if there comes to him the voice, "This night thy soul shall be required of thee," how little then has his hardness of heart availed him! how delusive will everything then prove that he has promised himself for this life! how vain everything that he has done for it alone! And so the Saviour rebukes the man who is not seeking after the kingdom of God, whose whole mind is set on the cheerful enjoyment of this short span of earthly life. He rebukes him, while He warns him of the end. He who knows and recognises nothing beyond this alternation between gaining and enjoying, however honourable his gains may be, however select and refined his pleasures, is still doing all only for himself, —for himself in this his earthly life, with his tastes for the enjoyment of earthly things, with his clinging to perishing possessions! And yet he cannot conceal from himself that even for him there is something better within reach; and so every thought of the end of this life reproaches him with his folly.

II. But we have not yet seen all that was in the mind of the man whom the Saviour sets before us. He had said to himself, What wilt thou do? thou hast no place where to lay up thy fruits! Well, thought he, I will pull down my barns and build greater, and in them will I bestow all my fruits and my goods; and not till then was to begin his easy life of enjoyment. But,—it would certainly have been a folly to pull down his barns and build greater for a single abundant harvest; therefore he must have been counting on similar ones to come. So we may conclude that he was one of those who thoroughly understand their business. He had improved his property, and applied all his faculties to his work; and now the fruit of all this painstaking began to be seen; now he could count with some probability on the continuance of this prosperity, and therefore wished to make arrangements for adapting his whole manner of life to his enlarged possessions. But as a man seldom attains to seeing such returns from his long-continued toils before he has reached middle age, and therefore whatever he builds then will in the natural order of things outlast him, he thinks, in his building, not only of himself, but of those who will afterwards live in his house and lay up in his barns; he thinks of the generations that may descend from him, and includes the life of his posterity in his own. Consider then how these words remind us of the great histories of human life that have taken place in our own land. Since the days of the remotest ancestors of whom we have any knowledge, how far have the operations of man on his mother earth extended, by the ever-renewed labours of successive generations! to what perfection have they reached almost before our own eyes! But how much has intervened from time to time which must have made manifest the folly of those who limited the aim of their life's work in the way we have spoken of! In the history of our own neighbourhood, without touching on the state of things before that dreadful war that desolated these lands two hundred years ago, we know how after its close all the labours of men on the soil were almost to begin anew. Then villages and towns rose again, but others remained lying in ruins, because there were not enough of men to rebuild them with profit. And after that time of terror was got over, how much was built, just as hopefully as by the man in our text, for future generations! how clearly do the monuments of that period proclaim the hope that where the builder lived and gathered treasure, his latest descendants should also live and amass in undiminished prosperty. But by-and-by times of war came again; for long years hostile armies swarmed over the land, and again many of the works of the elder generations perished in the storm. How little has history preserved to us of those who, between those two fateful times, lived and laboured, gathered and built! The names of those who in that interval shared the land and enjoyed the fruits of it are almost all unknown; and even when it is known here and there by whom a noble and stately mansion was built, it is very seldom the descendants of the founder who inhabit it. But after the devastation of the seven years' war, a splendid time of cultivation began once more; then tracts of land that had never before yielded anything to man were subdued by the plough, and began to bear crops; then the ancients forests were felled, that a yearly harvest might be drawn from the soil; marshes were drained, and regions that until then had only given forth noxious vapours became fertile and blooming; foreigners who had no room in their own country were attracted here, and we made them welcome, that our common prosperity might be increased by their help.

This, then, is cultivating in order to reaping: and how continuously has man been perfecting his dominion over his mother earth! how much more skilfully and successfully is this great business carried on among us! And though a far greater number of people than before now live in the same space, there has also been a constantly increasing development of mental powers, and life has altogether taken a fuller and nobler form. How well for those, then and now, who, in taking any active part in this progress, have rejoiced more in the ennobling of mankind than in the growing promise of wealth for their descendants; who have valued an improved state of worldly circumstances less for its own sake than because it leaves men more free and open to receive the kingdom of God. But if our case is only such as the Saviour represents in our text; if every one works only for himself and his successors, and wishes only himself and his family to reap the fruits of his industry, I have already sufficiently indicated how the folly of such a course punishes itself. How many a one in those past times, while labouring for himself and his descendants, may have looked far into the future and said to his soul, Take thine ease, and be merry; the name of thy race will never perish: he may have assured himself that what he had already made would suffice to maintain them in splendour and honour; that in the dwelling which he had built his children and his children's children would dwell, and that the fame of a race sprung from such an ancestor would be ever more widely spread; that the rights which he had acquired over others, and which placed him in so favourable a position for employing, not only his own powers, but far more those of others, to serve his ends, would be equally serviceable to those who came after him; that all would be an inviolable possession, and continue as it had been! But man is like a falling leaf, "as a flower of the field, so he flourisheth; the wind passeth over it, and it is gone"; and this is true, not only of individuals—it is true of races of men, it is true of all human plans. The most famous names pass away, and the scenes of their glory are no more. Poverty overtakes the richest families; and needy descendants, stripped of all the distinctions and prerogatives that adorned their ancestors, and far from their palaces, are often compelled to seek their bread of sorrow among strangers!

III. Thus we only now come to the full meaning of the question put to the man in the text by the heavenly voice: Whose shall the things be which thou hast prepared? Yes, whose shall they be? That is the question that always brings out the vanity of mere human wisdom; for there is none who can give the answer. If we look at the question in the sense that first of all occurs to every one, and in immediate connection with that stern sentence, This night thy soul shall be required of thee, it reminds us how so many, though perfectly aware that they have only a short and uncertain term of earthly life, and that what a man has worked for must go to those who come after him, yet neglect to arrange who shall have what they leave behind them, and that even when they have ample reason and motive for doing so. A most foolish fear of death makes many a man banish every thought of this kind from his mind; and if he brings himself to the point of setting about such an arrangement, he thinks he already hears the nails being driven into his coffin, and death whetting the scythe that is to cut him down. Foolish man! when there is really nothing—no agitation or satisfaction of mind, no feeling of hunger or thirst, of comfort or refreshment,—nothing that does not remind us how fleeting is our earthly life! Therefore let every one for himself get the mastery over this idea!

But this is not all: the question has a wider and deeper meaning. Whose shall these things be that thou hast gathered? These words remind us, further, of the various relations of human order and human law which protect our property and our possessions in the widest sense of the word. On these finally depend the things we have been considering to-day: they are, as it were, the hinges on which all work and business move. Most of those who have worked for their successors, who have wished to be able to count on their enjoying life in comfort, and on being honoured by them as faithful and considerate parents, have done so in the confidence that these social relations would remain unchanged. But how utterly mistaken they were! How even in our own district does the fleeting nature of all earthly things take hold of us! nay, how manifest it is here on the largest scale! We need only look back over a short period of history; for how short are a few hundred years, not only in the history of mankind in general, but in that of individual nations; and in that time what great changes have taken place in the legal relations of almost all the nations in this part of the world! There is no doubt of it—it is impossible that things should always remain as they have been.

Perhaps those relations originated in some great and undeniable inequality between one man and another; then, of course, where that inequality no longer exists, they can no longer serve the same purpose; and what was once justice may, in different circumstances, be the bitterest injustice. But if one party insists on defending such a change, while another opposes it, then what sad variance arises between forces that should work together! what endless quarrels between those who yet cannot get on without each other! And why? For this sole reason, that each one thinks only of himself and those belonging to him. The one knows that his predecessors have laboured for him, and he wishes at least to lay up something for those who come after him. But if he is to transmit gratefully what his fathers have made; if his own toil and trouble are not to be fruitless; his successors must have the same rights in regard to others which he has himself enjoyed; otherwise all his good beginnings are mistaken, and he is out in his reckoning. The other, on the contrary, knows that the adverse conditions under which his fathers groaned exist no longer; he notices in the affairs of men a tendency to change in his favour, and finds in this an inducement to work his way up to a better position. And so the two parties oppose each other, and strife and dissension break out. Those on the one side wish to keep what they have always had; those on the other struggle to win what they have not. But if the former are only actuated by the belief that they are called on to represent a special class in society and to defend its property, while the latter think that their work is to oppose this exclusiveness and to set up a new special class; what can there be but bitter strife and foolish disputes? What is this but that very selfishness which the Lord condemns when He says, "So is he that layeth up treasure for himself, and is not rich toward God"? For where there is debate and contention—a different kind of debate from that by which we seek in the spirit of love to find out the truth—there is also covetousness and selfishness; and there, too, is the folly of which the Lord says, "Thou fool, this night thy soul shall be required of thee; and the things which thou hast prepared, whose shall they be?" For mark well, even in the course of a single night, changes may take place in human things without your being consulted which entirely alter your position; and each one who, instead of concerning himself with the common good, and regarding himself as a part of the great whole, has limited his interest to some narrow circle, perhaps opposed to the private interest of some one else; every one has a soul which, with all its desires and joys, its treasures and possessions, may in a night be required of him! And the more keenly the strife has been carried on, the less sure can human wisdom be of any firm ground or of any certain issue; the more foolish would it be to undertake to answer the question, Whose shall those things be which thou hast provided, or hast wished to provide? But where instead of strife and wrangling, instead of self-seeking and covetousness, that rule of life and feeling guides men which makes them rich in God; in that God who makes His sun shine on the evil and on the good, and sends rain on the just and on the unjust; in that God before whom all are equal, His fatherly love going forth to all; whose wise decrees are indeed hidden from us, so that we can never for one short moment lift the veil that conceals them, but whose laws and will are clearly revealed and should be written on the hearts of those who confess the name of His Son;—among such people there is an end of this folly; each of them is willing that his soul should be called away at any moment; and such men know whose the things shall be which they have provided.

And now, my dear friends, after all this—with all this work and business which goes on, one day and one year like another; with that wider view of human things that extends from one generation to another; with the loving wisdom which seeks to answer without covetousness, according to the mind of God, the question whose the things shall be which we have provided; and so to preserve or establish anew all legal relations, that mutual love may rule over all, and that each may be able to rejoice in the common welfare without wranglings or disputes; after all, we are nothing more than stewards of God's earthly gifts. What are we as Christians? Stewards of His mysteries. But the

Saviour, in the words of our text, teaches us not to separate these two things. As stewards of God's earthly gifts we gather and are meant to gather treasure; but each of us not for himself, nor for those who are to come after him; not for that circle of society to which he specially belongs; but each for all, each for the whole, each regarding himself as belonging to the great family of man, which is to become one flock under one Shepherd. And we can only be faithful stewards of God's earthly gifts by being at the same time stewards of His mysteries; who, because we have risen from death to life by a living faith, seek, even in the work and toil of temporal things, only that which is eternal. And thus a pure joy in God's earthly blessings, undisturbed by any fear of death, is the portion of those alone who walk in that love which makes all men friendly with each other, and who are therefore each one ready to let his own interests stand aside for the greatest good of all. And thus only shall we be in a position to give in our account as to how we have helped forward the development of men's powers in our own neighbourhood, and how each of us has used his own powers only for the common good. But who can feel this, except he who looks beyond this earthly life, and keeps eternal things steadily in view? Thus, and thus only can he begin and continue such a life. Everything is foolishness, apart from that simple heavenly wisdom which He has taught us who is the Way and the Truth and the Life. He does not teach us to despise earthly things; He does not teach us to withdraw from the business of the world; for God has placed us in the world to make Him known. Thousands of worlds are rolling around us; but we do not know, though we may conjecture, that there is active, intelligent life there; but man is set in this world to make God ever more gloriously known—to glorify, by his life and his love, Him for whom and by whom he was created. Everything that we do on this earth is meant to subserve that end; and he who has this end in view does all not for himself—not for this one or that one: he does it from the eternal motive of love, and for eternity. May every new gift of God, then, which we receive from the hand of nature remind us afresh that the earthly exists only for the sake of the eternal, in order that the Divine Being may manifest Himself ever more clearly in men who are His offspring; and that the glory of His only-begotten Son and the gladsome life of His Spirit may shine ever more brightly out of all the works of men. If we do not use His gifts for this, we abuse them; if we are not setting this aim before us, we are with all our worldly wisdom only fools—fools who must be continually anxious about whose the things they have prepared shall be; who are ever clinging, as if it were to have no end, to that of which the end is coming so soon. May He be pleased to lead us all to this wisdom; and may every warning from history, everything that goes on before our eyes and close around us—all danger of death, as well as every glad sense of life, ever more powerfully impress us, that we may more and more understand this heavenly voice; that it may not need to reproach us as fools, but that in respect to this also His Spirit may bear witness with our spirits that we are His children.